MYTHS AND MAGIC IN THE MEDIEVAL FAR NORTH

ACTA SCANDINAVICA

CAMBRIDGE Studies in the early Scandinavian World

VOLUME 10

A series devoted to early Scandinavian culture, history, language, and literature, between the fall of Rome and the emergence of the modern states (seventeenth century) — that is, the Middle Ages, the Renaissance, and the Early Modern period (c. 400–1600).

Previously published volumes in this series are listed at the back of the book.

Myths and Magic in the Medieval Far North

Realities and Representations of a Region on the Edge of Europe

Edited by
STEFAN FIGENSCHOW
RICHARD HOLT
AND MIRIAM TVEIT

BREPOLS

British Library Cataloguing in Publication Data
A catalogue record for this book is available from
the British Library

D/2020/0095/151
ISBN 978-2-503-58823-0
E-ISBN 978-2-503-58824-7
DOI 10.1484/M.AS-EB.5.119411
ISSN 2466-586X
E-ISSN 2565-9170

Printed in the EU on acid-free paper.

Table of Contents

Introduction: Myths and Magic in the Medieval Far North
Stefan Figenschow, Richard Holt, Miriam Tveit   11

**Bearded Women and Sea Monsters: European
Representations of the Far North in the Early and High
Middle Ages**
Miriam Tveit   19

Myth, Magic, and Rituals in the Nordic World

**On the View of 'the Other' — Abroad and At Home: The
Geography and Peoples of the Far North, According to
*Historia Norwegie***
Lars Ivar Hansen   39

**The Ice Giant Cometh: The Far North in the Old Norse-
Icelandic Sagas**
Eleanor Rosamund Barraclough   71

**Fishermen in Trouble — *Grímnismál* and Elf Islands in
Northern Norway**
Petter Snekkestad   95

Sámi Myths and Medieval Heritage
Marte Spangen   119

**'I Hurl the Spirits of Gandul'. Pleasure, Jealousy, and Magic:
The Witchcraft Trial of Ragnhild Tregagaas in 1325**
Rune Blix Hagen   143

**The Meaning of Ale: Understanding Political Conflicts in the
North in Light of Cultural Practice**
Karoline Kjesrud   157

Myths and Representations in the Political Consolidation of the North

The Origins of Political Organization in the High North:
A Study of the Historical and Material Remains of Finnmǫrk,
Hálogaland, and the Mythical Ǫmð
Yassin Nyang Karoliussen   181

Norwegian or Northern: The Construction and Mythography
of Háleygr Identity, *c.* 800–1050
Ben Allport   197

The Formation of a Norwegian Kingdom: A Northern
Counter-Narrative?
Richard Holt   215

Approaches to Mythologized 'Others' in Norwegian
Expansion to the North
Stefan Figenschow   237

Index of People and Places   259

General Index   267

List of Illustrations

Maps

Map 1.   Map of Norway, showing key places named in the volume.   8
Map 2.   Map of Hálogaland, showing places named in the articles.   9

Figures

Fig. 1.   Stállo house ground in the mountain landscape of Saltfjellet,
          Nordland, Norway.   122
Fig. 2.   Pitfall trap for wild reindeer by Lake Láhpojohka in Kautokeino,
          Finnmark, Norway.   127
Fig. 3.   So-called 'circular offering site' by Lake Geaimmejávri in
          Karasjok, Finnmark, Norway.   130
Fig. 4.   'Fyn bracteate', Fyn in Denmark (Nat.mus. 8650, DR IK
          58). The runic inscription reads: Howar ('the high one')
          'laþu' … 'alu'.   162
Fig. 5.   Bone fragment from Horvnes, Alstahaug in Nordland (T
          22926/1-74, A372), which includes the inscription *aallu [u]*. 163
Fig. 6.   The Tune-stone from Tune in Østfold (C 2092, N KJ 72).
          The stone was erected in a burial field and was later included
          in the churchyard wall encircling the church of Tune. Now
          the stone is in the collections at Museum of Cultural History
          (KHM), Oslo.   165
Fig. 7.   The Årstad grave slab (C 3639, N KJ 58) was found in relation
          to a grave chamber at the farm Årstad in Sokndal, Rogaland
          in Norway.   166
Fig. 8.   The Bjarkøy cauldron (C18174) from Bjarkøy in Harstad,
          Troms.   170

Map 1: Map of Norway, showing key places named in the volume. Capitalized names indicate lesser regions, bold capitalized names indicate major regions. Map courtesy of Torger Grytå, UiT The Arctic University of Norway.

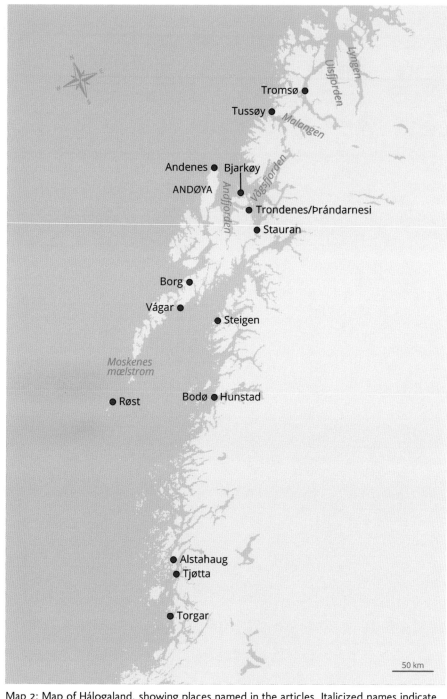

Map 2: Map of Hálogaland, showing places named in the articles. Italicized names indicate off-shore areas. Map courtesy of Torger Grytå, UiT The Arctic University of Norway.

STEFAN FIGENSCHOW, RICHARD HOLT,
MIRIAM TVEIT

Introduction: Myths and Magic in the Medieval Far North

Despite enormous interest in Viking-age Scandinavia, there is relatively little published material available in English for the early history of the northern parts of the continent — which we can call the Far North. Emphasis has more often been placed on the Scandinavian impact on Europe, on the colonization and formation of new societies, and only to a lesser degree on the contemporary evolution of structures of authority in the homelands. Furthermore, even the accounts that do deal with the latter tend to overlook the role of the Far North, especially the internal processes that took place *in situ* and also how the northern ethnic, political, and social conditions affected the wider processes of early Scandinavian state building, Christianization, and centralization in the area. That these are themes poorly represented in secondary literature is emphatically not a reflection of their importance in understanding wider aspects of the historical development of north-western Europe, nor is it justified by any particular lack of relevant sources. The written sources that are available, it is true, are later and often from outside the region, and the inherent difficulties they present are a challenge to the historian; but that is hardly a unique situation. And the Far North has a rich heritage of archaeological material from several thousand years of settlement.

It was to address this perceived neglect of research into the Far North that the research group *Creating the New North* came together at the University of Tromsø. With active partners from other universities both in Norway and elsewhere, the group was set up specifically to bring together scholars from a range of relevant disciplines who had a common interest in developing our understanding of historical developments in settlement, society, and identity in northern Norway specifically and in northern Fennoscandia generally.

Stefan Figenschow, UiT The Arctic University of Norway, stefan.figenschow@uit.no
Richard Holt, UiT The Arctic University of Norway, richard.holt@uit.no
Miriam Tveit, Nord University, miriam.tveit@nord.no

Myths and Magic in the Medieval Far North: Realities and Representations of a Region on the Edge of Europe, ed. by Stefan Figenschow, Richard Holt, and Miriam Tveit, AS 10
(Turnhout: Brepols, 2020), pp. 11–18
© BREPOLS ❧ PUBLISHERS   10.1484/M.AS-EB.5.120517

The group has now made good its claim to be among the leading centres of expertise regarding the Far North; and its central objective since its inception has been to develop a new understanding of how the most northerly areas of Europe grew from a situation of open interaction between different ethnic groups in the early Middle Ages to one which saw them become northern peripheries subject to emerging national states with administrative centres further south — hence the *New North* in the group's title.

The group's focus is far from being a narrow one, however, and in its research it has gone well beyond the bounds of its central objective. A recent interest has been the mythological and magical dimension of northernness, and this has developed to become a broad theme with relevance to other areas the group is studying. In essence, the theme takes its starting point in traditional ways of thinking about the Far North. There is a long tradition in European culture of treating it as a place with special attributes. With its remote location, harsh climate, boundless geography, complex ethnic composition, and often seemingly strange ways of life, the North has been considered as the hearth of evil — notably by St Augustine; as the end of the world, as the home of monsters and supernatural beings, as a hotbed of magic-wielding sorcerers, and as the last bastion of recalcitrant paganism. Elements of that picture are to be found in many historical and literary treatments of the North from the Middle Ages, even those from authors with first-hand knowledge and even experience. The familiar stereotypes were clearly too strong to be ignored; but it is also inescapable that elements of the northern myth contained enough truth that even those better-informed writers chose to perpetuate them.

And further to that: as Scandinavians were beginning to think about and record their past during the High Middle Ages, a new layer of myths and interpretations was being created, at least in part to support the development and expansion of national monarchies and the establishment of the Christian church, and to differentiate between what pertained to these structures and what did not. The mythological character of the North was already intertwined with the earliest tales of social relationships and structures, and of the first manifestations of the processes of political consolidation. That was not the end of the construction of myths concerning the northern aspects of these processes, and the medieval period saw the continued creation of origin and foundation myths. The effect was to have a profound influence on how the emergence of a Norwegian kingdom was understood and written about, and incidentally to reinforce how other Norwegians during and after the Middle Ages thought about the northern part of the kingdom and its inhabitants. It is quite clear that the products of these mythopoeic processes came to dominate the general perception of the Far North and its place in medieval Norwegian history; the consequence was an overshadowing of important characteristics and aspects of the North both in itself and as a part of wider, national developments. It is ironic, and historically significant, that while a considerable and growing body of both archaeological and documentary evidence confirms the North to have been economically and politically developed in the early Middle Ages, outsiders might still regard the region and its people as strange and backward.

The present volume is the result of the group's research to date on the themes of myth and magic, through studies in history, philology, and archaeology. The eleven papers each in their own way address questions around that theme, all with the common aim of contributing to our understanding of northern society. The volume thus presents new research on northern Fennoscandia, very much from a northern perspective. It explores the ways the Far North was represented in medieval sources, and how the emerging central authorities and the multi-ethnic population created their own myths, both as part of, and in reply to, the expansion of royal and ecclesiastical organizations.

The first chapter, by Miriam Tveit, explores the international context to draw out important themes that prepare for much that follows. Viewed from the outside, the Far North seemed a perilous place. Tveit presents the general reputation that the North had in Europe — the tales that could be told, and that were presumably believed. Despite already-established commercial contacts, the people of early medieval Christian Europe actually knew little of the North and its inhabitants. Fragments of knowledge about the natural conditions of the region, and its geography, were embedded into a confused mass of misunderstandings and pure fantasy. The effect was that the northern peoples appeared to be very different from their Christian counterparts further south. The North could thus be represented as a moral contrast, illustrating an order in the world that flattered the Christian regions. Perhaps it was this element, and no doubt the sheer entertainment value of such tales, that ensured that although more reliable information about the North became available with time, the fabulous nature of the tales only intensified. Even in the late eleventh century, Adam of Bremen was no less credulous, or at any rate seemed to be. There could have been ulterior motives for telling deliberately fanciful tales about the North: the anonymous author of the *Historia Norwegie* wrote for non-Norwegian readers but was most likely himself Norwegian, which casts particular doubts over his accounts both of sea monsters and of the magic of the Sámi. Incidentally, this fragmentary history is an important source for several of our contributors, as one might expect. It is difficult to date, although most historians place the composition of the text before 1200 rather than after; often to the middle years of the twelfth century, or in the decades following. The latter part is lost, but the earlier chapters of *Historia Norwegie* describing Norway and its peoples are a fortunate survival that have no Scandinavian parallel.

The following six chapters take up the general theme of myth, magic, and rituals in the Nordic world. And now the emphasis is on evidence from this world itself. Collectively, the chapters tell of a society retaining many cultural and social facets of a recent pagan past. Lars Ivar Hansen explores the identity of the inhabitants of the North, reducing Adam of Bremen's fanciful images to a patchwork of ethnicities. Within the northern geography there co-existed a variety of peoples living sometimes in harmony, sometimes in conflict with each other. Through the text of the *Historia Norwegie*, he presents the Sámi people as they were perceived by the Norwegians. Their nomadic lifestyle, their ways of living as hunters and gatherers in a landscape more often than not decked with snow, and their reputation as practitioners of a shamanistic magic made them 'others' to people who were themselves Christians and lived a settled life based on agriculture. At the same time there was an established relationship between Sámi and Norwegians for the purpose of the trade that benefited both of them; and that relationship, it seems, might entail a significant level of social contact. But the way *Historia Norwegie* might describe the inhabitants of the northern world was not the only literary — or indeed oral — genre to take up such matters. Turning to the chapter by Eleanor Rosamund Barraclough: we read of that world of the supernatural in the sagas written down in Iceland from the thirteenth century onwards, although the stories are older, perhaps far older: the written genre can hardly have sprung into existence fully formed without an oral prehistory, as Theodore Andersson forcefully argued.[1] Particularly the sagas grouped together by modern scholars as the *fornaldarsögur* tell of people and events in a legendary past in an unambiguously northern world, but a world full of supernatural beings, where intrepid people might meet gods, giants, and trolls. Taking in a variety of origin myths both of humans and non-humans, the sagas create a fantastic world that listeners might have been able to believe in; and the northernness of that world is an explicit recurrent theme, making the real North a place of mystery and the gateway to even more outlandish worlds that lay beyond. The mythical northern world contained elements of the geography of the Barents Sea and the White Sea, and there seem to be references to the Sámi people who lived in Hálogaland and more extensively in Finnmork. Increasing in its cold and inhospitality the further one went, their own north really was seen by Norse people as being beyond the bounds of the human world. Often trolls and giants were physical manifestations of a terrain dominated by rock and ice, a theme which is also taken up by Petter Snekkestad. Using folk tales recorded in early modern times from the fishing and farming population of Hálogaland, he reconstructs a traditional coastal geography, of islands and mountains with supernatural attributes. The abode of trolls, or themselves identified with trolls, these natural features became central to a mass of tales as well as serving a seafaring folk as aids to navigation. This system of folklore and belief is used by Snekkestad to inform an interpretation of *Grímnismál*, one of the poems of the Poetic Edda, and his discussion of the concept of *Utrøst* as a supernatural island but also perhaps as everything conceived of as a supernatural Otherworld.

Both Barraclough and Snekkestad point to specific or oblique references to the Sámi people of northern Norway in the essentially Norse narratives

---

1   Andersson, Theodore M., *The Problem of Icelandic Saga Origins* (New Haven: Yale University Press, 1964), p. 119.

and folklore they are interpreting. In the sagas that Barraclough writes about, they are the *Finnar*, located in the North but not so Far North as the inhuman beings whom she writes about. Snekkestad postulates a Sámi cultural element, sorcery, as part of the background of *Þokuvísur*, and a shamanistic aspect of *Grímnismál* has been suggested. Yet with the exception of the texts discussed by Hansen, the presence of the Sámi as a constant feature of northern Norwegian society and economy is under-represented in the historical record, and it is other disciplines such as archaeology or landscape studies that have more to say about their identity and culture. Marte Spangen's chapter examines such material, particularly in the light of how Sámi people themselves have interpreted earthworks and such features in the landscape shaped by their own forebears, and have woven legends around them, to give them mythical and ritual meaning. Whether the legends have had any basis in earlier events and practices is unknown and perhaps unknowable; the historical importance of the legends, moreover, lies more in the contemporary context of their telling than in any possible events of the past. Sites now accorded ritual significance, both by scholars and by Sámi people themselves, may have acquired that reputation only since the beginning of scientific study, with Sámi folk memory and belief being inspired by that work rather than the other way around. At the same time the recent proliferation of newly identified Sámi ritual sites has served both to demonstrate historic Sámi rights of land use and to confirm the persistent stereotype of the Sámi as historically a magical people, who even today are sometimes thought to have a special empathy with nature and natural forces.

Much of the literary evidence is of myths and the beliefs of a magical past recounted primarily for entertainment, it would seem, in the Iceland of the fourteenth century; but behind the literature, contemporary belief in Norway in the efficacy of magic was real enough. That surely is expressed in *Historia Norwegie*; and as we read in Rune Blix Hagen's chapter, there was a firm belief in the power of individuals to work magic to harm others. That the case of Ragnhild Tregagaas from 1325 is the earliest recorded witchcraft trial from Scandinavia only goes to illustrate the paucity of earlier records available to the historian. Ragnhild's spell cast 'the spirits of Gandul', or *gondol*, which appears to be a direct reference to the magical practices of the Sámi. Wherever in Norway Ragnhild had grown up, the Sørle Sukk who had taught her magic would seem to have been a Sáme. Again we see that association of the Sámi with magic and sorcery as being an explicit or implicit feature of their identity. But at the same time, a Norwegian woman could work magic; and there was more to northern magic than the rituals of the Sámi. By contrast with 'the spirits of Gandul', the genesis of magical, social, and political rituals surrounding the brewing and drinking of ale, and the significance of ale to social identity, could be characteristic only of a settled, agricultural society that grew barley or other grain with which to make malt. Ale and its significance were culturally purely Norse, therefore, although the Sámi were perhaps quick to learn: when the disputed king Sigurðr *slembidjákn* (the Rowdy) spent the winter of 1138 in Tjeldsund, on the northern island of Hinnøya, according to *Heimskringla*, the Sámi who were his hosts had ale for a feast in his honour. Simply the fact of drunkenness might be an attribute of creativeness in the skaldic tradition, but Karoline Kjesrud in her chapter has chosen to write about how ale was a crucial element in the culture of medieval Norway, an essential part of rituals marking all stages in life from birth to the grave in both the pre-Christian and the Christian periods. To find out why this was so, she demonstrates the antiquity of ale-rituals and their religious or magic significance; how drinking ale was a central aspect of social and political gatherings, and so how the control of trade in malt could even be a significant part of a royal strategy to confirm and consolidate central power. In that context, ale was just one of the factors making for social cohesion in a diverse society, and ultimately to political consolidation, and clearly a powerful factor with an enduring importance.

Kjesrud broaches the topic of political development, and the ultimate creation of a single Norwegian monarchy. The long, drawn-out processes of Norwegian political consolidation, and the worlds of legend and pseudo-history we must explore to elucidate those processes, are essential themes addressed in different ways by the remaining four chapters. All four address political realities in the North, in a broad chronological progression from the late Iron Age through to the fourteenth century. At the same time, the situation in the North is related to the emergence and early development of a Norwegian kingdom. An essential contextual element for these studies is that, like its Scandinavian neighbours, Norway emerged into the prevailing Christian culture significantly later than most of western Europe. That was a literate culture that brought with it the possibility and a sense of the desirability of commemorating events and people by means of the written word. By contrast with lands to the south, therefore, Norway had no early written history. Aspects of state formation and expansion, movements towards political consolidation which these chapters deal with, all began in Norway long before a written culture developed. Even when literacy came to the Far North, the preferred theme was fanciful tales and myths that contemporaries told of the past, which Norwegian and Icelandic authors weaved together to construct histories of kings and heroes who had existed in a world of wonders and of pagan magic. Furthermore, what they wrote down was selective and particular, and reflected the preoccupations and assumptions of their own time, the twelfth and thirteenth centuries. Contemporary concerns and interpretations dominate the early historical record of even earlier times, and perhaps inevitably misrepresent the true nature of situations and events. And it was not only myths from an oral culture of the past that they recorded. Many aspects even of later phases in the processes of political consolidation were the subject of new myths, created and designed to explain social and political developments.

Writing a coherent history of the early Far North in its Norwegian context has always proved a challenge, therefore, and in different periods that challenge has been met in different ways. Yassin Karoliussen's paper uses primarily archaeology to take us into a past which is poorly served by the historical record. Recorded in the kings' sagas as a place name, and apparently as a place of some importance, the Ǫmð of legend can be shown to have been an historical entity with its own chieftains or petty-kings already in the late Iron Age — though at the same time there has been disagreement as to its geographical extent, and just how important it might have been. The most recent research tends to confirm the conclusions of the nineteenth-century historian Peter Andreas Munch that Ǫmð was quite a large region comprising a variety of landscapes around Vågsfjorden, the region that in modern Norway constitutes the northernmost part of the county of Nordland and the southern part of the county of Troms, and in the early Middle Ages might be reckoned to have been the northernmost political unit with a Norse identity.[2] As such it was one of the building bricks of the consolidation of the whole northern part of what would become Norway into the early medieval jarldom of Hálogaland.

It is that process that is the theme of the next chapter, as Ben Allport examines an important preliminary phase in the evolution of a common Norwegian identity: that is, the evolution of regional identities, and in particular that of Hálogaland. Archaeological evidence for a hierarchy of central places and assembly sites, where disputes could be settled and authority mediated from a higher social level to the lower, seems to represent tiers of collective identity. For a long time, regional identity was more important in self-definition than any sense of being Norwegian might have been, Allport argues; using both literary evidence and archaeology to identify regional units of collective identity, he demonstrates that Hálogaland was identified as an entity very early both by outsiders and by the Háleygir, its people. Relative to other identifiable regions of what would become Norway, Hálogaland's emergence as a political unit with a developed economy was precocious, and it was early on participating in European trade networks both as an exporter and importer of luxury goods, and increasingly by 1000 as an exporter of fish. Its distinctive character also, it seems, gave it a reputation as a place of mystery. Distant and with more than a hint of the supernatural, the Háleygir people appeared to southern perceptions as inextricably associated with the magic-working Sámi.

Foundation myths of the Norwegian kingdom, and the participation of the Háleygir in that process, are the substance of Richard Holt's chapter. Allport concludes with the expansion of Háleygir authority in the tenth century further south into Þrœndalǫg, and the rise of the dynasty of the jarls of Hlaðir from their roots in Hálogaland. Holt takes the story further, re-examining the Norwegian national foundation myth, a pseudo-history that by the early twelfth century had begun to be written down in Iceland. The

---

2 Munch, Peter Andreas, *Det Norske Folks Historie*, 8 vols (Christiania: Tønsbergs forlag, 1852–1863), I, 88.

myth was perhaps the inevitable accompaniment of the establishment during the course of the eleventh century of a single dynasty of Norwegian kings, the sons and grandsons of King Haraldr Sigurðarson *harðráði* (hard-ruler) and their descendants. The essence of the myth was to assert that a single line of kings, descended from a King Haraldr *hárfagri* (fine-hair) had ruled a united kingdom of Norway since before 900, a line into which the Christianizing hero kings Óláfr Tryggvason and Óláfr Haraldsson, and other semi-historical earlier kings, could be inserted. Modern Norwegian historians have questioned most elements of the narrative but never jettisoned it altogether. Holt argues that the effect of the myth has been to play down the importance of Hálogaland and its resource base as factors in the creation of a Norwegian kingdom, a process more plausibly driven from the North than from the districts of southern Norway more traditionally seen as its cradle.

The final chapter, by Stefan Figenschow, takes the story further, with the expansion of the medieval Norwegian state and church north and eastward, deep into the north of Fennoscandia following on the reduction of the powerful chieftains of Hálogaland to dependence on the crown. The examples he takes up illustrate how the post-'Civil War' kings, their authority now consolidated within Norway, approached Sámi and other non-Norwegian ethnic groups. These peoples were still traditionally regarded as 'others', alien in their lifestyle and culture from Norwegians, although the relationship with the Sámi was both ancient and close, not least through their common participation in the economic exploitation of northern resources; the fact that the Sámi were pagans with a different lifestyle seems not to have had any deleterious effect on the possibilities of co-operation. Norwegian approaches to the northern peoples could be peaceable and nuanced, showing little sign of fear of 'otherness'. The promise of economic gain was a constant theme on the Norwegian side, through enhanced access to the rich resources of this vast wilderness, either directly or by taking tribute from the local population. Even so, contact with the northern peoples might have been as often amicable as it was exploitative; and a well-informed pragmatism in inter-ethnic relationships did not succumb to mythologized stereotypes.

MIRIAM TVEIT

Bearded Women and Sea Monsters: European Representations of the Far North in the Early and High Middle Ages

Introduction

In the Middle Ages, northern Fennoscandia constituted a periphery between the existing world and the beyond. Because the region was rich in natural resources, it was in regular commercial contact with other parts of Europe, although it remained largely unvisited and unknown. A number of accounts from learned European men describing the way of life and the inhabitants in the region do, however, exist. These southern representations were often confused and, to the modern reader, fantastic representations of the region as a peripheral area containing primitive, but noble, savages, wonders, and oddities. These representations contained a kernel of factual knowledge about the natural conditions of the Far North. This article will investigate the role of the Far North in a centre–periphery model in medieval European literature, where the northern periphery was the scene for the playing out of moral lessons. It will also examine how the conception of the supernatural North intensified over time.

To ancient and medieval writers alike, the Northern World was of indefinable size and uncertain physical dimensions. Moreover, what constituted northern and what constituted 'the Far North' was a matter of perspective. For some, all land north of the Alps might be far enough to include.[1] There is a low level of precision in the topographical descriptions in these accounts, and we should not expect to be able to pinpoint the positions in question on a map. The

---

[1] For instance, Protarcus (*c.* 392), who likened the Alps to the Riphean Mountains, the mountains said to be northernmost in Greco-Roman tradition; see Bridgman, *Hyperboreans*, p. 63. Paul the Deacon (*c.* 790) may have confused the German coast and the lands further north: see Foulke, *History of the Langobards*, pp. 3–4 n. 5.

Miriam Tveit, Nord University, miriam.tveit@nord.no

Myths and Magic in the Medieval Far North: Realities and Representations of a Region on the Edge of Europe: ed. by Stefan Figenschow, Richard Holt, and Miriam Tveit, AS 10
(Turnhout: Brepols, 2020), pp. 19–35
10.1484/M.AS-EB.5.120518

aim of these descriptions of the North was not to provide the reader with a trustworthy travel guide to the nature and peoples of the North. Trying to identify locations using the information we find in medieval accounts would therefore be an unrewarding task. It is rather the medieval authors' *idea* of the Far North that is fruitful to reconstruct, and thereby to analyse what the Far North represented to the centrally positioned European and what purpose the concept of the Far North served in the authors' writings.

Ancient and Medieval World Views

What constituted the centre of the world to medieval European writers was fluid and depended on the position of the author. Similarly, what constituted the periphery also depended on the author's perspective and position. Thus, we might assume that the mythical periphery retreated outwards as knowledge of the Northern World increased in continental Europe during the medieval period. The sources suggest quite the opposite, that representations of the lands of the North became more mythical in the high medieval sources than they had been in the early medieval accounts.

To some extent, we can read the medieval worldview from medieval maps. On the medieval European *mappae mundi*, the world was usually constructed in one of two main models, either as the T-O map or as a zonal map. T-O maps were arranged with the cardinal direction east on top, and often with a tripartite division of the land-mass where the map centres in the Mediterranean, with east on top and the north towards the left margin.[2] More complex versions of the T-O map could include visible positions of the centres of Christianity, Jerusalem, and Rome.[3] Zonal maps, also called macrobian maps, which were arranged in temperate zones in horizontal fields of land, traditionally placed north on top.[4] In some versions, the top- and bottom-most zones came with the description *inhabitabilis* (uninhabitable).[5] In both of these depictions, the early medieval world perspective saw the distance from the centre (the Mediterranean basin) as being inversely proportional to declining habitable environment. This emphasized the Christian order of the world, where the centre represented the normal and the extremes represented the abnormal. Depicting the 'otherness' at the peripheries may well have been the purpose of the written accounts.

Together with perceptions of 'otherness', the phenomena located in the Far North in medieval accounts are often what we today label 'supernatural', such as the existence of magic or people with abnormal physical attributes.

---

2 Bremner, 'The Underlying Projection of Mappaemundi', pp. 209–21.
3 Barber, 'Medieval Maps of the World', pp. 1–43.
4 See numerous examples in Hiatt, 'The Map of Macrobius before 1100', pp. 149–76.
5 For instance: Brussels, Bibliothèque royale, MS 10146, fol. 109^v (French, ninth–tenth century); Saint Petersburg, Russian National Library, MS lat. Q.v.XVII, no. 3, fol. 1^r (tenth–eleventh century); Leiden, Universiteitsbibliotheek, MS Gron 78, fol. 51^r (twelfth century).

Nevertheless, it was not a supernatural phenomenon to the medieval writer in the same sense. In medieval Christian beliefs, magic and monsters actually existed, both in the northern periphery and also in the centre, such as a dragon rising from the Tiber in the middle of Rome.[6] The supernatural was also a part of God's world order — if sometimes demonic — and therefore not always ungodly. Thus, a better collective term for what we perceive as supernatural in the medieval accounts might be 'extraordinary'.

In pre-Christian sources, the northern region was already described as a mythical landscape. In ancient Greek sources, demigods called Hyperboreans lived under a never-setting sun in the North without the toil of hunger and war.[7] This Greek myth, presented by Herodotus, positioned the Hyperboreans at the *ultima thule*, the outermost place in this world. The Romans continued the Hyperborean myth, but placed them beyond the accessible world of the North, as the elder Pliny (23–79 CE) wrote in his *Historia Naturalis* that behind the mountains of the Far North and beyond the north wind was the land of the 'gens felix' (happy people) called the Hyperboreans, who lived to be very old and who were known for their fantastic phenomena.[8] The medieval representations of the North were less positive.

Medieval writers perceived the world in terms of the centre–periphery model. The centre was order and civilization, and the periphery deviated from normality and possessed elements of chaos: the further the distance from the centre, the greater the difference from normality. All receptions and representations of 'otherness' similarly depicted how 'they' differed from 'us'. Since the Far North was beyond the borders of the known world, these regions were, to medieval scholars, the extreme limit, the fringe of the world, and a place where natural oddities blended with fantastic and mythological elements.

Origo

The knowledge of northern Europe demonstrated by ancient geographers, such as Pliny, disappeared in the first Christian accounts, according to Lars Hemmingsen.[9] Pliny himself mentioned the island of *Scatinavia* in his natural history, but deemed it to be unexplored by the Romans.[10]

---

6   On the plague serpents and a dragon rising from the Tiber, see Paul the Deacon, *Pauli historia Langobardorum*, ed. by Bethmann and Waitz, p. 104.

7   Mayer, 'Hyperboreer', pp. 2836–41; Casson, 'The Hyperboreans', pp. 1–3. Bridgman asserts that the Hyperboreans were really a confused image of the Celts, and not the Scandinavians; see Bridgman, *Hyperboreans*, pp. 101–56.

8   Pliny, *Historia Naturalis*, IV.12.89, p. 341.

9   Hemmingsen, 'Middelaldergeografien og *Historia Norwegie*', pp. 36–38.

10 Thompson, *The History of Ancient Geography*, p. 241. See Pliny, *Historia Naturalis*, IV.13.96, p. 345: 'qui Codanus vocatur, refertus insulis, quarum clarissima est Scatinavia, inconpertae magnitudinis, portionem tantum eius, quod notum sit, Hillevionum gente quingentis incolente pagis: quare alterum orbem terrarum eam appellant'.

Fennoscandia and the Baltic region then reappear in early medieval texts, although heavily indebted to the writers of Antiquity. In the sixth century, Jordanes — based in Constantinople — produced the *Getica*, his history of the Goths and their deeds before settling in the western provinces of the Roman Empire.[11] The *Getica* included a description of the area from which Jordanes saw the Goths as originating, which was the island of *Scandza*, now assumed to be a depiction of Scandinavia. On this island, Jordanes set a stage with many tribes that, according to him, 'Germanis corpore et animo grandiores, pugnabant beluina saevitia' (surpassed the Germans in size and spirit, and fought with the cruelty of wild beasts).[12]

The tale of *origo*-to-destination formed a part of the people's mythology of migration in the early Middle Ages. As many groups of people settled into new areas, they constructed stories of their origins and the events that happened en route to their current position in their newly formed kingdom. The Roman origin story famously descended from Troy and the Trojan hero Aeneas, and the Saxons in Britannia and the Franks also used myths of Trojan descent.[13] By boasting of a famous heritage, the *gens* elevated its own status in the contemporary environment, and Troy's famous heroes were excellent founding fathers in an origin myth. In the same way, several of the migrating peoples who settled in Western Europe claimed Scandinavian origins, although modern research proposes more easterly origins. Peter Hoppenbrouwers has pointed out how these origin myths usually speak of excellent breeding conditions and natural bravery, to elevate the descendants above other neighbours at their point of destination.[14] Being a good breeding ground for men was given as a reason why the people had to leave in the first place: the population grew too large and some had to bravely go out and find new land. In the then-Christian world, people's origins in a pagan society were enhanced by emphasis on the virtues and strength of the nation.[15] Jordanes revealed himself as a Goth in the final words of the *Getica*, which may have provided a motive to ascribe greater virtue to the Gothic race.[16] His own given reasons were, however, 'to condense in my own style in this small book the twelve volumes of Senator [Cassiodorus] on the origin and deeds of the *Getae* from olden time to the present day'.[17] The sober description of northern *Scandza*

---

11   Mierow, *The Gothic History of Jordanes*, pp. 11–12.

12   Jordanes, *Romana et Getica*, ed. by Mommsen, 3.24, p. 60; Mierow, *The Gothic History of Jordanes*, p. 57.

13   Hoppenbrouwers, 'Medieval Peoples Imagined', p. 47.

14   Hoppenbrouwers, 'Medieval Peoples Imagined', pp. 45–61.

15   Hoppenbrouwers, 'Medieval Peoples Imagined', p. 49; other stories tell of prophecy, like those suggested in the *Chronicon Gothanum* where the prophetess or sibyl Gambara 'declared to them their migration'. See also Foulke, *History of the Langobards*, 1.2 n. 8, and *Monumenta Germaniae Historica, Leges*, 4., p. 641.

16   Jordanes, *Romana et Getica*, ed. by Mommsen, 60.316, p. 138.

17   From Jordanes, 'Preface', in Mierow, *The Gothic History of Jordanes*, p. 51.

was an account of the authorities he cited. His sources for the origins of the Goths appear to be Cassiodorus (*c.* 490–*c.* 545), author, prefect, and counsellor to the young Ostrogothic king Athalaric (516–534).[18] Regarding *Scandza*, however, Jordanes cited the geographer Claudius Ptolemy (*c.* 100–*c.* 170).

The origin myth is also prominent in the opening of the *Historia Langobardorum* by Lombard historian Paulus Diaconus or Paul the Deacon (*c.* 720–799), dating to approximately 790.[19] The Lombard kingdom had given in to Frankish rule after its conquest by Charlemagne some fifteen years earlier, and the submission might have spurred the need for Paul to tell the glorious story of the Lombards, even in his privileged position at the Frankish court. Paul carefully abridged the document known as the *Origo Gentis Langobardorum*, in which the tribe emigrated from an island called *Scandanan*.[20] Like Jordanes, Paul began with the origin myth, and built up the image of stout Lombard nature resulting from the tribe's origins in a cold climate:

> Septemtrionalis plaga quanto magis ab aestu solis remota est et nivali frigore gelida, tanto salubrior corporibus hominum et propagandis est gentibus coaptata: sicut econtra omnis meridiana regio, quo solis est fervori vicinior, eo semper habundat et educandis minus est apta mortalibus.[21]

> (The region of the north, in proportion as it is removed from the heat of the sun and is chilled with snow and frost, is so much the more healthful to the bodies of men and fitted for the propagation of nations, just as, on the other hand, every southern region, the nearer it is to the heat of the sun, the more it abounds in diseases and is less fitted for the bringing up of the human race.)[22]

Paul goes on to position the origins of the Lombards in the North, on the island of *Scadinavia*, and again the North was associated with large populations of people.[23] The favourable breeding conditions attributed to the North could be part of the explanation for why the tribe had left its favourable northern origins, although it could also be remnants of a lasting fear in southern Europe based on the invasions in earlier centuries.

---

18 Jordanes' *Romana et Getica* is the only abridged remnant of Cassiodorus's Gothic history; in the *Variae* (ix.5), Cassiodorus comments on the origins of the Goths. See also Baldwin, 'Sources for the *Getica* of Jordanes', pp. 141–46.

19 Paul the Deacon, *Pauli historia Langobardorum*, ed. by Bethmann and Waitz, chap. 1.1 pp. 47–51.

20 Georg Waitz, ed., 'Origo Gentis Langobardorum', pp. 1–6.

21 Paul the Deacon, *Pauli historia Langobardorum*, ed. by Bethmann and Waitz, chap. 1.1, pp. 47–48.

22 Foulke, *History of the Langobards*, p. 1.

23 Oliver Thompson asserted that *Scadinavia* implied Scania or south Sweden, although Paul also mentioned the land beyond: Thompson, *Ancient Geography*, p. 241. The manuscript includes different spellings: *Scandinavia, Scadanavia*. As Bethmann and Waitz state: 'Fortasse ne in hoc quidem verbo scribendo sibi constans fuit Paulus', in *Pauli historia Langobardorum*, ed. by Bethman and Waitz, p. 48 n. g.

The sixth-century Roman writer Procopius (*c.* 500–554), however, tells of a central European tribe migrating *towards* the north, and prospering there, when he describes how the Heruli (Ἔρουλοι) migrated from their origo, and ʽπου τὰς ἐσχατιὰς τῆς οἰκουμένης ἱδρύσαντο' (settled at the very extremity of the world) at the island Θούλη (*Thule*).[24] To Procopius, Thule was the Scandinavian peninsula and what later authors called the island of *Scandza*.[25] Other writers have seen the island of Thule as positioned further beyond, perhaps being Iceland.[26] Procopius positioned Thule in the Far North, and described it as a barren land, much greater than Britain, and which was inhabited by thirteen different peoples, each with its own king.[27]

Again, the numerousness of men in the North was emphasized, even if the direction of migration in this tale was in the opposite direction.

In the late eleventh century, the German ecclesiastical writer Adam of Bremen gave a minute description of the regions constituting the archbishopric of Hamburg, including Scandinavia, in the *Gesta Hammaburgensis ecclesiae pontificum*.[28] The aim of Adam's work was not to provide a brave origin myth for the Scandinavians, but to tell the story of how the bishops had spread Christianity to the heathens in the Nordic regions. He was occupied with describing all the northern tribes, giving them extraordinary attributes, such as dogs' heads and deformities, as well as extraordinary lifestyles as Amazons and sorcerers. Adam's work is coloured by a mixture of disgust at the pagan ways and praise for the northerners' simple bravery. The fight against pagan beliefs might also be the reason for the many references to magic in Adam's text compared to the earlier Germanic writers.

The Northern Nature and Phenomena

The early medieval descriptions of nature in the peripheral parts of the world were for the most part limited to recognizable physical conditions. However, in the case of the Far North, we are given a frightening picture by Paul the Deacon of a land of eternal snow, and an ocean to the west with a great *vorago*, a whirlpool, that could swallow ships whole.[29] The latter is probably referring to the Moskenes maelstrom outside the Lofoten islands in northern Norway. Jordanes, too, had emphasized the chilling and dangerous aspects of northern nature. According to him, the Gulf of Bothnia would freeze over in winter,

24 Procopius, *The Gothic War*, trans. by Dewing, VI.xv, pp. 414–15.

25 Jordanes, *Romana et Getica*, ed. by Mommsen, 1.9, pp. 55–56. To Jordanes, Thule was a different island from Scandinavia, 'at the farthest bound of its western expanse it has another island named Thule': Mierow, *Gothic History*, p. 53.

26 Tacitus used this term of Shetland: Tacitus, *Agricola*, p. 10.

27 Procopius, *The Gothic War*, trans. by Dewing, VI.xv, 416–17.

28 Adam of Bremen, *Gesta*, pp. 1–286.

29 Paul the Deacon, *Pauli historia Langobardorum*, ed. by Bethmann and Waitz, chap. 1.6, pp. 50–51.

and the regions north of the gulf were inhospitable not only to humans but also to wild beasts, because he had heard that wolves crossing the frozen sea would go blind.[30]

The natural phenomena of the Far North were apparently well-known to early medieval writers. Procopius, having learnt of the midnight sun and the polar night, explained that in *Scandza* the sun never set for forty days during summer, but six months later, the sun was gone for forty days.[31] Procopius did not distinguish between the parts of Scandinavia that do not experience the polar night and those areas further north that do, but he was still obviously well informed about the spectacle.

While Paul the Deacon merely commented on the existence of the midnight sun and the winter darkness, we find again the notion of the forty days and nights in Jordanes.[32] He stated that

> In cuius parte arctoa gens Adogit consistit, quae fertur in aestate media quadraginta diebus et noctibus luces habere continuas, itemque brumali tempore eodem dierum noctiumque numero luce clara nescire.[33]

> (In the northern part of the island, the race of the Adogit live, who are said to have continual light in midsummer for forty days and nights, and who likewise have no clear light in the winter season for the same number of days and night.)[34]

Theodor Mommsen interpreted the *Adogit* people as a version of the *Halogios*,[35] the *Háleygir* population of the northernmost Norwegian province of *Hálogaland*. Sophus Bugge has another explanation: that *Adogit* was a corruption of *Andogii*, a people from the northern Norwegian island of Andøya.[36] What is the implication of this information? Topographically, it is the sixty-ninth parallel north that has approximately forty days without sun in the wintertime, corresponding roughly to Andøya in Norway, and the modern town of Nikel in Russia, high above the Arctic Circle. The specification of days need not, however, derive from natural observations at all, but may be of numerological significance corresponding to biblical spiritual numbers, where the number forty represents a trial or test, which such a period of darkness might represent.[37] A depiction of the North as the setting for trials of biblical proportions would give the periphery and its inhabitants a moral purpose: to sustain hardship, possibly as a counter-image to the comfortable way of life at the centre.

---

30 Jordanes, *Romana et Getica*, ed. by Mommsen, 3.18, p. 58.
31 Procopius, *The Gothic War*, trans. by Dewing, vi.xv, 417.
32 Paul the Deacon, *Pauli historia Langobardorum*, ed. by Bethmann and Waitz, p. 50.
33 Jordanes, *Romana et Getica*, ed. by Mommsen, 3.19, p. 58.
34 Mierow, *The Gothic History of Jordanes*, p. 56.
35 Mommsen, *Romana et Getica*, p. 164.
36 Sophus Bugge, 'Om nordiske folkenavne hos Jordanes', p. 98.
37 Christopher Butler, *Number Symbolism*.

In any case, it is not probable that the early medieval historian would have abandoned *his* comfortable life for an adventure at the fringes of the world. Procopius boasted that he would have liked to visit the island of Thule himself to observe these phenomena, but that, alas, he had never had the opportunity.[38] However, he claimed to have spoken to people from Thule and asked how they kept track of the days in the dark.[39] It is interesting to a contemporary reader that Procopious could claim acquaintance with people who originated from the North or knew people who did. It suggests a population in southern Europe maintaining contact with the northern world and thus a degree of travelling between the two. Procopius provides his informants' account of how the northerners celebrated the return of the sun after the forty days of darkness after winter solstice, where after thirty-five days, they tried to see the sun from the highest mountain, after which the whole community celebrated the return of the sun in the darkness. Procopius assumed that these inhabitants of Thule each year would become concerned that the sun did not return.[40] In this way, he points out both the frightening phenomenon of darkness and the naïve dispositions of the northern inhabitants. Jordanes on his side believed that the shifts between light and dark in the northern part of *Scandza* meant that the people living there had a different balance of good and evil from all other men.[41] This, too, was a reception ascribing moral purpose to the northern people, who coped with hardships different from those of the reader's known world. However, Jordanes still described the Far North as a world of plenty, with abundance of young game in the swamps (*palus*) that could feed a growing population.[42] Similarly, Procopius mentioned the abundant game in the Far North, as did Adam of Bremen in his eleventh-century account.[43]

Adam of Bremen described many arctic animals, among them a bear that lived underwater.[44] A polar bear, we would assume. One would think that Adam, in late eleventh-century Germany, had heard of the specimen brought from Greenland by Ísleifur, bishop of Iceland in 1052 — a bishop Adam himself mentioned.[45] Ísleifur gave the polar bear to Emperor Henry III before himself being consecrated in Bremen, probably in Adam's presence.[46] To Adam, the North was a region of magic, inhospitable nature, and odd creatures, and a proof of the challenges and deeds of the bishops in the Hamburg-Bremen archbishopric.

---

38 Procopius, *The Gothic War*, VI, 417.
39 Procopius, *The Gothic War*, VI, 417.
40 Procopius, *The Gothic War*, VI, 418–19.
41 Jordanes, *Romana et Getica*, ed. by Mommsen, 3.20, p. 58.
42 Jordanes, *Romana et Getica*, ed. by Mommsen, 3.21, p. 59.
43 Procopius, *The Gothic War*, VI, 418–19; Adam of Bremen, *Gesta*, p. 266.
44 Adam of Bremen, *Gesta*, 4.32, p. 267.
45 Adam of Bremen, *Gesta*, 4.36, p. 273 (*Isleph*).
46 Nedkvitne, *Norse Greenland*, p. 181.

The Monsters in the Far North

The early medieval perception of 'otherness' and the representation of the world was Eurocentric, but it also contrasted Christians with pagans, and civilization with barbarians. Yet another concept was used in European images of those dwelling at the fringes of the known world: 'the monstrous races'.[47] Medieval teratology used the outskirts of the known world as a tableau of their catalogues, such as Isidore's interpretations of the antipodes thought to live in the far south beyond the 'great heat'.[48] On the *mappae mundi*, the monsters on the fringe of the world are vivid, such as the *uniped*, with one foot, and the *blemmae*, described by Ptolemy, with faces on their torsos and which are numerous in the margins of the Hereford map from *c.* 1300.[49] The monsters at the fringes of the world were usually situated in the south-eastern parts of the world in the early Middle Ages. Later, they also frequented the northern parts. Still, the early medieval monstrous creatures also included those who were barely human, but still human. We find these semi-monsters in depictions of the North; describing a group's strange ways of eating, dressing, and living, and strongly underlining their disgusting habits was a way to animalize those groups as monstrous creatures. Most of the authors who described the North included an account of a people called *Skridfinns* (or some variation of that ethnonym), whom modern scholars take to be a group of the Sámi people due to the suffix *-finn* and because of the medieval correlation between the two, as seen in Alfred's *Orosius*, Saxo's *Gesta Danorum*, and Adam of Bremen.[50] The variations of the prefix, *skrid-*, *skrit-*, *scric-*, etc., probably derive from the Old Norse verb *skriða*, to 'stride' or 'glide', alluding to the activity of skiing. If that was the case, then the European writers would have received this exonym from Scandinavian informants, informants who may also have provided the other descriptions of the Far North.

In the medieval worldview, the barbarians and heathens formed what Hoppenbrouwers calls 'a buffer zone between Christendom and the monstrous races at the earth's periphery'.[51] The extraordinary existence of such monsters is thought not to have undermined Christian beliefs of all men under God, but rather to have demonstrated God's omnipotence. The people located in the Far North in these medieval accounts can accurately be said to have been perceived as monsters, given the animalized description of their way of life. Discussing the role of monsters in ancient and medieval Western culture,

---

47 Hoppenbrouwers, 'Medieval Peoples Imagined', pp. 54, 58–60; Kühnel, 'Das Fremde und das Eigene', pp. 415–28.

48 Kominko, 'New Perspectives on Paradise', pp. 151–52.

49 Buchholtz, 'Being (Non) Human', pp. 215–19.

50 Orosius, ed. by Thorpe, pp. 238–512, esp. p. 246: *Scride-Finnas*; Saxo, *Gesta Danorum*, 0.2.9: *skritfinni*; and Adam of Bremen, *Gesta* 4.24, p. 255 and n.f): scritefini, etc. See, e.g., northern Fennoscandia in Olaus Magnus, *Carta Marina*, 1539.

51 Hoppenbrouwers, 'Medieval Peoples Imagined', p. 59.

Jeffrey Cohen asserts them to be a significant destabilizing part of the logic of the world system, where the 'monstrous Other is […] absolutely essential to the production of the cultural self-same'.[52] Locating the monsters at the peripheries of the world meant they took on the role of vague reflections of intrinsic conflicts in the centre, thus making the monsters a moral depiction of potential degeneration in society. Cohen also finds that some of the monsters portrayed in Western accounts depict moral lessons of virtue, where the deviation of the monster also conferred on it a pious talent.[53] In the accounts of life in the Far North, it is skilfulness in hunting and living under onerous conditions that constitute such virtues, while most authors emphasize the oddities and ungodliness of the creatures there.

Procopius mentioned the northern tribe of the Σκριθίφινοι (Scrithiphini) that 'θηριώδη τινὰ βιοτὴν ἔχουσιν' (live a kind of life akin to that of the beasts).[54] According to him, they did none of the things fit for humans, as they wore neither clothes nor shoes, and did not drink wine or cultivate the land.[55] The Scritiphini only ate the flesh of the abundant game in the area. Similarly, Jordanes named the *Screrefennae* among the numerous peoples dwelling in the northern part of *Scandza*, writing also that they did not eat grain, but rather flesh of animals and birds' eggs.[56] In the eighth century, Paul the Deacon asserted that the *Scritobini* lived in a landscape with eternal snow, with midnight sun and winter darkness.[57] He described them as being not very different from animals, since they jumped around while hunting, ate raw flesh, and wore their prey as clothes. Paul tried to explain the etymology of the name *Scritobini* as deriving from the word 'jumping' in their own language, trying to explain the motion of skis in the snow.[58] The *Scritobini* would be skilful hunters. Paul mentioned 'animal cervo non satis absimile' (an animal not very unlike a stag), which is obviously a description of the reindeer roaming the Scandinavian peninsula.[59] He even claimed to have seen a tunic made from this animal's hide similar to what he claimed 'Scritobini utuntur' (the Scritobini use). While it is probable that the European historians never went to the North Sea or further north, it is apparent that Paul the Deacon also had contact with those who had knowledge of the northern regions.

---

52 Cohen, 'The Order of Monsters', p. 37.

53 Cohen, 'The Order of Monsters', p. 51.

54 Procopius, *The Gothic War*, VI, 418–19.

55 Procopius, *The Gothic War*, VI, 418–19.

56 Jordanes, *Romana et Getica*, ed. by Mommsen, 3.21, p. 59.

57 Paul the Deacon, *Pauli historia Langobardorum*, ed. by Bethmann and Waitz, chap. 1.5, pp. 49–50. There are a number variants in the manuscripts, e.g., *Scrittobini*, *Scriptofinni*, and *Cristobini*, among others. See *Pauli historia Langobardorum*, ed. by Bethmann and Waitz, p. 49 n. y).

58 Paul the Deacon, *Pauli historia Langobardorum*, ed. by Bethmann and Waitz, chap. 1.5, pp. 49–50.

59 Paul the Deacon, *Pauli historia Langobardorum*, ed. by Bethmann and Waitz, chap. 1.5, p. 50.

While the high medieval perceptions of the North were more apt to contain extraordinary elements than the early medieval works, Paul found room in the Far North for the well-known Christian and Islamic myth of the seven sleepers of Ephesus, sleeping in a cave, their bodies and clothes unharmed by time. The traditional myth originated in the East, and prophecies said that the seven sleepers would wake up when Christianity was acknowledged in certain lands. The story was also included in the Koran and mentioned by Gregory of Tours.[60] Paul, however, placed them 'in extremis circium versus Germaniae finibus, in ipso oceani littore, antrum sub eminenti rupe cospicitur' ([i]n the farthest boundaries of Germany towards the west-northwest, on the shore of the ocean itself, a cave is seen under a projecting rock).[61] This could be interpreted as being on the shore of the North Sea, but since Paul continues that 'Huic loco Scritobini […] vicini sunt' (the *Scritobini*, […] are neighbours to this place), it appears that Paul wanted the seven sleepers in the Far North.[62] He stated that the men would wake up one day and preach to the heathens up in the North and save their souls. In this way, the extreme north could function as a mythical land and the ideal setting for out-of-this-world stories.

The setting of the story of the seven sleepers was copied twice as scholia by Adam of Bremen in the *Gesta*.[63] Adam referred to, and clearly based much of his knowledge on, Paul the Deacon. He ultimately concluded that those who lived in Norway, in spite of their earlier violent and sinful and heathen ways, were now most pious people,[64] with the exception of those who lived by the sea farthest north, the *skritefingi*.[65] They were still engaged in witchcraft and soothsaying. Even worse, they were good at it. By murmuring spells, they could attract large sea mammals to the shore. The horrible North covered in eternal snow would be a perfect place for the *Skridfinns*: Adam declared that they could not live without snow and even ran faster than the wild animals they hunted in it. To Adam, then, the otherness of the northernmost people contrasted with the success of the Church in Christianizing the south.

Moreover, in Adam's account, the North was edged with the Riphean Mountains, where monsters lived, according to one of the comments inserted in the text (no. 137).[66] The myths of the Riphean Mountains may be a twisted version of Pliny's description from the first century, in which he placed the *Ripaean* Mountains close to the region called 'Pterophorus'

60 Foulke, *History of the Langobards*, p. 6 n. 1.
61 Paul the Deacon, *Pauli historia Langobardorum*, ed. by Bethmann and Waitz, chap. 1.4, p. 49.
62 Paul the Deacon, *Pauli historia Langobardorum*, ed. by Bethmann and Waitz, chap. 1.4, p. 49. Adam also understood him thus, Adam of Bremen, *Gesta*, 4.21, schol. 129, p. 250: 'Paulus in Gestis Longobardorum de fecunditate gentium septentrionalium et VII viris, qui in litore occeani iacent in provincia Scritefingorum'.
63 Adam of Bremen, *Gesta*, 4.21, pp. 250 and 4.32, p. 266.
64 Adam of Bremen, *Gesta*, 4.31, pp. 264–66.
65 Adam of Bremen, *Gesta*, 4.32, p. 266, also pp. 158, 223, 250, 255–56, and 274.
66 Adam of Bremen, *Gesta*, 4.25, shol. 137, p. 256.

(feather-bearer), because of the snow falling there being like feathers. This was a part of the world that according to Pliny lay under the 'munda damnata' (curse of nature) that was covered in dense fog, and unoccupied except for the work of frost and the north wind.[67] Adam added griffins and other monsters to the image.

A more puzzling description from Adam's *Gesta* is of the people neighbouring the *Skridfinns*. These were bearded women who lived in the mountains in the North, while the men lived in the woods and were rarely seen: 'In asperrimis, quae ibi sunt, alpibus audivi mulieres esse barbatas. Viros autem silvicolas raro se prebere videndos'.[68] It is often presumed that the 'bearded women' are a result of Adam's misunderstanding; perhaps he confused the Norse word for women, *kvenna*, with the group of people called *kvæn* (*cwenas, quene*) mentioned by Orosius in the fifth century and by Ohthere in the ninth.[69] However, Adam used the word *mulieres*, not *kvæns*.[70] Adam could, nevertheless, have been told this tall story by others who had made that mistake, and consequently wrote the infamous description of women in the Far North. *Barbatas* may also be scribal error for *barbaras*, savage women, or *barbaros*, as appears in some manuscript copies.[71] Adam did not explain why the women would have beards and the men hid in the woods, but this portrayal must have had a pedagogic function, demonstrating a twisted pagan society. Volke Scior suggests that these appearances in Adam's *Gesta* are an expression of the process of civilizing and a counter-image of the known, Christian world.[72] The Far North would be a fitting location to place such creatures and imagine a scary, upside-down world where women were in charge. To Adam, then, the Norse population consisted of scruffy but virtuous barbarians who slowly came into the faith, while the *Skridfinns*, together with the other northerners, constituted the monstrous races.

These outside receptions of the Far North include some fantastic elements. However, depictions of the North in texts where the author was positioned closer geographically to northern Scandinavia and therefore, one would think, ought to have had better knowledge of the region's physical conditions, often include even more exaggerated descriptions of the Far North.[73] The Icelandic legendary sagas are one example of this. Set in the age of the Vikings, but seemingly written in the twelfth and thirteenth centuries, these sagas portrayed the Far North as a fabled land. For instance, in the *Hrafnistasögur*, we meet

---

67 Pliny, *Historia Naturalis*, VI.12.88, p. 341.

68 Adam of Bremen, *Gesta*, 4.32, p. 266.

69 See, for example, Lönborg, *Adam af Bremen*, p. 147; See also Simek, 'The Shape of the Earth in the Middle Ages', pp. 293–303.

70 For instance, in Ohthere's Voyages, ed. by Thorpe, pp. 249–53, esp. pp. 250–51: *cwene*.

71 Schmeidler, *Gesta Hammaburgensis ecclesiae pontificum*, p. 266 n. b) and c).

72 Scior, *Das Eigene und das Fremde*, p. 127.

73 See examples from medieval Nordic literature in Simek, '"Monstra septentrionalia"', and Donecker, *Beiträge zum zirkumpolaren Norden*, pp. 55–75.

four generations of male protagonists, who venture north to *Finnmǫrk* in search of fish and game. In the North, the protagonist finds an abundance of supplies, but also many dangers, especially in his meetings with the Sámi population and other inhabitants of a more mysterious nature, as discussed by Eleanor Barraclough elsewhere in this volume. The sagas present the North as a terrible place of trolls, ghosts, death, and magic, which the hero must overcome to claim his reward from the abundant resources. In this way, the wonders of the magic North, along with the cleverness and bravery of the protagonist, would become part of the origin myths of the Icelanders, who claimed to be descended from Norwegian families.

Another source stemming from a northern writer is the anonymous work *Historia Norwegie*, which is a description of the regions and peoples of Norway and events in the eleventh and twelfth centuries.[74] It was written by an author thought to be a monk, thought by some to date possibly to the late twelfth century and by others to the early thirteenth. The opus gives a chilling picture of the North, in particular the waters outside *Hálogaland*, which are described as filled with terror and ice.[75] The author tells how nature spits icebergs into the sea, and sailors, when taking the route from *Hálogaland* to Greenland, were sometimes forced to sail into them, endangering life and ship. Whales lurked there that could capsize boats and swallow sailors. A one-eyed horse-whale could be found there, and the dreaded *hafstrambr*, a tree-trunk-like giant monster without head or tail that was considered a sign of peril for seafarers; further terrors included the *hafgufa* and the *hafrkitta*, the biggest of all sea monsters, and, according to the author, there were countless more.[76] The monster catalogue probably derived from a contemporary teratological notion of the northern seas.[77] It must have become a standard catalogue, as the sea monsters have clear resemblances to those depicted on the 1539 *Carta Marina* of Olaus Magnus. A distinct pattern in perceptions of the North was that, while the early medieval texts emphasized the marvels and inhumanity on this fringe of the world, the high medieval texts depicted its natural terror and ungodliness to a greater extent. The emphasis on extraordinary phenomena in high medieval accounts from northern Europe, such as Hamburg or Iceland, could be explained by anthropological theories about the centre–periphery on the establishment of a new centre, which would make it important to create a counter-image of the neighbours. When engaging in such positioning, the high medieval writer would need to distinguish their own dominant position at the centre and to emphasize the otherness of the proximate peripheries.

---

74 *Historia Norwegie*, ed. by Storm. The dating of the source is disputed, see Phelpstead, 'Introduction', pp. xvi–xvii.
75 *Historia Norwegie*, ed. by Storm, p. 79.
76 *Historia Norwegie*, ed. by Storm, p. 80.
77 Simek, '"Monstra septentrionalia"'.

Conclusion

In the early Middle Ages, the landscape of the North was described as cold, strange, and scary. The people dwelling in this frightening borderland between the known world and the outside were not seen as human because they lived in an uninhabitable land. They were therefore represented either as monstrous or as ungodly heathens with magic skills. Such extreme places challenged the established order of God in the centre, although it did not necessarily hinder the presence of Christianity, as we see in the descriptions of Paul the Deacon. As with other peripheries, the North comprised a fringe of the world where Christian writers based in central parts of Europe could stage 'otherness' and ungodliness, as well as a scene for lessons to those living within the civilized world.

It is clear that receptions of the Far North were based on first- or second-hand knowledge of people who had been there. It appears, however, that the later writers who were closer to this northern region, including Adam of Bremen and the author of the *Historia Norwegie*, included stories that were more fantastic than earlier accounts, and the writings from the High Middle Ages were filled with more extraordinary elements than the earlier texts, even though the later writers would have had easier access to actual knowledge about the region. Later writers, closer to the North, thus appear to be more disposed to create a division between the magic North and the normal South. For an author establishing himself in the centre, the need to create 'otherness' in the periphery was apparently greater than the forces of proximity.

Works Cited

Manuscripts and Archival Sources

Brussels, Bibliothèque royale, MS 10146, fol. 109^v (French, ninth–tenth century)
Saint Petersburg, Russian National Library, MS lat. Q.v.XVII, no. 3, fol. 1^r (tenth–eleventh century)
Leiden, Universiteitsbibliotheek, MS Gron 78, fol. 51^r (twelfth century)

Primary Sources

Adam of Bremen, *Gesta Hammaburgensis ecclesiae pontificum*, in *Adam von Bremen, Hamburgische Kirchengeschichte*, ed. by Bernhard Schmeidler, *Monumenta Germaniae Historica*, Scriptores rerum Germanicarum in usum scholarum separatim editi, 2 (Hannover: Hahn, 1917), pp. 1–286
Historia Norwegie, in *Monumenta historica Norvegiæ: Latinske kildeskrifter til Norges historie i middelalderen*, ed. by Gustav Storm (Kristiania: AW Brøgger, 1880), pp. 71–124

Isidore of Seville, *The Etymologies of Isidore of Seville*, ed. by Stephen A. Barney, W. J. Lewis, J. A. Beach, and Oliver Berghof (Cambridge: Cambridge University Press, 2006)

Jordanes, *Romana et Getica*, ed. by Theodor Mommsen, *Monumenta Germaniae Historica*, Auctores antiquissimi, 5.1 (Berlin: Weidmann, 1882)

'Origo Gentis Langobardorum', ed. by Georg Waitz, *Monumenta Germaniae Historica*, Scriptores rerum Langobardicarum et Italicarum saec., VI–IX 1 (Hannover: Hahn, 1878), pp. 1–6

Orosius, 'Alfred's Anglo-Saxon Version of Orosius', in *The Life of Alfred the Great: Translated from the German of Dr R. Pauli; to which is Appended Alfred's Anglo-Saxon Version of Orosius*, ed. by Benjamin Thorpe (New York: Bohn, 1873), pp. 238–512

Ohthere's Voyages, 'Alfred's Anglo-Saxon Version of Orosius', in *The Life of Alfred the Great: Translated from the German of Dr R. Pauli; to which is Appended Alfred's Anglo-Saxon Version of Orosius*, ed. by Benjamin Thorpe (New York: Bohn, 1873), pp. 249–53

Paul the Deacon, *Pauli historia Langobardorum*, in *Monumenta Germaniae Historica, Scriptores rerum Langobardicarum et Italicarum saec, VI–IX*, ed. by L. Bethmann and G. Waitz, 12–187 (Hannover: Hahn, 1878), pp. 12–187

Pliny the Elder, *Plinii, C. Secundi. Naturalis Historiae Libri XXXVII*, ed. by Karl Mayhoff, vol. I, books I– VI (Leipzig: Teubner, 1906)

Procopius, *The Gothic War*, in *History of the Wars*, trans. by H. B. Dewing, vol. III (Cambridge, MA: Harvard University Press, 1916)

Saxo, *Gesta Danorum*, ed. by Jørgen Olrik and Hans Ræder (Copenhagen: Royal Library, 1931)

Secondary Works

Baldwin, Barry, 'Sources for the Getica of Jordanes', *Revue belge de philologie et d'histoire*, 59.1 (1981), 141–46

Barber, Peter, 'Medieval Maps of the World', in *The Hereford World Map: Medieval World Maps and Their Context*, ed. by Paul D. A. Harvey (London: British Library, 2006), pp. 1–43

Bremner, R. W., 'The Underlying Projection of Mappaemundi', in *The Hereford World Map: Medieval World Maps and Their Context*, ed. by Paul D. A. Harvey (London: British Library, 2006), pp. 209–21

Bridgman, Timothy P., *Hyperboreans: Myth and History in Celtic-Hellenic Contacts* (New York: Routledge, 2004)

Buchholtz, Mirosława, 'Being (Non) Human, or on the Topography of "Monsters" Medieval and Modern', *Avant*, 8.2 (2017), 215–19

Butler, Christopher, *Number Symbolism* (New York: Routledge, 1970)

Bugge, Sophus, 'Om nordiske folkenavne hos Jordanes: optegnelser', *Fornvännen – Journal of Swedish Antiquarian Research*, 98 (1907), 98–101

Casson, S., 'The Hyperboreans', *The Classical Review*, 34.1–2 (1920), 1–3

Cohen, Jeffrey Jerome, 'The Order of Monsters: Monster Lore and Medieval Narrative Traditions', in *Telling Tales: Medieval Narratives and the Folk Tradition*, ed. by Francesca Canadé Sautman, Diana Conchado, and Giuseppe C. Di Scipio (New York: MacMillan, 1998), pp. 37–58

Dreyer-Eimbcke, Oswald, *Island, Grönland und das nördliche Eismeer im Bild der Kartographie seit dem 10. Jahrhundert* (Stuttgart: Steiner, 1987)

Foulke, William Dudley, *History of the Langobards (Historia Langobardorum) by Paul the Deacon (Paulus Diaconus)* (Philadelphia: University of Pennsylvania Press, 1907)

Fraesdorff, David, *Der barbarische Norden: Vorstellungen und Fremdheitskategorien bei Rimbert, Thietmar von Merseburg, Adam von Bremen und Helmold von Bosau*, v (Berlin: de Gruyter, 2005)

Hemmingsen, Lars, 'Middelaldergeografien og Histora Norwegie', in *Olavslegenden og den latinske historieskrivning i 1100-tallets Norge*, ed. by Inger Ekrem, Lars Boje Mortensen, and Karen Skovgaard-Petersen (Copenhagen: Museum Tusculanum Press, 2000), pp. 26–53

Hiatt, Alfred, 'The Map of Macrobius before 1100', *Imago Mundi*, 59.2 (2007), 149–76

Hoppenbrouwers, Peter, 'Medieval Peoples Imagined', in *Imagology: The Cultural Construction and Literary Representation of National Characters: A Critical Survey*, ed. by Manfred Beller and Joep Leerssen, Studia Imagologica, 13 (Amsterdam: Rodopi, 2007), pp. 45–62

Kominko, Maja, 'New Perspectives on Paradise. The Levels of Reality in Byzantine and Latin Medieval Maps', in *Cartography in Antiquity and the Middle Ages: Fresh Perspectives, New Methods. Technology and Change in History*, ed. by Richard J. A. Talbert and Richard W. Unger (Leiden: Brill, 2008), pp. 139–53

Kühnel, Harry, 'Das Fremde und das Eigene (Mittelalter)', in *Europäishe Mentalitätsgeschichte: Hauptthemen in Einzeldarstellungen*, ed. by P. Dinzelbacher (Stuttgart: Kröner, 1993), pp. 415–28

Lauha, Aarre, *Zaphon: Der Norden und Nordvölker im Alten Testament*, Vetenskapliga Samfundens Förlags expedition (Helsinki: Suomalainen Tiedeakatemia, 1943)

Lönborg, Sven Erik, *Adam af Bremen och hans skildring av Nordeuropas länder och folk* (Uppsala: Wretman, 1897)

Lutz, Henry L. F., *Plaga Septentrionalis in Sumero-Akkadian Mythology* (Berkeley: University of California Press, 1951)

Mayer, Maximilian, 'Hyperboreer', *Ausführliches Lexikon der griechischen und römischen Mythologie I–II*, ed. by Wilhelm H. Roscher (Leipzig: Teubner, 1884–1937), pp. 2836–41

Mierow, Charles C., *The Gothic History of Jordanes in English Version: With an Introduction and Commentary* (Princeton: Princeton University Press, 1915)

Molina Moreno, Francisco, 'Bilder des heiligen Nordens in Antike, Patristik und Mittelalter', in *Ultima Thule, Bilder des Nordens von der Antike bis zur Gegenwart*, ed. by Annelore Engel-Braunschmidt and others (Bern: Lang, 2001), pp. 47–65

Nedkvitne, Arnved, *Norse Greenland: Viking Peasants in the Arctic* (New York: Routledge, 2018)

Phelpstead, Carl, 'Introduction', in *A History of Norway and the Passion and Miracles of the Blessed Óláfr*, ed. by Carl Phelpstead, Viking Society for Northern Research Text, 13 (London: University College London, 2001), pp. xvi–xvii

Rapp, Adolf, 'Boreas', in *Ausführliches Lexikon der griechischen und römischen Mythologie I–II*, ed. by Wilhelm H. Roscher (Leipzig: Teubner, 1884–1937), pp. 804–14

Rix, Robert, *The Barbarian North in Medieval Imagination: Ethnicity, Legend, and Literature*, Routledge Studies in Medieval Religion and Culture, 11 (New York: Routledge, 2014)

Roscher, Wilhelm Heinrich, *Ausführliches Lexikon der griechischen und römischen Mythologie I–II* (Leipzig: Teubner, 1884–1937)

Scior, Volker, *Das Eigene und das Fremde: Identität und Fremdheit in den Chroniken Adams von Bremen, Helmolds von Bosau und Arnolds von Lübeck*, Orbis mediaevalis. Vorstellungswelten des Mittelalters, 4 (Berlin: de Gruyter, 2002)

Simek, Rudolf, '"Monstra septentrionalia": Supernatural Beings of the Far North', in *Imagining the Supernatural North*, ed. by Eleanor Rosamund Barraclough, Danielle Cudmore, and Stefan Donecker, Beiträge zum zirkumpolaren Norden, 3 (Edmonton: University of Alberta Press, 2016), pp. 55–75

——, 'The Shape of the Earth in the Middle Ages and Medieval Mappaemundi', in *The Hereford World Map: Medieval World Maps and their Context*, ed. by P. Harvey (London: British Library, 2006), pp. 293–303

Storm, Gustav, *Monumenta historica Norvegiæ: latinske kildeskrifter til Norges historie i middelalderen* (Kristiania: AW Brøgger, 1880)

Thompson, Oliver, *The History of Ancient Geography* (Cambridge: Cambridge University Press, 1948)

Myth, Magic, and Rituals in the Nordic World

LARS IVAR HANSEN

On the View of 'the Other' — Abroad and At Home: The Geography and Peoples of the Far North, According to *Historia Norwegie*[1]

In this discussion I want to focus a spotlight on what *Historia Norwegie* (hereafter H.N.) reports on relations in the Far North, on the Sámi and on the interaction between Norwegians and Sámi, as well as additional peoples further to the east in the North Calotte.[2] I shall concentrate on a summary of the peoples who were perceived, to a greater or lesser extent, as standing outside the Norse, Christian cultural complex. In this context I shall not, therefore, occupy myself with the populations of Iceland or the islands of the North Sea, which in H.N. are summarized using the term 'tributary islands' (*tributariae insulae*).

I shall seek to present the depiction of these peoples in the light of research results within the social sciences and humanities that relate to ethnic affiliation and ethnic demarcation. This includes how various groups of people relate to one another, use various aspects of their cultural property to mark their own identity and distinctiveness from others, and how they place different ethnic 'labels' and other 'characteristics' on one another in the course of these processes. Finally, I want to focus on the conclusions we can draw from this analysis regarding the work's provenance and the author behind the text. Before I embark on my main subject, however, I want to make some comments on the work itself, and try to place and characterize it as a textual source.

---

1 This article is a translation of Hansen, Lars Ivar 'Om synet på de "andre"—ute og hjemme. Geografi og folkeslag på Nordkalotten i følge Historia Norwegiae', in *Olavslegenden og den latinske historieskrivning i 1100-tallets Norge*, ed. by Inger Ekrem, Lars Boje Mortensen, and Karen Skovgaard-Petersen (Copenhagen: Museum Tusculanum Press, 2000), pp. 54–88, and published here by kind permission of Museum Tusculanum Press.
2 By the *North Calotte*, I here refer to northern Fennoscandia and parts of north-western Russia, i.e. the Kola peninsula and the White Sea region.

Lars Ivar Hansen, UiT The Arctic University of Norway, lars.ivar.hansen@uit.no

Myths and Magic in the Medieval Far North: Realities and Representations of a Region on the Edge of Europe, ed. by Stefan Figenschow, Richard Holt, and Miriam Tveit, AS 10 (Turnhout: Brepols, 2020), pp. 39–69
© BREPOLS ❧ PUBLISHERS   10.1484/M.AS-EB.5.120519

Historia Norwegie as a literary product

H.N. is an outstanding example of a genre of Latin-language texts authored by educated clerics in the early Middle Ages and High Middle Ages that include descriptions of a geographical and ethnographical character, as well as chronicle representations of historical events, principally linked to kings and other figures of authority as well as their kinship relationships and dynasties. Regarding texts of a comparable style preceding and contemporaneous with H.N., one might point to, for example, Adam of Bremen's account of *The History of the Archbishops of Hamburg-Bremen* (*Gesta Hammaburgensis ecclesiae pontificum*), and *Theodoric the Monk's History of the Kings of Norway from Antiquity* (*Historia de Antiquitate Regum Norwagiensium*), without at this stage making any decision concerning the mutual influence and interdependency between these texts and H.N.

From the first publication of this work, by P. A. Munch in 1850, and up until the aftermath of the Second World War in the mid-twentieth century, there was extensive discussion of the work's origins, the identification of the author, and the works, submissions, and traditions on which the author was building. A series of alternatives were launched throughout this debate concerning the probable dating of the text and the identity of the author; a wide range of circumstances were discussed regarding the origins of some of the reports and individual items of information, as well as both direct and indirect citations incorporated by the author in the text. The debate seemed to quieten down somewhat after about 1950, but central, significant contributions nonetheless continued to be submitted up until the turn of the century.[3]

The questions relating to the exact date of the work and its presumable author were thoroughly illuminated by Inger Ekrem (1998) who, besides a detailed historiographical review, made a persuasive argument that the work

---

3 Aside from the observations made by Munch in his edition, central contributions to the research debate have been made in the following works: Storm, in his edition of *Monumenta Historica Norvegiae*; Hægstad, 'Tillegg. Det norske skriftgrunnlaget i *Historia Norvegiae*'; Paasche, 'Norges og Islands litteratur indtil utgangen av middelalderen'; Skard, 'Målet i *Historia Norvegiae*'; Aðalbjarnarson, *Om de norske kongers saga*; Koht, *Innhogg og utsyn i norsk historie*; Koht, '1. Historia Norvegiae'; Hanssen, *Omkring Historia Norwegiae*; Steinnes, 'Ikring *Historia Norvegiae*'; Steinnes, 'Meir om *Historia Norvegiae*'; Robberstad, 'Ordet patria i *Historia Norvegiae*'; Nordal, 'Litteraturhistorie B. Norge og Island'; Ellehøj, *Studier over den ældste norrøne historieskrivning*; de Vries, 'Altnordische Literaturgeschichte, Bd. II: Die Literatur von etwa 1150 bis 1300. Die Spätzeit nach 1300'; Chesnutt, 'The Dalhousie Manuscript of the Historia Norvegiae'; Lange, 'Die Anfänge der isländisch-norwegischen Geschichtsschreibung'; Ekrem, *Nytt lys over Historia Norwegie. Mot en løsning i debatten om dens alder?*; Ekrem and Mortensen, *Historia Norwegie*. The principal views and main features of the older debate are summarized by Anne Holtsmark in a separate article about the work in *KLNM* (vol. VI, columns 585–87) and by Astrid Salvesen in the introduction to her translation, published in *Thorleif Dahls kulturbibliotek* (Salvesen, *Norges historie — Historien om de gamle norske kongene — Historien om danenes ferd til Jerusalem*).

must have come into existence before 1152/1153, and that this reflects Norwegian clerical endeavours to establish a Norwegian national ecclesiastical province (archdiocese).[4] So far, the most comprehensive presentation of H.N. and the discussion of the work's dating, place of origin, style, and narrative — as well as previous research — is the book by Inger Ekrem and Lars Boje Mortensen, published in 2003 bearing the title *Historia Norwegie*. It also contains an updated English translation by Peter Fisher.[5] Basing himself on various information given in the work, Mortensen sketches out various plausible time-spans for the work's origin: a completely certain interval between 1140 and 1265 AD; and a narrower, earlier one between 1150 and 1200 AD. However, he concludes that the period *c.* 1160–1175 appears most appealing.[6]

I shall not dwell further on this debate of identifying the exact date of the work or its likely author in my presentation, but concentrate on the overall picture that these investigations have been able to confirm concerning the profusion of texts, manuscripts, reported items, and points of view on which the author draws in assembling his manuscript. It has been observed, for instance, that the author quotes the Bible from the Vulgate version, and he gives the impression of having studied at a French or Anglo-Norman school. It is further assumed that he has knowledge of an Icelandic version of the genealogy of *Ynglingatal*,[7] and may have had access to a lost Latin work by Sæmundr *fróði*.[8] This latter work may also have served as a source for *Ágrip*. At any rate, it seems that H.N., *Ágrip*, and Oddr Snorrason the monk all drew on common sources, which may — according to Bjarni Aðalbarnarson — have included a lost 'Opplandssaga'.[9] The author also has a knowledge of an edition of the English line of kings (up to Henry I), which was included in the work *Liber de legibus Angliae* and incorporated in the annals of Roger of Hoveden.[10]

Of the more refined observations, one might single out Asgaut Steinnes's conclusion that the author must have had access to a Latin manuscript that was lost in the Fire of Copenhagen in 1728, of which we know the contents through diverse archive registrations, the so-called 'Sorø manuscript'. The contents of the Sorø manuscript included the following: 1) transcripts of parts of Adam of Bremen's work on the archbishops of Hamburg; 2) transcripts of two works by French theologian and author Honorius Augustodunensis[11]

4　Ekrem, '*Nytt lys over Historia Norwegie. Mot en løsning i debatten om dens alder?*'.

5　*Historia Norwegie*, ed. by Ekrem and Mortensen, pp. 49–105. The citations from H.N. in this article are quoted from Peter Fisher's translation in this edition.

6　Mortensen, 'Introduction', pp. 11–24.

7　*Ynglinga tal* is a skaldic poem presenting the genealogy of old — and mythic — Norse kings, cited by Snorre Sturlason in the first part of his work Heimskringla: the *Ynglinga Saga*. See Sturlason, *Heimskringla or The Lives of the Norse Kings*, pp. 1–35.

8　Holtsmark, 'Historia Norvegiae', column 586.

9　Steinnes, 'Ikring *Historia Norvegiae*'.

10　Storm, *Monumenta Historica Norvegiae, Latinske kildeskrifter til Norges Historie i Middelalderen*, ed. by Storm, p. xxi.

11　= from Autun, France.

(*c.* 1080–*c.* 1156): *Imago mundi* and *De philosophia et ratione mundi*; 3) excerpts from some works by the Roman geographer Solinus (third century); and 4) other, minor works, such as a genealogy of the kings of Denmark and a mnemonic for school purposes about the use of synonyms. The author of H.N. is guilty of confusing Honorius with Solinus, and believes himself to be citing Solinus when he is in fact referring to Honorius.[12] The reason for this is supposedly to be found in the Sorø manuscript, where the works of Honorius were quoted anonymously and inserted between the other texts in such a way that the mistake could be made.[13] On that basis, Steinnes maintains that the author of H.N. must himself have been resident in Roskilde (possibly in exile), became acquainted with the manuscript there and may even have prepared H.N. itself in these surroundings.

According to both Skard and Steinnes, a number of features are to be found in H.N. which the author appears to have borrowed or copied from *Imago mundi* by Honorius: several formulations appear in the introductions to both works, similarly several imitations of transitional forms between paragraphs.[14]

Of the remarkable accounts that are also to be found in a number of earlier works, the story of the 'beaver bondsman' may be singled out. In connection with an otherwise sober and factual account of the beaver's habitat and the furnishing of a beaver den, it is claimed that 'bondsmen', or slaves, are to be found among beavers, used amongst other things as work animals and a means of transport by the other beavers. Such bondsmen would supposedly lie on their backs and be used as a sledge to transport tree-trunks home to the den.[15] As early as the 1880 edition, Gustav Storm claimed that this story was a *Leitmotif* found in other sources dating from about the same time (or a little later, if we accept Ekrem's suggestion regarding the date of the text). Thus, the Welsh archdeacon Gerald of Wales (Giraldus Cambrensis) uses it in his *Topographica Hiberniae I* (dating from 1187), *Itinerarium Cambriae* (II, 3, dating from 1191) and his *Descriptio Cambriae* (I, 5, dating from 1194). According to Steinnes, the story is also included in a Danish book of history *Chronicon Lethrense*, written in Roskilde in 1170, or a little earlier.[16] It is further repeated in well-known historical summaries dating from succeeding centuries, including those of the thirteenth-century German scholar Albertus Magnus

---

12 In the section about earthquakes and other natural phenomena, under the description of Iceland.

13 Steinnes, 'Ikring *Historia Norwegiae*', pp. 17–30.

14 Skard, 'Målet i Historia Norwegiae'; Steinnes, 'Ikring *Historia Norwegiae*', p. 17.

15 'When the beavers have sweated a good deal gathering their winter provisions, they saw round lofty elms with their teeth (they are particularly fond of chewing the bark of this tree), and load the wood on to one of their slaves, who lies on his back holding a log between his forepaws; in this way, using him as a cart, they drag home a large stack of timber, for by gripping the log with their jaws on each side, they help to drag their porter along'. (*Historia Norwegie*, ed. by Ekrem and Mortensen, p. 61).

16 Steinnes, 'Meir om *Historia Norwegiae*', p. 176.

(*De Animalibus* liber XXII, tract. II, cap. I: *de castore*) and Olaus Magnus (*Historia de Gentibus Septentrionalibus…* , 1555, bk XVIII, chap. 5).

The work of foreign origin that it is perhaps easiest to find traces of in H.N. is Adam of Bremen's work on the archbishops of Hamburg. Researchers seem to agree that the author of H.N. had access to Adam's entire work. There is no doubt that material has been borrowed from the preface and the second book, and from the fourth and final book containing the geographical report of the Nordic countries.[17]

One curious example, which is of special interest in this context, is the interpretation of Kvenland as 'women's land', or *terra feminarum*. Kvenland as a place name is well-established in Norse sources; its localization in the coastal landscapes around the innermost and northernmost parts of the Gulf of Bothnia seems undisputed, not least following the investigations of Finnish historian Kyösti Julku (1986). After providing a sober description of the non-Christian peoples to be found to the east of Norway, the author of H.N. slips in the following, attributing the information to some errant seafarers:

> … they finally put in among Greenlanders and Bjarms, where, they claimed, they came upon people of extraordinary size,[18] and land of maidens, who are reputed to conceive when they have sipped water.[19]

This citation from H.N. is an abbreviated rendering of Adam's observations on 'the land of women', which he identified as the 'Land of Amazons', perceived partly as situated beyond the Land of the Swedes and partly as an island in the Baltic Sea:

> In this sea there are also very many other islands, all infested by ferocious barbarians and for this reason avoided by navigators. Likewise, round about the shores of the Baltic Sea, it is said, live the Amazons in what is now called the land of women. Some declare that these women conceive by sipping water. Some, too, assert that they are made pregnant by the merchants who pass that way, or by the men whom they hold captive in their midst, or by various monsters, which are not rare there. This explanation we also believe to be more credible.[20]

These examples serve to illuminate a phenomenon named *intertextuality* by literary theorists, as this appears in H.N.: through innumerable overt and obscure citations and allusions, references, reproductions of individual clarifications and entire reports, genealogies, and chronological histories, the

---

17 Steinnes, 'Ikring *Historia Norvegiae*', p. 17.
18 See also Adam of Bremen, *History of the Archbishops of Hamburg-Bremen*, trans. by Tschan, bk IV, chap. 41, where Frisian seamen are said to have encountered an island north of Iceland where there were '*homines mirae altitudinis*' (surprisingly tall men).
19 *Historia Norwegie*, ed. by Ekrem and Mortensen, p. 55.
20 Adam of Bremen, *History of the archbishops of Hamburg-Bremen*, trans. by Tschan, bk IV, chap. 19, p. 200.

account builds on earlier writings to varying degrees. This applies both to works of foreign origin and to works that form part of the oldest sections of Norwegian–Icelandic (Norse) Saga literature. Traditional material in general circulation was incorporated as well.

This is a methodological consideration to have in mind, when we are about to review items of information about other peoples — both near and far — and determine whether there is any system or 'inner logic' in the way they are depicted. If their depiction builds upon the compilation of a wide range of information from various works and different traditional sources then we cannot expect to find any great systemization or innate developed 'logic' in the way in which these peoples are depicted and presented.

H.N. is nonetheless not, in my opinion, presented in a purely *compilatory* fashion. As I now embark on a discussion of the Sámi, Norwegians and other peoples of the Far North, my working hypothesis will be twofold:

1) In the first place, the depictions of the Sámi and the author's overall perspective of them seem to be of a nature such that it is reasonable to assume that the author is here building on his own information, or upon a separate traditional source that it is not really possible to find a trace of anywhere else, neither in works of foreign origin nor within the roots of Norse Saga literature.

2) Secondly, there seems to be an essential difference between the way in which the author treats the Sámi — in respect of being one of the not-yet-Christian peoples who have the greatest contact with the Norwegians — and the other peoples located further east. In the case of the latter, their depiction seems to be based to a greater extent on the perpetuation of information provided by others, but nevertheless in a way revealing essential characteristics of how Christian northerners and these other peoples related to one another.

Apart from Inger Ekrem (2003), very few have addressed or focused on the ethnographical description of the Sámi and other peoples of the Far North with regard to an assessment of the provenance, authorship, and tradition behind H.N. True, Andreas Holmsen (1977) analysed H.N.'s geographical and ethnographical descriptions with regard to mapping relations between the Norwegians and the Sámi, and the broadening of Norwegian state power in the northern regions during this period. But the items of information contained in H.N. were then first and foremost used for charting the actual situation, and not for analysing the conceptual framework.

On the Labelling and Naming of Ethnic Groups

Traditional perceptions of ethnic groups, ethnic identity, and affiliation tended to link the question of ethnicity closely to culture, emphasizing the content or 'substantial' differences in the various cultural complexes manifested by ethnic groups. Cultural differences then tended to be perceived as determined and 'objective'.

Against this — since the 1960s within the social sciences sphere, and gradually and increasingly in humanities research — ethnic divisions have been regarded as social phenomena, as the results of communicative processes, essentially concerned with ethnic groups' categorization and delimitation in relation to one another. The focus is thus on the 'relational dimension', where ethnic differences have been regarded as the result of communication between the groups, and where cultural traits are emphasized, sustained, and altered due to changing needs for the consolidation of a group's own values internally, and a clear demarcation in relation to the values of other people's externally.[21] By means of these processes, some cultural traits acquire the character of symbols marking their own identity, unity, and consolidation within the group, at the same time as appearing to highlight external contrast and an identification of 'the Other'. At an external level, different traits such as language, costume traditions, architectural styles, and livelihood adaptation may act as markers of this kind. Regardless of historical origin and the possible borrowing of certain cultural elements from other groups, however, such symbols gain their own weight over time and form part of the overall cultural repertoire that each generation inherits from its forebears through a process of socialization.

This relational, dynamic perception of ethnicity and ethnic divisions has won through, partly on the basis of recognizing that the traditional substantive approach paid excessive regard to culture as a uniform, unwieldy, and almost predetermined entity of objectified cultural expressions. The traditional perception also tended to perceive ethnic identity as something static: something allocated once and for all.

In contrast to this, the relational approach emphasizes the dynamic aspects of both ethnicity and culture. This implies that the criteria for ethnic identity may change over time and space, and further offers opportunities for various choices and changes in ethnicity. On the contrary: instead of cultural standards, values, and peculiarities being allocated once and for all, they are subject to a continuous and extensive process of negotiation, both internally within the group and externally — a process of negotiation that covers both verbal and non-verbal expressions. In our own time, for example, discussions have been registered about what is, or should be, 'typically Norwegian'.

This perpetual discussion or process of negotiation is in the deepest sense historically situated. Firstly, the existing values, standards, and distinctive traits which serve as cultural building blocks do not, of course, emerge from nothing — from a social vacuum. They are primarily communicated,

---

21 Cf. Barth, *Ethnic groups and boundaries: the social organization of culture difference*; Odner, *Finner og terfinner*; Niemi and Hansen, 'Etnisitet'.

delivered, and deeply influenced by the traditionally transmitted values and perceptions of previous generations, enshrined in the current results of those generations' social practices, and they are to be found, internalized, in the younger generation through a process of socialization. Secondly, the existing realization that should be allocated to these values, standards, and distinctive traits is at all times largely determined by the existing situation in which the group of people finds itself — both in terms of its own conditions for cultural expression and with regard to the kind of relationship the group has with other actors and ethnic groups at the time. In other words, context plays a significant role in determining which concrete expressions an ethnic sense of affiliation or identity will assume at any time.

Such a perspective is, I think, also fruitful to resort to concerning the different ethnonyms or designation of peoples encountered in older sources. Ethnonyms are the designations of ethnic collectives, but simultaneously verbal cultural elements (cultural expressions) which form part of the reciprocal process of communication that takes place between ethnic groups, and internally within a group, and which may form part of the ongoing process of internal consolidation and external demarcation. This implies that it must be more important to try to obtain an overview of what comprehensive system of oppositions and relationships individual designated groups of people are included in, than to focus on the etymological roots of individual designations and their semantic content. If we glance at the designations at play in older sources, we might quickly conclude that these are far from 'commensurate'; that they cut across one and the same reading, and are thus based on the same type or similar criteria. In fact, the reverse is true: we find a blissful mixture of specific, self-referencing terms and their correct translations, as well as directly disparaging designations and names that are allocated from an outsider's perspective. Here, the outsiders may have taken vastly different phenomena into account in their naming practice: a people's lifestyle, for example, or their distinctive habitat, their particular religious identity, or administrative units, or landscape naming. In addition to names that seem to have functioned as fairly equivalent designations for collective ethnic units, as we know them in our own time, designations of association are also to be found of an economic-functional type, which may not necessarily be ethnic in their differentiation.

With this as a starting-point, it becomes clear that in the past, a 'name for a people', or a name for other social groups, did not necessarily have to demonstrate exact compliance with, or be able to be identified unambiguously with, the ethnic categories and labels known to us in our own time or from the immediate past. Nor did the use of language in previous centuries need to be reciprocal or symmetrical, in the sense that a group of people had specific designations for all the other groups of people in their vicinity, who in turn had their own specific designations. On the contrary: certain peoples used what might be called 'sack categories', into which they lumped a number of their neighbours.

Finally, one should also be aware of the relationship between 'in-group designations' (endonyms) and 'outside-group designations' (exonyms). This implies a significant difference, depending on whether the external designations represent a correct translation of a people's self-reference. A lack of compliance here *may* be an indication of asymmetry at other levels, for example exploitation through tribute or taxation, or other forms of dependence.

The Depiction of the Sámi in H.N.

If we now turn directly to H.N. and take into account the places where the author relates about the Sámi or the Finns — one of the closest 'foreign peoples' — we observe the reference at the beginning, in conjunction with three 'zones' into which the writer divides Norway lengthways. Initially, the author draws up a physical, geographical outline of the lands covered by the kingdom of Norway. This sketch is based on a longitudinal division of the country into three parts, three inhabited or habitable 'zones': *zona maritima, zona mediterranea,* and *zona silvestris,* i.e. 1) 'the coastal zone', 2) 'the middle zone', and 3) 'the wooded zone'. The forest zone — which also forms a section of Norway — is specifically itemized as comprising the settlement areas for the Sámi: *tertia silvestris, quae Finnis inhabitatur, sed non aratur*[22] ('... the third is wooded and populated by the Finns, but there is no agriculture there').[23]

There is thus a contradiction between Sámi settlement and agriculture: 'the Finns' do not practise agriculture, which corresponds with the stereotypical picture of the differences between the Norwegian and the Sámi way of life related in contemporaneous Norse sources.

In the next section — where the author describes in greater detail the division in areal and administrative (legal) terms of this 'tripartite settlement of Norway' — Hálogaland is depicted as the last of four *patriae* into which the coastal zone is divided. As far as the coastal zone is concerned, the designation *patria* has mostly been identified as *lagdømme* (law province).[24] We are informed that the fourth *patria* in the coastal belt is Hálogaland,

---

22 *Historia Norwegiae,* ed. by Storm, p. 73.

23 *Historia Norwegie,* ed. by Ekrem and Mortensen, p. 53.

24 The individual treatment of the 'Uplands' (*De montanis Norwegiae*) may, however, raise doubts as to how *patria* should be understood. Here it is maintained that the middle belt 'comprises four *patriae* and twelve *provinciae* [= counties?] and extends as far as Trondheim'. The four *patriae* are identified as follows: Romerike with Ringerike, Telemark, Hedmark, and Gudbrandsdalen. This division has caused Knut Robberstad to assert that the author selected *patria* in place of ON *lǫg,* which might also have indicated a smaller statutory area of law than in the case of a *lagdømme* (law province), Robberstad, 'Ordet patria i *Historia Norvegiae*', pp. 188–91; Helle, 'Norge blir en stat 1130–1319', pp. 47, 61.

Quarta Halogia, cujus incolae multum Finnis cohabitant et inter se
commercia frequentant; quae patria in aquilonem terminat Norwegiam
juxta locum Wegestaf, qui Biarmoniam ab ea dirimit.[25]

> (The fourth [law province] is Hålogaland, whose inhabitants dwell a
> good deal with the Finns, so there are frequent transactions between
> them; this law province forms the northern boundary of Norway next
> to Vegestav, which separates it from Bjarmaland.)[26]

Here it is implicitly stated that the Sámi are not considered as actual inhabitants of Hålogaland, but that these (Norwegian) inhabitants nevertheless
live together with the Sámi and pursue extensive trading transactions with
them.[27] At the same time we are told that 'this law province bounds Norway
in the north at a place called Vegestav, separating Bjarmaland from Norway'.

When the author subsequently starts to depict the Sámi separately, in a
section of their own called *De Finnis*, however, he begins by locating them in
an 'absolute wasteland' that stretches beside and up to Norway:

> Est igitur vastissima solitudo affinis Norwegiae. dividens eam per longum
> a paganis gentibus, quae solitudo Finnis et bestiis incolitur, quarum
> carnibus semicrudis vescuntur et pellibus induuntur. Sunt equidem
> venatores peritissimi, solivagi et instabiles, tugurea coriacea pro domibus
> insidentes, quae humeris inponentes levigatis asseribus pedibus subfixis
> (quod instrumentum ondros appelant) et per condensa nivium ac devexa
> montium agitantibus cervis cum conjuibus et parvulis ave velocius tran-
> feruntur. Est enim illorum incerta mansio, prout copia ferarum tempore
> instante eis dictaverit venationis loca. Ibi infinit numerositas bestiarum,
> scilicet ursorum, luporum, lyncum, vulpium, sabelorum, lutrearum,
> taxonum, castorum …[28]

> (On the borders of Norway is an immense wilderness, which divides
> the country along all its length and separates the Norwegians from
> the heathens. Only Finns dwell here and wild animals whose flesh
> they eat half-raw and whose skins they clothe themselves with. They
> are truly the most skillful huntsmen, patrolling alone and always on
> the move; for homes they occupy leather tents, which they carry
> on their shoulders; with smooth planks fastened beneath their feet,
> implements which they call '*ondrar*',[29] swifter than birds they are

---

25 *Historia Norwegiae*, ed. by Storm, p. 78.
26 *Historia Norwegie*, ed. by Ekrem and Mortensen, p. 57.
27 Håvard Dahl Bratrein has demonstrated that the Sámi must have been involved in
commercial fishing on a considerable scale as early as the twelfth century, see below.
28 *Historia Norwegiae*, ed. by Storm, pp. 82–83.
29 Regarding the use of the term *onder* to signify the shortest ski in a pair of different
lengths, related semantic content may be observed in the following Sámi words: the verbs
oandut (to be a little slow; to drag one foot slightly) and *oanedit* (to shorten; to pay off

conveyed with their wives and little ones, swept forward by their reindeer across packed snow and down mountain slopes. For they have no fixed abode, inasmuch as the supply of wild beasts dictates their hunting-grounds at any one time. In that region there live vast numbers of animals, including bears, wolves, lynxes, foxes, sables, otters, badgers and beavers [...]).[30]

Firstly, the Sámi are emphatically characterized as a hunting people and their mobile (actually semi-nomadic, cyclical) form of settlement is commented upon from the perspective of the residential, farming population. In addition to this, the greater part of the Sámi settlement area is evidently perceived as a territorially bounded area that borders the Norwegian polity, and so does not form part of the Norwegian *ríki* (realm) and is therefore not part of Hálogaland, either.

By portraying the Norwegian national unity in this way, as bordering to 'a great wasteland', the author is also conveying ancient Germanic notions of how a proper kingdom should be boundered. Curt Weibull,[31] amongst others, has pointed out that a kingdom should, in the Old Germanic perception, be surrounded by an extensive wasteland, which not only functions as the boundary of the dominion but also serves to the greatest possible extent as protection against enemy attacks, by constituting a hindrance to transport. Weibull selects statements about the Teutons in the work of Roman geographer Pomponius Mela (writing in the middle of the first century) and in the works of Caesar and Tacitus to illustrate this:

Civitatibus maxima laus est quam latissime circum se vastatis finibus solitudines habere. Hoc proprium virtutis existimant expulsos agris finitimos cedere neque quemquam prope se audere consistere; simul hoc se fore tutiores arbitrantur repentinae incursionis timore sublato.[32]

(It is most praiseworthy for states to be surrounded by wasteland to the greatest possible extent, with border areas kept free of people; they consider it a special sign of strength that the neighbours draw away, displaced from their fields, and with no-one daring to settle in the vicinity; thus they feel more secure, since the fear of sudden invasion is cleared away.)[33]

---

debt), as well as the adjective *oanehis* (short; short-term) and the adverb *oadni* (in short; scarce).

30 *Historia Norwegie*, ed. by Ekrem and Mortensen, pp. 59–61.

31 Weibull, 'Den älsta gränsläggningen mellan Sverige och Danmark. Gränsområde och gränslinje'. I owe thanks to Thomas Wallerström for drawing my attention to Weibull's article.

32 Gaius Julius Caesar, *Bellum Gallicum*, ed. by Guthardt, VI, chap. 23, p. 176.

33 Translated from the author's Norwegian translation of the original text.

Nonetheless, it is said that where these Sámi live, outside Hálogaland itself:

> Sunt etiam apud Finnos scuriones quam plures ac mustelae, de quarum omnium bestiarum pellibus regibus Norwegiae, quibus et subjecti sunt, maxima tributa omni anno persolvunt.[34]

>> (In Finnmarken there are also very large numbers of squirrels and ermines. From all these animals' pelts the people pay a large tribute every year to the Norwegian kings, who are their overlords.)[35]

Even the Sámi, who are outside the actual national unity that encompasses Hálogaland, are therefore required to pay tribute to the king of Norway. A perception of this distinct, forest-clad Sámi settlement area as spatially separated in relation to the area included within Norwegian state power, and thus in a certain sense adjoining Hálogaland, might fit in well with how 'Finnmǫrk' is referenced in Norse and Norwegian sources dating from that time or somewhat later.

In *Egils saga Skallagrímssonar*, for example, which is believed to have been written in the early thirteenth century, the region is described as follows:

> Finnmark is a vast territory, bordered by the sea to the west and the north, and all the way to east with great fjords, while Norway lies to the south of it. It extends as far south along the mountains as Halogaland does down the coast. East of Namdal lies Jamtland, then Halsingland, Kvenland, Finland and Karelia. Finnmark lies beyond all these countries, and there are mountain settlements in many parts, some in the valleys and others by the lakes. In Finnmark there are incredibly large lakes with great forests all around, while a high mountain range named Kjølen [= 'mountain ridge'] extends from one end of the territory to the other.[36]

The Icelandic documentary, handwritten text *Rímbegla*, which was compiled towards the end of the twelfth century, also portrays an apparently straightforward, spatially defined border, but this time at Malangen: 'Þá er fjǫrdr, er Malangr heitir, hann skilr Finnmǫrk vid búmenn' (Next there is a fjord called Malangen, it divides Finnmǫrk from settled men (= farmers.)).[37]

However, the author of H.N. is clearly capable of holding several apparently contradictory thoughts in his mind, and forcing readers to experience this as well — since he has simultaneously pointed out to us the existence of the Sámi in Hálogaland itself. This region (possibly this law province) is characterized precisely by the fact that its inhabitants 'live largely with the Sámi'. The interaction and the contact area between the peoples of Hálogaland

34 *Historia Norwegiae*, ed. by Storm, p. 85.
35 *Historia Norwegie*, ed. by Ekrem and Mortensen, p. 61.
36 *Egil's Saga*, ed. by Óskarsdóttir, trans. by Scudder, pp. 23–24.
37 *Alfrœði islenzk*, ed. by Kålund.

is also emphasized and made concrete by reporting particular events that took place between them.

Firstly, the text depicts a 'classic shaman séance', with all its associated elements — as far as we are able to judge by comparison with later material. Regarding the circumstances of this séance, the following is stated: *Quadam vero vice dum christiani causa commercii apud Finnos ad mensam sedissent, illorum hospital subito inclinata exspriavit; ...* [38] (Once when Christians who had come to trade had sat down at table with some Finns, their hostess fell forward all of a sudden and expired).[39]

It was also told that it happened, once, when some Sámi and Norwegians were fishing together:

[...] Item dum Finni unacum christianis gregem squamigeram hamo carpere attentassent, quos in casis fidelium pagani perspexerant, sacculis fere plenis unco suo de abysso attractis scapham cum piscibus impleverunt.[40]

(Again, when the Finns, together with the Christians, had gone about catching by hook a flock of fish such as these heathens had seen in Christian dwellings, they drew almost full traps out of the deeps with their wand, and so loaded the boats to capacity.)[41]

The fact that there was already extensive cooperation between the Sámi and the Norwegians by the end of the twelfth century regarding the commercial sale of fish is also covered in a contemporaneous work, *Passio et Miracula Beati Olavi*. Håvard Dahl Bratrein's article (1989) directs attention to information that appears in the report about one of these wonders: the story 'Concerning a youth cleansed of leprosy'.[42] This was an account of regular seasonal fishing — probably fishing in the spring, off west Finnmark — in which both Sámi and Norwegians participated as visiting fishermen. However, since the purpose of the report is to illustrate what luck with fishing the Christian Norwegians had, since they were helped by St Ólafr and addressed their prayers to God, the Sámi were consequently portrayed as pagan.

[...] He had recently come from pagan parts, where a great many Christians had gathered to fish, now that Lent was over [...] The pagan Lapps[43] who had also gathered there to fish, hearing the vow of the faithful, asked to

38 *Historia Norwegiae*, ed. by Storm, p. 85.
39 *Historia Norwegie*, ed. by Ekrem and Mortensen, p. 63.
40 *Historia Norwegiae*, ed. by Storm, pp. 86–87.
41 *Historia Norwegie*, ed. by Ekrem and Mortensen, p. 63.
42 *Passio et Miracula Beati Olavi*, ed. by Phelpstead and trans. by Kunin, pp. 69–73.
43 The Latin originals of H.N. and *Passio et Miracula Beati Olavi* render the old Norse designation '*Finn*' for the Sámi, and Peter Fisher's translation of H.N. in Ekrem and Mortensen (2003) follows this. However, the translation of both works by Devra Kunin (*Passio et Miracula Beati Olavi*, ed. by Phelpstead and trans. by Kunin) uses the term '*Lapp*', widely used in international scholarly literature. The term '*Lapp*' has probably its origin in

be permitted as fellows to this plan, but in such a way that their godlings should be no less honoured with the fruits of their vow than the blessed Óláfr with the offerings of the faithful. But since there is no concord between Christ and Belial, the wretches in their error were spurned.[44]

In H.N. we also find that the author is meticulous about characterizing the inhabitants of Hálogaland as Christians and believers (*fideles*), whereas the word primarily used to characterize the Sámi is *profani*, that is, 'sacrilegious', 'ungodly', or 'un-hallowed'. They are also referred to as 'this ungodly flock' (*profana secta*[45]) and are accused of exercising a 'devilish superstition in the magic arts' (*diabolica superstitio in magica arte*). They further possess an *intolerabilis perfidia* and perform countless magic tricks (*innumerae praestigiae*). A more detailed description is given of these magic tricks:

[…] There are some who are worshipped by the ignorant masses as though they were prophets, since, whenever questioned, they will give many predictions to many folk through the medium of a foul spirit which they call gand, and these auguries come true. Furthermore they attract to themselves desirable objects from distant parts in an astounding fashion and miraculously reveal hidden treasures, even though they are situated a vast distance away.[46]

The oppositions or dichotomies that the author of H.N. used to capture and characterize the relationship between Hálogaland's Norwegian inhabitants and the Sámi may thus be summarized as follows:

Farmers	hunters, trackers
Fixed settlement	mobile, (semi-)nomadic settlement
Hálogaland's inhabitants	Sámi
Norway	neighbouring wasteland (with Sámi settlement, still being subject to [*subjecti*] the King of Norway, in having to pay tribute to him)
Christians, believers	sacrilegious, ungodly [*profani*]

This last opposition was clearly the most fundamental and central for H.N.'s clerically educated author. The theme can be heard from the start, in the section where the author provides a general geographical introduction and figuratively 'places Norway on the map'. Concerning the countries and peoples surrounding Norway to the south and east (Denmark, as well as Svitjod,

the Ladoga region, and has been borrowed into Russian language ('*lop*') and into the Nordic languages. — Cf. Uibopuu, *Finnougrierna och deras språk*, p. 115; Ekrem, 'Essay on Date and Purpose', p. 181; Hansen and Olsen, *Hunters in Transition*, pp. 37–38.

44 *Passio et Miracula Beati Olavi*, ed. by Phelpstead and trans. by Kunin, pp. 70–71.
45 *Historia Norwegiae*, ed. by Storm, p. 87.
46 *Historia Norwegie*, ed. by Ekrem and Mortensen, p. 61.

Götaland, Ångermanland og Jämtland (all parts of present-day Sweden)),
he has this to say:

> Quas nunc partes (deo gratia) gentes colunt christianae. Versus vero
> septentrionem gentes perplures paganismo (proh dolor) inservientes
> trans Norwegiam ab oriente extenduntur, scilicet Kiriali et Kwæni, cornuti
> Finni ac utrique Biarmones.[47]

> > (The peoples who live in these regions, thanks be to God, are now
> > Christians. However, towards the north there are, alas, a great many
> > tribes who have spread across Norway from the east and who are in
> > thrall to paganism, that is, the Kirjarlers and Kvens, the Horned Finns
> > and two kinds of Bjarms.)[48]

The general perspective thus seems to have been as follows: the further north
and east one travelled, the stronger the heathendom. Similarly, the view that
the northern regions formed a centre and a bastion for paganism is found
both in the introduction to *Passio et Miracula Beati Olavi* and in Adam of
Bremen's writings:

> [...] Living in a region close to the north, it was the same north, from
> which comes every evil over the whole face of earth, that had possessed
> them all the more inwardly and gripped them all more firmly on the ice
> of unbelief.[49]

> All, indeed, who live in Norway are thoroughly Christian, except those
> who are removed beyond the arctic tract along the ocean. These people,
> it is said, are to this day so superior in the magic arts or incantations
> that they profess to know what every one is doing the world over. Then
> they also draw great sea monsters to shore with a powerful mumbling
> of words and do much else of which one reads in the scriptures about
> magicians.[50]

The formulation of the oppositions or dichotomies used to describe the
relationship with the Sámi might seem complicated and ambiguous if one
were expecting a clear correlation between ethnic and cultural divisions
and national boundaries. On the one hand, the Sámi inhabit the innermost,
wooded belt of land that constitutes Norway, and in Hálogaland, Norwegians
and Sámi lived together — clearly in a way that provided for extensive social
interaction. On the other hand, the Sámi were *not* considered to be inhabitants
(*incolae*) of Hálogaland, and the 'vast wasteland' that bordered it separated

---

47 *Historia Norwegiae*, ed. by Storm, p. 74.
48 *Historia Norwegie*, ed. by Ekrem and Mortensen, pp. 53–55.
49 *Passio et Miracula Beati Olavi*, ed. by Phelpstead and trans. by Kunin, p. 26.
50 Adam of Bremen, *History of the Archbishops of Hamburg-Bremen*, trans. by Tschan, bk IV,
    chap. 32, p. 212.

Norway as a state from the 'heathens'. And even though the opposition of the 'heathen Sámi' is emphasized to a great extent, this evidently does not prevent Norwegians and Sámi from sitting down to eat a meal together! It is also worth noting that linguistic differences are not mentioned at all, nor perceived as a problem, either in H.N. or the Norse sources.

Thus, in part, the ambiguities make it clear that the author was operating on several levels in his description. From one perspective, he was seeking to provide the most accurate geographical and ethnographical description of the extent of individual people's settlement and the characteristics of their habitat and forms of adaptation. From another perspective, he was also thinking in legal and institutional terms with regard to who could be considered subjects of the Christian kingdom of Norway as this was manifested in the jurisdiction, secular administration, system of defence, and Church organization. Discrepancies in relation to Norse sources dating from about this time become understandable when it is taken into account that a process was underway at exactly this time by which nationwide Norwegian social power — based on national kingship and the Church — was becoming ever more influential in Hálogaland. Important institutions such as the *lagting* (provincial court assembly), conscription for naval defences (*leidang*), and a centralized regional management system organized through administrative districts called *sysler* were being established at a local level, at the same time as Christianity was gaining a stronger foothold. In the course of such a process, there must have been a tension between how people's affiliation was defined and how social power over the same people was perceived: was such affiliation and power mainly linked to population characteristics or to those of individuals, through their affiliation in ethnic and religious terms, and might this have been linked to what type of livelihood they pursued? Or were affiliation and social power defined from a particular, well-defined, and delineated territory?

It may be further noted that the picture created in H.N. of Sámi settlement has, to an overwhelming extent, shown itself to be confirmed through settlement history studies in northern Norway. By means of a series of surveys from northern Nordland and up into northern Troms, it has been shown how the fjord areas and the coastal valleys during the early part of the Middle Ages constituted areas of purely Sámi use and settlement, which can thus be identified as the author's 'innermost, wooded belt'. In addition, however, there are also many places designated as Coastal Sámi settlements further out, side by side with those of the Norwegians.[51] As far as the king

---

51   Bertelsen, *Lofotens og Vesterålens historie*; Guttormsen, *Ressurser og bosetning i Andenes len og Sortland fjerding: fra ca 1000–1660 e.Kr.f.*; Schanche, *Nordnorsk jernalderarkeologi. Et sosialgeografisk perspekti'*; Bratrein, *Karlsøy og Helgøy Bygdebok: Folkeliv – Næringsliv – Samfunnsliv*, I: *Fra Steinalder til år 1700*; Hansen, *Samisk fangstsamfunn og norsk høvdingeøkonomi*; Nielssen, *Lødingen, Tjeldsund og Tysfjords historie*, IV; Andersen, *Ofuohtagat – Samer og nordmenn i Ofoten*.

of Norway's right to collect a tribute from the Sámi who lived beyond the kingdom itself is concerned, the information provided by the author also appears to equate to what we can glean from later sources. The king of Norway's taxation assertions led to, amongst other things, confrontation with Russian taxation interests, which in turn led to agreements in both 1250 (between Hákon Hákonarson and Alexander Nevsky) and 1326. In the latter agreement a common Norwegian–Russian area of taxation was defined, from Lyngstuva to the south-eastern coast of the Kola Peninsula, whereby both sides would have the right to tax the Sámi.[52]

Although the duality of statements in H.N. about the Sámi can mostly be explained by the concrete historical situation in Hálogaland, there is nonetheless a question of whether this ambiguity and duality might also reflect more fundamental and general problems in characterizing 'the Other', i.e. people who presented with a different cultural and social profile to that of the author himself.

In his book *Postmodern Ethics*, sociologist Zygmunt Bauman analyses the issue of relating to 'the Other' when the person concerned lives next door, i.e. when what is 'socially distant' and different is not separated by corresponding physical, geographical distance, but is intrusively close.[53] On a scale, or within a space whose boundaries are marked by intimacy on the one hand and anonymity on the other, 'it' or 'the Other' may be located at varying distances according to how much and how complementary the knowledge is that 'we ourselves' possess of the person concerned. Depending on how comprehensive our familiarity is, and the number of situations in which we have experienced 'the Other', the person concerned may appear as 'the intimate Other', 'the alien Other', or 'the completely anonymous Other' who exists beyond our social horizon or outside our social space. 'Classes' and 'categories' of person come into existence in precisely this space, this tension between the extremes of intimacy and anonymity. According to Bauman, it is our varying and partially flawed knowledge of the behavioural norms followed by 'the Other' that attracts our attention and reflection. We react to the fact that in various situations, 'the Other' does not behave normally and 'naturally', based on our own norms and values.

Disturbing behaviour occurs, however, when the coordination between physical and social (cognitive) proximity is broken; when 'the stranger' is made physically manifest within the boundaries of everyday life; when the person concerned lives in the house or on the farm next door. Not only does 'the stranger' pose the threat of incorrect classification; what is even more frightening is that the person concerned poses a threat to the classification itself.

---

52 Cf. Hansen, 'Interaction between Northern European Sub-Arctic Societies during the Middle Ages', pp. 68–69, 76–79.
53 Bauman, *Postmodern Ethics*.

Thus, in trying to maintain a unity of physical and social proximity, a 'stranger' may be treated in — broadly speaking — three different ways, according to Bauman:

1) The person concerned may be perceived as an *enemy*, to be fought and chased away.

2) The person concerned may be defined as a casual *guest*, to be received in accordance with the rules of civilization and hospitality, implying the expression of a set of rituals that isolate the person concerned and place him or her in a very distinct position.

3) Alternatively, the person concerned may be defined as a *prospective neighbour*, and then one must ensure as soon as possible that the person concerned is acting like a proper neighbour.

I think this perspective may serve as an approach to understanding the discussion of the Sámi in H.N. Since Sámi and Norwegians lived mostly side by side in Hálogaland and had extensive interaction with each other, the Sámi could not be treated as complete 'strangers', let alone as 'enemies' or 'casual guests'. They were within the social space, so to speak. Yet they were not 'proper neighbours' either, given that they appeared distinctive in a cultural and cognitive sense. The solution was to treat them according to the third alternative, as 'prospective neighbours' who, in the long run, would be won over to Christianity and thus incorporated fully into the community. There is an essential difference, in my opinion, between the way the Sámi are presented in H.N. and the depiction of the 'other heathens' who extended themselves towards Norway from the east. The depiction of the Sámi settlement area in the 'wasteland' to the east of Norway may also be understood in the sense that the author perceives this as a buffer zone between the Norwegian kingdom and these truly 'foreign' peoples. Unlike the Sámi, these peoples may be said to be located beyond the social horizon.

Other, 'Foreign' Peoples Depicted in H.N.

In his geographical introduction, the author of H.N. also enumerates these heathen peoples in the North: there are 'Karelians and Kvens, Horned Finns and two kinds of Biarmians' (*scilicet Kiriali et Kwaeni, cornuti Finni ac utrique Biarmones*).[54] In the final part of this discussion I shall take a closer look at the presumed location of these different groups, who go by different 'people's names', and their distinguishing characteristics in general.

---

54 *Historia Norwegiae*, ed. by Storm, pp. 73–75.

The Kvens

The location of this group's area of origin and habitat and their functional relations with the Sámi appear to be relatively well clarified. However, the etymological background to the designated names they have been allocated and the question of their ethnic status have undergone a thorough discussion.

The oldest written sources from the West agree that Kvenland is located east of the Norwegians' land — especially along the northern part of it — and is more specifically located in the coastal regions around the northernmost parts of the Gulf of Bothnia. In Ohthere's account, the Kvens and the Norwegians are depicted as opponents, who sometimes carry out raids on one another. The Kvens are said to prefer small, light boats, which they pull overland and use in the lakes in the interior of northern Fennoscandia. From the end of the twelfth century onwards, Norse texts depict Kvenland regularly as an area on a par with Finland and Karelia, placing it between Hälsingland and Finland. The description in *Egils saga Skallagrímssonar*, dating from the first half of the thirteenth century, gives a general impression of Norwegians and the Kvens as competing collectors of Sámi furs, but it also relates that these two groups collaborated and sometimes entered into alliances against other stakeholders, such as the Karelians. Regarding their economy, the Kvens stand out during this period as a group that had specialized in trade and bartering with the inland Sámi, but who also carried out raids and plundering against them. The more exact geographical location of Kven settlement, in the coastal lands around the upper and innermost part of the Gulf of Bothnia, has been demonstrated by the investigations of Finnish scholar Kyösti Julku (1986).

Despite certain phonological issues, most researchers now seem to concur with an interpretation that links the Nordic term 'kven' to a Norse word rendered as *hvein* in Old Norse and as *hven / hvene* in Swedish and Danish dialects. This word must have signified 'low-lying, marshy area' and, to some extent, 'thin grass'/'area with thin grass'. Thus, it must have been a terrain-descriptive word applicable to the topography of the coastal region. On the Finnish side, the Kvens are termed *kainulaiset* and the area around the upper part of the Gulf of Bothnia was called *Kainu* or *Kainuunmaa* in ancient times. This term is also found in Russian in the form of *kajani*, and in the name *Kaiano more* (the Kajan Sea), applied to the innermost part of the Gulf of Bothnia.[55] Linguistically, the Norse and Finnish terms are so far apart that there can be no question of direct borrowing or synchronous influence. It has, however, been suggested that the Finnish *kainu* was borrowed earlier, from Old German, to signify 'low-lying land'. The Finnish historian Jouko Vahtola (1980) has suggested that the low-lying coastal regions along the inner part of the Gulf of Bothnia have been named independently from two sides — from

---

55 Cf. the Russian language version of the Swedish-Russian border treaty of 1323 (see Gallén and Lind, 'Nöteborgsfreden och Finlands Medeltida Östgräns').

two separate linguistic naming environments. On one hand, the Norse *hvein* may have been taken up by the Norwegians, who undertook trade and hunting expeditions in the interior of northern Fennoscandia and down to the Gulf of Bothnia. At the same time, the Finnish term may have been used as a place name by Finnish ethnic groups who came from the south-eastern areas of Finland — Karelians and Savonians, who were following the same pursuits.[56]

In his doctoral dissertation of 1995, Swedish archaeologist Thomas Wallerström has turned sharply towards the view that the Kvens must have formed an ethnic group in their own right. In a detailed discussion of the corresponding Russian term *kajani*, Wallerström's perception is that both this and the equivalent Finnish and Nordic terms relate to population elements that played a key role within a widespread economic system built around the fur trade with the Sámi and hunters. This system extended from Norrbotten and eastwards to the Onega and Dvina regions. 'Kvens' is thus conceived as a general term linked to economic functions within this trading system, and as such may comprise elements from several different peoples.

Regardless of how this may relate to the etymological basis for the naming of the Kvens, it seems to be most fruitful to emphasize their regional associations and economic functions throughout the early part of the Middle Ages. What can certainly be concluded from medieval sources is that 'the Kvens' is used as a term for the inhabitants of a specific area around the northern Gulf of Bothnia coastal regions, an area that demonstrated certain territorial and topographical peculiarities in relation to the surrounding areas. These inhabitants further seem to have practised a special economic adaptation in which hunting and trade with the Sámi and other neighbouring peoples played a major role, running concurrently with a partial basis in agriculture and livestock. It is also worth noting that the last mention of the Kvens (*kvenene*) in a medieval context was in 1271,[57] while the *Birkarler* group, which preserved exactly corresponding economic functions throughout the late Middle Ages and modern period, was mentioned for the first time in 1328, in the context of the Swedish Crown undertaking an affirmation and appraisal of their rights in relation to the people of Hälsingland.[58] This raises the question of whether one is to do with a continuity of the actual economic functions, while the terms themselves changed. During the sixteenth century, Finnish-speaking population groups from the inland river valleys — which included some of the Birkarler — were also referred to as Kvens in Norwegian material ('*hwener*' or '*øst*(eastern)-*hvener*'). There is nothing to suggest that the Kvens, during *later* historical processes, could not have formed a separate ethnic identity

56 Vahtola, *Tornedalens historia*, p. 209ff; cf. Niemi, 'Kven'.
57 It is related that in this year, Kvens and Karelians laid waste in Hålogaland: 'Þa gorþu Kereliar ok Kvénir mikit hervirki á Hálogalanndi' (cf. *Islandske annaler*, ed. by Storm, p. 138).
58 The so-called 'Täljestadgan' of September 5, 1328, published in, amongst others, *Fellman* III, 336.

for themselves in such a way that it becomes reasonable to characterize them as an ethnic group. During the eighteenth and nineteenth centuries, the term 'Kvens' became established as the term for Finnish-speaking immigrants from the river valleys who settled down along the coast in the north and west, not least along the coast of Finnmark.

The Karelians

These people, likewise, do not seem to offer any significant problems with regard to identification and location during the period in question. From an original heartland north and west of Ladoga (cf. the expression 'the Karelian Isthmus'), Karelian settlement seems to have expanded to the north-west, north and north-east as early as the twelfth century. In the north-west they approached Savolax, and in 1143 there were reports of clashes with the Finnish population group *Häme* or *Hämäläiset*.[59] Elsewhere, Karelian expansion continued northwards, penetrating what had originally been Sámi settlement areas. Throughout this expansion, these areas were transformed into what would later become East Karelia, and during the fifteenth century the west coast of the White Sea was referred to as the 'Karelian shore' (*Korel'skij bereg*). But as late as the second half of the sixteenth century there was still considerable Sámi settlement in this region.[60]

By the beginning of the fourteenth century, Karelian expansion seems to have reached so far north as to offer contact with the Sámi on the Kola Peninsula. Regarding the treaty of 1326 between Norway and Novgorod regarding joint taxation of Sámi in the area stretching from Lyngen to Kola, this seems to have confirmed an older agreement, according to which the King of Norway had the right to collect taxes from the eastern end of Kola 'where there are half-Karelians or half-Sámi, who have had a Sámi mother' (*huar sem halfkarelar æða halfinnær ero, þeir sem finska moðor hafua aat*).[61] This seems to indicate that contact between the Karelians and the Sámi had already been so extensive that it provided a basis for marriage between these ethnic groups.

A peace treaty between Sweden and Novgorod three years earlier (in 1323) delineated at the same time a common Swedish–Russian taxation area covering most of the Sámi settlement in present-day northern Finland.[62] Both along the northern coast and in the interior of the northern Fennoscandia, the Sámi settlements could thus be integrated into Novgorod's economic system, based on trade and taxation. And both Karelian and Russian merchants had an important role to play in this traffic from the eastern side. The eastern

---

59 *The Chronicle of Novgorod*, trans. by Knud Rahbek Schmidt, p. 43.
60 Lukjančenko, Rasselenie Kol'skikh Saamov v XVI–XVII vv.
61 *Norges gamle Love* III, 151–52.
62 Gallén and Lind, *Nöteborgsfreden och Finlands Medeltida Östgräns*.

Karelians, in particular, who came under the rule of Novogorod following a military settlement at the end of the High Middle Ages, came to play a key role in increasing Novgorod's influence among the Sámi, linking them more closely to Novgorod's system of trade.

Throughout the late Middle Ages and the sixteenth century, both Norse and Russian sources dating from that time portray Karelians and Norwegians as the main opponents and rivals in trade and taxation in the North. Norwegian pillaging raids to the White Sea are known from the years prior to 1326, as well those of 1419 and 1445. Conversely, the Karelians, especially, pursued their interests along the coasts of Troms and Finnmark, and Norwegian sources reveal eleven Karelian incursions along the northern Norwegian coast during the period 1250–1444.[63] The clashes are depicted as purely warring expeditions in these sources, but it is most likely that they were expressions of rival trade interests.

The 'Horned Finns'

This term should probably be viewed in the context of ethnic differentiation processes that took place in prehistoric times in the present-day Finnish region. As far as the complex ethnic situation on the North Calotte is concerned, archaeologists, historians, and language researchers maintain increasingly that the various ethnic identities have arisen through long-term differentiation and 'ethnification processes' among original heterogeneous groups of hunters and gatherers in northern Fennoscandia. According to this dynamic view of the emergence and maintenance of ethnic affiliation, these processes must have been reciprocal, in the sense that Sámi ethnic affiliation has been developed in interaction and contemporaneous with the establishment and generalization of a corresponding Finnish and North German ('Nordic') ethnic identity in other parts of Fennoscandia. Regarding the much-discussed question of the relationship between the ancestors of those who became the Sámi and the people of Finland, most researchers today reckon that an original population which existed in the present-day area of southern Finland — who may be regarded as the ancestors of both the Sámi and the people of Finland — initiated a process of linguistic and cultural differentiation during the course of the last two millennia before Christ. Encouraged by increased contact with Baltic and Germanic groups, some of this population adopted agricultural and livestock techniques, eventually becoming the precursors ('Proto-Finns') of the latter-day people of Finland, while the others continued with their old hunter / gatherer adaptation and were the ancestors of the Sámi ('Proto-Sámi').[64] In tandem

---

63   Bratrein, *Karlsøy og Helgøy Bygdebok: Folkeliv – Næringsliv – Samfunnsliv*, 1: *Fra Steinalder til år 1700*, p. 235; cf. Hansen, 'Interaction between Northern European sub-Arctic Societies during the Middle Ages', pp. 57, 61.

64   Hansen and Olsen, *Hunters in Transition*, pp. 22–31; cf. Odner, *Finner og terfinner*.

with this, the original common Finnish-Sámi source language split during the period 1500–1000 BC into Proto-Sámi and Proto-Finnish language forms.[65]

It may seem as if there is still a linguistic memory of this originally common origin in the self-referential terms with which the Sámi and a Finnish people operate. Both the Sámi's own self-referential *sámi / sápmi / sápmelaš* and the old term for the Finnish group, *hämäläiset*, date back to a common original form *šämä*, which must have existed in the Sámi-Finnish language of origin. *Hämäläiset* — known in English as *Tavastians* — maintained close and institutionalized trading relations with the Sámi during the Iron Age.[66]

This perception of a cultural and linguistic differentiation between the ancestors of the people of Finland and the Sámi generates a certain reverberation when we look at the exonyms used in Nordic languages to denote the Sámi and the people of Finland. A characteristic ambiguity is known to exist here regarding the expression 'Finn' (*finn(e)*). This ambiguity created difficulties as early as the Middle Ages, for example in Snorri's *Heimskringla*, whose *Óláfs saga helga* cites a lay (a short lyric poem) by Sigvatr skáld in which the term *finnlender* is used to distinguish the inhabitants of Finland. It is also worth noting that European, continental writers describing geographical conditions and the peoples of the Nordic region seem, from the sixth century onwards, to need to distinguish the Sámi from 'the other Finns'. For this purpose they adopt a new term, *skriðfinner*.[67]

In my opinion, it is through such an interaction and differentiation perspective that the term *hornfinner* (Horn Finns) in H.N. should be viewed.[68] The participle *cornuti* or 'equipped with horns' should be perceived as a distinguishing characteristic that is applied in order to distinguish this group from other 'Finns'. Two primary possibilities exist here: it may either have served to distinguish the ancestors of the people of Finland, delimiting them from the Sámi, who were consequently called 'Finns' (*finni*). In this interpretation it is telling that neither Finland nor its inhabitants, in the modern sense of *finnlendere* (people of Finland), are mentioned anywhere else in H.N. This may also match the order of the geographical listing. But the term could also have served to specify one of the Proto-Finnish peoples in relation to others. This leads us to consider as an option the *hämäläiset* or *Tavastians*, who had close and well-organized trading connections with the

---

65 Hansen and Olsen, *Hunters in Transition*, pp. 133–39; cf. Uibopuu, *Finnougrierna och deras språk*, pp. 92–97; Strade, 'Suomalainen etnogeneesi kielihistorian valossa', p. 575.
66 Hansen and Olsen, *Hunters in Transition*, p. 36; Uibopuu, *Finnougrierna och deras språk*, p. 115.
67 Cf. Hansen and Olsen, *Hunters in Transition*, pp. 35–37, 126.
68 As Gustav Storm (*Historia Norwegiae*, ed. by Storm, p. 74) observed, the term was also used in a piece in 'Nökkur blöð úr Hauksbók'. There, this group is mentioned in connection with 'Kvenland' and an explanation is provided which is also linked to a discussion on satyrs: *Heitir enn Quennland, þar ero oft orrostr miclar oc eigo þar sialfar iafnan bardaga ... Er su þioð er Hornfinnar heita, þeim er horn niðrbiugt i enni oc ero mannetor.*

Sámi in Finland as early as the Iron Age. The term may have been used to distinguish this group, amongst other things in the delimitation of *suomalaiset*, which were settled longer to the south-west, in the region later known as 'real Finland'. It is interesting to note that Gustav Storm, too, in the notes system of his 1880 edition, tentatively identified *cornuti Finni* with precisely *Hæmmerne*, or *hämäläiset*.[69]

'Two kinds of Biarmians'

According to the oldest Western sources (Ohthere, *Heimskringla*, *Hákonar saga Hákonarsonar*) the 'Biarmian' settlement area appears to extend to the south coast of the White Sea, as well as the northern parts of the Dvina river valley. But in the same way as for the Kvens, the potential status of the 'Biarmians' as an ethnic group in their own right and the etymology behind this term are widely discussed.

Based on Ohthere's remark that 'he thought the Finns and the Biarmians spoke almost the same language', the following alternatives have been posited concerning identification with earlier and later known peoples:[70]

1) The Permyak-speaking ancestors of the Komi people of our time.
2) Identification with a Baltic Finnish-speaking people: either the Votes, the Vepsians or the Karelians.

Etymologically, the name 'Biarmian' has been associated with both the Baltic-Finnish word *perä-maa*, which denotes a 'faraway, remote country',[71] and the Komi-Zyrian word *parma*, meaning 'wilderness', 'wasteland'.[72]

Through the works of the Finnish researcher Matti Haavio (1965) and the Norwegian historian Håkon Stang (1977), it now seems probable that the Biarmians should be largely identified with the Baltic–Finnish people the Vepsians, referred to in ancient Russian sources as *ves'* and in Arabic as *Wīsū*. The Vepsians' original settlement area seems to have been the areas of land between Lake Ladoga, Lake Onega, and the Beloozero region. From this heartland they shall, however, have moved northwards and eastwards, establishing themselves in the River Dvina's fluvial basin — possibly as early as the tenth century, but certainly during the course of the eleventh century. In Russian this area was called *Zavoločje*, i.e. 'the country beyond the isthmus or the watershed'.

---

69 *Historia Norwegiae*, ed. by Storm, p. 74.
70 Bergsland, 'Utredning for Skattefjällsmålet om de sydlige sameområders historie til omkring 1751', p. 8; Stang, 'Bjarmene — deres identitet, eksistensgrunnlag og forbindelser med andre folkeslag', p. 97.
71 Sjögren, *Gesammelte Schriften*, p. 295; Stang Stang, 'Bjarmene — deres identitet, eksistensgrunnlag og forbindelser med andre folkeslag', pp. 106–09, 120.
72 Carpelan, 'Bjarmerna', p. 231.

From the Russian side, the Vepsians might be referred to as *Čud'* or 'Chud'.[73] This term, however, was not only applied to the Vepsians but also to a series of Baltic–Finnish peoples with whom the Russians associated, including the *Votes* and the *Estonians* in the west. Indications of direction or area names — like *Zavoločje* — were therefore used to distinguish between the various groups of people.

The Russian term 'Chud' was thus an overall term and did not provide any precise ethnic identification in itself. Perhaps we might venture to consider the Norse 'Biarmians' as an equivalent 'sack category'? In that case, we should renounce the linking of 'the Biarmians' unilaterally to some later known people, and rather view the term in line with 'Birkarler' and 'the Kvens': as an amalgamation of traders who served distinct economic functions with regard to the Sámi, the Norwegians, and the Russians, playing a role as intermediaries within a trading network that would eventually be dominated by Novgorod.[74] If 'Biarmian' should be perceived as such a functional term, deriving from a distinct economic adaptation, then this group may well have included several population elements of various ethnic origins. Aside from the Vepsians, the group may also have included Karelians and Permyak-speaking people who comprised the ancestors of the present-day *Komi*.

Such an approach also raises the possibility that the concrete ethnic composition of the 'Biarmian' group may have changed over time: the Vepsian population element may have been very strong in the early Middle Ages, whereas the Karelians grew during the course of the High Middle Ages and became dominant during the late Middle Ages — in line with Karelian expansion towards the White Sea region. Such a course of development would chime with later source statements. A Russian source dating from 1419 takes it for granted that Karelians are present in 'the Zavoločje country',[75] and an English ambassador to Russia in 1618–1620 reports knowledgeably that 'the people around Kholmogory were in times gone by called the Chud, and spoke a different language from the Samoyeds and the Sámi, but now they are not there anymore'.[76]

This course of development may also lie behind the reference made by the author of H.N. to the 'two kinds of Biarmians', or *utrique Biarmones*. A similar distinction relates back to Saxo Grammaticus (*c.* 1200), which refers to *Biarmia*

---

73 Etymologically, the term *Čud'* may itself be derived from an assumed pre-Slavic form **tjudjo* (foreign), which may in turn have been borrowed from the Gothic *þiuða*, or the Germanic **þeuðo* (Melnikova and Petrukhin, 'The Origin and Evolution of the Name Rus'. The Scandinavians in Eastern-European Ethno-Political Processes before the 11th Century', pp. 223–25). Cf. the Old Norse term *þjóð* (people; nation). Although this may have been the original etymology, new and distinct connotations have nonetheless been attached as a result of the interaction between Slavic and Finno-Ugrian peoples.

74 Carpelan, 'Bjarmerna'.

75 Gejman, *Materialy po Istorii Karelii XII–XVI vv.*

76 Simoni, Zametki Rikarda Džemsa o čudi, loparjakh, samoedakh i čeremisakh. Iz rukopisi 1618–20 gg, p. 126.

ulterior (farther Biarmia / Biarmaland), and thus also requires a *Biarmia citerior* (nearer Biarmia / Biarmaland).[77] This distinction is later referred to by Olaus Magnus (*Historia de Gentibus Septentrionalibus…* , 1555, bk 1, chap. 1). The 'one Biarmaland' is thus identifiable with the lower areas of the Dvina river valley, where Norse expeditions encountered the Biarmians during the early Middle Ages, but where Karelian settlement established itself more strongly during the High Middle Ages. The 'second Biarmaland' may refer to other areas where Karelian settlement gained a foothold during the High Middle Ages, for example along the west coast of the White Sea or along the south coast of the Kola Peninsula. If the Norse term 'Biarmians' is to be perceived as being in tandem with the Russian term 'Chud', it may also be the case that the differentiation between the 'two kinds of Biarmians' followed on from an original Russian distinction between various types of 'Chud': either between the western and the northern 'Chud', or between the Vepsians ('the Chud'), who were still living in their heartland, and those who in the early Middle Ages had moved to the Dvina river valley.

Conclusion

If, finally, we return to the question of the instigator of H.N., this review should enable us to draw the following conclusions about the author's knowledge and background. He seems to be very well informed about the geographical and ethnographical conditions in the North, presenting an overview that seems to match both the facts and the knowledge status within the best-informed circles of that time — as far as it is possible to attest to this from contemporaneous and subsequent sources. He nonetheless adapts this information to the prevailing 'paradigmatic' views as to how an organized and well-ruled 'kingdom' should be territorially defined, according to Old Germanic thinking. In his depiction of the peoples who stand outside the Norse cultural community, he draws a relatively clear distinction between the Sámi, who are still 'within the social horizon' and live largely side by side with the Norwegians in Hálogaland, and the other peoples who extend themselves towards the kingdom from the north and the east, and who are partly separated from the kingdom because of the buffer zone created by the 'wasteland' to the east. These peoples appear more distant, while the Sámi are, as it were, defined as 'prospective neighbours' who should be won over to Christian religion and the cultural community. The well organized and Christian kingdom of Norway is thus assigned a clear missionary task, primarily as far as the Sámi are concerned, but subsequently also vis-à-vis the 'other heathen peoples' in the North.

Since the author also reproduces eyewitness descriptions of situations interacting with the Sámi, it is reasonable to assume that he has — at least

---

77 Cf. Gustav Storm in the notes system to his edition of *Historia Norwegiae*, p. 75.

for periods of time — resided in reasonable proximity to the Sámi settlement areas. We are thus close to being able to guess that we are dealing with a cleric who has served in central or northern Norway, possibly in Niðaróss.

Works Cited

Primary Sources

Adam of Bremen, *History of the Archbishops of Hamburg-Bremen*, trans. with introduction and notes by Francis Joseph Tschan and new introduction and selected bibliography by Timothy Reuter, Records of Western Civilization, 53 (New York: Columbia University Press, 2002)

Alfræði íslenzk, Islandsk encyclopedisk litteratur III, ed. by Kristian Kålund (Copenhagen: Møllers Bogtrykkeri, 1917–18)

Gaius Julius Caesar, *Bellum Gallicum: Vollständige Ausgabe*, ed. by Alois Guthardt, Aschendorffs Sammlung Lateinischer und Griechischer Klassiker (Münster: Aschendorff, 1973)

The Chronicle of Novgorod = *Den første Novgorod-krønike, ældste affattelse*, trans. by Knud Rahbek Schmidt, in *Skrifter. Selskabet til historiske kildeskrifters oversættelse*, XIII–15 (Copenhagen: Munksgaard, 1964)

Egil's Saga, ed. by Svanhildur Óskarsdóttir, trans. by Bernard Scudder (London: Penguin Books, 2004)

Historia Norvegiae = 'II. *Historia Norvegiae*', in *Monumenta Historica Norvegiae, Latinske kildeskrifter til Norges Historie i Middelalderen*, ed. by Gustav Storm (Kristiania: Brøgger, 1880), pp. 71–124

Historia Norwegie, ed. by Inger Ekrem and Lars Boje Mortensen, trans. by Peter Fisher (Copenhagen: Museum Tusculanum Press, 2003)

Islandske Annaler indtil 1578, ed. by Gustav Storm (Christiania: Grøndahl & Søns Bogtrykkeri, 1888)

Norges gamle Love indtil 1387, ed. by Rudolf Keyser, Peter Andreas Munch, Gustav Storm and Ebbe Carsten Hornemann Hertzberg, 5 vols (Christiania 1846–1895)

Norges historie, in *Norges historie – Historien om de gamle norske kongene – Historien om danenes ferd til Jerusalem*, trans. by Astrid Salvesen, Thorleif Dahls kulturbibliotek (Oslo: Aschehoug, 1969), pp. 17–47

Olaus Magnus, *Historia de Gentibus Septentrionalibus* ... Translation and commentary by John Granlund. In *Historia om de nordiska folken* ... (Stockholm: Gidlund, 1976; originally published Rome, 1555.)

Passio et Miracula Beati Olavi = 'The Passion and the Miracles of the Blessed Óláfr', trans. by Devra Kunin, in *A History of Norway and The Passion and Miracles of the Blessed Óláfr*, translated by Devra Kunin, ed. and notes by Carl Phelpstead, Viking Society for Northern Research Text Series, 13 (University College London: London, 2001), pp. 26–75

Skard, Eiliv (trans.), *Passio Olavi, lidingssoga og undergjerningane åt den heilage Olav.* (Samlaget, repr. 1995)

Snorre Sturlason, *Heimskringla or The Lives of the Norse Kings*, ed. by Erling Monsen, trans. with the help of A. H. Smith (New York: Dover, 1990)

Secondary Works

Aðalbjarnarson, Bjarni, *Om de norske kongers saga*, Skrifter utgitt av Det Norske Videnskaps-Akademi i Oslo, II, Hist.-Filos. klasse No. 4 (Oslo: Dybwad, 1937)

Andersen, Oddmund, *Ofuohtagat – Samer og nordmenn i Ofoten*, unpublished master's thesis in archeology, University of Bergen, 1992

Barth, Fredrik, ed., *Ethnic Groups and Boundaries: The Social Organization of Culture Difference* (Bergen: Universitetsforlaget, 1969)

Bauman, Zygmunt, *Postmodern Ethics* (Oxford: Blackwell, 1993)

Bergsland, Knut, 'Utredning for Skattefjällsmålet om de sydlige sameområders historie til omkring 1751', in *Samernas Vita bok* III, 1: *Fyra utlåtanden i hovrätten i Skattefjällesmålet*, ed. by Svenska Samernas Riksförbund (Stockholm: Svenska Samernas Riksförbund, 1975), p. 573

Bertelsen, Reidar, *Lofotens og Vesterålens historie*, vol. 1: *Fra den eldste tida til ca. 1500 e.Kr* (Stokmarknes: Kommunene i Lofoten og Vesterålen, 1985)

Bratrein, Håvard Dahl. *Karlsøy og Helgøy Bygdebok: Folkeliv, Næringsliv*, vol. 1: *Fra Steinalder til år 1700* (Hansnes: Karlsøy commune, 1989)

Bratrein, Håvard Dahl, '*Passio Olavi* – et kildested om finnmarksfisket på 1100-tallet', *Håløygminne*, 20 (1998), 117–21

Carpelan, Christian, 'Bjarmerna', in *Finlands historia*, vol. 1, ed. by Torsten Edgren and Lena Törnblom (Ekenäs: Schildts, 1993), pp. 231–33

Chestnutt, Michael, 'The Dalhousie Manuscript of the Historia Norvegiae', *Bibliotheca Arnamagnaeana* 38, *Opuscula*, 8 (1985), 54–95

Ekrem, Inger, *Nytt lys over Historia Norwegie. Mot en løsning i debatten om dens alder?* (Bergen: Museum Tusculanum Press, 1998)

——, 'Essay on Date and Purpose', in *Historia Norwegie*, ed. by Inger Ekrem and Lars Boje Mortensen, trans. by Peter Fisher (Copenhagen: Museum Tusculanum Press, 2003), pp. 155–226

Ellehøj, Svend, *Studier over den ældste norrøne historieskrivning*, Bibliotheca Arnamagnaeana, 26 (Copenhagen: Munksgaard, 1965)

Fellman, Isak, *Handlingar och Uppsatser angående Finska Lappmarken och Lapparne* I–IV (Helsingfors: Svenska Litteratursällskapet i Finland, 1910–1915)

Gallén, Jarl and Lind, John, *Nöteborgsfreden och Finlands medeltida östgräns: andra delen*, maps, appendices (Helsingfors: Svenska Litteratursällskapet i Finland, 1991)

Gejman, V. G., *Materialy po Istorii Karelii XII–XVI vv* (Petrozavods: Naučno-Issledovatel'skij Institut Kul'tury Karelo–Finskoj SSR, 1941)

Guttormsen, Helge, *Ressurser og bosetning i Andenes len og Sortland fjerding: fra ca 1000–1660 e.Kr.f.*, unpublished master's thesis, University of Tromsø, 1983), Tromsø

Haavio, Martti, *Bjarmien vallan kukoistus ja tuho. Historiaa ja runoutta* (Helsinki: WSOY, 1965)

Hansen, Lars Ivar, 'Interaction between Northern European Sub-Arctic Societies during the Middle Ages: Indigenous Peoples, Peasants, and State Builders', in *Two Studies on the Middle Ages*, ed. by Magnus Rindal, KULTs skriftserie, 66 (Oslo: Kult, 1996), pp. 31–95

—— *Samisk fangstsamfunn og norsk høvdingeøkonomi* (Oslo: Novus, 1990)

Hansen, Lars Ivar, and Bjørnar Olsen, *Hunters in Transition: An Outline of Early Sámi History* (Leiden: Brill, 2014)

Hanssen, Jens S.Th., *Omkring Historia Norwegiae*, Avhandlinger utgitt av Det Norske Videnskaps-Akademi i Oslo, II, Hist.-Filos. Klasse, 2 (Oslo: Dysbwad, 1949)

Hederyd, Olof, and Yrjö Alamäki, *Tornedalens historia I. Från istid till 1600-talet* (Malung: Tornedalskommunernas historiebokskommitté, 1991)

Helle, Knut, *Norge blir en stat 1130–1319*, Handbok i Norges historie, 3 (Bergen: Universitetsforlaget, 1974)

Holmsen, Andreas, 'Finnskatt og nordmannsskatt', in *Samenes og sameområdenes rettslige stilling historisk belyst*, ed. by Knut Bergsland, The Institute for Comparative Research in Human Culture, *Serie A: Forelesninger*, 28 (Oslo: Universitetsforlaget, 1977), pp. 56–77

Holtsmark, Anne, 'Historia Norvegiae', in: *Kulturhistorisk leksikon for nordisk middelalder fra vikingetid til reformationstid*, vol. VI, ed. by Johannes Brøndsted (Copenhagen: Roskilde og Bagger, 1961), cols 585–87

Hægstad, Marius, 'Tillegg. Det norske skriftgrunnlaget i *Historia Norwegiae*', in *Edda. Nordisk tidsskrift for litteraturforskning* 17, ed. by Francis Bull and Gerhard Gran (Kristiania: Aschehoug, 1919–1920), pp. 118–21

Julku, Kyösti, *Kvenland – Kainuunmaa*, Studia Historica Septentrionalia, 11 (Rovaniemi: Societas Historica Finlandiae Septentrionalis, 1986)

Koht, Halvdan, *Innhogg og utsyn i norsk historie* (Kristiania: Aschehoug, 1921)

——. '1. Historia Norvegiae', *Historisk Tidsskrift*, 35 (1949), 49–56

Lange, Gudrun, *Die Anfänge der isländisch-norwegischen Geschichtsschreibung*, Studia Islandica, 47 (Reykjavik: Bókaútgáfa Menningarsjóðs, 1989)

Lukjančenko, T. V., 'Rasselenie Kol'skikh Saamov v XVI–XVII vv', in *K Istorii Malykh Narodnostej Evropejskogo Severa SSSR*, ed. by G. M. Kert Kozlova (Petrozavodsk: Karel'skij filial AN SSSR, 1979)

Melnikova, E. A. and V. J. Petrukhin, 'The Origin and Evolution of the Name Rus'. The Scandinavians in Eastern-European Ethno-Political Processes before the 11th Century', *Tor*, 23 (1990–1991), 203–33

Mortensen, Lars Boje, 'Introduction', in *Historia Norwegie*, ed. by Inger Ekrem and Lars Boje Mortensen, trans. by Peter Fisher (Copenhagen: Museum Tusculanum Press, 2003), pp. 11–24

Nielssen, Alf Ragnar, *Lødingen, Tjeldsund og Tysfjords historie*, vol. IV: *Fra steinalderen til 1700-tallet* (Lødingen: Tjeldsund og Tysfjord kommuner, 1990)

Niemi, Einar, 'Kven', in *Norsk historisk leksikon: kultur og samfunn ca. 1500–1800*, ed. by Steinar Imsen and Harald Winge, 2nd edn (Oslo: Cappelen akademisk forlag, 1999), pp. 226–30

Niemi, Einar and Hansen, Lars Ivar, 'Etnisitet', in *Norsk historisk leksikon: kultur og samfunn ca. 1500–1800*, ed. by Steinar Imsen and Harald Winge, 2nd edn (Oslo: Cappelen akademisk forlag, 1999), pp. 102–04

Nordal, Sigurður, *Litteraturhistorie B. Norge og Island*, Nordisk Kultur VIII:B (Stockholm: Bonnier, 1953)

Odner, Knut, *Finner og terfinner. Etniske prosesser i det nordlige Fenno-Skandinavia*, Oslo Occasional Papers in Social Anthropology, 9 (Oslo: University of Oslo, 1983)

Paasche, Fredrik, 'Norges og Islands litteratur indtil utgangen av middelalderen', in *Norsk litteraturhistorie*, vol. I, ed. by Francis Bull and Frederik Paasche (Kristiania: Aschehoug, 1924)

Robberstad, Knut, 'Ordet patria i *Historia Norvegiae*', in *Historisk Tidsskrift*, 35 (1950), 187–91

Schanche, Audhild, 'Nordnorsk jernalderarkeologi. Et sosialgeografisk perspektiv' (unpublished master's thesis, Univiversity of Tromsø, 1986)

Simoni, P. K., 'Zametki Rikarda Džemsa o čudi, loparjakh, samoedakh i čeremisakh. Iz rukopisi 1618–20 gg.', in *Sbornik Leningradskogo Obščestva Issledovatelej Kul'tury Finno-Ugorskikh Narodnostej* (Leningrad: Loikfun, 1929)

Sjögren, J. Andreas., *Gesammelte Schriften*, Hist.- etnographische Abhandl. über den russ.-finn. Norden (St Petersburg: Wiedemann, 1861)

Skard, Eiliv, *Målet i Historia Norwegiae*, Skrifter utgitt av det Norske Videnskaps-Akademi i Oslo II, Hist.-Filos. klasse no. 5 (Oslo: Dybwad, 1930)

Stang, Håkon, 'Bjarmene — deres identitet, eksistensgrunnlag og forbindelser med andre folkeslag. Et problem i Nord-Russlands forhistorie. En sammenlignende kulturhistorisk studie med utgangspunkt i arabiske kilder' (unpublished master's thesis, University of Oslo, 1977)

Steinnes, Asgaut, 'Ikring *Historia Norvegiae*', *Historisk Tidsskrift*, 34 (1946), 1–61

——, 'Meir om *Historia Norvegiae*', *Historisk Tidsskrift*, 35 (1950), 173–87

Storm, Gustav, *Monumenta Historica Norvegiae, Latinske kildeskrifter til Norges Historie i Middelalderen* (Kristiania: Brøgger, 1880)

Strade, Norbert, 'Suomalainen etnogeneesi kielihistorian valossa. [Zusammenfassung: Die finnische Ethngenese im Licht der Sprachgeschichte]', in: *Suomen varhaishistoria*, ed. by Kyösti Julku, Studia Historica Septentrionalia, 21 (Rovaniemi: Societas Historica Finlandiae Septentrionalis, 1992), pp. 568–75

Uibopuu, Valev, *Finnougrierna och deras språk: kapitel om de finsk-ugriska folkens förflutna och nutid* (Lund: Studentlitteratur, 1988)

Vahtola, Jouko, *Tornionjoki- ja Kemijokilaakson asutuksen synty. Nimitieteellinen ja historiallinen tutkimus*, Studia Historica Septentrionalia, 3 (Rovaniemi: Societas Historica Finlandiae Septentrionalis, 1980)

Vilkuna, Kustaa, *Kainuu – Kvänland, ett finsk-norsk-svenskt problem*, Acta
    Academiae Regiae Gustavi Adolphi, 46 (Uppsala: Kvänland, 1969)
de Vries, Jan, *Altnordische Literaturgeschichte*, Bd. II: Die Literatur von etwa 1150
    bis 1300. Die Spätzeit nach 1300, Grundriss der germanischen Philologie, 16
    (Berlin: de Gruyter, 1942 [revised edition 1967])
Wallerström, Thomas, *Norrbotten, Sverige och Medeltiden. Problem kring makt och
    bosättning i en europeisk periferi*, Lund Studies in Medieval Archaeology, 15:1–2
    (Stockholm: Almqvist & Wiksell, 1995)
——, 'De historiska källornas "folknamn" som analysenheter och projektet
    "State, Religion and Ethnicity in the North AD 700–1990"', in *Stat, etnisitet,
    religion*, ed. by Bjørn-Petter Finstad, Lars Ivar Hansen, Henry Minde, Einar
    Niemi, and Hallvard Tjelmeland, Skriftserie Senter for Samiske studier, 4
    (Tromsø: Senter for Samiske studier, 1997), pp. 383–424
Weibull, Curt, 'Den älsta gränsläggningen mellan Sverige och Danmark.
    Gränsområde och gränslinje', *Historisk Tidskrift för Skåneland*, 7 (1917), 1–18

ELEANOR ROSAMUND BARRACLOUGH

The Ice Giant Cometh: The Far North in the Old Norse-Icelandic Sagas

Introduction

Associations between the supernatural and the inhabitants of the North are deeply rooted in medieval Norse texts, particularly the sagas. This is true of the depiction of non-Norse human populations often associated with the North, such as the *Finnar*.[1] The further north the sagas take us, the more human inhabitants give way to non-human beings such as trolls and giants. In what follows, the focus is on the depiction and function of this type of far-northerner. Plotting a trajectory through Old Norse literature describing Norwegian origin myths and fantastical tales set in supernatural kingdoms, my aim is to address the following questions: who were the inhabitants of the Far North in the Norse cultural imagination, and why?

Firstly, some background to the sources. Broadly speaking, the Old Norse sagas began to be recorded in Iceland during the thirteenth century, although many of them have longer-lived oral components stretching back across the centuries and beyond Iceland. Today, they are typically divided according to literary genres such as the *Íslendingasögur* (sagas of Icelanders), *konungasögur* (kings' sagas), *fornaldarsögur* (legendary sagas), and *riddarasögur* (chivalric sagas). The first two of these are often considered to be more realistic in tone and more rooted in historical reality, while the third and fourth categories

---

1 *Finnar* is the Norse word for the people who can be broadly equated with the ancestors of today's Sámi. In Old Norse texts, they have a reputation for magic, particularly with regard to shape-shifting, soothsaying, and controlling the weather. See Lindow, 'Supernatural and Ethnic Others'; Mundal, 'The Perception of the Saamis and their Religion', p. 98; Hermann Pálsson, 'The Sami People in Old Norse Literature', pp. 29–53; Cardew, '"Mannfögnuður er oss at smjöri þessu"', pp. 146–58; Lindow, 'Cultures in Contact', pp. 89–109, esp. 91–106; Aalto, 'Alienness in *Heimskringla*'; DeAngelo, 'The North and the Depiction of the *Finnar* in the Icelandic Sagas', pp. 257–81.

Eleanor Rosamund Barraclough, Durham University, e.r.barraclough@durham.ac.uk

Myths and Magic in the Medieval Far North: Realities and Representations of a Region on the Edge of Europe, ed. by Stefan Figenschow, Richard Holt, and Miriam Tveit, AS 10
(Turnhout: Brepols, 2020), pp. 71–94
10.1484/M.AS-EB.5.120520

tend to be more fantastical in terms of their content, set in a chronologically unfixed, quasi-legendary past. Yet by no means all of these genres are medieval in origin, and there is considerable overlap in terms of thematic preoccupations and narrative style, regardless of the genres to which specific sagas are assigned. Indeed, the texts designated *fornaldarsögur* were only brought together as a genre in the nineteenth century, edited in three volumes by Carl Christian Rafn and given the title *fornaldarsögur norðurlanda* (sagas of ancient times from northern lands). We cannot be certain that the original medieval saga writers and audiences would have grouped these sagas together in the same way as we do today. Therefore, while a good proportion of the sagas addressed below are classed as *fornaldarsögur*, I will not attempt to ascribe too much significance to their genre categorization. Indeed, as I have demonstrated elsewhere, by addressing the full spectrum of texts regardless of genre, it is possible to see just how widespread the association between the Far North and the supernatural actually is, regardless of whether one focuses on its human or non-human inhabitants.[2]

As Ármann Jakobsson has investigated, there is a significant degree of terminological and semantic overlap between Old Norse terms such as *jǫtunn* (giant) *risi* (giant), *trǫll* (troll), and *þurs* (troll).[3] While I will not be adding to that debate here, it is worth pointing out that the following assessment of far-northern supernatural beings in the sagas does nothing to simplify the picture. While some of the texts are at pains to create a coherent internal geography of the non-human kingdoms, it is also true that no consistent, comprehensive map of the Far North and its inhabitants can be drawn from the corpus as a whole. Perhaps this should not come as a surprise, for as the Canadian literary scholar Sherrill E. Grace has written, 'North is multiple, shifting, elastic; it is a *process*, not a condition. It is, above all, Other, and as such emphatically a construction of southerners'.[4] Even given the northerly location of the Nordic cultures compared to the rest of the medieval European world, the same was true in their collective cultural imagination. So who — or what — lived north of the Northmen in the saga writers' imagination?

Origin Myths

Two texts incorporate variations on a founding myth that roots the origins of Norway and several prominent ruling families in the Far North amongst the giants. The opening chapters of *Orkneyinga saga* (*The Saga of the Orkney*

---

2 See Barraclough, *Beyond the Northlands*; Barraclough, 'Arctic Frontiers'. For more on this general trend, see Barraclough, Cudmore, and Donecker, eds, *Imagining the Supernatural North*.

3 See Ármann Jakobsson, 'The Good, the Bad, and the Ugly', pp. 1–15; Ármann Jakobsson, 'Identifying the Ogre', pp. 181–200.

4 Grace, *Canada and the Idea of North*, p. 16.

Islanders), also known as *Fundinn Noregr* (*The Founding of Norway*), is likely the older version, but the information is closely paralleled in *Hversu Noregr byggðist* (*How Norway was Settled*) preserved in the Icelandic manuscript Flateyjarbók (*c*. 1387). The founding figure is Fornjótr, and while neither text identifies him as a giant (in fact *HNb* calls him a man), Fornjótr is listed as a *jǫtunn* (giant) in Snorri Sturluson's *Edda* (*c*. 1220). This is how *FN* begins:

> Fornjótr hefir konungr heitit; hann réð fyrir því landi, er kallat [er] Finnland ok Kvenland; þat liggr fyrir austan hafsbotn þann, er gengr til móts við Gandvík; þat kǫllu vér Helsingjabotn. Fornjótr átti þrjá syni; hét einn Hlér, er vér kǫllum Ægi, annarr Logi, þriði Kári; hann var faðir Frosta, fǫður Snæs ins gamla. Hans sonr hét Þorri; hann átti tvá syni; hét annarr Nórr, en annarr Górr; dóttir hans hét Gói.[5]
>
> > (There was a king called Fornjótr. He ruled over those lands that are called Finland and Kvenland, east of the seabed that goes northward towards Gandvík [the White Sea]; we call this Helsingjabotn [the Gulf of Bothnia]. Fornjótr had three sons; the first was called Hlér [Sea], whom we call Ægir, the second Logi [Fire], the third Kári [North Wind]. He [Kári] was the father of Frosti [Frost], the father of Snær [Snow] the Old. His [Snær's] son's name was Þorri; he [Þorri] had two sons, one was called Nórr and the other Górr; his daughter's name was Gói.)[6]

The story with its elemental protagonists then homes in on the last generation. When Gói is abducted, her brothers set out separately to find her. Nórr's journey in particular is deeply rooted in the weather and landscapes of the Far North; he waits for the snows to fall on the moors, then skis all the way to where the *Finnar* live on the far side of Finnmǫrk.[7] Having scared the *Finnar* away with magic, Nórr and his men continue west, claiming land wherever they can. When they reach the Uplands they find Gói, who has been abducted by King Hrólfr, 'sonr Svaða jǫtuns norðan af Dofrum' (son of the giant Svaði from Dovrefjell in the North).[8] Having made peace with his sister's abductor, Nórr journeys back north and rules the lands that he has claimed, which are afterwards called Norway.

In *HNb*, new characters are introduced into the lineage, also named for their elemental associations with the North. Kári's son is Jǫkull (Glacier), who in turn becomes the father of Snær (Snow). Snær now has four children, including two girls called Drífa (Driving Snow) and Mjǫll (Powdered Snow). This is not

---

5   *Orkneyinga saga*, ed. by Finnbogi Guðmundsson, p. 3.
6   Translations my own unless otherwise specified.
7   The medieval region of Finnmǫrk is not synonymous with modern-day Finnmark, the northernmost province in Norway, although there is some overlap. Finnmǫrk literally means the 'forest' or 'borderland' of the *Finnar*. For more, see Barraclough, 'Arctic Frontiers'.
8   *Orkneyinga saga*, ed. by Finnbogi Guðmundsson, p. 5.

the only text in which we will meet Snær and his daughters; elsewhere their supernatural nature is more pronounced, as will be returned to later. What is significant is that in both versions of this foundation myth, as has been argued by, amongst others, Preben Meulengracht Sørensen, this is a lineage that 'personif[ies] the Nordic winter and northern nature'.[9] Margaret Clunies Ross has traced references to Fornjótr and his family elsewhere in the Old Norse textual corpus, such as in fragments of a poem called *Norðrsetudrápa* (*Poem of the Northern Seat*, likely a reference to Greenland's 'Northern Hunting Grounds' beyond the Arctic Circle). Here, the 'hostile sons of Fornjótr' are said to 'blow drifting snow', thus emphasizing their far-northern characteristics.[10] As Clunies Ross states, 'A number of giant-names, which occur in Eddaic verse […] signal a close association between giants and cold weather', and the same is demonstrably true of the names of Fornjótr's kin in both *Fundinn Noregr* and *Hversu Noregr byggðist*.[11]

It has been noted that this foundation story contrasts with the better-known euhemerized narrative presented by Snorri Sturluson in his *Edda* and *Ynglinga saga* (*The Saga of the Ynglings*), the first saga in his *Heimskringla* compilation.[12] Here, the Norse pagan gods are humans who start out in the far south as Trojan warriors, before travelling to northern Europe and being feted as gods. By contrast, scholars have suggested that the function of both versions of the far-northern myth is to legitimize the alternative rulership of various lineages: specifically the earls of Orkney in *Fundinn Noregr*.[13] As Gro Steinsland argues, this is a genealogy that 'stresses that the earls originated in the most northerly areas of Scandinavia, and that their history reaches back to the beginnings of time'.[14] Moreover, as Ian Beuermann notes,

> With their descent from Fornjótr, the ancestors of the earls of Orkney are shown to be exclusively Nordic. They stem from an ancient native race hailing from a mythical past, and — to put it in somewhat racist terms — their blood had not been diluted by southern immigrants.[15]

This argument is complicated by the fact that, when the euhemerized framework is removed from Snorri's *Edda*, the underlying myth of creation is still rooted in ice and cold. As is stated in *Gylfaginning* (*The Tricking of Gylfi*), the northern part of Ginnungagap (the primeval void) was filled with ice and rime, while the

---

9   Meulengracht Sørensen, 'The Sea, the Flame, and the Wind', p. 213. See also Beuermann, 'Jarla sögur Orkneyja', p. 115; Langeslag, *Seasons in the Literatures of the Medieval North*, p. 44; Clunies Ross, 'Snorri Sturluson's Use of the Norse Origin-Legend', pp. 47–66.

10   Clunies Ross, 'Snorri Sturluson's Use of the Norse Origin-Legend', p. 48.

11   Clunies Ross, 'Snorri Sturluson's Use of the Norse Origin-Legend', p. 50.

12   Meulengracht Sørensen, 'The Sea, the Flame, and the Wind', p. 229; Steinsland, 'Origin Myths and Rulership', p. 58.

13   See Rowe, 'Origin Legends and Foundation Myths in Flateyjarbók', pp. 198–216.

14   Steinsland, 'Origin Myths and Rulership', p. 50.

15   Beuermann, 'Jarla sögur Orkneyja', p. 116.

southern part faced the intense heat of Múspellsheimr. In the space between, the frozen rime from the rivers of Élivágar (icy / stormy waves) combined with the heat and fire of Múspellsheimr to create Ymir, father of the *Hrímþursar* (frost giants). Moreover, the ancestor of the gods was also born of ice, for as the cow Auðumbla licked at the salty frozen blocks a man's head emerged: Búri, grandfather of Óðinn. Significantly, Óðinn himself was of part-giant descent, since his mother was Bestla, daughter of the frost giant Bǫlþorn. Therefore, in terms of establishing a long-standing and legitimate lineage in the medieval north, perhaps it was enough that far-northern elements and frost giants formed the core of the origin myth for the world itself.

An alternative Norwegian foundation myth also rooted in giant ancestry can be found in *Háleygjatal* (*c.* 985), Eyvindr *skáldaspillir's* praise poem to Jarl Hákon recounting the origins of the jarls of Hlaðir (Lade) (Hákon's lineage). This myth is different, for here the original progenitors are Óðinn himself and the giantess Skaði, the latter described in the poem as *ǫndurdís* (ski-goddess) and *járnviðja* (giant-woman). This stanza is preserved in *Ynglinga saga*:

> Þann skjaldblœtr | skattfœri gat | Ása niðr | við járnviðju, | þás þau mær |
> í manheimum | skatna vinr | ok Skaði byggðu, | sævar beins, | ok sunu
> marga | ǫndurdís | við Óðni gat.

> (The shield-worshipped kinsman of the Æsir <gods> [= Óðinn] begat that tribute-bringer [Jarl = Sæmingr] with the female from Járnviðr, when those renowned ones, the friend of warriors [= Óðinn] and Skaði [giantess], lived in the maiden-lands of the bone of the sea [rock> giantess> = Jǫtunheimar 'Giant-Lands'], and the ski-goddess [= Skaði] bore many sons with Óðinn.)[16]

This 'tribute-bringer' is Sæmingr, the son of Óðinn and Skaði and reputed ancestor of Jarl Hákon. While the giant figure, Skaði, is not traditionally associated with climes as far northern as Fornjótr (rather she is said to come from Dovrefjell, a well-known giant haunt in central Norway also mentioned in *Fundinn Noregr*), it is nevertheless true that, as Gro Steinsland has pointed out, the poet Eyvindr was well aware of her association with snowy winter landscapes. Indeed, since the original powerbase of the jarls of Hlaðir was said to be in Hálogaland, the northernmost province inhabited by the medieval Norse, this may be another giant-oriented origin myth with northern roots in which, as Steinsland suggests, 'the giants of the old origin myths are re-defined into the native population, and the northern regions of Norway are depicted as the genuine Nordic landscape'.[17] More specifically, she notes, there may be a Sámi element in this myth, expressed particularly in the figure of Sæmingr, meaning that, 'whether it was created in the skaldic milieu at Hlaðir, or

---

16 Eyvindr *skáldaspillir* Finnsson, *Háleygjatal*, p. 199.
17 Steinsland, 'Origin Myths and Rulership', p. 60.

perpetuates older traditions, might express an awareness of the integration of two people, the Sami and the Scandinavians'.[18]

Giants as the original inhabitants of the Far North also feature in *Hervarar saga ok Heiðreks* (*The Saga of Hervǫr and Heiðrekr*), a saga that may date to the early thirteenth century but is now extant only in later manuscripts and paper copies. In the U-redaction of the saga (preserved in a seventeeth-century manuscript described by its modern editor as 'ill-written and extremely corrupt'), the *Jǫtunheimar* (Giant Worlds) are said to lie north of Gandvík (perhaps meaning 'Sorcery Bay'), the Norse name for the White Sea.[19] *Ymisland* — likely named for Ymir, mythical progenitor of the frost giants — is located between there and Hálogaland:

> Svá finnsk ritat í fornum bókum, at Jǫtunheimar váru kallaðir norðr um Gandvík, en Ymisland fyrir sunnan í millum Hálogalands. En áðr Tyrkjar ok Asíamenn kómu í Norðrlǫnd byygðu norðrhálfurnar risar ok sumt hálfrisar; gerðisk þá mikit sambland þjóðanna; risar fengu sér kvenna ór Mannheimum, en sumir giptu þangat dœtr sínar.[20]

> (It is found written in ancient books that to the north beyond Gandvík it was called Jǫtunheimar and Ymisland to the south between there and Hálogaland. But before the Turks and the men of Asia came to the Northlands giants dwelt in the northern regions, and some were half-giants; there was a great mingling of races in those days, for the giants got themselves wives out of Mannheimar, and some married their daughters to men from that country.)

As the text develops its theme this mingling of races continues, with the abduction of females from both Jǫtunheimar and Ymisland:

> Maðr hét Arngrímr, hann var risi ok bergbúi; hann nam ór Ymislandi Ámu Ymisdóttur ok gekk at eiga hana. Sonr þeira hét Hergrímr, er kallaðr var hálftrǫll; hann var stundum með bergrisum en stundum með mǫnnum; hann hafði afl sem jǫtnar; hann var allfjǫlkunnigr ok berserkr mikill. Hann nam ór Jǫtunheimum Ǫgn álfasprengi ok gekk at eiga hana; þau áttu þann son, er Grímr hét.[21]

> (There was a man named Arngrímr, a giant, who dwelt in the mountain rocks; out of Ymisland he carried off Áma Ymir's daughter and made her his wife. Their son's name was Hergrímr, who was called Halftroll; at times he dwelt among the mountain-giants, but at other times among men. His strength was that of giants, and he had deep knowledge of

18 Steinsland, 'Origin Myths and Rulership', p. 61.
19 *Hervarar saga ok Heiðreks*, ed. by G. Turville-Petre and Christopher Tolkien, p. xvii.
20 *Hervarar saga ok Heiðreks*, ed. by G. Turville-Petre and Christopher Tolkien, p. 66.
21 *Hervarar saga ok Heiðreks*, ed. by G. Turville-Petre and Christopher Tolkien.

magic arts; he was a great berserk. Out of Jǫtunheimar he carried
off Ǫgn Álfasprengi and married her; they had a son called Grímr.)

Here, too, are elements of cosmographical geography: Hergrímr Halftroll is
said to have abducted Ǫgn when her fiancé goes *norðr yfir Élivága* ('north over
Élivágar', the frozen rivers of North mythology).[22] But there are also connections
to historical regions of the Far North, for Grímr later sets himself up on the
island of Bólm in Hálogaland. In the H-redaction of the same saga, human
and giant geographies are even more closely intertwined: here Jǫtunheimar
is located *in* Finnmǫrk rather than to the north of it.[23]

The same text also includes information about the migration of the
euhemerized gods from the south: 'Þessu samtíða kómu austan Asíamenn
ok Tyrkjar ok byggðu Norðrlǫnd. Óðinn formaðr þeira átti marga sonu'
(It was about this time that the men of Asia and the Turks came out of the
east and settled in the Northlands. Óðinn their leader had many sons).[24]
Significantly, this information is preceded by information about the giants
of the Far North and their encounters with mankind: they are clearly set
up as the first inhabitants of Norway. The idea of Norway being inhabited
by giants before men also appears in the version of *Óláfs saga Tryggvasonar*
(*The Saga of Óláfr Tryggvason*) originally thought to have been written by the
twelfth-century Icelandic monk Oddr Snorrason. The king is sailing up the
coast when a red-bearded man asks to be taken on board. He turns out to be
the pagan god Þórr in disguise, for he tells the king:

> Herra land þetta er ver siglum firir var bygt forðum af risum nocquorum.
> En þat barsc at at þeir risarnir fengu nocquorn braðan bana oc dó þeir sua
> at eigi varð fleira eptir en konur ij. Siþan gerþiz þat herra. at menn tocu
> at byggia land þetta þeir er menndskir voro. or austr halfu heimsins.[25]

> (Lord, the land that we are sailing past was formerly inhabited by
> certain giants. But it came about that the giants suddenly died so
> that none remained except two giantesses. Then it happened, lord,
> that men from the eastern part of the world began to settle this land.)

In such stories about Norway's ancient origins, giants are present from its
conception. They are the first inhabitants of the land even before the arrival
of the Norse pagan gods and humans, or the ancestors of ruling lineages.
More generally in Norse texts, the north is not the only cardinal direction
to which they are linked, for they are also present in the east (indeed this
is where Þórr can often be found bashing giantesses). Ármann Jakobsson

---

22 *Hervarar saga ok Heiðreks*, ed. by G. Turville-Petre and Christopher Tolkien, p. 67.
23 *Hervarar saga ok Heiðreks*, ed. by G. Turville-Petre and Christopher Tolkien, p. 66 n. 2.
24 *Hervarar saga ok Heiðreks*, ed. by G. Turville-Petre and Christopher Tolkien, p. 67.
25 *Saga Óláfs Tryggvasonar af Oddr Snorrason Munk*, ed. by Finnur Jónsson, pp. 173–74.

has tried to disentangle these associations in Snorri's *Edda*, but in doing so demonstrates its lack of systematic consistency, for:

> if Iotunheimar are indeed to the North, we might infer that the natural abode of the giants is the coldness of the North, which fits in with the notion of frost-giants. However, as it turns out, North is not always the direction where giants can be found.[26]

This makes sense given that while Jǫtunheim(ar) appears in both the singular and plural form (i.e., 'giant world' or 'giant worlds'), the fact that it *can* appear in the plural may indicate that, as John Lindow points out, 'there were multiple areas inhabited by giants. […] In the world of humans there were multiple places where the trolls might live: mountains, forests, and so forth — any of the unsettled areas surrounding the farmstead'.[27] The giants, in other words, inhabited *útgarðar* (literally 'out-yards'), the location of external and dangerous cosmological forces.[28] Such regions are very often found in the Far North, where the physical topography is not suited to most types of human habitation (at least by European standards).

Jǫtunheim(ar)

Like the example of *Hervarar saga* above, there are a number of sagas in which a geographical system of supernatural giant kingdoms is placed in the Far North. But here we find no enumeration of a primeval giant genealogy rooted in the deep mythological past. Most of these stories are classed as *fornaldarsögur* and seem to be concerned more with outlandish literary entertainment and folktale motifs borrowed and shared between each other. As Rudolf Simek puts it, 'In descriptions of countries on the fringe of the northern hemisphere the actual geographical facts, as experienced by travellers there, strangely mingle in most of these sagas with a more mythical-literary geography'.[29]

The presence of this mythical-literary geography does not necessarily denude the *fornaldarsögur* of deeper purpose and significance. Margaret Clunies Ross has pointed out that while these texts cannot be read as realistic narratives, they nevertheless deal with 'deep and disturbing issues that cannot

---

26 Ármann Jakobsson, 'Where Do the Giants Live?', p. 106. As Ármann Jakobsson explains elsewhere, '*Snorra Edda* leaves us unsure where the giants live. They may live in the woods of the East. They may live on the shore. They may live in the North, being frost-giants. […] What is their relationship with the frost-giants or the wood-giantesses? *Snorra Edda* offers no explanation. To Snorri, they seem to be of the same pack', Ármann Jakobsson, 'The Good, the Bad, and the Ugly', p. 4.

27 Lindow, *Norse Mythology*, p. 206.

28 Gro Steinsland makes much of the importance of alliances with 'útgarðar' women in origin myths associated with the Far North; see Steinsland, 'Origin Myths'.

29 Simek, 'Elusive Elysia', p. 251.

be approached from the perspective of the mundane world but must rather be enacted in a literary world in which often taboo subjects can be raised and aired, though not necessarily resolved. They may also be treated in a comic or parodic vein'.[30] There may be an element of this in the treatment of trolls and giants as inhabitants of the Far North: the literary manifestation of a cold, distant geographical region where humans rarely thrive or survive for long.

Jǫtunheim(ar) itself has already featured in several of the sagas discussed here, and in its various manifestations it puts in appearances both in eddic verse and Snorri's *Edda*. Its far-northern location is particularly well established in the sagas, for, as Simek notes:

> In later prose literature, when Jötunheim has been firmly established as a literary motif and as the realm of the giants, it was no longer thought to be situated in the east and indeed it moved further and further to the north as the increasingly empirically understood geographical picture of the world demanded.[31]

In *Egils saga einhenda ok Ásmundar berserkjabana* (*The Saga of One-Handed Egill and Ásmundr the Berserk-Killer*), the giant lands are ruled over by Queen Arinnefja (Eagle Beak), skinless nymphomaniac and former lover of the pagan gods Óðinn and Þórr. Her lands lie to the far north of Russia, and throughout this outlandish saga we see giant politics at play in the High Arctic. The meat of the story concerns two human heroes and their quest to find the Russian princesses who have been captured (it turns out by giants). The affable if grotesque queen helps them in their attempt and is rewarded at the end of the saga with a 'smjörtrog svá mikit sem hún gat lyft, ok sagði hún, at sá gripr mundi torgætr þykkja í Jötunheimum' (butter-trough so big she could only just lift it, and she said that such a gift would be thought a rare one in Jötunheimar).[32] She is also given two flanks of bacon weighing a ton: 'Þótti kerlingu þessir gripir betri en þótt þeir hefði gefit henni byrði sína af gulli' (the old woman thought this was a better gift than if she had been given a load of gold).[33] The encounter is thus of a type typical to human–giant interactions in the sagas, whereby a giant acts as the human hero's helpmate and may help to shield them from the more unsavoury supernatural inhabitants of the country.

Risaland and Dumbshaf

In addition to *jǫtunn*, another Old Norse word for 'giant' is *risi*. Risaland, another giant kingdom, appears in a small number of texts including *Samsons*

---

30 Clunies Ross, *The Cambridge Introduction to the Old Norse-Icelandic Saga*, p. 77.
31 Clunies Ross, *The Cambridge Introduction to the Old Norse-Icelandic Saga*, p. 180.
32 *Fornaldar sögur norðurlanda*, ed. by Guðni Jónsson, III, 363.
33 *Fornaldar sögur norðurlanda*, ed. by Guðni Jónsson, III, 363.

saga fagra (*The Saga of Samson the Fair*), *Örvar-Odds saga* (*The Saga of Arrow-Oddr*), *Bárðar saga Snæfellsáss* (*The Saga of Barðr, God of Snæfellsnes*), and *Valdimars saga* (*The Saga of Valdimar*). In *Samsons saga* this kingdom is clearly located in the north-east, and connected once again to Jǫtunheimar:

> Risaland liggr til austurs ok nordurs af Austurueginum ok þadan til landnordurs Þa liggr þat land er Iotunheimar heita ok bua traull ok ovætter. enn þadan til mozs vid Grænlanz obygder geingr þat land er Sualbardi heiter. þat byggia ymissar þioder. þar eru þeir einer at þeir verda .cc. vetra enn sialldan eiga þeir fiolberni.[34]

> > (Risaland lies to the east and north of the 'Eastern Way' (Baltic countries) and from there further northeast. There is a country there called Jǫtunheimar, which is inhabited by giants and trolls. Svalbard extends from there to the deserts of Greenland. There live Ymir's people. There are those who live 200 winters and seldom have children.)

Although 'Ymisland' is not named here as it is in *Hervarar saga*, the effect is much the same; if its inhabitants are descended from the mythological ur-being Ymir, then we might conclude that this is the land of the frost giants. Furthermore, the Svalbard of this passage more likely refers to Jan Mayen than the archipelago known today as Svalbard, but its inclusion takes us decidedly into the High Arctic; appropriately enough *Svalbarði* translates as 'cold coasts' or 'cold shores'.[35] In *Bárðar saga Snæfellsáss* (*The Saga of Bárðr, God of Snæfellsnes*), this same region is given a supernatural ruler, King Dumbr, who 'réð fyrir hafsbotnum þeim, er ganga af Risalandi í landsuðr, en fyrir sunnan gengr þat haf, sem nú er kallat Dumbshaf' (ruled over the gulfs that stretch from Risaland in the south-east, and stretch north to the sea that is now called Dumbshaf).[36] From this and other references to Dumbshaf, this seems to be the Arctic Ocean. *Bárðar saga* is a particularly unusual text; despite generally being classified as one of the *Íslendingasögur*, it opens with another supernatural lineage in the Far North, although this one blends trolls and giants in its heritage:

> Hann var kominn af risakyni í föðurætt sína, ok er þat vænna fólk ok stærra en aðrir men, en móðir hans var komin af tröllaættum, ok brá því Dumbi í hvárutveggju ætt sína, því hann var bæði sterkr ok vænn ok góðr viðskiptis ok kunni því at eiga allt sambland við mennska menn. En um þat brá honum í sitt móðurkyn, at hann var bæði sterkr ok stórvirkr ok umskiptasamr ok illskiptinn, ef honum eigi líkaði nökkut; vildi hann einn ráða við þá, er norðr þar váru, enda gáfu þeir honum konungs nafn, því at þeim þótti mikil forstoð í honum vera fyrir risum ok tröllum og óvættum;

---

34   *Samsons saga fagra*, ed. by Wilson, pp. 31–32.
35   See Jón Jóhannesson, *A History of the Old Icelandic Commonwealth*, p. 109.
36   *Bárðar saga*, ed. by Þórhallur Vilmundarson and Bjarni Vilhjálmsson, p. 101.

var ok hann inn mesti bjargvættr öllum þeim, er til hans kölluðu. Hann tók tólf vetra konungdóm. Hann nam í burtu af Kvenlandi Mjöll, dóttur Snæs ins gamla, ok gekk at eiga hana. Hon var kvenna fríðust ok nær allra kvenna stærst, þeira sem mennskar váru.[37]

> (He [Dumbr] was descended from giants through his father, a handsome people who were bigger than other men, but his mother came from the race of trolls. Both sides of his ancestry were evidence in Dumbr, because he was both strong and handsome, as well as good-natured, and so was easily able to mix with humans. From his mother's side he inherited his strength and ability to perform great deeds, as well as his changeability and bad temper if something wasn't to his liking. He wanted to be the sole ruler of the north, and so they gave him the name of king because it seemed to them that he would be a powerful protector against giants and trolls and evil creatures. He was also the greatest supernatural guardian of all those who called on him for help. He was twelve winters when he took up the kingdom. From Kvenland he abducted Mjöll, daughter of Snær the Old, and made her his wife. She was the fairest of women, and almost the largest of all those who were human.)

Note that towards the end of this passage we are reintroduced to characters who also appear in the Fornjótr origin myth from *Hversu Noregr byggðist*. Snær and Mjöll are even correctly positioned in Kvenland, although here Mjöll is specifically identified as 'human'. This is not the case in the other saga in which she makes a guest appearance, *Sturlaugs saga starfsama* (*The Saga of Sturlaugr the Industrious*), where she is presented as the daughter of King Snær of Finnmǫrk. Her precise nature is never spelled out, but she can move faster than the wind and is described as so dangerously *fjölkunnig* (skilled in magic) that she is burned to death.[38] The episode initially plays out like a northern chivalric romance: Sturlaugr sends one of his companions, Frosti (Frost), on a mission to visit King Snær and befriend his daughter, but this is a trap. Frosti is said to be a Swede, but in addition to his giant-like wintry name he himself displays supernatural traits and is burnt to death together with Mjöll.

Returning to *Bárðar saga*, Mjöll gives birth to Bárðr, the hero of the saga. While Bárðr is off further south in Dovrefjell being fostered by Dofri (the most famous of giant foster-fathers, also said to have fostered King Haraldr Fairhair), a civil war breaks out between the Arctic giants and trolls. King Dumbr is killed, at which point the inhabitants of this troll-giant kingdom in the Arctic Ocean relocate to Hálogaland in northern Norway and live amongst humans. Mjöll marries again, but her new husband is Rauðfeldr, the son of a giant. As Ármann Jakobsson has pointed out, she may be classed as human

---

37 *Bárðar saga*, ed. by Þórhallur Vilmundarson and Bjarni Vilhjálmsson, p. 101.
38 *Fornaldar sögur norðurlanda*, ed. by Guðni Jónsson, III, 151.

by the saga writer but 'she seems more at ease with giants than humans and is thus perhaps more Other than human'.[39] In Hálogaland, troll-giant hybrids mix happily with humans and even migrate together in order to become settlers in Iceland.

Occasional references to Dumbshaf, the Arctic Ocean, can be found elsewhere in the saga corpus. In the aforementioned *Egils saga einhenda*, the human heroes Egill and Ásmundr are enchanted by Queen Arinnefja so that they appear as giants, and given the names Fjalar and Frosti (both typical giant names). Their cover story is that they are 'synir Dumbs konungs ór Dumbshafi, — "ok munu slíkir men varla finnast í Jötunheimum"' (the sons of King Dumbr of Dumbshaf, and you'll hardly find their equal in Jötunheimar).[40] In *Ketils saga hœngs* (*The Saga of Ketill Trout*), the human hero is in the Far North when he meets a troll woman on her way to a troll assembly: 'Þar kemr Skelkingr norðan ór Dumbshafi, konungr trölla, ok Ófóti ór Ófótansfirði ok Þorgerðr Hörgatröll ok aðrar stórvættir norðan ór landi' (Skelkingr, king of the trolls, is coming north from Dumbshaf, and Ófóti from Ófótansfjörðr, and Þorgerðr Hörgatröll, and other powerful creatures from the north of the land).[41] Þorgerðr Hörgatröll (Altar-Troll) is a particularly significant figure. Elsewhere in the Norse textual corpus she is given alternative nicknames such as *Hölgabrúðr* (Hölgi's Bride) and *Hörgabrúðr* (Altar-Bride). Her nature and origins have been much debated: sometimes identified as a giantess and sometimes as a *landvættr* (land spirit) or *fylgja* (fetch), it is possible that she may have been the focus of cult activity (as the nickname 'Altar-Troll' implies).[42] There seems to have been a particularly close connection between the figure of Þorgerðr and Jarl Hákon of Hlaðir: Gro Steinsland, amongst others, has suggested that she was most closely associated with the Háleygjar, the people from Hálogaland in northern Norway.[43] Once again, therefore, it is possible to see a close relationship and identity between the Norse living in this part of the country and supernatural entities, in this case benevolent.

Helluland

Sometimes located in Dumbshaf is the island of Helluland, which also becomes the setting for supernatural encounters in multiple *fornaldarsögur*. Helluland (literally 'Stone Slab Land') was initially the Norse name for Baffin Island in Arctic Canada, and it appears in both of the Vínland sagas as one of the — historically realistic and non-supernatural — locations visited by

---

39 Ármann Jakobsson, 'The Good, the Bad, and the Ugly', p. 8.

40 *Fornaldar sögur norðurlanda*, ed. by Guðni Jónsson, III, 357.

41 *Fornaldar sögur norðurlanda*, ed. by Guðni Jónsson, II, 173.

42 See Motz, 'The Family of Giants', pp. 216–36; McKinnell, 'Þorgerðr Hölgabrúðr and Hyndluljóð', pp. 265–90; McKinnell, 'Two Sex Goddesses', pp. 268–91.

43 Steinsland, 'Det hellige bryllup og norrøn kongeideologi'.

the Norse explorers from Greenland as they make their way down the North American coastline. But in later texts, there are times when Helluland becomes detached from its original location in the far west and makes its way up to the Arctic Ocean.[44]

Returning to *Bárðar saga*, a far-northern Helluland is the location for a showdown between Gestr, Bárðr's son, and the dead pagan zombie-king Raknarr. Dumbshaf, which they sail across to reach Helluland, is a place of monsters and pagan gods in disguise. The one featured in this passage seems to be a cross between Óðinn and Þórr because of his one eye and the colour of his moustache, but is later identified as the former:

> Er þeir kvámu norðr fyrir Dumbshaf, kom maðr af landi ofan ok réðst í ferð með þeim; hann nefndist Rauðgrani; hann var eineygr; hann hafði bláflekkótta skautheklu ok kneppta niðr í milli fóta sér. Ekki var Jósteini presti mikit um hann. Rauðgrani taldi heiðni ok forneskju fyrir mönnum Gests ok taldi þat bezt at blóta til heilla sér.[45]

> (When they were north of Dumbshaf, a man came out from the shore who joined the voyage with them. He called himself Rauðgrani [Red-Moustache]. He was one-eyed, and he wore a blue-spotted cape with a hood that buttoned all the way down to his feet. Jósteinn the priest didn't like him. Rauðgrani preached heathen beliefs and lore to Gestr's men and said it was best to sacrifice to bring themselves luck.)

Helluland and King Raknarr also feature in *Hálfdans saga Eysteinssonar* (*The Saga of Hálfdan Eystein's Son*). In this instance, not only giants and pagan gods but also dragons inhabit Dumbshaf. The further north the saga takes its readers, the more supernatural the encounters become. We are introduced to two brothers, the sons of the king of Gästrikland on the eastern coast of Sweden:

> Hét annarr Raknarr, en annarr Valr. Þeir váru víkingar ok lágu úti í Dumbshafi ok herjuðu á jötna. […Valr] lá í Dumbshafi, ok er mikil saga af honum. […] Valr hafði drepit Sviða ok lagt undir sik Kirjálabotna. Hann hafði fengit svá mikit gull, at þess kunni engi markatal, ok tók hann þat af Svaða jötni, er bjó í fjalli því, sem Blesanergr heitir. Þat er fyrir norðan Dumbshaf. Svaði var sonr Ása-Þórs.[46]

> (One was called Raknarr, the other Valr. They were Vikings and set out for Dumbshaf [the Arctic Ocean] where they harried the giants. […Valr] stayed in Dumbshaf, and there is a great story about him. […] Valr had killed Sviði, and taken control of Kirjalabotn. He had

---

44 For further discussion of this, see Barraclough, *Beyond the Northlands*, pp. 161–64; Barnes, *Viking America*, p. 34; Grove, 'The Place of Greenland in Medieval Icelandic Saga Narratives', p. 45.

45 *Bárðar saga*, ed. by Þórhallur Vilmundarson and Bjarni Vilhjálmsson, p. 163.

46 *Fornaldar sögur norðurlanda*, ed. by Guðni Jónsson, IV, 283.

acquired so much gold that it couldn't be counted, and he took it from the giant Svaði, who lived in the mountain Blesanergr. That is north of Dumbshaf. Svaði was the son of the god Þórr.)

When Hálfdan, the saga's eponymous hero, comes north to fight Valr, the latter dives down into a waterfall with his sons to where his treasure is hidden, 'ok lögðust á gullit ok urðu at flugdrekum ok höfðu hjálma á höfðum, en sverð undir bægslum, ok lágu þeir þar, til þess at Gull-Þórir vann fossinn' (and lay down on the gold, and became winged dragons. They had helmets on their heads and swords under their flippers. They lay there, until Gull-Þórir took possession of the waterfall).[47] A variation on same story, also set in Helluland up in Dumbshaf, is told in *Gull-Þóris saga* (*The Saga of Gold-Þórir*). Once again, a rich Viking called Valr, together with his sons, is said to have travelled north to a cave at Dumbshaf with vast quantities of gold. They lie on the gold and turn into dragons with helmets on their heads and swords under their wings.

Finally, in *Hálfdans saga Brönufóstra* (*The Saga of Hálfdan Brana's Foster-Son*), the hero is washed off course on the way to Bjarmaland, east of Gandvík. That he ends up on a glacier in the wastes of Helluland suggests that once again Helluland has been transposed to the Far North. There he finds two man-eating trolls. The male asks the female:

> 'Er nokkut eftir, Sleggja', segir hann, 'af þeim hálfum þriðja tigi manna, er ek seidda hingat í fyrra vetr?' Hún segir alllítit um þat. Hún gekk þá innar eftir hellinum ok kom svá aftr, at hún hafði sinn mann undir hvorri hendi sér, ok leggr niðr hjá eldinum ok segir, at eigi váru fleiri eftir.[48]

> ('Is there anything left, Sleggja', he said, 'of the twenty-five men, whom I brought here by enchantment last winter?' She said very little about that. She went into the cave and then came back with a man in each of her hands, and laid them down by the fire and said that there were not many left.)

Man-eating monsters lurk in the northern waste. They live in landscapes where humans cannot survive: on glaciers, under waterfalls, in the Arctic Ocean itself. What all these sagas underline is that the further north we travel in the imagination of the medieval Icelandic saga writers, the more suitable the setting becomes for wild tales of trolls and giants, as well as the occasional enchanted dragon and abandoned pagan god.

Guðmundr of Glæsisvellir

At other times, the focus is not on the geographical configuration of far-northern giant kingdoms, but on the individual who rules them. King Guðmundr of

---

47 *Fornaldar sögur norðurlanda*, ed. by Guðni Jónsson, IV, 284–85.
48 *Fornaldar sögur norðurlanda*, ed. by Guðni Jónsson, IV, 298.

Glæsisvellir is a case in point. He appears several times in the *fornaldarsögur*, although the nature and location of his kingdom varies, as Rudolf Simek has explored.[49] Guðmundr and Glæsisvellir are mentioned in texts already introduced in this analysis, such as *Hervarar saga*, following the opening paragraph describing the 'great mixing of races' that went on between giants and humans before the Turks and the men of Asia came north:

> Guðmundr hét hǫfðingi í Jǫtunheimum; bœr hans hét á Grund, en heraðit Glasisvellir. Hann var ríkr maðr ok vitr, ok varð svá gamall ok allir hans men, at þeir lifðu marga mannsaldra.[50]

> (Guðmundr was the name of a lord in Jǫtunheimar; his dwelling place was at Grund, in the region of Glæsisvellir. He was a mighty man, and wise, and so old were he and his people that their lives lasted through many generations of men.)

Again, although Guðmundr is not specifically said to be a giant, he is a lord of the giant lands and supernatural in a broader sense of the word, since he has the gift of foresight and he — and his subjects — live unnaturally long lives. Elsewhere in the *fornaldarsaga* corpus, *Þorsteins saga bæjarmagns* (*The Saga of Þorstein Mansion-Might*) notes that Guðmundr is a dependant of Risaland, a tax-paying tributary of the king of Jǫtunheim, while the aforementioned *Samsons saga* locates it east from Jǫtunheim. As I have discussed elsewhere, Guðmundr's character shifts from saga to saga: in *Þorsteins saga*, he is just starting out in the world of giant politics, in *Bósa saga ok Herrauðs* (*The Saga of Bósi and Herrauðr*) he dances drunkenly at wild feast whilst toasting the pagan gods, while in *Helga þáttr Þórissonar* (*The Tale of Helgi Þórir's Son*) he is described as 'mjök fjölkunnigr ok illu megi helzt við hann skipta' (very skilled in magic and bad to deal with).[51] When Helgi, the hero of the saga, returns to the human world after a blissful sojourn in Glæsisvellir as the lover of Guðmundr's daughter, his eyes have been ripped out of his head. Helgi's father rejoices that his son has been freed 'ór trölla höndum' (from the clutches of trolls), but Helgi makes it clear that he would return to the Far North in a heartbeat.[52]

Encounters in the Wilderness

Not all trolls and giants live in kingdoms presided over by rulers such as Guðmundr, Dumbr, and Arinnefja. Elsewhere, they are creatures of the wilderness, either living alone or in small family packs. Once again, they are

49 Simek, 'Elusive Elysia'.
50 *Hervarar saga ok Heiðreks*, ed. by G. Turville-Petre and Christopher Tolkien, p. 66.
51 *Fornaldar sögur norðurlanda*, ed. by Guðni Jónsson, IV, 351.
52 *Fornaldar sögur norðurlanda*, ed. by Guðni Jónsson, IV, 353.

not confined to the Far North, but it is nevertheless true that saga heroes frequently encounter them there. Returning to *Sturlaugs saga*, a series of meetings between the human hero and giant women take place off the coast of Arctic Norway, the hero and his companions having sailed 'norðr fyrir Hálogaland ok Finnmörk ok Vatnsnes ok inn á Austrvík ok kasta akkerum' (north via Hálogaland and Finnmörk and Vatnsnes and into Austrvik and cast anchor).[53] While the word 'giant' is never used, we are left in no doubt as to who these creatures are: on one occasion an enormous female climbs into the boat and Sturlaugr rows them out across the sound before she tells him that from there, 'má ek vel vaða til lands' (I can easily wade to land).[54] A little later, another creature he is ferrying in his boat lifts up her skin skirts and steps overboard telling him, 'eigi þarftu nú lengra út at flytja mik, eru nú þeir einir álar til lands, at ek get vel vaðit' (you don't need to transport me any longer, it's now just a few ells to shore and I can wade that just fine).[55] Another is capable of changing her size, for as Sturlaugr watches she grows until she has stretched herself up to the cliff.

Several generations of a family from Hrafnista, an island off the coast of Hálogaland, also experience supernatural encounters in the Far North beyond their already northern home. We have already met one of these, Ketill, the hero of the first so-called *Hrafnistasögur* (*Hrafnista sagas*), who encounters a troll woman on her way to a troll assembly in the High Arctic, with names on the guest list including King Skelkingr of Dumbshaf and Þorgerðr Hörgatröll. During his various adventures in the Far North, Ketill meets a host of giants, trolls, and other monsters, including Surtr the man-eating giant, who has clearly had past dealings with Ketill's father, Hallbjörn Half-Troll, since he refers to Hallbjörn as *vinr minn* (my friend).[56] Later on during a famine in Hálogaland, Ketill travels north and meets a giant woman called Forat, who rises from the sea black as pitch and dressed in bearskin. They exchange a series of verses, beginning with Ketill:

Hvat er þat flagða, | er ek sá á fornu nesi | ok glottir við guma? | At uppiverandi sólu, | hefi ek enga fyrr | leiðiligri litit.[57]

(Who is that ogress | who I see on the far peninsula | sneering at men? | Under the rising sun, | I have never seen before | one so loathsome.)

53 *Fornaldar sögur norðurlanda*, ed. by Guðni Jónsson, III, 132.
54 *Fornaldar sögur norðurlanda*, ed. by Guðni Jónsson, III, 133.
55 *Fornaldar sögur norðurlanda*, ed. by Guðni Jónsson, III, 134.
56 *Fornaldar sögur norðurlanda*, *Fornaldar sögur norðurlanda*, ed. by Guðni Jónsson, II, 156. Hallbjörn's nickname is a matter of dispute: it may suggest that he is partly descended from the *Finnar* (Sámi), or it may suggest that he has close connections to the trollish inhabitants of the Far North. (For more, see Barraclough, *Beyond the Northlands*, p. 82, and the discussion in Hermann Pálsson 'The Sámi People in Old Norse Literature').
57 *Fornaldar sögur norðurlanda*, ed. by Guðni Jónsson, II, 169.

The creature replies:

> Forað ek heiti. | Fædd var ek norðarla | hraust í Hrafnseyju, | hvimleið búmönnum, / ör til áræðis, | hvatki er illt skal vinna.[58]

> (I am called Forað. | I was brought up in the north | valiant in Hrafnsey, | loathsome to farmers | who attack me with arrows. | Each evil thing shall conquer.)

Thus far, two generations of Hrafnista men have had dealings with supernatural creatures in the Far North: Ketill and Hallbjörn. This continues into the next generation and the next saga, with Ketill's son Grímr. When another famine strikes Hálogaland, Grímr goes north like his father before him, and sails to Gandvík (the aforementioned White Sea). He wakes in the night to find two women trying to shake his ship to pieces. When he asks them who they are, one replies, 'Feima ek heiti | fædd var ek norðarla, | Hrímnis dóttir | ór háfjalli' (Feima is my name, | I was born in the north, | Hrímnir's daughter | from the high mountains).[59] If the reader was in any doubt as to the nature of this pair, the name of her father, Hrímnir, might give us a clue, since this is another typically giant name that may call to mind the Far North and the winter (the meaning is either 'hoar frost' or 'sooty'). Hrimnir puts in guest appearances elsewhere in Norse mythological texts, including Snorri's *Edda*, the eddic poems *Hyndluljóð* and *Skírnismál*, and *Vǫlsunga saga*.

The next generation of the Hrafnista family, Oddr, will be returned to presently, but in the final and fourth saga, *Áns saga bogsveigis* (*The Saga of Án Bow-Bender*), Án returns to his family home in Hrafnista expressly 'at berja um þær skinnkyrtlur norðr þar, ok þótti hann inn mesti maðr' (to fight skin-wearing trolls there in the north, and he was thought of as the most accomplished of men).[60] In one redaction of the saga, it is even said that he had a lot of trouble from a gang of ogresses when he lived in Hrafnista.[61]

Returning to Ketill, when addressing both Forað and the troll woman on her way to the assembly, he calls them 'foster-mother'. Since one is determined to rip him to bits and the other wants him to stop bothering her, the nomenclature is likely ironic, but elsewhere trolls and giants form close connections of exactly this sort. As Marlene Ciklamini has noted, giants can be both 'intimate and hostile' in their relations with humans, and once again while this is not limited to the Far North, it is certainly true that a great number of these stories are set there.[62]

58 *Fornaldar sögur norðurlanda*, ed. by Guðni Jónsson, II, 169.
59 *Fornaldar sögur norðurlanda*, ed. by Guðni Jónsson, II, 187.
60 *Fornaldar sögur norðurlanda*, ed. by Guðni Jónsson, II, 402.
61 Leslie, 'The Matter of Hrafnista', p. 189.
62 Ciklamini, 'Grettir and Ketill Hængr the Giant Killers', p. 146.

Intimate Relations: Lovers and Foster-Mothers

Troll and giant women can be notoriously man-hungry and scantily clad; often the effect is intentionally shocking and comical. In *Jökuls þáttr Búasonar* (*The Tale of Jökul Búi's Son*), the hero is washed up in the Greenlandic wilderness after a shipwreck and wakes to hear two troll girls deciding what to do with him, either force him to marry one of them or kill him. The description of what they are wearing suggests that not much is left to the imagination:

> Skinnstökkum vóru þær klæddar, síðum í fyrir, svó þær stigu að mestu á þá, en bak til fylgdu þeir ofanverðum þjónhnöppum; þær skelldu á lærin og fóru mjög ókvenliga.[63]
>
> > (They were dressed in skin cloaks that were so long at the front that they almost stepped on them but at the back reached down only to the tops of the buttocks; they slapped their thighs and carried on in a very unlady like way.)

Jökull is unmoved by their overtures, but by no means all such potential sexual encounters between human heroes and supernatural women are so one-sided. *Örvar-Odds saga* (*The Saga of Arrow-Oddr*) is the third of the *Hrafnistasögur* (and the one missing from the line-up above). Many of Oddr's travels are in the Far North, and on one occasion he ends up in the land of giants — this time Risaland — where he has a relationship with a giant woman called Hildigunnr. The fruit of this encounter is their son, Vignir, whose mixed heritage is clear from early on. When Oddr next meets his son he is only ten years old, but the first thing he does is 'rær svá hart at skipum Odds, at hvervetna brotnaði þat, er fyrir varð' (row so hard towards Oddr's ship that anything in the way would have broken)[64] and call his dad 'lítill ok smáskítligr' (a tiny little shit).[65]

Oddr and Hildigunnr's relationship gets off to an unusual start: since he is so small, she assumes he is a baby, lays him in a cradle, and sings him lullabies. When he gets restless she puts him in the bed next to her and wraps her arms around him, and the upshot is that 'Oddr lék allt þat, er lysti; gerðist þá harðla vel með þeim' (Oddr played all the games he liked, and things went very well between them).[66] Erotic undertones — or more often overtones — in this sort of care-giving relationship between a giant woman and a human hero are present in other sagas, including the aforementioned *Hálfdans saga Brönufóstra*, where the hero is washed up in the wastes of a Helluland relocated to the Arctic and rescued by Brana. She herself has mixed heritage of the type described in the origin myths that opened this discussion,

---

63 *Jökuls þáttr Búasonar*, ed. by Jóhannes Halldórsson, p. 49.
64 *Fornaldar sögur norðurlanda*, ed. by Guðni Jónsson, II, 286.
65 *Fornaldar sögur norðurlanda*, ed. by Guðni Jónsson, II, 287.
66 *Fornaldar sögur norðurlanda*, ed. by Guðni Jónsson, II, 274.

for as she tells Hálfdan: 'mennsk er ek í aðra ætt, því at móðir mín var dóttir Vilhjálms konungs ór Vallandi. Járnhauss, faðir minn, nam hana í burt. Átti hann mik við henna, ok bregðr mér meir til hennar, en þó nokkut til hans' (I was human in another lineage, because my mother was the daughter of King Vilhjálmr of Valland. My father Járnhauss kidnapped her. He had me with her, and I take after her more, but a bit after him).[67] First the two become lovers before she helps him to win an English princess for a wife, but ever afterwards he is known by the nickname 'Brana's Foster-Son'.

Sometimes the helpful creature is a human under enchantment. In *Gríms saga loðinkinna*, the second of the Hrafnista sagas, Grímr's fiancée is spirited away by her stepmother who turns out to be a Finnmǫrk troll in disguise. The stepmother tells her young charge: 'þu verðir at inni ljótustu tröllkonu ok hverfir norðr til Gandvíkr ok byggir þar afhelli ok sitir þar í stóðrenni við Hrímni, bróður minn' (you shall become the ugliest troll-woman and go off north to Gandvík and live right next to Hrímnir, my brother).[68] In the far north of Finnmǫrk, Grímr is wounded during a fight over a whale, and saved from certain death by a monstrous creature who turns out to be his enchanted fiancée:

> Hún var eigi hæri en sjau vetra gamlar stúlkur, en svá digr, at Grímr hugði, at hann mundi eigi geta feðmt um hana. Hún var langleit ok harðleit, bjúgnefjuð ok baröxluð, svartleit ok svipilkinnuð, fúlleit ok framsnoðin. Svört var hún bæði á hár ok á hörund. Hún var í skörpum skinnstakki. Hann tók eigi lengra en á þjóhnappa henni á bakit. Harðla ókyssilig þótti honum hún vera, því at hordingullinn hekk ofan fyrir hváftana á henna.[69]

> (She was no taller than a seven-year-old girl, but so fat that Grímr doubted he could even get his arms around her. She was long-faced and hard-faced, hook-nosed and shoulder-hunched, dark-faced and pinch-cheeked, filthy-faced and bald at the front. Her hair and skin were black. She wore a shrivelled skin smock, which didn't come down below her buttocks. She's not exactly kissable, thought Grímr, as snot dripped down her cheek.)

The fact that Grímr even thinks about this creature in terms of her kissability is telling, for indeed the monster will only save his life once she has extracted a promise from him that he will kiss her and share her bed. This breaks the spell and she is returned to her human form, much to Grímr's relief.

Sagas of this type are generally assigned to the *fornaldarsaga* genre for good reason, but not all relationships of this kind are so fantastical in terms of the wider thematic preoccupations of the story. *Hauks þáttr hábrokar* (*The Tale of Haukr High-Breeches*) is preserved in the same manuscript

---

67 *Fornaldar sögur norðurlanda*, ed. by Guðni Jónsson, IV, 302.
68 *Fornaldar sögur norðurlanda*, ed. by Guðni Jónsson, II, 193.
69 *Fornaldar sögur norðurlanda*, ed. by Guðni Jónsson, II, 191.

Flateyjarbók that contains *Hversu Noregr byggðist*, and as such is a fitting text to bring us full circle. The tale concerns King Haraldr Fairhair, who united Norway under him according to saga tradition, and his foster-mother Heiðr. Haraldr asks his men Haukr and Vígharðr to visit her at her home 'norðr við Gandvík' (north by the shores of Gandvík).[70] At first glance, her nature is uncertain: while others describe her as 'svá mikit tröll, at slíku hefir ek eigi fyrr mætt' (the greatest troll I have ever encountered), Haraldr only refers to her as his foster-mother.[71] Yet the location of her home and appearance aligns her strongly with the trolls and giants encountered in other sagas: she is dressed 'í skinnkyrtli, ok tóku ermar at olboga' (in a skin tunic with sleeves down to the elbows),[72] and seems to them 'heldr munnljót, þvíat önnr vörin tók niðr á brínguna, en önnr breiddist upp á nefit' (rather ugly in the mouth, because one lip hung down to her chest while the other spread up to her nose).[73] Furthermore, Haukr brings her butter and bacon as gifts from Haraldr, which may seem unremarkable, except that identical gifts were also given to Queen Arinnefja of *Egils saga einhenda*, in exchange for her help in rescuing the princesses. Once again, sex lurks not far below the surface of this exchange. While one of her visitors is horrified when she asks him to kiss her — 'hann biðr öll tröll kyssa hana' (he said that all the trolls could kiss her)[74] — the other is happier to oblige: 'hún færði Hauk or klædunum, ok þreifaði um hann, ok mælti: þu ert þrekligr ok hamíngjusamligr; hún bað hann kyssa sik, ok svá gerði hann' (she removed Haukr's clothes and touched him all over, and said 'You're stout-hearted and lucky'. She asked him to kiss her, so he did).[75] Later on, Haukr returns to Heiðr to be healed from injuries sustained in battle, and there seems to be genuine affection between the pair, for 'hún lætr vel yfir at hann er aptr kominn' (she was glad that he had come back).[76] Despite her ambiguous nature, therefore, Heiðr fulfills many of the characteristics and functions assocated with encounters between humans and trolls or giants in the Far North: she is grotesque, wears skins, and is sexually predatory, but she is also a foster-mother, helper, healer, and lover.

Conclusion

Throughout the sagas, the Far North is the domain of trolls, giants, and their kind. Certain named locations become particularly associated with these

---

70 *Þáttr Hauks Hárbrokar*, in *Fornmanna saga*, p. 204.
71 *Þáttr Hauks Hárbrokar*, in *Fornmanna saga*, p. 203.
72 *Þáttr Hauks Hárbrokar*, in *Fornmanna saga*, p. 204.
73 *Þáttr Hauks Hárbrokar*, in *Fornmanna saga*, pp. 204–05.
74 *Þáttr Hauks Hárbrokar*, in *Fornmanna saga*, p. 205.
75 *Þáttr Hauks Hárbrokar*, in *Fornmanna saga*, p. 205.
76 *Þáttr Hauks Hárbrokar*, in *Fornmanna saga*, p. 206.

supernatural inhabitants, such as Dumbshaf, Gandvík, and Helluland, but there is no consistent typology across the corpus. In many of the texts classed as *fornaldarsögur*, the main aim of these stories seems to be entertainment, although as Margaret Clunies Ross points out, they can also be a conduit through which to explore disturbing or taboo subjects through comic or parodic means. The presence of thematic cross-currents across the sagas certainly suggests a collective body of literary or folkloric motifs associated with human heroes who journey to the Far North and encounter supernatural beings. In other texts — notably *Hversu Noregr byggðist, Fundinn Noregr,* and to some extent *Hervarar saga* and *Óláfs saga Tryggvasonar* — the non-human inhabitants of the Far North play fundamental roles in the creation of origin myths, attached either to powerful ruling families or to the creation of Norway itself. These seem to chime with deeper cosmological patterns related to the creation of the world according to Norse mythology, which may well be the basis of their legitimacy. The common denominator in all these stories is the link between the Far North and its non-human inhabitants.

What does this association tell us about how medieval Nordic cultures — and the Icelandic saga writers in particular — perceived the Far North? As they experienced it, this was a geographical region physically unsuitable for most human habitation. Located so far north themselves, the Norse knew this better than most. To their south lay historical civilizations, farmable lands, learned cultures, religious centres. To their north lay increasingly sparse populations, long winters, and wastelands. It is true that trolls and giants are not confined to the Far North in the sagas. More generally, their natural habitats are the wildernesses beyond where humans naturally live, in the uninhabitable rocky wastes and high mountains. Yet the Far North was especially rich in such spaces, and therefore especially rich in such inhabitants in the saga imagination. The further north the saga writers take us, the more fitting the inhospitable geographical setting becomes for tales of giants, trolls, and other non-human beings. In many texts trolls and giants become the physical and metaphorical manifestation of such terrains; arctic coldness personified and named for the frost, snow, and ice. In the cultural imagination of the medieval Nordic world, where human beings could not survive, inhuman beings thrived.

Works Cited

Primary Sources

Bárðar saga, in *Harðar saga, Bárðar saga, Þorskfirðinga saga, Flóamanna saga, Þórarins þáttr Nefjólfssonar, Þorsteins þáttr Úxafóts, Egils þáttr Síðu-Hallssonar, Orms þáttr Stórólfssonar, Þorsteins þáttr Tjaldstöðings, Þorsteins þáttr Forvitna, Bergbúa þáttr, Kumlbúa þáttr, Stjörnu-Odda draumr*, ed. by Þórhallur Vilmundarson and Bjarni Vilhjálmsson, Íslenzk fornrit 13 (Reykjávik: Hið Íslenska Fornritafélag, 1991), pp. 99–172

Eyvindr *skáldaspillir* Finnsson, *Háleygjatal 2*, ed. and trans. by Russell Poole, in *Poetry from the Kings' Sagas 1: From Mythical Times to c. 1035*, ed. by Diana Whaley, Skaldic Poetry of the Scandinavian Middle Ages, 1 (Turnhout: Brepols, 2012), p. 199

Fornaldar sögur norðurlanda, ed. by Guðni Jónsson, 4 vols (Reykjavík: Íslendingaútgáfan, 1950)

Hervarar saga ok Heiðreks, ed. by G. Turville-Petre and Christopher Tolkien, Viking Society for Northern Research Text Series, 2 (London: Viking Society for Northern Research, UCL, 1956 [repr. 2014])

Jökuls þáttr Búasonar, in *Kjalnesinga saga, Jökuls þáttr Búasonar, Víglundar saga, Króka-Refs saga, þordar saga Hredu, Finnboga saga, Gunnars saga Keldugnúpsfifls*, ed. by Jóhannes Halldórsson, Íslenzk fornrit, 14 (Reykjávik, 1959), pp. 45–59

Oddr Snorrason *munkr*, *Saga Óláfs Tryggvasonar af Oddr Snorrason Munk*, ed. by Finnur Jónsson (Copenhagen: G. E. C. Gad, 1932)

Orkneyinga saga, ed. by Finnbogi Guðmundsson, Íslenzk fornrit 34 (Reykjávik, 1965)

Samsons saga fagra, ed. by John Wilson (Copenhagen: Jørgensen, 1953)

Þáttr Hauks Hárbrokar, in *Fornmanna sögur, eptir gömlum handritum*, vol. x (Copenhagen: Norræna Fornfræða Félags, 1835), pp. 198–209

Secondary Works

Aalto, Sirpa, 'Alienness in *Heimskringla*: Special Emphasis on the *Finnar*', in *Scandinavia and Christian Europe in the Middle Ages: Papers of the 12th International Saga Conference, Bonn / Germany, 28th July–2nd August 2003*, ed. by Rudolf Simek and Judith Meurer (Bonn: University of Bonn, 2003), pp. 1–7

Ármann Jakobsson, 'The Good, the Bad, and the Ugly: *Bárðar saga* and its Giants', *Mediaeval Scandinavia*, 15 (2005) 1–15

——, 'Identifying the Ogre: The Legendary Saga Giants', *Fornaldarsagaerne: Myter og virkelighed*, ed. by Annette Lassen and others (Copenhagen: Museum Tusculanum, 2009), pp. 181–200

——, 'Where Do the Giants Live?', *Arkiv för nordisk filologi*, 121 (2006), 101–12

Barnes, Geraldine, *Viking America: The First Millennium* (Cambridge: Brewer, 2001)

Barraclough, Eleanor Rosamund, 'Arctic Frontiers: Rethinking Norse-Sámi Relations in the Old Norse Sagas', *Viator*, 48.3 (2017), 2–25

——, *Beyond the Northlands: Viking Voyages and the Old Norse Sagas* (Oxford: Oxford University Press, 2016)

Barraclough, Eleanor Rosamund, Danielle Cudmore, and Stefan Donecker, eds, *Imagining the Supernatural North* (Alberta: University of Alberta Press, 2016)

Beuermann, Ian, '*Jarla sögur Orkneyja*: Status and Power of the Earls of Orkney According to their Sagas', in *Ideology and Power in the Viking And Middle Ages: Scandinavia, Iceland, Ireland, Orkney and the Faeroes*, ed. by Gro Steinsland and others (Leiden and Boston: Brill, 2011), pp. 109–62

Cardew, Phil, '"Mannfögnuður er oss at smjöri þessu": Representation of the Finns within the Icelandic Sagas', in *Text and Nation: Essays on Post-Colonial Cultural Politics*, ed. by Andrew Blake and Jopi Nyman (Joensuu: Joensuun yliopisto, 2001), pp. 146–58

Ciklamini, Marlene, 'Grettir and Ketill Hængr the Giant Killers', *Arv*, 22 (1966), 136–55

Clunies Ross, Margaret, *The Cambridge Introduction to the Old Norse-Icelandic Saga* (Cambridge: Cambridge University Press, 2010)

——, 'Snorri Sturluson's Use of the Norse Origin-Legend of the Sons of Fornjótr in his *Edda*', *Arkiv för Nordisk Filologi*, 98 (1983), 47–66

DeAngelo, Jeremy, 'The North and the Depiction of the *Finnar* in the Icelandic Sagas', *Scandinavian Studies*, 82.3 (2010), 257–81

Grace, Sherill E., *Canada and the Idea of North* (Montreal: McGill-Queen's University Press, 2002)

Grove, Jonathan, 'The Place of Greenland in Medieval Icelandic Saga Narratives', in *Norse Greenland: Selected Papers from the Hvalsey Conference 2008*, ed. by Jette Arneborg and others, Special Volume 2 of *Journal of the North Atlantic* (Steuben: Eagle Hill, 2009), pp. 30–51

Hermann Pálsson, 'The Sami People in Old Norse Literature', *Nordlit*, 5 (1999), 29–53

Jón Jóhannesson, *A History of the Old Icelandic Commonwealth: Íslendinga saga* (Winnipeg: University of Manitoba Press, 2007)

Langeslag, Paul, *Seasons in the Literatures of the Medieval North* (Woodbridge: Brewer, 2015)

Leslie, Helen F., 'The Matter of Hrafnista', *Quaestio Insularis*, 11 (2010), 169–209

Lindow, John, 'Cultures in Contact', in *Old Norse Myths, Literature and Society*, ed. by Margaret Clunies Ross, The Viking Collection, 14 (Odense: University Press of Southern Denmark, 2003), pp. 89–109

——, *Norse Mythology: A Guide to the Gods, Heroes, Rituals and Beliefs* (Oxford: Oxford University Press, 2002)

——, 'Supernatural and Ethnic Others: A Millennium of World View', *Scandinavian Studies*, 67.1 (1995), 8–31

McKinnell, John, 'Two Sex Goddesses: Þorgerðr Hölgabrúðr and Freyja in *Hyndluljóð*', in *Essays on Eddic Poetry*, ed. by Donata Kick and John D. Shafer (Toronto: University of Toronto Press, 2014), pp. 268–91

———, 'Þórgerðr Hölgabrúðr and Hyndluljóð', in *Mythological Women: Studies in Memory of Lotte Motz 1922–1997*, ed. by Rudolf Simek and Wilhelm Heizmann (Vienna: Fassbaender, 2002), pp. 265–90

Meulengracht Sørensen, Preben, 'The Sea, the Flame, and the Wind: The Legendary Ancestors of the Earls of Orkney', in *The Viking Age in Caithness, Orkney and the North Atlantic*, ed. by Colleen E. Batey and others (Edinburgh: Edinburgh University Press, 1993), pp. 212–21

Motz, Lotte, 'The Family of Giants', *Arkiv for nordisk filologi*, 102 (1987), 216–36

Mundal, Else, 'The Perception of the Saamis and their Religion in Old Norse Sources', in *Shamanism and Northern Ecology*, ed. by Juha Pentikäinen (Berlin: de Gruyter, 1996), pp. 97–116

Rowe, Elizabeth Ashman, 'Origin Legends and Foundation Myths in *Flateyjarbók*', *Old Norse Myths, Literature and Society*, ed. by Margaret Clunies Ross, The Viking Collection, 14 (Odense: University Press of Southern Denmark, 2003), pp. 198–216

Simek, Rudolf, 'Elusive Elysia, or: Which Way to Glæsisvellir? On the Geography of the North in Icelandic Legendary Fiction', in *Sagaskemmtun: Studies in Honour of Hermann Pálsson on his 65th Birthday, 26 May 1986*, ed. by Rudolf Simek and others (Vienna: Bóhlau, 1986), pp. 247–75

Steinsland, Gro, *Det hellige bryllup og norrøn kongeideologi: En analyse av hierogami-myten i Skírnismál, Ynglingatal, Háleygjatal og Hyndluljóð* (Oslo: Solum, 1991)

———, 'Origin Myths and Rulership. From the Viking Age Ruler to the Ruler of Medieval Historiography: Continuity, Transformations and Innovations', in *Ideology and Power in the Viking and Middle Ages: Scandinavia, Iceland, Ireland, Orkney and the Faeroes*, ed. by Gro Steinsland and others, The Northern World, 52 (Leiden: Brill, 2011), pp. 15–67

PETTER SNEKKESTAD

Fishermen in Trouble — *Grímnismál* and Elf Islands in Northern Norway

Introduction

In Sophus Bugge's seminal work *Studier over de nordiske Gude- og Heltesagns Oprindelse*, he argued that the prose framework of *Grímnismál* was informed by folklore that had only survived in northern Norway.[1] According to Bugge, tales of supernatural islands recorded in Hálogaland bore a resemblance to the motif of the two stranded brothers in the Eddic poem. The body of lore that Bugge referred to can be called the 'Utrøst complex', consisting of 'Utrøst tales' that in one form or another tell of supernatural islands. The only systematic study of the complex was undertaken by Jan Byberg in 1970.[2] He distinguished between 'Utrøst tales' more broadly and the more specific 'joyous island' group in Norwegian tradition, the latter of which was the focus of his investigation. They appear in several regions in Norway, yet their frequency in northern Trøndelag and northwards is striking: more than twice as many 'joyous island' tales are found in Hálogaland as in the rest of the country. More than two-thirds of the overall material was found in northern Trøndelag and Hálogaland. In the Iron Age, these two areas were more or less understood as one, Hálogaland, and corresponded to a stretch of the Norwegian coast known for extensive seasonal fishing, with Lofoten as its nexus.

In the following, *Grímnismál*, *Þorleifs þáttr jarlaskálds*, and the 'Utrøst tales' will be discussed against the background of the peculiar fisherman-farmer culture of Hálogaland. A general picture of fishermen's superstitions will be offered, arguing that folklore recorded in northern Trøndelag and Hálogaland from the 1800s and the following century sheds light on Geirrøðr's fate in *Grímnismál*.

---

1 Bugge, *Studier over de nordiske Gude- og Heltesagns Oprindelse*, I, 25–26.
2 Byberg, *Dei lukkelege øyane*.

Petter Snekkestad, Nordlandsmuseet, petter.snekkestad@nordlandmuseet.no

Myths and Magic in the Medieval Far North: Realities and Representations of a Region on the Edge of Europe, ed. by Stefan Figenschow, Richard Holt, and Miriam Tveit, AS 10
(Turnhout: Brepols, 2020), pp. 95–117
  10.1484/M.AS-EB.5.120521

The poem opens a window onto the wider question of how supernatural islands were understood by people in pre-modern Hálogaland and elsewhere. The picture is messy, and Eldar Heide's study of how holy islands and godly abodes were reached by waterways in Old Norse literature — placed both horizontally and vertically, that is, under the surface of the sea and up in the sky — is therefore instructive. His general category will be applied here: these places are all an 'Otherworld beyond water'. This Otherworld encapsulates all the supernatural places one could arrive at by water, usually through mist and storm.[3] Utrøst was just one of these places, but this term was by far the most commonly used name for such an Otherworld in Hálogaland. I will therefore discuss the word *útrǫst* in a stanza by Eyvindr *skáldaspillir* Finnson (the Poet-spoiler), a Háleygr, and ask whether Utrøst can be understood as a place not just denoting a supernatural island west off the Røst archipelago, which is the modern understanding of Utrøst, but as a general noun referring to an Otherworld.

The sources deserve a brief comment. *Grímnismál* is an Eddic poem written down in the 1200s and was probably composed in the Viking Age. The description of what is here interpreted to be an Utrøst-like island is found in the prose framework in *Grímnismál*, which can be much younger than the poem itself. The motif of an otherworldly man visiting a 'ruler' ignorant of the visitor's powers — a motif that arguably is found also in the legendary *Þorleifs þáttr jarlaskálds* from the *Flateyjarbók* manuscript dating to the late 1300s and in the 'take your time' strand of 'Utrøst tales' from northern Norway in the 1800s and the following century — is however found in the poem and is the setting for its performance by Óðinn. In the *þáttr*, Þorleifr is pitted as the otherworldly man against a jarl, and the story neither begins nor ends with this event. In the 'take your time' stories, on the other hand, the story begins and ends with such a meeting. *Þorleifs þáttr jarlaskálds* is relevant because it is to my knowledge the only Old Norse text that, apart from *Grímnismál*, so clearly makes use of the motif in question. And since we are here interested in Far North traditions, the possibility that the *þáttr* contains traditions from Hálogaland is key to our discussion. Although we do not know from where Þorleifr's Norwegian family emigrated, he was brought up in Svarfaðardal, the land-taking of Þorsteinn *svarfaðr* and Hilda daughter of Þráinn *svartaþurs* from Namdal in northern Trøndelag. Namdal was more or less understood as a part of Hálogaland in the Viking Age, and the milieu in Svarfaðardal therefore arguably had the characteristics of Far North traditions. The marriage of Þorleif's sister with a grandson of the land-takers implies tight bonds between the two families. We should also note that the nickname of Hilda's father, 'black-troll', may indicate a Sámi background.[4] We need not believe anything that is told in *Þorleifs þáttr jarlaskálds* in order to entertain

3 Heide, 'Holy Islands and the Otherworld', pp. 57–80.
4 Nielssen, *Landnåm fra nord*, pp. 86–94, 143–45.

its possible northern motifs and themes. However, we need to trust that the Svarfaðardal folk recounted in *Landnámabók* are historical and that the *þáttr* is based on a tradition from that part of Iceland settled by folk from Namdal.

In discussing the word *útrǫst* in a stanza thought to belong to the poem *Háleygjatal*, I rely on an understanding of the word *rǫst* as documented in skaldic poetry and as recorded in northern Norway in the 1800s and 1900s, namely a current. It must be stressed that *útrǫst* is not used in this sense in the Old Norse material. The word features in four letters from the southern part of Norway spanning 1398–1449 with the meaning 'outlying area' in relation to a farm. Still, in attempting to make sense of the kenning in which it features, and addressing the conspicuous likeness of *útrǫst* and Utrøst, I believe that this elusive word is worth discussing in light of late sources. An analogy to *útrǫst* interpreted as 'the outlying current' is found in Ottar Grønvik's reading of the Eggum Stone from the late 600s. Although Grønvik spent some two decades contemplating the stone, writing four articles adjusting his initial conclusions in a 1985 book, his interpretations should be viewed as persuasive yet far from certain or definitive. Its state of preservation has forced all its interpreters, Grønvik being the latest, to reconstruct missing parts. He builds, however, a strong case for the claim that the rune-stone describes a shipwreck. Interestingly, he relied partly on a little-known dictionary of northern Norwegian dialect words to arrive at the meaning of the important *ím* in his *firney-ím* ('current over the outlying island').[5] To be clear, the arguments in this article are predicated on the assumption that certain traditions recorded fairly recently in northern Norway reflect medieval traditions in an unbroken line. There is little to imply that the 'Utrøst tales' discussed below are corrupted by literary influence.

The Economy and Fishermen's Superstitions

Compared to its Scandinavian neighbour Denmark, Norway's rocky and fjord-pierced geography does not allow for extensive growing of crops. That is even more the case in Hálogaland, with its lack of suitable land and short growing seasons. Those who chose to settle here relied on extensive fishing and hunting to compensate. Thus, a peculiar fisherman-farmer culture emerged that, over time, became to an extent dependent on the import of grain from the south. From *c.* 1100 AD, a boom in the export of stockfish led to a further specialization in fishing. While the winter fisheries around the Lofoten Isles — the biggest seasonal fishery in the world — had probably attracted many fishermen from at least the early Iron Age, the increased demand served to cement Hálogaland as a supplier of fish and at the same time heavily dependent on imported grains. To illustrate, in Snorri Sturluson's

---

5 Grønvik, *Runene på Eggjasteinen*, pp. 82–83. The dictionary in question is Hveding, *Håløygsk ordsamling*.

Heimskringla, the spiral of revenge that led to Óláfr Haraldsson's (St Olaf's) fall in 1030 AD was instigated by his refusal to allow a Hálogaland chieftain to bring home grain from the west coast. As a rule of thumb, chieftains in the Far North were all located on farms most suitable for crop growing within each chieftaincy. In the Iron Age, some magnate farms were situated in the fjords to secure ties with suppliers of furs and skins, especially the Sámi. The export of fish, however, overshadowed the export of inland wares during the 1100s, and the elites all settled on the outer coast.

Folk traditions were bound to take on a maritime flavour in the North. From the early Iron Age and beyond, people commuted between islands and across fjords, women gathered seaweed for husbandry, and men spent months each year at desolate fishing stations, the so-called *vær*. They hunted seals and smaller whales, and fowlers and down pickers frequented skerries and towering bird cliffs on the outer coast. The Lofoten cod fishing season lasted for three months during the winter, while halibut and pollack were caught in the spring and summer. Many also rowed to Finnmark to fish in the spring. We are not sure, however, when this sort of intensive fishing came about. Herring, which visit the coast at unpredictable times, feature in a handful of *lausavísar* by Eyvindr *skáldaspillir* Finnsson, lamenting his failed crops after a snowy summer in the late 900s. He had to acquire herring by barter, what he called 'husbandry of the sea', revealing that they were caught in narrow bays and perhaps farmed.

Seamen's Lore

Just as beings and spirits were thought to inhabit the land, sea folk believed in their maritime counterparts. The ethnologist Eilert Sundt observed in 1850 that 'sea peasants' believed that the ocean was inhabited by beings — he called them *Havets Vætter* — that could not stand hearing human language and therefore had invented an alternative tongue in order not to upset them.[6] These beings lived in a *hulderland* (land of the hidden people) or *alveland* (land of elves). The fishermen's 'secret language' out at sea is the most widespread cultural trait we find along the Norwegian coast. Fish, birds, equipment, land animals, women, and mountains were either not spoken about or not called by their correct name. A gaff would become 'the wood with iron in it' and had to be wrapped before being brought onto the boat. A halibut would be referred to as 'she'.[7] A failure to speak carefully would result in the spirits refusing to allow their fish to be caught. There are grounds to believe that, while out at sea, offerings were made to gods and other spirits. There are many later accounts of trivial 'acts of reverence' addressed at certain holmes

---

6 Sundt, 'Beretning om Fante- og landstrygerfolket i Norge', p. 128.
7 Eidnes, 'Fiske og fordom', pp. 499–500.

and skerries, seemingly intertwined in a tradition of novices being lured into committing foolish acts. Flatbread and the like might be offered, and these threatening skerries could have names such as 'the ox' or 'the lady'. Sticking knives into the boat when passing holmes such as Galten (the galt), may reflect a tradition of offerings.[8] Young, inexperienced fishermen, so-called 'raven boys', would offer their first catch, as reflected in a saying: 'the first catch belongs to the raven'.[9] In some instances, foodstuffs were offered outright to a particular being.[10] Some mountains were greeted, for instance Vågakallen (the man of Vågan) and Svolværkjerringa (the lady of Svolvær). Other folkloric accounts attribute offerings to particular trolls living on or in a mountain, such as the one on Reinesfjellet in Helgeland who was believed to suck in and spew out vicious gales.[11] These accounts are all late and have not been studied thoroughly.

'Troll' is a common term for a number of supernatural beings, whose names are overlapping and used indiscriminately. A rough distinction has been made between the *jǫtnár*, *þursar*, and *bergrisar* who feature in the Eddic poems and who quarrel with the gods, and a group of *gýgr*, *flagð*, *flagðkona*, and *jǫtunn* denoting either good-willed or malevolent giants. These last four often lived in mountains far to the north.[12] However, the terminology is rather topsy-turvy, and a number of hard-to-define troll names could be added: *smyl*, *kóna*, *gerðr*, *grýla*, *fála*, *mǫrn*, and so on. The *gýgr* appear most frequently in the place names of Nordland, while no names in the four *þulur* concerning *trollkvenna heiti* can confidently be associated with any mountains or place names in northern Norway. In later folklore, the *gýgr* are female giants with a male counterpart in the *jutul*, called a *rise* if he was of exceptional size. Their foul behaviour, such as hurling giant rocks or moving about islands and headlands, would explain topographical peculiarities. They were also unambiguously associated with paganism and abhorred Christians and their building of churches. How these *gýgr* were understood in relation to their counterparts of the sea, *sjógýgr*, *margýgr*, *sjókona*, *sækona*, and so on, is not clear. Misbehaving troll women in the Far North are probably attested to by the skald Hofgarða-Refr Gestsson in the first decades of the eleventh century. According to one interpretation of a stanza in *Ferðavisur*, Refr refers to an event in *Ǫrvar-Odds saga*, where Oddr encounter stone-hurling giants on his sea journey to Bjarmaland.[13] Sailing from his home in Namdal, these events were thus thought to take place either in Hálogaland or further north in Bjarmaland.

---

8   Solheim, *Nemningsfordomar*, pp. 141–55.
9   Hveding, 'Astøingsvisa', pp. 18–19.
10 Strompdal, *Gamalt frå Helgeland*, p. 119.
11 Løkås, 'Heilag Olav og Reines-trollet', pp. 322–23.
12 KLNM, XVIII, pp. 655–57.
13 Marold, ed., 'Hofgarða-Refr Gestsson', p. 248.

The *gýgjar* are attested in names of coastal mountains in Nordland in the forms Gjura, Jura, Juret, and so on.[14] But a much larger group of mountains have taboo names to shroud their 'real' trollish identity. Here, a possible *gýgr* or other troll is renamed in order not to upset the spirit world. Most of them are female, called *kjerring* (woman), *møy* (maiden or young woman), *kone* (wife, woman), and *jomfru* (virgin). In rare cases, the mountains are understood as male: a *kall* or *karl* (man) or variations of *mannen* (the man). Perhaps also names containing *hest* (horse) or *løve* (lion) are also euphemisms for trolls. The most informative example is the island Landegode (the Good Land) outside Bodø. Here we find a conjunction of the names Gjura and Landegodekjerringa (Lady of the Good Land), showing clearly how a *gýgr* mountain would be renamed to *kjerring*. Oral tradition among locals is telling; its real name, Gygrøy or Giggerøy (Island of the Gýgr), could only be whispered or talked about with great caution.[15]

These troll-fells often possess features that make them stand out. Yet the most peculiar among them often lack a troll name. The stub names of some mountainous islands, such as Hugla, Tomma, Torga, Bolga, Aldra, Træna, Lovund, and perhaps Alsten, are philologically inseparable from their same-named mountains. These names are also thought to be of great antiquity. For seamen, their foremost concern when naming places on the coast was to find peculiarities not to be missed by their peers. Uncanny resemblance seems to trump the need to 'bewitch' mountains — although a combination was sometimes a possibility. So 'Torga' was so named for its hole, 'Træna' because of its three shafts as seen from the west, and 'Lovund' because of its 'hanging' cliffside. 'Tomma' can be understood as relating to a thumb-like shaft if viewed from the south. The knoll-shaped mountain of 'Kunna' in Meløy can illustrate the ambiguity of such names. As a name group, it is convincingly interpreted as 'one which is easily recognizable', relating to Old Norse *kunnr*.[16] Yet the much-travelled stretch of sea around the mountain is the most turbulent in Nordland, something that invites a troll association. 'Kunna' in the Froan archipelago in Trøndelag was thought to be a troll woman, as laid out in the tale of Gurri Kunna.[17] This can be understood as 'the *gýgr* of Kunna'. A fisherman informant associated this Kunna with an underwater skerry or shallow on which a troll woman lived.[18]

14   *Gýgr* fells are barely discerned on maps and in historical records; they no longer provide the name of the summits in question, but rather to an adjacent scree, ridge, or cliffside.

15   Gudbrandson, *Bodin bygdebok*, II, pt. I, 351–52.

16   Sandnes and Stemshaug, ed., *Norsk stadnamnleksikon*, p. 269.

17   Aasen, *Norske minnestykke*, p. 74.

18   Solheim, *Nemningsfordomar*, p. 167. This Guri Kunna was also thought to reside on Utfrovær, an Utrøst-like island or archipelago off Froan in northern Trøndelag. See Stemshaug, *Havbrua*, p. 28.

The Utrøst Complex

Jan Byberg studied the 'Utrøst complex' in a 1970 Norwegian thesis translated as 'The Joyous Islands in Norwegian Tradition — A Study of Motifs'.[19] He systematized the many motifs of supernatural islands and compared them to similar traditions abroad. Utrøst, which was thought to lie outside the Røst archipelago in Lofoten, is just one of many such islands, but is by far the most central. Others are Utvega off Vega, Sandflesa off Træna, Utfroan off Froan, and so on. Some are also found south of Trøndelag, on the western and south-western coasts. Among Byberg's 161 stories, seventeen Sámi and fourteen Nordic stories (excluding Norwegian) were discussed separately, and among the rest another thirty-five were not filed under the 'joyous island' group, but under two related groups; *samror med huldrefolket* (fishing with elves) and *Halten-segna* (Halten lore), named after the fishing bank of Halten in northern Trøndelag. The two groups deviate primarily in their lack of visits to a paradise-like island. Their concern is rather an encounter or intermingling with supernatural beings on or from such an island. The remaining ninety stories, then, were grouped into two main strands: (I) fifty-four epic and non-epic stories of the existence of supernatural islands, and (II) thirty-six epic and non-epic stories of visits to these islands. It is notable that seventy-two of the total number (group I and II) are found in northern Trøndelag and Hálogaland. A meagre two accounts of the non-epic material, with the first recorded in Nordland in 1591, are found outside this area. Byberg argued that the epic material had spilled over from Nordland to Trøndelag as fishermen from the latter area took part in the Lofoten fisheries.[20]

I will pay special attention to one of the two groups under (I), the epic motif *Tenk i tóm* (take your time). Byberg found six examples, with four in Hálogaland and one in northern Trøndelag. He noted that the Old Norse catchphrase 'tenk i tóm' hinted at a time far in the past, most often not understood by later tellers. Here, a stranger from the outer sea, named variously *Utrøst-mannen* (the Utrøst man), *fiskarkallen* (the fisherman), and so on, visits a priest's house. The stranger either has a request or he wants to reveal a secret to the priest, whose hesitation and failure to respond adequately thwarts the revelation. The wavering priest is told that he will not see the man's abode, usually called Utrøst, until Doomsday. One version does not include this 'spell'.[21] Similarly, a version from Gildeskål in Nordland, not discussed by Byberg, also lacks the 'take your time' phrase. A stranger wearing a black cloak stands before

---

19 Byberg, 'Dei lukkelege øyane'.
20 Byberg, 'Dei lukkelege øyane', pp. 9–85, 124–25. Byberg underlines that the high number of 'joyous island' tales in Hálogaland could partly be attributed to an initiative in the first issue of the journal *Håløygminne* in 1920 to collect tales that were thought to reflect northern Norwegian cultural tradition, especially 'Utrøst tales'. This cannot, however, account for the lack of 'Utrøst tales' in other regions.
21 Byberg, 'Dei lukkelege øyane', pp. 28–31.

the priest in his parlour. He realizes too late that a rolled-up piece of paper was about to be presented him. Suddenly the stranger is gone.[22] The first recorded 'take your time' story was published in 1879.[23]

On one level, the 'take your time' motif revels in a priest's failure to recognize supernatural forces out to sea. He is a landlubber, and he does not grasp such forces and therefore misses a chance to enrich himself or attain vital knowledge. Those who knew the outer sea were imbued with knowledge that was unavailable to the priest. This distinction between one in authority and a fisherman can be expanded if we look closely at the 'Utrøst tales' that tell of visits to the 'joyous island' (II). *Skarvene fra Utrøst* (*The Cormorants from Utrøst*), first published in 1852 by Peter Christian Asbjørnsen, can serve as an example of the 'joyous island' type, yet it does not represent the tradition as a whole.[24] A poor fisherman, Isak, is caught in a storm and is blown to Utrøst. On his way into the Otherworld, he sees three cormorants on a log. Arriving on the lush island of Utrøst, Isak meets a farmer who explains that the cormorants are his sons who have been out fishing. Isak stays on the island and fishes with the sons. Eventually, they travel to Bergen with the fish, and Isak becomes rich. He travels back to his family on Værøy (near Røst) and helps out the family of his rich neighbour, who bullied Isak and had now drowned. Isak's story is one that underlines a very consistent theme in the 'Utrøst tales': the visitor to a supernatural island is always a fisherman or someone of humble standing, and the stay benefits him in the end. This can be contrasted with the outcome for men of some authority, be they priests, magnates, or Isak's rich neighbour, who wished to keep Isak from using their shared harbour. The upper strata of society lack access to or understanding of Utrøst. Even skippers, the often-affluent owners of cargo ships, *jekts*, could not fully enjoy a visit to Utrøst. This is made particularly clear in one tale of a ship's landing on a supernatural island, on which the skipper refused to allow his crew to tread. He turned down 'the key to Utrøst' and proclaimed that he would never settle there.[25] In another tale, Tom, the skipper of a *jekt*, was helped by *draugen* (the sea ghost) in a storm, but fled his island and rejected him a second time outside a church (the 'take your time' motif is mixed in), and, from that day on, he was called Idiot-Tom (*Tomsing*) for not settling on 'Utrøst'. An observant listener would foresee Tom's sorry end; he is introduced as a not-so-brave sailor.[26] Asbjørnsen writes in his introduction to *The Cormorants from Utrøst* that, according to the northerners, only the *'fromme eller fremsynte'* (the pious or foresighted) would catch sight of Utrøst. The cultural historian Roald Kristiansen found this detail crucial for

22   Mo, 'Dagar og år', pp. 94–95.
23   Nicolaissen, *Sagn og Eventyr fra Nordland*, p. 29.
24   Asbjørnsen and Moe, *Norske Folke- og Huldreeventyr*, pp. 67–72.
25   Hveding, *Folketru og folkeliv på Hålogaland*, pp. 88.
26   Ruud, 'Segna om Utrøst', pp. 20–25.

understanding the religious attitudes of fisherman-farmers in Hálogaland. The poor fisherman Isak is a pious Christian, yet also acutely aware that beings and forces out at sea had to be respected. Isak was in that sense both pious *and* foresighted. Kristiansen also found this peculiar fisherman religiosity recorded in the writings of northern Norwegian priests in the 1800s.[27] I will return to this observation below as we discuss the possible relation between Utrøst and the Vanir gods.

Grímnismál and Utrøst

The prose framework of *Grímnismál* introduces Agnarr and Geirrøðr, two brothers who are out fishing and seek refuge on an island. They are taken care of by a husband and his wife, Óðinn and Frigg in disguise. Before leaving on a ship, the man whispers into Geirrøðr's ear (although what is whispered is unknown), but when they arrive at their father's farm, Geirrøðr sends his older brother out to sea: *Farðu nú, þar er smyl hafi þik* (Fare to where trolls will have you). Geirrøðr becomes king after his father and Agnarr lived on what we must take to be a mountainous island out to sea. As Óðinn points out to tease Frigg: *Sér þú Agnar, fóstra þinn, hvar hann elr börn við gýgi í hellinum* (Look at Agnarr, your foster-son, how he breeds children with a *gýgr* in a cave). Frigg retorts that Geirrøðr is miserly with food. Óðinn then seeks to investigate the matter and travels to Geirrøðr's hall in disguise. He is placed between two fires without food and drink, until Geirrøðr's son, Agnarr, named after his uncle, hands him a drink. At this point, the prose framework ends and Óðinn's poem about the gods begin. When Geirrøðr finally discovers that the tortured man is Óðinn, he stands up, stumbles onto his sword, and dies.

The first thing that springs to our attention is how the brothers were stranded on an otherworldly island. Agnarr is even stranded a second time on a troll island. The former event is similar to Byberg's type of visits to the 'joyous island' (II), reminiscent of Isak on Utrøst. The latter falls under the 'Halten lore' heading, not strictly part of the 'joyous island' group. A scheming brother is enthroned at the cost of his brother being left to fish and hunt on a trollish island. *Tuftefolket på Sandflæsa* (*The Elves on Sandflæsa*), first published in 1851, is an early and well-known carrier of this motif.[28] 'Sandflæsa' translates to 'the sand-skerry' or 'the sandy skerry'. One detail in the 'Halten lore' is worth keeping in mind — the stranding benefits the 'good' brother and he eventually takes his rightful place on the throne. The 'evil' brother's attempt to inhabit or exploit this troll island fails. In *Grímnismál*, the 'good' brother Agnarr stays on the island and is 'written

---

27 Kristiansen, 'Om å være from og fremsynt', pp. 73–84.
28 Asbjørnsen and Moe, *Samlede eventyr*, I, 92–97.

out' of the story. The brothers attain two different sets of knowledge: Agnarr is taken care of by Frigg, and Geirrøðr by Óðinn. According to Jere Fleck, Óðinn's whispering into the ear of his protégé is no small matter; Geirrødr was imbued with numinous knowledge associated with sacred kingship of the kind young Agnarr was offered in the hall.[29] On the other hand, Agnarr is left to the female and trollish realm — twice over, it may seem. In Gro Steinsland's reading, Geirrøðr received secret ruler-knowledge from Óðinn, while the older Agnarr received erotic knowledge — two complementary aspects of princely wisdom. She discusses the issue of Agnarr in the cave and understands his breeding with a troll as an erotic encounter in a sort of *Útgarðr* — something outside the farm in an uncultured world. This theme is common among future rulers, namely their adventure and entanglement with females of other races: 'Erotisk forening med en kvinne fra Utgård hører sammen med overtakelse av kongeverdigheten' (Erotic union with a woman from Utgård [*Utgarðr*] is connected with the attaining of royal prestige).[30] For Steinsland, who paid particular attention to origin myths in the light of holy marriages, *hieros gamos*, the stranded brother's ordeal can be seen as a faint reflection of this motif. How we should understand the possible merging of Agnarr's erotic knowledge and his nephew's newly attained ruler-knowledge is, however, not clear.

An island far out to sea can then be understood as an *Útgarðr* where knowledge could be attained. This is in line with the 'Utrøst tales'. Agnarr was removed from the agricultural context of his father's farm. Instead, although not stated, Agnarr had little else to do on the island other than to fish and hunt. Living in a cave with a troll woman is to say that he lived outside the sphere of farming; he was carried away from the aristocratic milieu of his father by Geirrøðr. We can therefore reasonably say that he became a fisherman. His name — Agnarr features in the poem, not only in the prose framework — may even suggest such association.[31] The prose framework enigmatically relates the stranded Agnarr with the boy who became king. By stating that he was named after his uncle, we may ask if the young Agnarr offering Óðinn a drink represents the stranded brother in a manner not well understood. According to Carolyne Larrington, Agnarr received holy ruler-knowledge by offering Óðinn the drink, and possibly also by removing the kettles, aligning the right relationship between worshipper and the worshipped, and, unlike his father, obeying the divine laws of hospitality and sacrifice.[32] But again, given that both erotic / otherworldly knowledge and ruler-knowledge was needed for

29 Fleck, 'The "Knowledge-Criterion" in the *Grímnismál*', pp. 58–65.
30 Steinsland, *Det hellige bryllup og norrøn kongeideologi*, pp. 257–59; Steinsland, *Mytene som skapte Norge*, p. 87, my translation.
31 The etymology of the first name Agnarr is contested. According to Eivind Vågslid it was originally a nickname for a fisherman: 'stridsmann med agn beita og upphavleg tiln. på fiskar'. See Vågslid, *Norderlendske fyrenamn*, p. 24.
32 Larrington, 'Vaþruðnismál and Grímnismál', pp. 72–75.

succession, where did the young Agnarr attain the former if not through some unstated relation to his stranded uncle? Naming Geirrøðr's son Agnarr (or naming the brother after the young Agnarr) may be, on a speculative note, an attempt to connect the attained knowledge of the 'fisherman' Agnarr with his nephew's good sense in the presence of an otherworldly being.

Geirrøðr does not understand the otherworldly. He did not enjoy the mystical tutelage of Frigg, or attain erotic knowledge on a troll island, and he failed to recognize an otherworldly being in his hall. Whatever his flaw, it was serious enough for him to fall out of Óðinn's favour. Being miserly with food was not the issue. Frigg's claim was false, the introduction assures us. Here it will be proposed, perhaps daringly, that an analogy to the 'take your time' motif is key to our understanding of Geirrøðr's fatal misstep. Just as Geirrøðr recognized too late the presence of a sorcerer, the slow-thinking priests in Nordland failed to acknowledge the 'Utrøst man'. Óðinn's role as the 'man on Utrøst' (erase blue-clothed) in the introduction is not here of prime interest. It is rather the unambiguous favouring in the 'Utrøst tales' of those accepting and experiencing the Otherworld out at sea. The 'take your time' motif is the sharpest articulation of a message that one must be open to the unexpected, disorderly, and chaotic reality 'out there'. Ruler-knowledge is not enough. Along Norway's coast, this 'out there' was placed far out to sea. On the surface, the tales catered to a fisherman identity that took the forces out at sea seriously: Isak is foresighted and accepts the Otherworld. The 'take your time' catchphrase is even suited to pit the bookish landlubber against a quick-witted seaman, whose life relied on fast and firm decisions when encountering storms and squalls on the open sea. Yet, under the surface, so to speak, a lack of observance of the disorderly and unknown by an authority representing order touches on a much deeper motivation. For now, however, we can simply focus on the claim that the 'take your time' motif reflects Geirrøðr's situation in the hall. Further, the folkloric motif can help us understand the nature of Geirrøðr's flaw: it is not only his failure, according to Larrington, to 'align the right relationship between god and worshipper', but also, or perhaps primarily, to understand and respect the forces outside his guarded sphere of the farm, of order, and of the known.

To develop this point, the legend-like *Þorleifs þáttr jarlaskálds* in *Flateyjarbók* from *c.* 1387 can be interpreted as a playful send-up of the events in *Grímnismál.*[33] Þorleifr *jarlsskáld* Rauðfeldarson performs a poem called *Jarlsníð* in the hall of Hákon Sigurðarson, jarl of Hlaðir, in Niðaróss. The partly magical poem was performed to avenge Hákon's looting and burning of a ship in Oslofjorden. Like Óðinn, he doubles as an old beggar and is deprived of food and drink by the jarl. Only one *helmingr* of the poem has survived, and the *þáttr* says it belonged to the beginning of a section called *Þokuvísur* ('Fog Vísur') in *Jarlsníð.*

---

33 Vikør, trans., 'Tåtten om Torleiv jarlsskald', pp. 355–62.

Þoku dregr upp it ýtra;
él festisk it vestra
(mǫkkr mun náms) af nøkkvi
(naðrbings kominn hingat).

> (Fog rises up on the outer side; a storm gathers in the west for some reason; the cloud from the taking of the adder-bed must have come this way).[34]

The poem has a similar jarring effect to that of Óðinn's speech in *Grímnismál*. The jarl falls sick, and moving weapons kill his retinue. Þorleifr then escapes in the mist created by the poem. We recognize the corrupt authority, namely Hákon, and his inability to detect a sorcerer, which follows *Grímnismál* closely. Þorleifr is not stranded on an island, but he is taught 'forlorn knowledge' from his foster-father and father in his native Iceland. They were said to be well versed in sorcery. Seen from Niðaróss, where the poem was performed, Iceland serves here almost as an Utrøst-like island in the west where secret knowledge could be attained. Thus, one could argue that the theme of rearing by a foster-father on such an island is present. The burning of Þorleifr's ship is also worth notice. Learning about Hákon's misdeed, Þorleifr dwells in a verse on how his ship had turned into charcoal on a sandy spit. He does not fail to mention the robbing in the *Þokuvísur* stanza either, and the smoke from Hákon's misdeed seemingly blends with, or causes, the brewing storm. If we dare assume a pattern, we can ask whether the 'seaman's revenge' in Hákon's hall extends to that of Geirrøðr — implying that mistreatment of those who are imbued with otherworldly knowledge can have dire consequences. The source of knowledge or means to smite a land-based authority through word-sorcery is found on an island in the west: Þorleifr from his foster-father in Iceland, the 'Utrøst man' who inhabits such an island, and Óðinn from the supernatural island on which the brothers were stranded. Óðinn is of course a skilled sorcerer irrespective of his island dwelling, and in *Grímnismál* it is not clear whether he takes the role as an avenger from the sea.

The *Þokuvísur* stanza deserves an extensive study, greater than it can be accorded here. I dare only point to a possibility that the emerging *él*, which could also mean a swift-moving rain-cloud, recalls a dramatic weather shift. A sudden change in weather was a serious matter for sea folk — not so much for those on land. Stories of Lofoten fishermen and their observance of slight alterations in wind, movement of water, and fog-topped mountains is a recurring theme in northern Norwegian storytelling. These were signs only a seasoned seaman would interpret, and only a determined and swift reaction could save

---

34 Heslop, 'Jarlsnið', p. 372. Note that, according to Bo Almqvist, the *helmingr* perhaps originally belonged to the setting in Oslofjorden, following the burning of Þorleifr's ship. Almqvist contended that the *nið* could be older than the *þáttr* itself. Almqvist, *Norrön Niddiktning*, pp. 194–198.

one's life. The portrayal of one such brewing storm, placed in an Utrøst tale, gives a sense of the drama so effectively expressed in the *Þokuvísur* stanza:

> '«Eg ser det på sjyen», sa han Per Jonsa, høvedsmannen på fembøringen, og ennu før karene var ferdige med linedragningen, begynte det å tetne til ute i horisonten. Tunge, truende skyer track hurtig op, himmelen blev mørkere og mørkere, og det var som om en gråsort mur vokste opp mot vest. En liten mørk sky blev revet løs, og fór som en jaget hest over himmelen. Nordvesten kom som sloppet ut av en sekk. Sjøen hadde på få minutter vokset seg krapp og stygg og blev snart som en eneste heksegryte, full av hvitskummende, fresende bølger. Det var ikke annet å gjøre enn å kappe linen og prøve å komme seg op til været.'

> > ('I see it on the sea', said Per Jonsa, skipper of the *fembøring* boat, and even before the men had hauled in the longline, the horizon was filling up. Heavy, threatening clouds appeared, the sky became darker and darker, and it was as if a greyish-black wall was building up in the west. A small, gloomy cloud detached itself and flew like a driven horse over the sky. The northwestern gale blew up as if it was emptied out of a sack. In minutes the sea had become choppy and foul, and soon resembled a witch's cauldron of white-foaming and spitting waves. There was nothing for it but to cut the fishing-line and head for land).[35]

They were caught in the storm and drifted for days until they landed on an Utrøst-type island west of Træna in Nordland. Fishermen from Trøndelag and Hálogaland who took part in the fishing around Lofoten each storm-ridden winter were especially vulnerable to such squalls.

Utrøst and the Vanir

Returning to the issue of a maritime *Útgarðr* in the imagination of northerners, it is necessary to underline the very modest agricultural yields in Hálogaland. In northern Nordland and beyond, specialization in fishing was taken to an extreme, to a point where the *utmark* — that is the uncultivated resources such as grass, timber, turf, and hunting — associated with a traditional farm model stopped making sense. On marginal Iron Age settlements in Hálogaland the *utmark* was out to sea, not in the forest or mountains. This is a very different mode of subsistence compared with most European contexts, and people living from the sea grew in numbers as the stockfish trade blossomed from *c.* 1100 AD.

---

35 Christiansen, *Norske sagn*, pp. 85–87. The piece is called *Et sagn om Utrøst* (A Legend About Utrøst), told by Robert Danielsen in Salten, Nordland; my translation.

The name Utrøst is worth a second look. We should distinguish between the proper noun Utrøst, understood as the Otherworld off the Røst archipelago, and the Old Norse *útrǫst*, which has been interpreted as an outlying tract or *utmark*.[36] Yet, the word *rǫst* or *røst* can also take on another meaning, as documented in skaldic poetry and as recorded in northern Norway — namely, a part of the sea that is disturbed by a current.[37] The Røst archipelago is generally believed to be named after strong currents north of the islands.[38] 'Utrøst' would in that sense mean 'the outlying current' or 'the outermost current'. Ottar Grønvik's authorative interpretation of the A3 section of the runic inscription on the Eggum Stone in Sogn in western Norway may suggest that this understanding of *útrǫst* is meaningful.[39] The rune stone eulogizes a ship's crew lost at sea some time before 700 AD. They were seemingly brought to an underwater island by a fish-like creature:

Gotna fiskr
ór firney-ím,
svimande foki
af fænjunga lande

36 Poole, 'Háleygjatal', p. 201; Fritzner, *Ordbog over det gamle norske Sprog*, III, 153. See DN II, 784; DN V, 435; DN VIII, 224; DN XII, 206 for the earliest, apart form Eivindr's poem, uses of the word *útrǫst* (outlying tract) in Old Norse sources. The earliest letter dates to 1396 or 1397 (DN VIII, 224) with the others dating to 1404, 1441 and 1449. They were written in the southern part of Norway.

37 See for example Gade, ed., 'Haraldr harðráði Sigurðarson', pp. 52–53. A ship's carved frame (cross-piece) shook in the currents (*ristin rǫng skalf í rǫstum*). See also Bondevik and others, *Målsamlingar 1851–1854 av Ivar Aasen*, p. 13. Aasen recorded *røst* in Lofoten as 'Strømsø, en Række af Strømbølger, f. Ex. Ved et Næs' ('a part of the sea defined by currents, a series of waves caused by currents, F. ex. close to a headland'). Around Andøya in Vesterålen, Myrvang understood *røst* as identical to a *straumrand* (current-stripe), alluding to how water in a current behaved as if falling off an underwater cliff. He also notes *røss* and *skavlrøss* as a type of wave that suddenly appears when a current is forced up from the seabed and to the surface. *Straum-imen* is of a gentler kind, when the current is made visible by 'light, humble waves'. See Myrvang, *I havsauga*, pp. 9, 16. The words *røst* and *rås* are related. Hovda noted that on the west coast of Norway (from Jæren to Stad) *rås* means 'a strong current-belt' off the outer-most skerries. *Straumrås* apparently has the same meaning, following Hovda, and is recorded in a number of places in Trøndelag and northern Norway. In these tracts *rås*, however, mostly refers to open sea-stretches suitable for sailing, with strong currents (in the case of fishing spots) only as an additional sense. See Hovda, *Norske fiskeméd*, pp. 150–53. Notably, one of Hovda's informants, a fisherman from Rogaland, Norway, explained in 1962 that waking mackerel shoals created *småbårar*, 'light waves', that were called *imen* (determinative) and which the fisherman likened to *straumrås*. The latter then seems to mean the same as Aasen's *røst* and Myrvang's *røst, røss*, and *straum-imen*, and Grønvik's interpretation of *im*, that is, (light) waves or lines in the water surface caused by a current. Hovda's unpublished notes are referenced in Grønvik, *Runene på Eggjasteinen*, p. 82.

38 Sandnes and Stemshaug, ed., *Norsk stadnamnleksikon*, p. 377.

39 Grønvik, *Runene på Eggjasteinen*, pp. 79–89; Grønvik, 'Om Eggjainnskriften', pp. 36–47; Grønvik, 'Om Eggjainnskriften enda en gang', pp. 5–22; Grønvik, 'Om Eggjainnskriften – Epilog', pp. 29–34.

The man-fish
from the currents of Firney
swimming fast
from the land of fen-folk[40]

If Grønvik's interpretation is correct, the description of *firney* accords, as he is aware, with several details in the much later 'Utrøst tales'. Just as Utrøst was thought to almost dip under the surface — fishermen would pluck out corn straws from their rudders if passing over it, according to Asbjørnsen's introduction to *The Cormorants from Utrøst* — the *ím*, which he understood as a current over a shallow, covers *firney*, meaning 'the outlying island'.[41] Likewise, *útrǫst*, an 'outlying current', would be a clear alternative name for a submerged island — a shallow in an otherwise open ocean. The *gotna fiskr* that, according to Grønvik, led the dead to *firney* do not find parallels elsewhere.[42]

It is worth noting that the first documented use of the word *útrǫst* is found in one of the stanzas of the Nordland native Eyvindr *skáldaspillir* Finnsson, generally accepted as belonging to Eyvindr's poem *Háleygjatal*. Here he enumerates the forefathers of Hákon Sigurðarson, jarl of Hlaðir, in Hálogaland and Trøndelag:

Þás útrǫst
jarla bági
Belja dolgs
byggva vildi

> (When the adversary of jarls wished to settle the outlying tract of the enemy of Beli).[43]

The stanza has been understood to refer to the outlying tract that is Freyr's. Finnur Jónsson asked if this could be interpreted as a coastal island or a coast, but he did not offer any grounds for such an assumption.[44] Poole reasonably called the kenning (*útrǫst Belja dolgs*) 'enigmatic' in his detailed analysis of

---

40 Grønvik, *Runene på Eggjasteinen*, p. 163. The third line was amended to *svimandi foki* and the last line was amended to *fœnjunga lande*, as presented here, in Grønvik, 'Om Eggjainnskriften enda en gang', pp. 5–22; my translation.

41 See Hveding, *Håløygsk ordsamling*, p. 54, for the word *ím* in northern Norwegian use.

42 Grønvik, *Runene på Eggjasteinen*, pp. 79–89, 160–63.

43 Poole, 'Háleygjatal', p. 201. Finnur Jónsson guessed that the jarl in question was Goðgestr and was not quite certain whether it was Freyr or the jarls who had an adversary: '[Usikkert om hvem, Godgest?]. da jarlernes modstander vilde bebo Freys udrast (søkyst eller ø ved kysten; eller: da Freys modstander [Surt, jætten] vilde bebo jarlens udrast?)'. See Finnur Jónsson, *Den Norsk-Islandske Skjaldedigtning*, 1, 60. I follow Poole's assertion that introducing a giant, Surtr, into the realm of humans in *Háleygjatal* is unlikely. Finnur's first and preferred alternative is therefore the likely one.

44 Finnur Jónsson, *Den Norsk-Islandske Skjaldedigtning*, 1, 60.

the poem.[45] If Freyr appeared in myths unknown to us, his 'outlying tract' can then mean a great many things. The enemy of the jarls is perhaps the Ynglingr dynasty, but this also is dubious.[46] What we do know is that the kenning *útrǫst Belja dolgs* must refer to concrete and worldly geography. Interpreting *útrǫst* plainly as 'the outlying current' would be an unlikely place for 'the adversary of jarls' to settle. But what if Eyvindr twisted the meaning of *útrǫst* as it was perhaps understood in contemporary coastal Norway? That is, if it was understood as an underwater island of otherworldly beings revealed by the shallow currents passing above it. If we place Freyr on *útrǫst*, which is indeed a daring proposition, the kenning will in my view make sense. For men, *útrǫst* was an Otherworld of elves, but for Freyr, perhaps submerged, glancing back from far out at sea, the coast settled by men was *his* 'outlying current' — or rather, *his* Otherworld. This would provide the kenning with a needed kick. Freyr's outlying current would then mean a coast or something similar, as suggested by Finnur Jónsson. This coast is of course tricky to place, not knowing either the temporal or geographical context of Eyvindr's verse.[47] Two observations may buttress the interpretation *útrǫst Belja dolgs* = Freyr's outlying current = coast. Firstly, Eyvindr's kenning for 'Icelanders', *álhimins lendingar* (dwellers of the 'sky of the eel'), reveals his fondness for a similar reversed perspective. Just as he takes an eel's vantage point from the bottom of a lake, the poet invites us to take a god's outlook from an Otherworld. Secondly, a key element of the otherworldly in the 'Utrøst complex' and elsewhere is how reality is twisted. On entering the Otherworld, things are turned upside down. Isak realized on Utrøst that the three cormorants on a log were really three brothers in a boat. In a Sámi 'Utrøst tale', a boy on a supernatural island saw fishing lines dropping from the sky. His family's fish-catch now looked like goats.[48] The elf world is not what it seems, and nor is the human world for elves. Their eyes being somehow turned inside out, a common theme in folktales, is perhaps a useful analogy. As Reidar Christiansen puts it: '...etter vanlig folketro er det noe vrangt ved huldrefolks syn' (according to common folk-belief, there is something skewed about the eye-sight of elves).[49] Their strange language, attested by the fishermen's superstition treated above, is also part of the picture.

---

45 Poole, *Háleygjatal*, p. 201.
46 According to the *Ynglinga saga*, they moved into Norway from Sweden prior to the Viking Age, and Harald Fairhair, Óláfr Tryggvason, and Óláfr Haraldsson were claimed to be of this kin. The former two, at least, were in an unstable relationship with the jarls, involved in struggles of political control in northern and southern Norway.
47 Some suggestions could be the Coastal Land (*Zona itaque maritima*) as recounted by the twelfth-century *Historia Norwegie*, the coastal stretch from Stad northwards, corresponding with the Háleygir jarl's coastal realm in the late Viking Age (Møre, Trøndelag, and Hálogland), or, even more uncertain, Hálogaland, if *útrǫst* was associated with the region by the 900s. These can only be viewed as very uncertain guesses.
48 Friis, *Lappiske Eventyr og Folkesagn*, p. 22.
49 Christiansen, 'Sagnstudier', pp. 77–78.

Is it reasonable to place a Vanir on *útrǫst*? The question can only be touched upon briefly here. Grønvik proposed that Freyja inhabited *firney*, as he believed that the Eggum runic inscription referred to a death-world called *fænjunga land* (the land of fen-folk). He relied on the assertion that Frigg, whose abode is Fensalir (the fen-hall), was identical to Freyja by the late Iron Age (600–1050 AD). The rune carver thus placed Freyja and her *fænjunga* on a submerged island while keeping her mire-dwelling association.[50] Also intriguing is the man-fish, who 'always brings about luck'.[51] The Vanir are associated with prosperity, but then again it is not clear who or what the *gotna fiskr* is. The maritime association of the Vanir is unquestionable. Njǫrðr's abode Nóatún, 'farmyard of ships', his daughter Freyja's alternative name, Mardǫll, and her brother Freyr's ship, Skiðblaðnir, are some examples of this. According to the *Prose Edda*, Njǫrðr was to be called upon for seafaring and fishing — a role attested to in at least one traditional account in Norway.[52] If indeed Freyr had taken Njǫrðr's place in the late Iron Age, he, too, is a god for fishermen. Yet little supports situating them far out to sea. Njǫrðr gave name to at least five islands in Norway — three of them in Trøndelag and Hálogaland, the only theophoric place names attested in the latter area — and all of them are located near the coast-line.[53] In making a fruitful proposition of the Vanir's possible relation to *útrǫst*, we should look to what they represent in relation to a broader understanding of the 'joyous island' in a Western and Far East tradition. Three common traits are discernable: the island belongs to the dead, it cannot be found, and it is joyful.[54] The Vanir's dual role as gods of both death and fertility (joy, prosperity) is not irrelevant here. So is their claimed chthonic nature, in this case under water, and the way in which they are closely associated with, or even identified as, elves, if we accept Jens Peter Schjødt's contention. His discussion of the ideological relation between the Vanir and Æsir is striking when seen through the lens of 'Utrøst tales'. The Vanir represent the 'other' world, the latent, hidden, and mystical (*'den anden verden'*, *'det latente'*, *'det dulgte'*, *'det mystiske'*), while the Æsir represent the reigning culture (*'den egentlige kultur'*), that which is high,

---

50 Grønvik, 'Om Eggjainnskriften enda en gang', pp. 12–13.

51 Grønvik, 'Om Eggjainnskriften — Epilog', p. 32.

52 Opedal, 'Makter og menneske', v, 49. A woman, Gunnhild Reinsnos, born in 1746, thanks 'Njor' for a good catch: 'No ska han Njor ha takk fý denn' vændo'.

53 See Olsen, 'Det gamle norske ønavn Njarðarlǫg'. Nærøy in Namdal would fall under Hálogaland according to the old definition of the region. The second Nærøy is found in Øksnes in Nordland. Olsen entertains the possibility of a third 'Njǫrðr's island' outside Bodø, called Godøy, or the Goðeyjar by Snorri. Other theophoric names may have been renamed due to being taboo. As Magnus Olsen points out, Njǫrð named more islands than any other god in Norway. In Hálogaland, we find no firmly attested theophoric place names associated with the Æsir. Possible exceptions are local traditions of a Torshov (Thor's temple) and Torshaugen (Thor's mound) on Rødøy in Nordland. These names are, however, only attested very late.

54 Holbek and Piø, *Fabeldyr og sagnfolk*, pp. 243–54.

orderly, and protective of life. In contrast, the Vanir stand for something pre-cultural, backwards, and outside (*'prækulturelt'*, *'forud'*, *'Uden for'*), all draped in death, disorder, and the low.[55] In the folktales, Utrøst embodies this hidden, low death-world which is also joyful and enriching for those who settle and perhaps return to the human world. That this Otherworld is indeed a death-world is attested to in Grønvik's *hitt lant* on the the Eggum Stone.[56] As noted, Isak was both pious *and* foresighted, perhaps balancing 'the reigning culture' of Christianity and age-old superstition, which aided him among the chaotic forces of the sea. Geirrøðr seems to represent the high and orderly kingship associated with the Æsir, but he either ignored or did not have its opposite bestowed on him: the dangerous, Vanir-like chaos and travel into the unknown that one must face to renew one's authority. If Frigg and Freyja are then one and the same, Agnarr's tutelage was probably one step closer to the low, mystical realm of the Vanir, in line with his fate as someone breeding with a *gýgr* in trollish lands. If the gods are indeed conflated, it would also place a Vanir, Freyja, on a supernatural island in the prose framework of *Grímnismál*. Óðinn does not fit in as an island dweller. We dare say, as an Æsir, he does not belong there.

Admitting that the Norse literary corpus does not support the situating of Freyr on a submerged island, the confusing snippets of information about the Vanir's homes do not, however, make it a wholly unlikely proposition either. The familial bond between Njǫrðr, Freyr, and Freyja can have been extended hypothetically to their homes. Lately, scholars have adapted to the often local characteristics of mythology in Scandinavia, with local variations as to where gods were understood to dwell. In that sense, the leap from Freyja inhabiting *firney* in the late 600s to Freyr inhabiting *útrǫst* in the late 900s is not unbridgeable. They were both placed somewhere off the Norwegian coast and, as proposed above, refer to the same Otherworld under a current.

Conclusion

Despite the popularity in northern Norway enjoyed by *The Cormorants from Utrøst* and other 'Utrøst tales', little regard has been paid to their possible ideological bearings — not to mention whether gods were once thought to inhabit the island. Firstly, an overview was provided of fisherman-farmer superstition in northern Norway in order to show that belief in underwater beings was a markedly common cultural trait. The *hulderland*, the land of elves, defined speech and attire out at sea. The unforgiving nature, its skerries

---

55   Schjødt, 'Relationen mellem aser og vaner', pp. 303–19. See also a discussion of the word *Algrǫn* (All-Green) from *Hárbarðsljóð* in the context of a lush, supernatural island in Lundberg, *Ön Allgrön*, pp. 5–27.
56   Grønvik, 'Om Eggjainnskriften — Epilog', pp. 31–32.

and towering island peaks, was female, with the *gýgr* as the most common term for a troll woman. Secondly, the 'Utrøst complex' and its relationship to *Grímnismál* was presented. The brothers' visit to a supernatural island and the later stranding of Agnarr bear resemblance to two motifs in this complex. According to Jan Byberg, the former belongs to the 'joyous island' type, while in a strict sense the latter falls outside the 'Utrøst complex'. The lines, however, are fuzzy, and for our purpose, the 'Halten lore' motif, along with the 'Utrøst tales', is represented overwhelmingly in northern Trøndelag and Hálogaland, in the cultural sphere of fishermen-farmers visiting Lofoten in the winter. These motifs belong to the prose framework, which might be secondary to the actual poem. On the other hand, the 'take your time' motif arguably reflects a defining situation in the poem, namely Geirrøðr's fatal mistreatment of Óðinn. Just as the king fails to recognize a sorcerer or otherworldly being in his hall, the priests in Nordland hesitate when approached by the 'Utrøst man'. In the 'take your time' motif, the visitor arrives from the sea. This maritime thread is amplified in *Þorleifs þáttr jarlaskálds*, where Þorleifr's mystical tutelage on Iceland enables him to cast a spell in Niðaróss on Hákon Sigurðarson, earl of Hlaðir. Iceland is here Utrøst, so to speak, and the setting of Þorleifr's revenge (for the burning of his ship) follows *Grímnismál* closely. If we also address how the 'Utrøst tales' favour without exception low-status seamen who hold the Otherworld in high regard, it is fair to ask whether Geirrøðr's end has something to do with a *disregard* for these maritime forces.

Thirdly, I discussed whether Eyvindr's kenning *útrøst Belja dolgs* means 'Freyr's outlying current', which refers to a coast. This interpretation necessitates that the Vanir should be associated with Utrøst. If accepted, the forces that Geirrøðr disregarded now perhaps emerge. Or rather, the forces these gods were thought to represent are embodied in the stranded 'fisherman' Agnarr. As a side note, the enigmatic word pair *vilbiǫrg vaka* in *Grímnismál* 45 may benefit from a future discussion in light of the barely submerged *útrøst* and *firney*. Noting that *vilbiǫrg* could mean 'a desirable rescue' or 'saving' that surfaces or becomes visible (*vaka*), it would fit as a taboo name for a supernatural island.[57] The context is puzzling, and we are seemingly in Ægir's company out at sea.

Concerning *Grímnismál*'s possible conception in Hálogaland, it is difficult or even meaningless to make such an argument based on folklore. Yes, the 'Utrøst tales' do find parallels in the prose framework, and the 'take your time' motif appears perhaps in the poem as well. Þorleifr's upbringing in a land-taking by Namdal folk is also worth mentioning. In that sense, *Grímnismál* might

---

57 Heggstad, 'Gamalnorsk ordbok', pp. 770, 804. *Vilbiǫrg* is interpreted as 'ynskjeleg berging, frelsa' (a desirable rescue, saving). *Vaka* has several meanings: to wake up or to be awake, to move or become visible, and to swim on the water surface. *Vakka* means to drift around. Larrington, 'Vaþruðnismál.and Grímnismál', p. 73, understood *vilbiǫrg* as a 'wished-for sustenance', linking the word to sacrificial feasting.

have taken on some Háleygir colours. Yet the traditions on which the poem and prose framework rests must have a historical depth that goes far beyond the timeframe discussed above. The clear over-representation of 'Utrøst tales' in northern Trøndelag and Hálogaland may in part be attributed to an unprecedented specialization in fishing from around 1100 AD that continues into our age. Prior to that, these traditions were probably shared by the coastal population further south in western Norway and beyond, to which the Eggum Stone serves as a testament.

In conclusion, I am aware that the thoughts presented above plunge headlong into intricate scholarly discourses concerning the nature of the Vanir and the tricky relationship between Norse literature and much later folklore. The purpose of this discussion has been to state clearly what *Grímnismál* looks like through the Utrøst prism. To speculate on what *Grímnismál* is *really* trying to tell us based on studying the 'Utrøst tales' is a tall order. Yet, beating a path for future study, it is in my view hard to overlook Jungian approaches to myth and lore, where Jordan Peterson's extensive treatment of 'The Hostile Brothers' motif can serve as an example.[58] Peterson, who did not analyse *Grímnismál*, stressed how many ancient stories seem to address the human balancing act between chaos and order. Agnarr's breeding with a *gýgr* on a desolate island implies that he inhabited the realm of the archetypal Great Mother, with the potential for creativity and destruction. Geirrøðr becomes the Great Father, with the potential for order and tyranny. The brothers thus occupy two extremes, both devoured by negative archetypal potential: destruction and tyranny. Agnarr is trapped in the chaos out at sea, not able to utilize its potential knowledge, while Geirrøðr becomes a tyrant. Is this to say that 'Vanir-knowledge' bestowed on Agnarr by Frigg (given that she is identical to Freyja) and 'Æsir-knowledge' passed on from Óðinn had to be balanced against each other? That the one cannot do without the other? It is intriguing that the young Agnarr seems to have placed himself in the middle of chaos and order; he is imbued with numinous ruler-knowledge by way of welcoming the otherworldly. Is he like Isak, both 'pious and foresighted'? I think these questions ought to be asked in order to challenge Larrington's claim that Geirrøðr's punishment is first and foremost invoked for his failure to sacrifice to a god, having 'prejudiced the relationship between human and divine'.[59] Or that Geirrøðr's death is non-functional, even 'overkill', as suggested by Fleck, stressing young Agnarr's ritual education.[60] His end can just as well express a necessary divine correction for not being observant to the powers of chaos that entered his hall.

---

58 Peterson, *Maps of Meaning*, pp. 324–29.
59 Larrington, 'Vafþrúðnismál and Grímnismál', p. 73.
60 Fleck, 'The "Knowledge-Criterion" in the *Grímnismál*', pp. 60–61.

Works Cited

Primary Sources

Aasen, Ivar, *Norske minnestykke* (Oslo: Norsk folkeminnelag, 1923)

Asbjørnsen, Peter Christian, and Jørgen Moe, *Samlede eventyr: norske kunstneres billedutgave*, 3 vols (Oslo: Universitetsforlaget, 1965)

——, *Norske Folke- og Huldreeventyr* (Oslo: Universitetsforlaget, 1962)

Bondevik, Jarle, Oddvar Nes, and Teje Aarset, ed., *Målsamlingar 1851–1854 av Ivar Aasen* (Bergen: Norsk bokreidingslag, 1999)

Christiansen, Reidar, *Norske sagn* (Oslo: Aschehoug, 1938)

DN = *Diplomatarium Norvegicum. Oldbreve til Kundskab om Norges indre og ydre Forhold, Sprog, Slægter, Sæder, Lovgivning og Rettergang i Middelalderen*, ed. by Christia. C. A. Lange and others, 23 vols (Christiania: Mallings Forladshandel, 1847–2011)

Myrvang, Finn, *I havsauga – Andøya i stadnamn og kysttradisjon* (Værøy: Lofotboka, 1981)

Nicolaissen, Oluf, *Sagn og Eventyr fra Nordland* (Kristiania: Mallings boghandel, 1879)

Secondary Works

Almqvist, Bo, *Norrön Niddiktning — Traditionshistoriska studier i versmagi*, 2 vols, Nordiska texter och undersøkningar, 21 (Uppsala: Almqvist & Wiksell, 1965–1974)

Bugge, Sophus, *Studier over de nordiske Gude- og Heltesagns Oprindelse*, 2 vols (Christiania: Cammermeyer, 1881–1889)

Byberg, Jan, 'Dei lukkelege øyane i norsk tradisjon – ei motivgransking' (unpublished master's thesis, University of Bergen, 1970)

Christiansen, Reidar, 'Sagnstudier', in *Eventyr og sagn* (Oslo: Norli, 1946 [1941]), pp. 71–100

Eidnes, Hans, 'Fiske og fordom', *Håløygminne*, 71 (1940), 497–503

Finnur Jónsson, *Den Norsk-Islandske Skjaldedigtning*, 2 vols (Copenhagen: Rosenkilde og Bagger, 1973 [1912])

Fleck, Jere, 'The "Knowledge-Criterion" in the *Grímnismál*: The Case against "Shamanism"', *Arkiv för nordisk filologi*, 86 (1971), 49–71

Friis, Jens A., *Lappiske Eventyr og Folkesagn* (Kristiania: Cammermeyers, 1871)

Fritzner, Johan, *Ordbog over det gamle norske Sprog*, 3 vols (Kristiania: Den norske forlagsforening, 1886–1896)

Gade, Kari Ellen, ed., 'Haraldr harðráði Sigurðarson, Lausavísur 11', in *Poetry from the Kings' Sagas 2*, ed. by Ellen Kari Gade, Skaldic Poetry of the Scandinavian Middle Ages, 2 (Turnhout: Brepols, 2009), pp. 52–53

Grønvik, Ottar, 'Om Eggjainnskriften', *Arkiv för nordisk filologi*, 103 (1988), 36–47

——, 'Om Eggjainnskriften enda en gang', *Arkiv för nordisk filologi*, 115 (2000), 5–22

————, 'Om Eggjainnskriften — Epilog', *Arkiv för nordisk filologi*, 117 (2002), 29–34

————, *Runene på Eggjasteinen: En hedensk gravinnskrift fra slutten av 600-tallet* (Oslo: Universitetsforlaget, 1985)

Gudbrandson, Terje, *Bodin bygdebok*, 2 vols (Bodø: Bodø kommune, 1961–2004)

Heggstad, Leiv, *Gamalnorsk ordbok — med nynorsk tyding* (Oslo: Det norske samlaget, 1930)

Heide, Eldar, 'Holy Islands and the Otherworld: Places Beyond Water', in *Isolated Islands in Medieval Nature, Culture and Mind*, ed. by Gerhard Jaritz and Torstein Jørgensen (Bergen: Central European University, 2011), pp. 57–80

Heslop, Kate, '*Jarlsníð*', in *Poetry from the Kings' Sagas 1: From Mythical Times to c. 1035*, ed. by Diana Whaley, Skaldic Poetry of the Scandinavian Middle Ages, 1 (Turnhout: Brepols, 2012), pp. 375–76

Holbek, Bengt, and Iørn Piø, *Fabeldyr og sagnfolk* (Copenhagen: Politikens, 1967)

Hovda, Per, *Norske fiskeméd — landsoversyn og to gamle médbøker* (Oslo: Universitetsforlaget, 1961)

Hveding, Johan, *Astøingsvisa — med innleiing og ordtyding* (Harstad: Hålogaland historielag, 1961)

————, *Folketru og folkeliv på Hålogaland* (Oslo: Norsk folkeminnelag, 1935)

————, *Håløygsk ordsamling* (Bodø: Nordland boktrykkeri, 1968)

Kristiansen, Roald E., 'Om å være from og fremsynt — Nordnorsk natur og religiøsitet', in *Mellom sagn og virkelighet i nordnorsk tradisjon*, ed. by Marit Anne Hauan and Ann Helene Bolstad Skjelbred (Stabekk: Vett og viten, 1995), pp. 73–84

Kulturhistorisk leksikon for nordisk middelalder, 22 vols (Oslo: Gyldendal, 1956–1978)

Larrington, Carolyne, 'Vaþruðnismál and Grímnismál', in *The Poetic Edda: Essays on Old Norse Mythology*, ed. by Paul Acker and Carolyne Larrington (New York: Routledge, 2002), pp. 59–77

Lundgren, Oskar, *Ön Allgrön — är Eddans Harbardsljod ett norskt kväde?*, Arctos Svecica, 2 (Stockholm: Gebers, 1944)

Løkås, Ole, 'Heilag Olav og Reines-trollet', *Håløygminne*, 32 (1951), 322–23

Marold, Edith, ed., 'Hofgarða-Refr Gestsson, *Ferðavísur* 5', in *Poetry from Treatises on Poetics*, ed. by Kari Ellen Gade and Edith Marold, Skaldic Poetry of the Scandinavian Middle Ages, 3 (Turnhout: Brepols, 2017), pp. 248

Mo, Ragnvald, *Dagar og år — segner frå Salten* (Oslo: Norsk folkeminnelag, 1936)

Nielssen, Alf Ragnar, *Landnåm fra nord* (Stamsund: Orkana akademisk, 2012)

Olsen, Magnus, *Det gamle norske ønavn Njarðarlǫg*, Christiania Videnskabs-Selskabs Forhandlinger, 5 (Christiania: Dybwad, 1905)

————, 'Helkunduheiðr', in *Norrøne studier* (Oslo: Aschehoug, 1938 [1932]), pp. 87–101

Opedal, Halldor O., *Makter og menneske*, 17 vols (Oslo: Norsk folkeminnelag, 1930–88)

Peterson, Jordan, *Maps of Meaning* (New York: Routledge, 1999)

Poole, Russell, ed., 'Háleygjatal', in *Poetry from the Kings' Sagas 1: From Mythical Times to c. 1035*, ed. by Diana Whaley, Skaldic Poetry of the Scandinavian Middle Ages, 1 (Turnhout: Brepols, 2012), pp. 195–212

Ruud, Edvard, 'Segna om Utrøst', *Håløygminne*, 72 (1941), 20–25

Sandnes, Jørn, and Ola Stemshaug, ed., *Norsk stadsnamnleksikon* (Oslo: Samlaget, 1997)

Schjødt, Jens Peter, 1991 'Relationen mellem aser og vaner og dens ideologiske implikasjoner', in *Nordisk hedendom: et symposium*, ed. by Gro Steinsland (Odense: Odense Universitetsforlag, 1991), pp. 303–19

Solheim, Svale, *Nemningsfordomar* (Oslo: Det Norske Videnskaps-Akademi, 1940)

Steinsland, Gro, *Det hellige bryllup og norrøn kongeideologi: en analyse av hierogami-myten i Skírnismål, Ynglingatal, Háleygjatal og Hyndluljóð* (Oslo: Solum, 1991)

——, *Mytene som skapte Norge* (Oslo: Pax, 2012)

Stemshaug, Ola, 'Havbrua', in *Årbok for Fosen*, 50 (2011), 25–34

Strompdal, Knut, *Gamalt frå Helgeland* (Oslo: Norsk folkeminnelag, 1929)

Sundt, Eilert, 'Beretning om fante- eller landstygerfolket i Norge', in *Fante- eller landstrygerfolket i Norge*, ed. by H. O. Christophersen, Nils Christie, and Kaare Pettersen (Oslo: Gyldendal, 1974 [1850]), pp. 1–285

Vikør, Lars S., trans., 'Tåtten om Torleiv jarlsskald', in *Islendingesagaene*, ed. by Jon Gunnar Jørgensen and Jan Ragnar Hagland, 5 vols (Reykjavík: Saga, 2014), pp. 355–62

Vågslid, Eivind, *Norderlendske fyrenamn* (Eidsvoll: self-published, 1988)

MARTE SPANGEN

Sámi Myths and Medieval Heritage

Introduction

There is a reciprocal relationship between humans and their surroundings: people create their cultural landscapes as they use and observe them, while landscapes, topographies, and non-human actors also shape people, practices, and beliefs. This has been studied in a number of ways within subjects such as history, geography, psychology, social anthropology, and archaeology. Various aspects and theoretical approaches have been emphasized, including the *longue durée* effects of natural conditions on society, the cultural creation of place, the affordance of landscapes and topographies for certain human activities, and the ever-present interconnections between people, animals, and other non-human actors.[1] Moreover, the concept of *materiality* and how things affect human behaviour and being-in-the-world has been frequently discussed in archaeology over the last fifteen years.[2]

Even before this concept was adopted, researchers within archaeology had a lasting interest in studying how the remains of the past, which continue to linger in the landscapes around us, have affected people in different places and time periods and shaped their understanding of the world and themselves.[3] Investigations show, not surprisingly, that large, conspicuous, and enigmatic monuments in particular tend to call for an explanation. Consequently, such structures are integrated into the existing

---

1 Braudel, *The Mediterranean and the Mediterranean World*; Tuan, *Space and Place*; Gibson, *Ecological Approach to Visual Perception*; Ingold, *Perception of the Environment*.
2 Olsen, 'Material Culture after Text', pp. 87–104; Olsen, *In Defense of Things*; Svestad, 'The Impact of Materiality on Sámi Burial Customs and Religious Concepts', pp. 39–56.
3 For example, Burström, *Mångtydiga fornlämningar*; Burström, Winberg, and Zachrisson, *Fornlämningar och folkminnen*; Gazin-Schwartz and Holtorf, *Archaeology and Folklore*; Andrén, 'Places, Monuments, and Objects', pp. 267–81; Lund and Arwill-Nordbladh, 'Divergent Ways of Relating to the Past in the Viking Age', pp. 415–38.

Marte Spangen, UiT The Arctic University of Norway, marte.spangen@uit.no

Myths and Magic in the Medieval Far North: Realities and Representations of a Region on the Edge of Europe, ed. by Stefan Figenschow, Richard Holt, and Miriam Tveit, AS 10
(Turnhout: Brepols, 2020), pp. 119–142
© BREPOLS ❧ PUBLISHERS   10.1484/M.AS-EB.5.120522

local worldviews, and the mythical and mythological complexes of the time. Such explanations often suggest construction by giants or other non-human creatures, but many stories also relate monuments to more or less specific historical events.[4]

The Sámi in northern Fennoscandia are no exception. They have observed more or less unexpected features in their familiar landscapes and interpreted them within their frames of reference at the time. This article will focus on some medieval activities in Sámi landscapes and the known Sámi myths about these. Three examples will discuss the Sámi interpretation of so-called 'Stállo' house grounds, of pitfall traps for reindeer hunting, and of a type of structure called 'circular offering sites'. Archaeologists have studied these features, considering such aspects as construction details, dating, and placement in the landscape. Over the last three decades, these studies have led to new theories about the initial function, dating, and social context of these archaeological types.[5] Local Sámi interpretations of the structures have been discussed, too, with varying degrees of influence on the ethnographic and archaeological understanding of their original use.[6]

Over the last few decades there has been a growing awareness of the relevance and problematics related to the use of such sources in archaeological interpretations, especially in indigenous contexts such as that of the Sámi.[7] The history of studies of archaeological features started with a fascination for ancient monuments as early as the Middle Ages. The credibility of such sources as myths and folklore, as well as the saga literature and similar written sources, regarding such monuments has changed over time.[8] The value they have been credited with has depended, in part, on the context. Indigenous people have been perceived to have a more static culture, and thus to be more likely to preserve actual historical information through traditions than the supposedly modern and progressive cultures of the West. To some extent, this has led to a somewhat indiscriminate use of oral traditions as a source

---

4 For example, Klintberg, *Svenska folksägner*, pp. 26–27; Burström, Winberg, and Zachrisson, *Fornlämningar och folkminnen*, pp. 96–103, 107–09, 114–30.

5 Storli, '*Stallo*'-boplassene; Liedgren and Bergman, 'Aspects of the Construction of Prehistoric Stállo-Foundations and Stállo-Buildings', pp. 3–26; Sommerseth, 'Villreinfangst og tamreindrift i Indre Troms'; Spangen, *Circling Concepts*.

6 Manker, *Fångstgropar och stalotomter*; Kjellström, 'Är traditionerna om stalo historiskt grundade?', pp. 155–78; Vorren and Eriksen, *Samiske offerplasser i Varanger*; Wepsäläinen, *Stalotomterna*.

7 Burström, *Mångtydiga fornlämningar*; Burström, Winberg, and Zachrisson, *Fornlämningar och folkminnen*; Solli, *Narratives of Veøy: An Investigation into the Poetics and Scientifics of Archaeology*; Solli, 'Narratives of Veøy. On the Poetics and Scientifics of Archaeology', pp. 209–27; Gazin-Schwartz and Holtorf, *Archaeology and Folklore*; Nilsen, *Brytninger mellom lokal og akademisk kulturminnekunnskap*; Damm, 'Archaeology, Ethno-history and Oral Traditions', pp. 73–87; Skandfer, 'Ethics in the Landscape', pp. 89–102.

8 Cf. Klindt-Jensen, *A History of Scandinavian Archaeology*; Hastrup and Sørensen, *Tradition og historieskrivning*.

for explaining the historical past in indigenous contexts, sometimes as far back as the Stone Age.[9]

It is important that archaeologists acknowledge the value of traditional information for understanding landscape use and worldviews of indigenous groups in the past.[10] Such an approach corresponds with the recognition of the rights of indigenous groups to define their own cultural heritage.[11] However, while myths may include elements of ancient historical realities, one-to-one interpretations of their content to explain archaeological features and historical situations are problematic because they run the risk of reinforcing reactionary stereotypes about a static culture for the indigenous groups they concern.[12]

The following exploration of Sámi myths about three types of medieval monuments will exemplify the questions that arise in relation to the use of different myths and legends as sources of knowledge about the historical past as this is constituted in modern Western academic traditions. It will also exemplify the importance such narratives have for negotiating Sámi past and present identities today.

'Stállo' House Grounds

The 'Stállo' house grounds are found in the high mountain areas, mainly in the mountain range marking today's border between Norway and Sweden. There are around 470 recorded house grounds of this type between the 64th and 69th parallel. The house grounds are oval or rounded rectangular, with widths of 2 to 5 m and lengths of 2 to 6.5 m. They are usually clearly visible due to their size, their semi-subterranean construction, where the floor level is dug down to a level beneath the surrounding terrain surface, and the surrounding embankments of surplus soil or sand from the floor area. Their location in mountain areas with limited vegetation contributes to rendering the traces clearly visible even today (Fig. 1). There is some debate over the construction details of the walls and roof the embankments must have supported, but convincing arguments have been made for a construction similar to the Sámi *bealljegoahti*, a round turf hut with curved wall / roof posts (a so-called 'bow-pole framework'), whether these were covered with turf or with materials such as bark or cloth. An important difference from the usual *bealljegoahti* is that the Stállo house grounds are often distinctly larger.

---

9   Flood, *Archaeology of the Dreamtime*; Ecko-Hawk, 'Forging a New Ancient History for Native America', pp. 88–102; cf. Damm, 'Archaeology, Ethno-history and Oral Traditions', p. 78.

10 For example, Schanche, 'Horizontal and Vertical Perceptions of Saami Landscapes', pp. 1–10; Barlindhaug, 'Cultural Sites, Traditional Knowledge and Participatory Mapping'.

11 Skandfer, 'Ethics in the Landscape'.

12 Spangen, *Circling Concepts*.

Fig. 1: Stállo house ground in the mountain landscape of Saltfjellet, Nordland, Norway. Photo by Bjørnar Olsen.

They also have a conspicuous internal relation; where the sites include three or more house grounds, these are usually organized in rows.[13]

Radiocarbon dating suggest that some of the Stállo house grounds may have been constructed as early as the seventh century, but the main phase of use was between *c.* 800 AD and 1050 AD, with continued use into the fourteenth century on some sites. In addition, in several regions examples indicate that certain houses were reused in the seventeenth century or later. The datings are mainly based on samples of charcoal from hearths within the houses. The excavated house grounds have produced only a few finds of animal bones and objects. [14]

There have been lengthy discussions about the cultural and economic context of these house grounds.[15] Today, most researchers relate them to the

13 Storli, '*Stallo*'-*boplassene*; Mulk, *Sirkas*; Bergman and others, 'Kinship and Settlements: Sami Residence Patterns', pp. 97–114; Liedgren and Bergman, 'Aspects of the Construction', pp. 3–26.

14 Mulk, *Sirkas*; Storli, '*Stallo*'-*boplassene*; Liedgren and others, 'Radiocarbon Dating of Prehistoric Hearths', pp. 1276–88; Sommerseth, 'Villreinfangst og tamreindrift i indre Troms', pp. 234–35.

15 Also summarized by Mulk and Bayliss-Smith, 'The Representation of Sámi Cultural Identity on the Cultural Landscape of Northern Sweden'.

Sámi, though with contrasting views of whether they were used during wild reindeer hunts or in early reindeer herding.[16] The emergence of reindeer pastoralism or herding in Sámi societies is an extensive debate in itself, and many researchers believe this development happened after the main period of use of the Stállo houses.[17] Based on the manner in which the houses were constructed, others have suggested that the Stállo sites were in fact winter dwellings for reindeer herders.[18] However, studies of the landscape context of recorded house grounds, and the climatic and environmental conditions during their main period of use, render this theory somewhat unlikely. Considering the harsh weather, lack of firewood, and limited grazing opportunities in the high mountains during winter, this time of year seems less than ideal for reindeer and herders to stay in the areas in question.[19] An alternative explanation is that reindeer herders used the houses in summer or early autumn,[20] but there is no conclusive evidence for this. Investigation of landscape use during the Middle Ages in the Lule Sámi area, Sweden, and in Troms county, Norway, argues rather convincingly for the use of these sites as housing for Sámi autumn hunting expeditions into the mountains. In the fifteenth century, the Stállo house grounds are replaced by scattered hearths in what is known from later times to be grazing lands for reindeer in these areas, suggesting an increased importance of reindeer herding.[21]

An entirely different interpretation is presented by researchers that have used both archaeological comparisons and folkloristic sources to argue that the house grounds are *Norse* settlements related to taxation of and trade with the Sámi.[22] This interpretation is based on comparisons with the house building techniques in Iceland, L'Anse aux Meadows, and other unmistakably Norse settlements, arguing for a similar construction of the Stállo houses with solid turf walls. According to this theory, the walls have later deteriorated to the extent that there is nothing left of them today.

The Sámi name for these unusually large turf house grounds, *Stállo* houses, has been used as a further argument for this interpretation. The idea is that Norse tax collecting practices included violence and coercion that may have caused the remains of their house to be associated with danger and hence

---

16 Manker, *Fångstgropar och stalotomter*; Mulk, *Sirkas*; Storli, 'Stallo'-boplassene'; Liedgren and Bergman, 'Aspects of the Construction of Prehistoric Stállo-Foundations and Stállo-Buildings'; Sommerseth, 'Villreinfangst og tamreindrift i Indre Troms'.

17 Mulk, *Sirkas*; Sommerseth, 'Villreinfangst og tamreindrift i Indre Troms'; Salmi and others, 'Tradition and Transformation in Sámi Animal-Offering Practices', pp. 472–89.

18 Liedgren and Bergman, 'Aspects of the Construction of Prehistoric Stállo-Foundations and Stállo-Buildings'.

19 Storli, 'Stallo'-boplassene', p. 60; Sommerseth, 'Villreinfangst og tamreindrift i Indre Troms', p. 245.

20 Storli, 'Stallo'-boplassene'.

21 Mulk, *Sirkas*; Sommerseth, 'Villreinfangst og tamreindrift i Indre Troms'.

22 Hansen and Olsen, *Hunters in Transition. An Outline of Early Sámi History*, p. 48.

the well-known Sámi mythical troll or ogre figure Stállo.[23] The explanation emphasizes the nineteenth-century interpretations of the Stállo character as related to historical experiences of attacks and robberies. For instance, the famous Sámi preacher Lars Levi Læstadius noted, in the margins of a manuscript about Stállo traditions, that originally this character was nothing other than old Vikings and thieves who settled in desolate woods and sometimes robbed the Sámi of their reindeer.[24] The Norwegian linguist and ethnographer Jens Andreas Friis concurred with this and repeated the opinion about the Viking / robber origin of the Stállo character. He believed the name probably stems from *Staalmanden* (Norwegian for the Steel Man, or the Iron Clad), referring to the Sámi word for steel as *stalle*. He notes that Stállo sometimes appears in a *ruovdegakte* (Sámi), an iron jacket (*-gakte* being part of the Sámi traditional dress). According to Friis, this probably reflects old memories of berserks, the infamous Norse elite warriors, in coats of mail or similar armour[25] (though this is contradictory to the usual description of berserks specifically *not* wearing armour).

Some early twentieth-century researchers also argue that the Stállo house grounds may have been houses for Norse / Germanic people who hunted wild reindeer in nearby reindeer pitfall traps.[26] However, the Swedish ethnographer Ernst Manker rejects this because he found nothing in the Sámi myths about Stállo hunting anything other than beaver.[27]

The arguments for a Norse origin of the house grounds based on a link between Norse tax collectors, Vikings, or villains, and the mythological Stállo, has been criticized for assuming too high a degree of historicity in these myths.[28] The recorded Stállo stories and notions are of relatively late date. Manker notes that none of the seventeenth-century sources on Sámi beliefs even mention the word or name 'Stállo'. The notion of Stállo is, however, explained in the earliest Sámi dictionaries in the eighteenth century as a ghost or a giant, with definitions Manker believes reflect older traditions.[29] Nevertheless, the variation in both Stállo myths and ideas about the Stállo house grounds indicates a more complex relationship between a historical reality of the Middle Ages and the narratives and notions recorded from the eighteenth century onwards. Several of the authors recording such stories note that the Stállo traditions are manifold and vary geographically.[30] In the nineteenth century, recorded descriptions portray him as a large human-like

23 Kjellström, 'Är traditionerna om Stalo historiskt grundade?'; Wepsäläinen, *Stalotomterna*.
24 Cf. Manker, *Fångstgropar och stalotomter*, p. 219.
25 Friis, *Lappiske eventyr og folkesagn*, pp. 75.
26 For example, Drake, *Västerbottenslapparna under förra hälften av 1800-talet*, p. 318.
27 Manker, *Fångstgropar och stalotomter*, p. 228.
28 For example, Holm, 'Review of: A. Wepsäläinen, Stalotomterna', pp. 62–64.
29 Leem, *Beskrivelse over Finmarkens Lapper 1767*; Lindahl and others, *Lexicon Lapponicum*; cf. Manker, *Fångstgropar och stalotomter*, p. 217.
30 Læstadius, *Fragmenter i Lappska Mythologien*; Manker, *Fångstgropar och stalotomter*, p. 219.

creature who was strong and hungry for human flesh, but dimwitted and easy to fool. His paraphernalia were a silver belt, a purse, a staff, and a dog (thus not necessarily an iron shirt or jacket). The Sámi are quoted to think either that Stállo was created at the beginning of time or that he was a human who had washed off his baptism and had sworn to serve Satan.[31] Thus, the association of Stállo with a Norse population is not specifically mentioned in Sámi traditions, and in many cases there is no reason to assume this connection.

A prerequisite for the connection between the Stállo figure and Norse tax collection is that the latter was associated with some sort of danger and force. Over the last forty years of Sámi archaeology and history, the view of the tax collection as a situation where the Norse pressured the Sámi to pay these taxes has been modified by emphasizing the bilateral relationship of exchange, where both parties had something to gain. The Sámi are suggested to have been involved in a redistributive chieftain economy. Besides, they could easily 'disappear' in the vast forests, plains, and mountain areas to avoid direct violence from the Norse.[32] The fact that Sámi languages contain an Old Norse loanword for 'gift', *skeaŋka*, has been suggested to illustrate a more peaceful and mutually rewarding relationship between the two groups. In a Norse Viking Age context, the word meant 'poor' or 'serve', and gift-giving was often related to drinking.[33] Still, it should not be dismissed that the Norse collecting of tax or tribute may have included at least elements of direct or indirect threats of violence and coercion, which may have caused anxiety and conflict both between the two communities and within the Sámi societies.

This external and internal pressure related to increased integration into a Norse redistribution system, as well as the 'taxation' involved in these relations, played out at the same time as the Stállo houses were in use. This may have caused the association of these houses with an uncomfortable situation and thus the unpleasant and even dangerous Stállo.[34] However, the sagas indicate that the trips to collect taxes and trade took place during winter,[35] when transport of goods was easier with sleighs on the snow, and there is no conclusive evidence to suggest that these meetings happened in the Stállo houses in the harsh mountain areas. It is more likely that meetings took place at Sámi winter habitation or gathering sites, whether these were villages where all *siida* (group) members lived for a while or the more sporadic meeting and market places known from later periods in the Swedish inland and in the fjords along the Norwegian coast.[36]

31 Læstadius, *Journal af Petrus Laestadius*; Fellman, *Anteckningar under min vistelse i Lappmarken*, pp. 160–61; cf. Manker, *Fångstgropar och stalotomter*, pp. 217–18.

32 Odner, *Finner og terfinner*; Hansen, *Samisk fangstsamfunn og norsk høvdingeøkonomi*.

33 Schanche, *Graver i ur og berg*, pp. 333–34.

34 Hansen, *Samisk fangstsamfunn og norsk høvdingeøkonomi*, p. 200.

35 *Egilssoga*, chap. 14.

36 Hansen, 'Trade and Markets in Northern Fenno-Scandinavia', pp. 47–79; Bergman and Edlund, 'Birkarlar and Sámi', pp. 52–80.

Thus, neither the association between Stállo and Norse actors, nor the connection between Norse trade and taxation activity and the Stállo house grounds are entirely convincing. Why some Sámi groups have associated this medieval heritage with Stállo will be discussed further below.

Reindeer Pitfall Traps

Reindeer pitfall traps are found all over the historical Sámi areas in northern Fennoscandia and beyond. Thousands have been recorded, and substantial numbers of new sites are discovered every year during archaeological surveys. Estimates suggest that tens of thousands are still to be found spread across the landscape.[37] Today, the structures are usually visible as oval depressions in the ground, with variable depth and circumference, somewhat depending on the topography and degree of erosion after they fell into disuse (Fig. 2). Originally, most pits were built with a narrow rectangular wood case in the bottom, which locked the reindeer's feet so that it had no room to manoeuvre back up out of the pit. Apart from this, the construction details vary, as some have traces of wood cladding further up along the outward sloping walls, while others appear to have had only soil walls. The pits were placed in systems consisting of rows of up to hundreds of traps, and they had fences made from wood or shrubberies between them. The reindeer were led to an opening in the fence and into a concealed pitfall. A few investigated pits have featured pointy rocks at the bottom, and some written sources mention spears and sharpened poles placed at the bottom to kill the animal, but the latter is unknown from archaeological sites.[38] In addition, and especially in the mountain areas of mid- and southern Norway and Sweden, there are many stone-clad pitfall traps with low stone fences leading the animals into them.[39]

Such trapping systems have a long history in Fennoscandia, but there are very few written sources describing Sámi use of pitfalls for reindeer hunting.[40] Traps in Sámi areas have been radiocarbon dated back to the Stone and Bronze Ages. However, many of these datings are uncertain because carbon samples have been taken from the original ground surface under embankments of soil that were thrown out of the pits during the digging of the traps. Hence samples are not usually taken from material directly related to the building or use of the traps, as the organic building materials have often deteriorated completely. Though it is likely that pitfall traps do date far back in time, the majority of radiocarbon datings on construction details and contextual

---

37 For example, Ramqvist, 'Fem Norrland. Om norrländska regioner och deras interaktion', p. 170.

38 Lundius, 'Descriptio Lapponiæ', p. 22; Fellman, *Anteckningar under min vistelse i Lappmarken*, p. 222; Manker, *Fångstgropar och stalotomter*, pp. 205–06.

39 Bang-Andersen, 'Prehistoric Reindeer Trapping by Stone-Walled Pitfalls', pp. 61–69.

40 Though see Niurenius, 'Lappland; eller beskrivning över den nordiska trakt'; Knag, 'Matricul oc beschrifuelse ofuer Findmarchen', p. 21.

Fig. 2: Pitfall trap for wild reindeer by Lake Láhpojohka in Kautokeino, Finnmark, Norway. Photo by Anders Vars.

evidence indicate a main phase of building and use in the Middle Ages.[41] The majority of pitfall traps in Sámi areas of Sweden have been constructed and used between the first and the eleventh century, with a peak in the Viking Age (*c.* 800 AD–*c.* 1050 AD).[42] In the far north-east of Norway, extensive pitfall trap systems are related to turf house grounds that have been dated to the fifteenth and sixteenth centuries, and written sources document wild reindeer hunts in the area into the sixteenth and seventeenth centuries.[43]

The Sámi oral traditions about reindeer pitfall traps were mainly collected in Sweden in the early twentieth century but still contain significant variation. The discrepancies are probably due to a variation in the time elapsed since the traps in different Sámi areas fell into disuse, and thus to the extent their original use was remembered. However, the variations also relate to the local cultural context within which these monuments have been interpreted. In the mid-twentieth century, some Sami informants said that their ancestors had called them traps for elk or reindeer, while others, predominantly in the Pite Sámi area of northern Sweden, said they had been told that they were

41 Manker, *Fångstgropar och stalotomter*; Mulk, *Sirkas*, pp. 167–68; Furset, *Fangstgroper og ildsteder i Kautokeino kommune*; Furset, *Fangstgroper i Karasjok kommune*; Halinen, *Prehistoric Hunters of Northernmost Lappland*; Klaussen, 'Strategisk villreinfangst i Troms', pp. 39, 47; Sommerseth, 'Villreinfangst og tamreindrift i Indre Troms'.
42 Ramqvist, 'Fem Norrland. Om norrländska regioner och deras interaktion'.
43 Odner, *The Varanger Saami*, p. 86; Munch and Munch, 'Utgravningene på Boplassen på Gållevarri'; Vorren, *Villreinfangst i Varanger fram til 1600–1700 årene*, p. 28.

underground houses where their ancestors had hidden from Norse, Russian, and Karelian attackers, or the so-called *Čud*.[44] It may be relevant to mention that the Pite Sámi area features fewer pitfall traps than territories further south.[45]

Čud is a term that has been used in West Sámi contexts about anyone coming from the east to raid and rob them. The exonym is likely to have its origin in the historically documented raiding by Russian and Karelian groups in the thirteenth to fifteenth centuries.[46] At this time, the city-state of Novgorod, situated by Lake Ilmen south of present-day St Petersburg in western Russia, was a major trade centre for fur. Novgorod also had the right to collect taxes from the Sámi as far west as the Lyngen fjord in northern Troms, Norway. To reinforce this right, Novgorod employed Finno-Ugric speaking Karelians as intermediaries. The Russians called all their Finno-Ugric speaking neighbours by the blanket name *Čud* or *Chudes*.[47] Apparently, the Sámi who encountered these groups adopted the term, but it took on a somewhat different meaning and subsequently gained an additional mythical content. There are abundant local legends about the danger of the *Čud* and how the Sámi have avoided or fallen victim to them. One recurring legend is about a young man who outwits the *Čud* by pretending to guide them through the landscape when, in fact, he leads them off a cliff.[48] The frequently recurring *Čud* prefix in Sámi place names is partly related to such legends,[49] but, equally, it provides evidence of the actual presence of Karelian and Russian groups in Sámi areas in the Middle Ages. The fact that the Sámi related unfamiliar aspects of the landscape to this particularly popular mythical concept is hardly surprising.

The folklore related to the pitfall traps has not had much bearing on the archaeological and ethnographic interpretations of these sites. As described above, some researchers have suggested that the ones situated close to Stállo house ground sites may have been used by Norse groups, while discussion has been lacking about whether the traditional association with the *Čud* could indicate a historical connection between Russian or Karelian groups and the trapping systems. In any case, the traditional explanations are concentrated on the pits as Sámi hiding places rather than suggesting foreigners from the east used them. The discussion below will consider why the Sámi related these features in their landscapes specifically to this threat and the Sámi handling of it.

44 Johansson, 'Om vildrensfångst på Kebnekaisemassivet', pp. 6–7; cf. Manker, *Fångstgropar och stalotomter*, pp. 19–20.

45 cf. Ramqvist, 'Fem Norrland. Om norrländska regioner och deras interaktion', fig. 10.

46 For example, 'Oddveria Annall' and 'Henrik Høyers Annaler', in *Islandske Annaler indtil 1578*, ed. by Storm, pp. 70, 73, 483–84; *DN* I, no. 670 (1420); Hansen, 'Interaction between Northern European Sub-Arctic Societies during the Middle Ages', pp. 31–95.

47 Hansen and Olsen, *Hunters in Transition*, pp. 146–50.

48 The myth was popularized in the Oscar-nominated film *Pathfinder* (Norw. *Veiviseren*), directed by Nils Gaup.

49 Bratrein, 'Russesagn i Nord-Norge'.

'Circular Offering Sites'

The 'circular offering sites' currently operates as a very wide category, covering a large variety of smaller and larger stone circles and other more or less similar constructions. A recent study of 161 suggested circular offering sites in present-day Norway indicates that the structures included in the category feature substantial variation in size, morphology, topographical placement, landscape, and cultural contexts. A majority of sites are not confirmed as ritual or offering sites by archaeological finds, historical sources, ethnographic evidence, or place names. These should be reconsidered in terms of original function and use, which may include fireplaces, graves, turf- or haystack foundations, house grounds, tent rings, results of children's play, and natural features, to mention some substantiated reinterpretations.[50]

However, certain structures in the counties of Finnmark and northern Troms do indeed form a defined category with clearly standardized measurements and construction details that cannot be explained by such alternative functions (Fig. 3). A total of forty-two recorded sites in northern Norway are considered to fall within this uniform category, whereof twenty-five are confirmed by surveys and other investigations. Apart from three examples of somewhat larger enclosures, these structures measure between 470 and 760 cm in inner diameter. They are placed in rocky terrain and feature solidly built stone dry walls of up to 140 cm in extant height and with substantial widths. The walls are built from rocks and slabs taken from the enclosed area, creating semi-subterraneous floor levels. Where pole photography or more systematic measurements have been available, it is clear that the structures tend to have an angular inner shape (often pentagonal or hexagonal). The walls are thought to have been much higher than today's eroded remains, some probably reaching 2 m or more. Remains of wood in some of the structures indicate additional wooden fences. There are usually no signs of entrances, fireplaces, or burials. Apart from the remains of wood, documented finds are normally limited to a variety of animal bones. Datings indicate that these stone-wall enclosures were established from the fourteenth, or possibly even the thirteenth, century onwards, and that they fell into disuse sometime between 1450 AD and 1650 AD. However, some have signs of reuse in later centuries, including newer depositions of coins and other objects in the late twentieth and early twenty-first century.[51]

Since the nineteenth century, it has been accepted, both in local and academic discourse, that the structures were remains of Sámi ritual places, functioning as offering sites. However, no older written sources support this interpretation. In fact, none of the sources that otherwise describe Sámi offering sites or offering-site types mention stone circles. The historiography

---

50 Spangen, *Circling Concepts*.
51 Spangen, "'It Could Be One Thing or Another'"; Spangen, *Circling Concepts*.

Fig. 3: So-called 'circular offering site' by Lake Geaimmejávri in Karasjok, Finnmark, Norway. Photo by author.

from around 1850 onwards is highly inter-referential, with little or no new evidence coming to light to support the offering-site explanation. Furthermore, it is unclear whether the nineteenth-century descriptions were, in fact, informed by local Sámi traditions. While it cannot be positively refuted that the stone dry-wall enclosures in question were used as ritual or offering sites in the Middle Ages, the documented uncertainties have resulted in alternative hypotheses. A recent study concludes that the construction details, topographical positions, and assemblages of animal bones in the structures are highly compatible with historical and ethnographic descriptions of traps for wolves and other large predators, like fox and wolverine. This is further substantiated by certain place names and recorded traditions about the use of equivalent constructions as wolf traps.[52]

There are limited local traditions about the sites in question, but some local Sámi individuals or groups today are considering the remains of particular

52 Spangen, "'It Could Be One Thing or Another'", pp. 67–80. Magnus, *Historia om de nordiska folken*, chap. 18:13; Qvigstad, *Lappiske eventyr og sagn fra Varanger*, pp. 535, 537; Itkonen, *Suomen Lappalaiset Vuoteen*; Henriksson, *Popular Hunting and Trapping in Norrland*, p. 48; Álvares and others, 'Os Fojos Dos Lobos Na Península Ibérica', pp. 57–77. Spangen, *Circling Concepts*; Spangen, 'Anomaly or Myth?'.

importance and treat them with a certain reverence. If we were to consider this as a reminiscence of a medieval sacredness, it would entail a Sámi tradition preserved throughout the centuries. However, the question remains as to the extent such traditions are inspired by more recent scholarly studies and explanations of the sites, instead of the other way around. It can be argued that the noted traditions are concentrated in areas and at sites where there has been an active dissemination of the offering-site explanation through writing, museum work, school teaching, ethnographic field work, and tourist information in the nineteenth and twentieth centuries. In one case, datings made evident that depositions in an enclosure only went back to the time of the official recording of this site as a Sámi offering site in 1973.[53] This emphasizes the complexity of tradition-making and the difficulty of separating 'original' or ancient traits from newly incorporated knowledge.

One may or may not agree with the wolf-trap explanation for the original building and use of the larger, standardized stone dry-wall enclosures; the prolific adding of often highly dissimilar structures to the same category from around 1950 onwards, especially in Norway and Sweden over the last twenty years,[54] is still highly interesting. This practice reflects the specific socio-political climate in the Sámi areas in question during these decades, where there has been a pronounced demand from the majority societies that Sámi groups prove their (pre-) historic presence to obtain property and usufruct rights. The emphasis on an offering-site interpretation can be related to a persistent stereotype, and to some extent to an auto-stereotype, of the Sámi as particularly 'ritual' and 'close to nature', arguably amounting to a central myth about the Sámi in the past and present.[55] The idea of 'typical' Sámi (ritual) use of such constructions has contributed to proliferating and maintaining the interpretation of increasing numbers of various stone circles as ritual sites.[56] This ascribed meaning has substantial significance for the understanding of the Sámi, their religion, culture, and landscape use during the Middle Ages.

Archaeology and Oral Traditions

The relationship between oral traditions and other alternative interpretations on the one hand, and the academic interpretations of heritage sites on the

53 Teigmo, 'Samisk-etnografisk avdelings undersøkelser i forbindelse med de planlagte reguleringer i Skibotnvassdraget'; Äikäs and Spangen, 'New Users and Changing Traditions', pp. 95–121; Spangen, *Circling Concepts*.
54 For example, Manker, *Lapparnas heliga ställen*, pp. 25–26; Vorren and Eriksen, *Samiske offerplasser i Varanger*; Huggert, 'A Church at Lycksele and a Sacrificial Site on Altarberget', pp. 51–75; Edvinger and Broadbent, 'Saami Circular Sacrificial Sites in Northern Coastal Sweden', pp. 24–55.
55 Cf. Schanche, 'Kulturminner, identitet og etnisitet', pp. 55–64.
56 Spangen, *Circling Concepts*.

other has been widely debated in archaeology, especially within branches that may be defined as 'public archaeology' or 'indigenous archaeology', including studies in Sámi contexts.[57] Especially in non-literate societies, the oral traditions pertaining to monuments of the past *are* the local, indigenous history. According to post-colonial theoretical approaches, the inclusion of such ethno-histories in Western academic discourse can benefit the democratization and decolonization of archaeology and other scientific projects and practices. A growing number of researchers are of the opinion that cooperation with local communities before, during, and after research projects may be beneficial, not only for ethical reasons, but also in terms of opening up new epistemological and methodological approaches. However, the practical implementation of this aim can be complicated, and there is no singular correct method for combining archaeology and local traditions about the past.

One aspect is the necessary ethical considerations concerning local participation and the ownership and use of traditional knowledge.[58] On a more practical level, a precondition for integrating local traditions in archaeological studies is to gain an understanding of what these traditions represent. It is a basic acknowledgment that oral traditions are generally part of a different discourse than academic knowledge, a discourse that has a multitude of other narrative functions beyond producing a 'truth' about the past.[59] Furthermore, such narratives are continuously adjusted to changing contexts and local environments. Adjustments tend to happen according to how groups and societies wish to portray themselves through their myths and legends (a central topic to discussions about collective memory) and according to what narratives individual storytellers identify with.[60] Modifications often concern aspects of the tradition that are perceived as less important to the main message. The remaining core ideas, and quite often even the structure and plot, can plausibly be identified as that which has been central and influential to the community.[61] This means that individual storytellers can influence traditions, but folklore is also a group-defining practice. Knowledge about certain types of stories, as well as when and how to tell them, may reflect or define the individual's in-group position.[62]

---

57 Burström, *Mångtydiga fornlämningar*; Solli, *Narratives of Veøy*; Gazin-Schwartz and Holtorf, *Archaeology and Folklore*; Damm, 'Archaeology, Ethno-history and Oral Traditions'; Skandfer, 'Ethics in the Landscape'.

58 For example, Barlindhaug, 'Mapping Complexity'.

59 Cf. Damm, 'Archaeology, Ethno-history and Oral Traditions'. Solli, 'Narratives of Veøy. On the Poetics and Scientifics of Archaeology'.

60 Eskeröd, *Årets äring. Etnologiska studier i skördens och julens tro och sed*; Dégh, 'The Approach to Worldview in Folk Narrative Study', pp. 243–52; Eriksen and Selberg, *Tradisjon og fortelling*, pp. 59, 220; Halbwachs, *On Collective Memory*; Hodne, 'Eventyrfortellerne som forskningsfelt', pp. 25–40.

61 Damm, 'Archaeology, Ethno-history and Oral Traditions', p. 77 with references.

62 Dundes, *Interpreting Folklore*.

By extension, folklore can serve to define an opposition to other groups. In Antonio Gramsci's view, folklore can even function as part of class struggle, when understood as the culture of oppressed groups like workers and peasants in opposition to the hegemonic bourgeois culture and worldview.[63] Mikhail Bahktin agrees that folk culture can function as social critique, but emphasizes its role as an accepted way of expressing frustrations — an outlet that most often *does not* create lasting social change.[64] Thus, oral traditions and myths of an indigenous group in a colonized situation may convey social critique, cultural subversiveness, and the venting of frustration in difficult situations. Importantly, the same stories may thematize different social, religious, or political antagonisms according to the specific time and place where they are retold. This may be done by, for instance, changing who is ascribed the role as protagonist or villain in otherwise seemingly stereotypical stories.[65]

The way indigenous people and other local groups relate to their own traditions versus scholarly narratives about the past vary both between groups and within communities. The encounter between two knowledge systems can be more, or less, problematic. Studies show that in some cases new and even contrasting archaeological evidence and interpretations may be incorporated as parallel storylines into local discourses without diminishing existing narratives.[66] However, we should be wary of reproducing a stereotypical opposition between the local or indigenous worldview or discourse and the (predominantly Western) academic narratives. In Sámi contexts, the rather harsh assimilation measures during the nineteenth and twentieth centuries have partly resulted in alienation from previous traditions and relatively extensive integration of academic knowledge. Despite examples of oral traditions that are clearly of substantial age, many older narratives have been preserved primarily through academic recording.[67] Again, different individuals and communities will necessarily be differently influenced by traditional and academic narratives, respectively, and this affects the maintenance and adjustments of oral traditions.

Understanding oral traditions therefore includes exploring the changing cultural and historical context and significance of any given myth, and the role that different groups and individuals have in maintaining, but also in changing, these traditions over time. Importantly, even enduring and widespread folklore and traditions are usually less unchanging or uniform than they may seem at first glance.

---

63 Gramsci, *Selections from Cultural Writings*, p. 195; Eriksen and Selberg, *Tradisjon og fortelling*, p. 22.
64 Bakhtin, *Rabelais och skrattets historia*.
65 Eriksen and Selberg, *Tradisjon og fortelling*, p. 221.
66 For example, Solli, *Narratives of Veøy*; Nilsen, *Brytninger mellom lokal og akademisk kulturminnekunnskap*.
67 For example Qvigstad, *Lappiske eventyr og sagn*.

As is evident from the literature cited above, a focus on fairytales and myths as extremely old remains of cultural facts preserved in the 'people'[68] is an outdated understanding of folklore in general. However, there is still a tendency to implicitly view indigenous oral traditions as especially archaic and well preserved, and thus as better sources for historical facts than traditions in what is understood as contrasting, modern, Western communities.[69] It is all the more important to emphasize that Sámi worldviews and values, and in turn their myths and folklore, have obviously varied, developed, and changed over time, too. The chronological and geographical variations in ideas about, for instance, medieval monuments may still be interesting to explore as potential sources for historical facts about these sites, but equally as sources for the Sámi (local) social and cultural situation, worldview, and self-understanding over time.

Sámi Myths, Medieval Realities, and Modern Stereotypes

The examples described in this article illustrate that the Sámi have constructed legends and myths about remains from the past and enigmatic features in the landscape in a variety of ways. Some of these traditions include elements of historical facts, but overemphasizing the historicity of the narratives equals an implicit understanding of the Sámi as more 'traditional' than other people. Hence, it is important that the historicity, as well as the multilayered and complex purpose and context of local narratives about monuments and the past, are evaluated in each specific case.

The myths and legends related to the Stállo house grounds, reindeer pitfall traps, and 'circular offering sites' describe different aspects of the Sámi pasts and Sámi understanding of the world and themselves. In general, the Stállo myths can be seen to articulate chaotic forces that the Sámi have dealt with in different ways. Stállo is somewhat undefined and has a changing character in different stories, but he represents a definite danger that has to be avoided, usually through wit rather than force. Relating this figure specifically to a group of Norse tax collectors or roaming villains in the Viking Age is not a plausible understanding, even if elements such as the notion of an 'iron shirt' may have derived from meetings with warriors in chain-mail at this time, or at some later point in history.

I find the interpretation of the Stállo house grounds as specialized medieval Sámi hunting stations convincing. The main phase of use for the houses was the ninth to the fifteenth century. The construction, placement, and internal row organization would have represented a relatively foreign social and economic adaptation by the seventeenth or eighteenth century. This, and

---

68   Dundes, 'The Devolutionary Premise in Folklore Theory', p. 6.
69   Eriksen and Selberg, *Tradisjon og fortelling*, p. 45.

the mere size of the houses, may explain the association with mythical giants, a typical explanation known from other cultural contexts, too. Hence, this mythical connection probably falls within a category that is not especially useful either to specific archaeological studies of the house grounds or the historical context of the Sámi at the time.

The myths about the pitfall traps as hiding places from the Čud have not been used in archaeological interpretations of these sites; they have only been noted as a local historical background. The regional variations are noteworthy, as some Sámi in the early twentieth century were cognizant of the historical information that these pits had been used for trapping reindeer (or elks). It could be interesting to compare these variations with traces of actual Russian / Karelian medieval activity, correlated with the age of the pitfall traps in each area. It is, however, similarly interesting to evaluate whether the (early) modern situation of the Sámi have been particularly difficult in areas were the legend of the Čud connection has been maintained, for instance, due to harsh measures during the intensified Christianization and state integration in the seventeenth and eighteenth centuries, or the assimilation processes in the nineteenth and twentieth centuries. Such contemporary hardships may well have made these legends about past difficulties more relevant in some regions than others.

The background for the understanding of the 'circular offering sites' as ritual sites is unclear, as it may have been based on local Sámi traditions or a scholarly interpretation. It has certainly spread and become general 'knowledge' today because of scholarly and popular scientific discussions, publications, and other dissemination. In any case, the increased use of the categorization over the last few decades has to be seen in the context of a socio-political situation where the Sámi have been under pressure to prove their past use of certain landscapes through archaeological means, in scientific, political, and legal contexts, including court cases.[70] Durable ritual sites present a particularly efficient argument in this discourse, due to a lasting stereotype, and auto-stereotype, from the Viking Age onwards of the Sámi as particularly 'prone to magic', or today rather as spiritual people in close contact with nature. These stereotypes are so prevalent that they can be argued to be part of the Sámi 'central myth',[71] which influences the view and understanding of their history, including their 'medieval selves'. Without diminishing the importance of rituals and sacred landscapes in Sámi culture, I would claim that the promotion of this sort of explanation may obscure the diversity of Sámi landscapes, culture, and history.[72]

---

70 Bull, 'Samisk forhistorie og samiske rettigheter i et juridisk perspektiv', pp. 40–49; Zachrisson, 'Fanns det samer i Härjedalen i äldre tid?', pp. 56–61.
71 Schanche, 'Kulturminner, identitet og etnisitet', p. 55.
72 Spangen, Circling Concepts; Spangen, 'Anomaly or Myth? Sami Circular Offering Sites in Medieval Northern Norway'.

Conclusion

The materiality of archaeological remains, especially large, clearly visible, and enigmatic constructions, tends to generate myths and legends among the people who interact with them in the landscape. This may involve historically accurate traditions, since place and specific landscape features are aids to maintain such common memories over time. These are actualized every time individuals or groups encounter the same or similar features.

However, the repetition of myths and legends include a constant renegotiation of these traditions, since a story is never only retold, but reconfigured and reintroduced to the audience. In addition to individual influences, oral traditions are also shaped by group dynamics, current hardships that highlight certain topics, and other time- and place-specific conditions. The multilayered information contained in myths therefore has to be interpreted in view of the local social and historical context. Only from such a contextual understanding is it possible to identify in what way and to what extent myths can inform archaeological interpretations or questions.

Without denying the occurrence of ancient traditions, I find it important to oppose a lingering notion that indigenous oral traditions in general are particularly well preserved and therefore better sources for ancient historical facts than their 'Western' equivalents. On the contrary, indigenous folklore is, of course, equally dynamic and contextual, functioning as a multi-levelled instrument of self-identification and social negotiation. The examples in this article demonstrate this point in terms of how Sámi myths about their medieval cultural heritage sites are also constant reinterpretations of their past and present identities, including their 'medieval selves'.

Works Cited

Primary Sources

DN = Diplomatarium Norvegicum. Oldbreve til Kundskab om Norges indre og ydre Forhold, Sprog, Slægter, Sæder, Lovgivning og Rettergang i Middelalderen, ed. by Christian C. A. Lange and others, 23 vols (Christiania / Oslo: Mallings Forlagshandel, 1847–2011) <https://www.dokpro.uio.no/dipl_norv/diplom_felt.html> [accessed 3 October 2017]

Egilssoga, trans. by Leiv Heggstad and Magne Heggstad, in Ættesoger. Egilssoga. Soga om Gisle Sursson, ed. by Hallvard Magerøy, Odd Nordland, and Per Tylden, Den norrøne litteraturen, 3 (Oslo: Samlaget, 1962)

Islandske Annaler indtil 1578, ed. by Gustav Storm (Oslo: Norsk historisk kjeldeskrift-institutt, 1977)

Leem, Knud, Beskrivelse over Finmarkens Lapper: 1767, ed. by Asbjørn Nesheim (Copenhagen Rosenkilde og Bagger, 1975)

Læstadius, Lars Levi, *Fragmenter i Lappska Mythologien*, ed. by Nilla Outakoski. NIF Publications, 37 (Åbo: Nordiska institutet för folkdiktning, 1997)

Læstadius, Petrus. *Journal af Petrus Laestadius för andra året af hans tjenstgöring såsom missionaire i Lappmarken* (Stockholm: Zacharias Häggström, 1833)

Lindahl, Eric, Johan Öhrling, and Johan Ihre, *Lexicon Lapponicum cum Interpretatione Vocabulorum Sveco-Latina et Indice Svecano Lapponico* (Holmiae: Joh. Georg. Lange, 1780)

Lundius, Nicolaus, 'Descriptio Lapponiæ', in *Berättelser om Samerna i 1600-talets Sverige. Faksimileutgåva av de s.k. prästrelationerna m.m. först publicerade av K. B. Wiklund 1897–1909*, ed. by Karl Bernhard Wiklund, Kungl. Skytteanska Samfundets Handlingar, 27 (Umeå: Skytteanska samfundet, 1983)

Niurenius, Olaus Petri, 'Lappland; eller Beskrivning över Den Nordiska Trakt, som Lapparne Bebo i de Avlägsnaste Delarne av Skandien eller Sverge', in *Berättelser om Samerna i 1600-talets Sverige. Faksimileutgåva av de s.k. prästrelationerna m.m. först publicerade av K. B. Wiklund 1897–1909*, ed. by Karl Bernhard Wiklund, Kungl. Skytteanska Samfundets Handlingar, 27 (Umeå: Skytteanska samfundet, 1983)

Secondary Works

Äikäs, Tiina, and Marte Spangen, 'New Users and Changing Traditions — (Re) Defining Sami Offering Sites', *European Journal of Archaeology*, 19.1 (2016), 95–121

Álvares, Francisco, Pedro Alonso, Pablo Sierra, and Francisco Petrucci-Fonseca, 'Os Fojos dos Lobos na Península Ibérica. Sua Inventariação, Caracterização e Conservação', *Galemys*, 12 (2000), 57–77

Andrén, Anders, 'Places, Monuments, and Objects: The Past in Ancient Scandinavia', *Scandinavian Studies*, 85.3 (2013), 267–81

Bakhtin, Michail, *Rabelais och skrattets historia. François Rabelais' verk och den folkliga kulturen under medeltiden och renässansen*, trans. by Lars Fyhr (Gråbo: Anthropos, 1986)

Bang-Andersen, Sveinung, 'Prehistoric Reindeer Trapping by Stone-Walled Pitfalls: News and Views', in *From Bann Flakes to Bushmills. Papers in Honour of Professor Peter Woodman*, ed. by Nyree Finlay, Sinead McCartan, Nicky Milner, and Caroline Wickham-Jones, 61–69 (Oxford: Oxbow, 2009), pp. 61–69

Barlindhaug, Stine, *Cultural Sites, Traditional Knowledge and Participatory Mapping: Long-Term Land Use in a Sámi Community in Coastal Norway* (Tromsø: University of Tromsø, 2013) <https://munin.uit.no/ handle/10037/5405> [accessed 22 April 2014]

——, 'Mapping Complexity: Archaeological Sites and Historic Land Use Extent in Sami Community in Arctic Norway', *Fennoscandia Archaeologica*, 29 (2012), 105–24

Bergman, Ingela, and Lars-Erik Edlund, 'Birkarlar and Sámi — Inter-Cultural Contacts beyond State Control: Reconsidering the Standing of External

Tradesmen (Birkarlar) in Medieval Sámi Societies', *Acta Borealia*, 33.1 (2016), 52–80

Bergman, Ingela, Lars Liedgren, Lars Östlund, and Olle Zackrisson, 'Kinship and Settlements: Sami Residence Patterns in the Fennoscandian Alpine Areas around AD 1000', *Arctic Anthropology*, 45.1 (2008), 97–114

Bratrein, Håvard Dahl, 'Russesagn i Nord-Norge', *Ottar: Naboer ved Ishavet*, 94–95 (1977), 5–12

Braudel, Fernand, *The Mediterranean and the Mediterranean World in the Age of Philip II: 1* (London: Collins, 1972)

Bull, Kirsti Strøm, 'Samisk forhistorie og samiske rettigheter i et juridisk perspektiv', in *Samisk forhistorie. Rapport fra konferanse i Lakselv 5.-6. September 2002*, Várjjat Sámi Musea Čállosat, 1 (Varangerbotn: Varanger samiske museum, 2004), pp. 40–49

Burström, Mats, *Mångtydiga fornlämningar. En studie av innebörder som tillskrivits fasta fornlämningar i Österrekarne härad, Södermanland*, Stockholm Archaeological Reports, 27 (Stockholm: Institutionen för arkeologi, University of Stockholm, 1993)

Burström, Mats, Björn Winberg, and Torun Zachrisson, *Fornlämningar och folkminnen* (Stockholm: Riksantikvarieämbetet, 1997)

Damm, Charlotte, 'Archaeology, Ethno-history and Oral Traditions: Approaches to the Indigenous Past', *Norwegian Archaeological Review*, 38.2 (2005), 73–87

Dégh, Linda, 'The Approach to Worldview in Folk Narrative Study', *Western Folklore*, 53.3 (1994), 243–52

Drake, Sigrid, *Västerbottenslapparna under förra hälften av 1800-talet — etnografiska studier*, Lapparne och deras land, 7 (Uppsala: Almqvist & Wiksell, 1918)

Dundes, Alan, 'The Devolutionary Premise in Folklore Theory', *Journal of the Folklore Institute*, 6.1 (1969), 5–19

——, *Interpreting Folklore* (Bloomington: Indiana University Press, 1980)

Ecko-Hawk, Roger, 'Forging a New Ancient History for Native America', in *Native Americans and Archaeologists: Stepping Stones to Common Ground*, ed. by Nina Swidler, Kurt Dongoske, Roger Anyon, and Alan Downer (Walnut Creek: Altamira, 1997), pp. 88–102

Eriksen, Anne, and Torunn Selberg, *Tradisjon og fortelling. En innføring i folkloristikk* (Oslo: Pax, 2006)

Eskeröd, Albert, *Årets äring. Etnologiska studier i skördens och julens tro och sed*, Nordiska museets handlingar, 26 (Stockholm: Nordiska museet, 1947)

Fellman, Jacob, *Anteckningar under min vistelse i Lappmarken*, II: *Ur lappsk mytologi och lappländsk sägen* (Helsingfors, 1906)

Flood, Josephine, *Archaeology of the Dreamtime* (Sydney: Collins, 1983)

Friis, J. A., *Lappiske Eventyr og Folkesagn* (Christiania: Cammermeyer, 1871)

Furset, Ole Jakob, *Fangstgroper i Karasjok kommune. Rapport fra forskningsutgraving 3/7-4/8 1995*, Stensilserie B, 39 (Tromsø: Arkeologiseksjonen, Institutt for samfunnsvitenskap, University of Tromsø, 1996)

——, *Fangstgroper og ildsteder i Kautokeino kommune. Rapport fra forskningsutgraving 24. juli-3. september 1994*, Stensilserie B, 37 (Tromsø:

Arkeologiseksjonen, Institutt for samfunnsvitenskap, University of Tromsø, 1995)

Gazin-Schwartz, Amy, and Cornelius Holtorf, *Archaeology and Folklore* (London: Routledge, 1999)

Gibson, James J., *The Ecological Approach to Visual Perception* (Boston: Houghton Mifflin, 1979)

Gramsci, Antonio, *Selections from Cultural Writings* (London: Lawrence and Wishart, 1985)

Halbwachs, Maurice, *On Collective Memory*, ed., trans. and with an introduction by Lewis A. Coser, The Heritage of Sociology Series (University of Chicago Press, 1992)

Halinen, Petri, *Prehistoric Hunters of Northernmost Lappland: Settlement Patterns and Subsistence Strategies*, Iskos, 14 (Helsinki: Finnish Antiquarian Society, 2005)

Hansen, Lars Ivar, 'Interaction between Northern European Sub-Arctic Societies during the Middle Ages: Indigenous Peoples, Peasants and State Builders', in *Two Studies on the Middle Ages*, ed. by Magnus Rindal, KULTs Skriftserie, 66 (Oslo: Research Council of Norway, 1996), pp. 31–95

——, *Samisk fangstsamfunn og norsk høvdingeøkonomi* (Oslo: Novus, 1990)

——, 'Trade and Markets in Northern Fenno-Scandinavia AD 1550–1750', *Acta Borealia*, 1.2 (1984), pp. 47–79

Hansen, Lars Ivar, and Bjørnar Olsen, *Hunters in Transition: An Outline of Early Sámi History*, The Northern World, 63 (Leiden: Brill, 2014)

Hastrup, Kirsten, and Preben Meulengracht Sørensen, *Tradition og historieskrivning. Kilderne til Nordens ældste historie*, Acta Jutlandica, 63.2 (Århus: Aarhus Universitetsforlag, 1987)

Henriksson, Heidi, *Popular Hunting and Trapping in Norrland*, Early Norrland, 6 (Stockholm: Kungl. Vitterhets-, historie- och antikvitetsaka, 1978)

Hodne, Ørnulf, 'Eventyrfortellerne som forskningsfelt', in *Kunnskap om kultur. Folkloristiske dialoger*, ed. by Knut Aukrust and Anne Eriksen (Oslo: Novus, 1999), pp. 25–40

Holm, Olof, 'Review of: A. Wepsäläinen, Stalotomterna. En kritisk granskning av forskningsläget rörande en omdiskuterad fornlämningstyp', *Fornvännen*, 111.1 (2016), 62–64

Huggert, Anders, 'A Church at Lycksele and a Sacrificial Site on Altarberget: The Two Worlds of the Saami', *Acta Borealia*, 17.1 (2000), 51–75

Ingold, Tim, *The Perception of the Environment: Essays on Livelihood, Dwelling and Skill* (London: Routeledge, 2000)

Itkonen, Toivo Immanuel, *Suomen Lappalaiset Vuoteen 1945*, II (Porvoo: WSOY, 1948)

Johansson, Carl, 'Om vildrensfångst på Kebnekaisemassivet', *Samefolkets egen tidning*, 1950 (1), pp. 6–7

Kjellström, Rolf, 'Är traditionerna om Stalo historiskt grundade?', in *Fataburen 1976* (Stockholm: Nordiska museet, 1976), pp. 155–78

Klaussen, Monica, *Strategisk villreinfangst i Troms. En analyse av fangstgropanlegg og deres beliggenhet, oppbygging og bruk* (Tromsø: University of Tromsø, 2008) <https://munin.uit.no/handle/10037/1760> [accessed 20 May 2013]

Klindt-Jensen, Ole, *A History of Scandinavian Archaeology*, The World of
    Archaeology (London: Thames and Hudson, 1975)
Klintberg, Bengt af, *Svenska folksägner* (Stockholm: PAN / Norstedt, 1977)
Knag, Niels, 'Matricul oc Beschrifuelse ofuer Findmarchen for Anno 1694', in
    Finnmark Omkring 1700. Aktstykker og Oversikter, 1, Nordnorske Samlinger, 1
    (Oslo: Etnografisk museum, 1932), pp. 1–32
Liedgren, Lars, and Ingela Bergman, 'Aspects of the Construction of Prehistoric
    Stállo-Foundations and Stállo-Buildings', *Acta Borealia*, 26.1 (June 2009), 3–26
Liedgren, Lars G., Ingela M. Bergman, Greger Hörnberg, Olle Zackrisson, Erik
    Hellberg, Lars Östlund, and Thomas H. DeLuca, 'Radiocarbon Dating of
    Prehistoric Hearths in Alpine Northern Sweden: Problems and Possibilities',
    Journal of Archaeological Science, 34.8 (2007), 1276–88
Lund, Julie, and Elisabeth Arwill-Nordbladh, 'Divergent Ways of Relating to
    the Past in the Viking Age', *European Journal of Archaeology*, 19.3 (July 2016),
    415–38
Manker, Ernst, *Fångstgropar och stalotomter. Kulturlämningar från lapsk forntid*, Acta
    Lapponica, 15 (Stockholm: Geber, 1960)
——, *Lapparnas heliga ställen. Kultplatser och offerkult i belysning av nordiska
    museets och landsantikvariernas fältundersökningar*, Acta Lapponica, 13
    (Stockholm: Almqvist and Wiksell, 1957)
Mulk, Inga-Maria, *Sirkas: Ett samiskt fångstsamhälle i förändring Kr.f.-1600 e.Kr.*
    (Umeå: Umeå University, 1994)
Mulk, Inga-Maria, and Tim Bayliss-Smith, 'The Representation of Sámi Cultural
    Identity in the Cultural Landscape of Northern Sweden', in *The Archaeology
    and Anthropology of Landscape*, ed. by Robert Layton and Peter Ucko
    (London: Routledge, 1999), pp. 358–96
Munch, Jens Storm, and Gerd Stamsø Munch, 'Utgravningene På Boplassen På
    Gållevarri', in *Villreinfangst i Varanger fram til 1600–1700-årene*, ed. by Ørnulv
    Vorren, Tromsø Museums Skrifter, 28 (Stonglandseidet: Nordkalott-forlaget,
    1998), pp. 106–33
Nilsen, Gørill, *Brytninger mellom lokal og akademisk kulturminnekunnskap. En
    analyse av fortidsforestillinger i Nord-Troms og Lofoten* (Tromsø: University of
    Tromsø, 2003)
Odner, Knut, *Finner og terfinner. Etniske prosesser i det nordlige Fenno-Skandinavia*
    (Oslo: University of Oslo, 1983)
——, *The Varanger Saami. Habitation and Economy AD 1200–1900*, Instituttet for
    Sammenlignende Kulturforskning, Serie B, Skrifter, 86 (Oslo: Scandinavian
    University Press, 1992)
Olaus Magnus, *Historia om de nordiska folken* (Stockholm: Gidlund / Nordiska
    museet / Stockholms universitet, 1976)
Olsen, Bjørnar, *In Defense of Things. Archaeology and the Ontology of Objects*
    (Lanham: AltaMira, 2010)
——, 'Material Culture after Text: Re-membering Things', *Norwegian
    Archaeological Review*, 36.2 (2003), 87–104
Qvigstad, Just, *Lappiske eventyr og sagn fra Varanger* (Oslo: Aschehoug, 1927)

Ramqvist, Per H., 'Fem Norrland. Om norrländska regioner och deras interaktion', *Arkeologi i Norr*, 10 (2007), 153–80

Salmi, Anna-Kaisa, Tiina Äikäs, Marte Spangen, Markus Fjellström, and Inga-Maria Mulk, 'Tradition and Transformation in Sámi Animal-Offering Practices', *Antiquity*, 92.362 (2018), 472–89

Schanche, Audhild, *Graver i ur og berg. Samisk gravskikk og religion fra forhistorisk til nyere tid* (Karasjok: Davvi girji, 2000)

——, 'Horizontal and Vertical Perceptions of Saami Landscapes', in *Landscape, Law and Customary Rights*, ed. by Michael Jones and Audhild Schanche, Diedut, 3 (Kautokeino: Nordic Saami Institute, 2004), pp. 1–10

——, 'Kulturminner, identitet og etnisitet', *Dugnad*, 19.4 (1993), 55–64

Skandfer, Marianne, 'Ethics in the Landscape: Prehistory Archaeology and Local Sámi Knowledge in Interior Finnmark, Northern Norway', *Arctic Anthropology*, 46.1–2 (2009), 89–102

Solli, Brit, *Narratives of Veøy. An investigation into the poetics and scientifics of archaeology*, Universitetets Oldsaksamlings Skrifter, n.s., 19 (Oslo: Universitetets oldsaksamling, 1996)

——, 'Narratives of Veøy. On the Poetics and Scientifics of Archaeology', in *Cultural Identity and Archaeology: The Construction of European Communities*, ed. by Siân Jones, Clive Gamble, and Paul Graves-Brown, Theoretical Archaeology Group (TAG) (London: Routledge, 1996), pp. 209–27

Sommerseth, Ingrid, 'Villreinfangst og tamreindrift i Indre Troms. Belyst ved samiske boplasser mellom 650 og 1923' (Tromsø: University of Tromsø, 2009) <https://munin.uit.no/handle/10037/2376> [accessed 3 May 2012]

Spangen, Marte, 'Anomaly or Myth? Sami Circular Offering Sites in Medieval Northern Norway', in *Religion, Cults and Rituals in the Medieval Rural Environment*, ed. by Christiane Bis-Worch and Claudia Theune, Ruralia, 11 (Leiden: Sidestone, 2017), pp. 39–51

——, *Circling Concepts. A Critical Archaeological Analysis of the Notion of Stone Circles as Sami Offering Sites* (Stockholm: Department of Archaeology and Classical Studies, Stockholm University, 2016)

——, '"It Could Be One Thing or Another" — On the Construction of an Archaeological Category', *Fennoscandia Archaeologica*, 30 (2013), 67–80

Storli, Inger, *'Stallo'-boplassene. Spor etter de første fjellsamer?*, Instituttet for sammenlignende kulturforskning, 90 (Oslo: Novus, 1994)

Svestad, Asgeir, 'The Impact of Materiality on Sámi Burial Customs and Religious Concepts', *Fennoscandia Archaeologica*, 28 (2011), 39–56

Teigmo, Mari, 'Samisk-etnografisk avdelings undersøkelser i forbindelse med de planlagte reguleringer i Skibotnvassdraget. Rapport fra arbeid sommeren 1973' (Topographical archive: Tromsø Museum, 1973)

Tuan, Yi-Fu, *Space and Place: The Perspective of Experience* (Minneapolis: University of Minnesota Press, 1977

Veiviseren, dir. by Nils Gaup (SF Norge, 2005)

Vorren, Ørnulv, *Villreinfangst i Varanger fram til 1600–1700-årene*, Tromsø Museums Skrifter, 28 (Stonglandseidet: Nordkalott-forlaget, 1998)

Vorren, Ørnulv, and Hans Kr. Eriksen, *Samiske offerplasser i Varanger*, Tromsø Museums Skrifter, 24 (Stonglandseidet: Nordkalott-Forlaget, 1993)

Wennstedt Edvinger, Britta, and Noel D. Broadbent, 'Saami Circular Sacrificial Sites in Northern Coastal Sweden', *Acta Borealia*, 23.1 (2006), 24–55

Wepsäläinen, Anders, *Stalotomterna. En kritisk granskning av forskningsläget rörande en omdiskuterad fornlämningstyp* (Uppsala: Kungl. Gustav Adolfs akademien för svensk folkkultur, 2011)

Zachrisson, Inger, 'Fanns det samer i Härjedalen i äldre tid? Om rättsprocesser och arkeologi', in *Samisk forhistorie, rapport fra konferanse i Lakselv 5.–6. september 2002*, ed. by Mia Krogh and Kjersti Schanche (Varangerbotn: Varanger samiske museum, 2004), pp. 56–61

RUNE BLIX HAGEN*

'I Hurl the Spirits of Gandul'. Pleasure, Jealousy, and Magic: The Witchcraft Trial of Ragnhild Tregagaas in 1325

A woman called Ragnhild Tregagaas (*Ragnhildr tregagás*) is first mentioned in Norwegian documents dating from the year 1325. She was probably born towards the end of the thirteenth century and lived some parts of her life in Fusa parish, south-east of Bergen, the largest town in Norway at the time and located in western part of Norway. Ragnhild was married, but by 1325 she had become a widow. The content of the surviving documents suggests that she might have been descended from the lower aristocracy or at least from the upper end of society, which could have had some influence on the legal handling of her case. Other biographical details are unknown.

The purpose of this short article is twofold: first, to give an account of a church court case, based on the Latin text of a document dating from February 1325, the full text of which is printed at the end of this article. Following this account, I shall discuss briefly some features relating to the case in a synchronic and chronologically comparative context. Even though this case took place in the western part of Norway, the content of the court stories has strong connections to both Hálogaland and Finnmǫrk in the Far North. This is likewise evident when discussing the kind of magic that the accused woman was supposed to have been practising. The 'northernness' of the magical rituals seems to be related to the magic practices of the Sámi

*   I wish to thank Adam Grimshaw, Ingrid Agnete Medby, Catherine Rider, Richard Holt, and the members of CNN — Creating the New North — for useful comments. Before the IMC session in July 2013, this paper was discussed at a CNN seminar in Tromsø on 13 June 2013. I also thank those attending the IMC sessions in 2013 for their fruitful comments on my paper. Thanks also for their comments to scholars who took part in a paper seminar at UiT — The Arctic University of Norway in April 2017. I am also grateful for all the comments from Mary Katherine Jones on the final version of my text.

Rune Blix Hagen, UiT The Arctic University of Norway, rune.hagen@uit.no

Myths and Magic in the Medieval Far North: Realities and Representations of a Region on the Edge of Europe, ed. by Stefan Figenschow, Richard Holt, and Miriam Tveit, AS 10
(Turnhout: Brepols, 2020), pp. 143–155
10.1484/M.AS-EB.5.120523

population living in the North, and to the established and long-standing reputation of the Sámi as clever sorcerers.

A trial was conducted against this woman called Ragnhild, according to the single Norwegian charter of the late Middle Ages that deals with magic, witchcraft, and diabolism. The trial was also 'the first documented case of witchcraft to take place in the Nordic world'.[1] This woman was also known as 'Tregagaas'. The nickname 'Tregagaas' may allude to a vindictive woman who creates difficulties and obstacles, or to a person who is mentally deranged. According to the documents, she was found guilty of a number of serious offences: love spells, charm magic, incest or illicit sexual relationships, extramarital intercourse, and for having conjured up impotence by means of black magic. Bishop Andulfinus Audfinn Sigurdsson of Bergen (d. 1330) contended that she had 'been led astray by heretical superstition'.[2]

The Court Case: Confession and Verdict

The case was tried in two stages. First, Ragnhild is said to have confessed on 3 November 1324 at Fusa's parsonage. Burning with jealousy, she allegedly used magical objects and conjuring to weaken her ex-lover's genitals, thereby ruining his fertility and love life. The intense pleasure experienced with her former lover and second cousin, Baard, had ended, and he had married another woman called Bergljot. On their wedding night, Ragnhild had hidden five peas and five loaves of bread in the newlyweds' bed. The intention was to provoke discord between the happily married couple. A sword was also laid close to the bed. The meaning of the sword was to create division between the newlyweds: the peas would inhibit Baard from begetting children, and the loaves would strengthen Ragnhild's curse. From her hiding place in the bedroom, she murmured a 'loathsome curse', written down almost as rhyming lines:

'I hurl the spirits of Gandul;	Ritt ek i fra mer gondols ondu.
One bites you in your back,	Æin Der i bak biti
Another one bites your chest,	Annar i briost der biti
And the third afflicts you	Dridi snui uppa dik
With hatred and envy'.	Hæimt oc ofund.[3]

The Fusa confession and charges attracted attention, and word spread quickly. The clergy in Bergen soon heard the rumours and the bishop decided to investigate. At the end of January 1325, Ragnhild was summoned to appear at the ecclesiastical court in Bergen. There she was confronted by rumours and gossip that she had made Baard impotent. She was probably imprisoned

1 Mitchell, *Witchcraft and Magic*, p. 169.
2 *Diplomatarium Norvegicum*, ed. Lange and others, IX, 113; see Appendix 1.
3 *Diplomatarium Norvegicum*, ed. Lange and others, IX, 113; see Appendix 1.

while the clergy gathered reliable witnesses. At the beginning of February, four men from the nearby parish of Os were summoned to testify about Ragnhild's confession three months earlier. Threatened by the stipendiary magistrate — probably after imprisonment — she was led in chains to her 'true confession' on 8 February 1325. Her admission of guilt confirmed everything the witnesses had told.

Ragnhild also stated that she had enjoyed great erotic pleasure, and that she had had intimate relations with Baard while her own husband was still alive. By giving herself to the Devil, and calling upon his help, she had managed to sow discord and disagreement between Baard and Bergljot. With the Devil's help, she had made her lover impotent so he could not have sex with Bergljot. Because of the impotence caused by Ragnhild's magic, Baard and Bergljot divorced, and he travelled northward to Hálogaland (Halogiam). Ragnhild followed after him to the Far North. By her own admission, she controlled his life and death. In her husband's lifetime, if Baard had not bowed to her will she would have told everything to her husband, who would been at liberty to kill Baard for adultery and incestuous activity. According to her confession, a person called Sørle Sukk had taught her 'heretical conjuring' in her youth.[4]

At this time, Hálogaland was seen as the border area to Finnmǫrk in the Arctic region of Norway. Hálogaland was regarded as a region with a primarily Norwegian population; the indigenous Sámi people of that time were living to the north of this area, even though contemporaneous sources stated that the inhabitants of Hálogaland 'often live together with the Sámi and have frequent commerce with them'.[5] Faraway regions such as Lofoten and Vesterålen, amongst others, were demographically characterized by a mixed settlement of Norse and Sámi people.[6] In the first half of the fourteenth century there were also tight networks and interaction between the western part of Norway and the Far North areas, due to expanding trade traffic to the north, including the import of grain from the Baltic, via merchants in Bergen. In this context it is, of course, tempting to suggest that Ragnhild had learnt some kind of magic rituals from people up in the North, who might have been related to the Sámi population. Sørle Sukk, her teacher of magic, may very well have been of Sámi origin, or at least acquainted with Sámi magic. Ragnhild's confession and the whole content of the case may to a certain degree substantiate such an interpretation, though there is no surviving archival or other supporting evidence for such a conclusion.

Bishop Audfinn Sigurdsson wrote in a letter that Ragnhild returned to sensibility after a long incarceration in the bishop's prison (*carceri nostro*). This was a gradual process that she paid for by nights spent awake, together with

---

4 *Diplomatarium Norvegicum*, ed. Lange and others, IX, 114; see Appendix 1.
5 *Historia Norwegiae*, ed. and trans. by Kunin, pp. 2–5, 7. See the discussion in Figenschow 'The Rise and Extent of Commercial Stockfish Production', p. 6.
6 Nielssen, *Landnâm fra nord*, pp. 66–67.

tears, incessant prayers, and fasting. She was also said to have been moonstruck when performing her evil deeds (*non compotem mentis ut lunatica*). Since she had renounced her shortcomings, and since she had been of unsound mind when the crimes were committed, the bishop sentenced her with pity, leniency, and mercy. Her punishment was to be regarded as 'beneficial penitence'. Upon the advice of the canons, prelates, and monks of Bergen, Ragnhild was told by the bishop to fast on bread and water a couple of times a week, and on other days of the year. She was admonished to leave on a seven-year pilgrimage to holy sites in other countries as well. If she did not obey the clerical decree her case would be turned over to the temporal authorities for criminal prosecution, and thus she would be regarded as guilty, because of her relapse into heresy. According to the historian Stephen A. Mitchell, she would presumably have been condemned by the secular authorities for her heretical wickedness, punishable by execution.[7]

The Sámi's 'gand' and the Spirits of Gandul

The 1325 case against Ragnhild comprises several interesting aspects. It was treated more as a heresy case than as a witchcraft case. This context suggests that the difference between the two sins was not clearly defined during the late Middle Ages in Norway, like everywhere else in Europe at the time. In Europe, and especially papal Avignon, in the early fourteenth century there was a learned discussion going on among canon lawyers and theologians about how to define harmful sorcery and magic rites. Even though magic rituals as actions were not considered to be a kind of heresy, it was declared by many that magic actions entailed an underlying heretical belief.[8]

In the Latin text (see Appendix 1) relating to the case of 1325, medieval Norwegian law codes (1274–1276) on *trolldom* (sorcery) are not referred to at all. Nor are words such as *trolldom* or magic mentioned in the bishop's account. In fact, there is not a single surviving concrete criminal case from Norway during the medieval period in which *trolldom* or *trollfolk*, the native words for sorcery and sorcerers, are explicitly mentioned. The word *gondols* (*Gandul*), on the other hand, mentioned in the first part of Ragnhild's 'loathsome curse', is of interest.[9] Gondols is a word derived from *gand* or *gandr*, referring to a kind of demonic spirit (*diabolicus gandus*) or magical projectile known from quite a few early modern witchcraft trials in Norway, especially in the Far North, when the native Sámi people were involved in this kind of persecution. The alleged sorcerers among the Sámi were often renowned and convicted for their use of *gand-trolldom*.

---

7   Mitchell, 'Heresy and Heterodoxy', pp. 43–44.
8   Bailey, *Fearful Spirits*, pp. 78–79; Hutton, *The Witch*, pp. 162–64.
9   Heide, *Gand, seid og åndevind*, pp. 34–35.

From the thirteenth century onwards, the so-called witches of Lapland were known all over Europe for casting their evil spells across vast distances. It was said that such spells could be carried upon the north wind and result in illnesses among people far to the south in Europe. Shootings or the conjuring of spells 'on the wind' were well-known as a form of malevolent magic across most of northern Scandinavia. The *gand* was imagined to be something physical. The shooting of 'Lap shot' was perceived as small lead darts, which the Sámi could shoot across great distances. Olaus Magnus (1490–1557), for instance, described this kind of spell as using small lead arrows in the mid-sixteenth century. The northern Norwegian priest, Petter Dass (1646/47–1707), at the end of the seventeenth century described this Sámi spell as using vile, dark blue flies — otherwise known as Beelzebub's flies. Court records from northern Norwegian witch trials offer specific descriptions and actual illustrations of the Sámi's '*gand*'.[10] One passage affirms that the *gand* resembles a mouse with a head at both ends. Consequently, the Sámi were known to bewitch by casting spells upon people. This kind of spell-casting is the kind of bewitching that is reported upon in the Sámi sorcery trials of the seventeenth century. However, the use of *gand* does not relate exclusively to the indigenous people of northern Europe. 'Gand' seems to be a word of Norse provenance.[11]

Turning back to the 1325 case against Ragnhild Tregagaas, the expression *gondols ondu* could refer to the spirits connected to this kind of *gand* shooting. From a great distance, when cast out, these spirits were supposed to bite, scratch, or otherwise harm the victim of the curse.

As mentioned earlier, the 1325 case was the first of its kind — not only in Norway but in all the Scandinavian countries — that can be labelled as a case of witchcraft where the role of magically induced impotence plays an important role. However, these kinds of cases and debates among theologians on magical impotence were quite well-known in other European countries during the late medieval period: in Germany, for instance.[12] According to British historian Catherine Rider, the story of Ragnhild's use of impotence magic to gain power over her former lover 'seems to reflect a widespread belief'.[13] This is also true in a Norse context.[14]

---

10 See Andersen, *Hr. Petter, Signe-Folk og Satans Træl*, p. 35, where her text contains an
    illustration of the *gand* drawn from the original eighteenth-century court book. The fire-and-
    brimstone preacher Petter Dass wrote about the Sámi use of poisoned Beelzebub's flies in his
    poem *The Trumpet of Nordland* (Nordlands Trompet), first published in the 1730s. The poem
    was published in English in 1954, see Dass, *The Trumpet of Nordland*, pp. 72–73. See also
    Olaus Magnus, *A Description of the Northern Peoples*, pp. 173–74.
11 Thuv, *Trolldom*, p. 46; Heide, *Gand, seid og åndvind*, p. 173; Hagen, *The Sami*, pp. 9–11, and
    'Witchcraft and Ethnicity', pp. 148–51.
12 Kieckhefer, 'Magic and its Hazards', pp. 20–24.
13 Rider, *Magic and Impotence*, p. 98.
14 Heide, *Gand, seid og åndevind*, p. 173.

Bishop Audfinn, Canon Law, and Papal Avignon

The bishop's ruling shows that the Church held jurisdiction over cases of this kind; only in the case of a recurrence was Ragnhild to be transferred to the secular authorities. The ruling also indicates how sceptical the ecclesiastical authorities of the Middle Ages were towards narratives relating to magic and sorcery. The Catholic Church showed little interest in heresy grounded in demonic magic at this time. However, attitudes towards magic among the literate elite underwent important changes during the late medieval period, from about 1300 onwards, and discussions and actions against sorcery blossomed in papal Avignon. The Avignon Pope John XXII, who was pope between 1316 and 1334, is said to have been obsessed with the performance of magical conspiracies, 'more consumed with the problem of magic than any other medieval pope'.[15] He even set up a commission to root out magic from his court in Avignon, and from other parts of France. British historian Ronald Hutton writes that the pope's concerns seem to have had a knock-on effect in different parts of Europe when he and his court tried to categorize magic with heresy in the early part of the fourteenth century.[16]

Before becoming Bishop of Bergen, from 1314 until his death in 1330, Audfinn Sigurdsson studied theology and canon law in France. He took part in the Council of Vienne in south-eastern France in 1311–1312, a council whose primary concern was heresy.

Audfinn is renowned for his insistence on the jurisdiction of the Church, and for his knowledge of canon law. The case against Ragnhild could be attributed to some kind of individual zeal on the part of Bishop Audfinn Sigurdsson, possibly inspired by his continental learning and ideas about demonic sorcery. Similarly, Pope John XXII's concern about magic and alleged sorcerers may have reached as far as the western part of Norway. Aside from this case against Ragnhild Tregagaas, records have been lost to history, so there is little evidence to support possible links between papal Avignon and Norway.

There are, however, some similarities between Pope John XXII's concerns about magic and the Norwegian case in 1325, at least when it comes to magical rituals. As we have seen, one part of Ragnhild's magic rites was to hide five loaves of bread in the wedding bed of Baard and Bergljot to strengthen her curse. A conspiracy and plot against Pope John XXII in 1317 was said to have been carried out using poison and image magic. Three large loaves of bread were hollowed out and a waxen image was placed inside each of the loaves. A small container of arsenic was also added to each of the loaves. After the conspirators had been arrested, their loaves of bread were discovered.[17]

---

15 Decker, *Witchcraft and the Papacy*, p. 23.
16 Hutton, *The Witch*, p. 163.
17 Decker, *Witchcraft and the Papacy*, pp. 25–27.

Magic Rites and Gender

The case against Ragnhild Tregagaas supports the proposition that women were more likely than men to be placed on trial for using some very special kinds of magic relating to sex and love. This was especially true with regard to magical curses that were intended to break up relationships and cause married couples to be unable to have sex.[18] Similar cases from other Nordic and European countries have also shown that medieval magic was often associated with frustrated love, jealousy, and impotence. In the words of American scholar Stephen A. Mitchell, '[o]ther notorious witch trials from the later Scandinavian Middle Ages generally focus on sex, love, and more sex, but always in the context of love triangles where passions of the heart are clearly at the forefront…'.[19] In this case, Ragnhild Tregagaas had used impotence magic to prevent her lover from having sex and, consequently, from consummating his marriage with another woman. This kind of impotence magic was associated with women. According to Catherine Rider, a pattern is visible when it comes to love magic: '[m]en are most commonly mentioned as using magic to seduce women, while women are most often depicted as using magic on their own husbands or making men impotent, perhaps in the hope of preserving their own relationship with them'.[20] The 1325 case from the western part of Norway during the late medieval period fits this pattern quite well.

Ragnhild Tregagaas is the only person we know of from medieval Norway who was charged and convicted for conjuring magic — more than 250 years before the witch-hunts started in Norway, which were then carried out with entirely different levels of intensity and brutality than those expressed in the 1325 conviction. The seriousness of Ragnhild's magic curses is evident, but in 1325 there were few signs of the stereotypical perceptions of the evil, satanic witch of early modern demonology. This long-term transition in dealing with cases like this relates to different kinds of developments in demonology, and in transforming witchcraft into a secular crime to be dealt with by secular courts. This 1325 case from Norway has obvious similarities with later witch trials and demonology, not least when it comes to a pact with the Devil being essential for all kinds of effective magic. Indeed, the story and confession of Ragnhild Tregagaas come very close to pact-witchcraft. During the late medieval period, however, cases like this often combined heresy, diabolism, and magic in a context that is not connected in any clear way to the early modern trials for diabolic magic. This case from the fourteenth century is important in throwing some light on the essential shift from heresy via sorcery to demonic magic.

---

18 Rider, 'Women, Men and Love Magic', pp. 191, 197.
19 Mitchell, 'Blåkulla and its Antecedents', p. 85.
20 Rider, 'Women, Men and Love Magic', p. 208.

American historian Stephen A. Mitchell is so far the only scholar who has systematically conducted research on sorcery and witch-hunts in the Nordic countries during the pre-Reformation period. He uses saga texts, ancient legislation and diploma materials dating from the Middle Ages. On the basis of his findings, Mitchell argues that the persecution of sorcerers before the era of witch-burning occurred in all the Nordic countries without exception, albeit limited in scope. Sentencing was relatively mild and women were, for the most part, treated more leniently than men. Magic-related activities during the late Middle Ages were clearly linked to gender: women were often accused of magic connected to love and of offences connected to sexuality, while typical accusations against men concerned heresy and acts linked to a political agenda. In contrast to later centuries, women did not form a clear majority among the few who were punished for sorcery-related activities prior to the Reformation. Prior to the publication in 2011 of his book on witchcraft and magic in the Nordic Middle Ages, Mitchell's line of research attracted little attention among Nordic researchers, but there is reason to believe that the topics covered in his book are now starting to arouse greater interest among historians in the Nordic countries.

Proposals for Further Study

At about the same time as Ragnhild's trial, the case against Dame Alice Kyteler in Kilkenny, Ireland in 1324 was an early instance of the later stereotype of the evil diabolic witch, but this case was also treated like a heresy trial. The documents from this case, like those from the Norwegian one, were written by a bishop, Richard Ledrede, bishop of Ossory from 1317 to about 1360, and thus a contemporary of Avignon Pope John XXII. For a period of time he was also based in Avignon during the pope's reign. Alice Kyteler was a wealthy woman who married three times. Her case concerns topics including inheritance, possessions, and dowry. During an inheritance dispute, Alice and a few other women were accused of practising heretical sorcery. The charges against the women relate to a denial of the Christian faith, meetings with sacrifices to and advice from demons, nocturnal gatherings, and displaying love and hate magic through the use of candles, potions, powder, and ointments. Sexual intercourse with a demon was one of the accusations against Alice. Alice managed to escape, but one of her accomplices, Petronilla of Meath, was convicted and burnt alive in Kilkenny on 2 November 1324.[21] A discussion of possible interesting parallels between the two cases in Norway and Ireland might be one idea to expand further the content and context of this article. A systematic comparison might provide new and interesting perspectives in both cases, by highlighting continuities and contrasting elements, as well as regional differences.

---

21   Bradley, "Kyteler, Alice", pp. 613–15.

Another interesting question relating to the 'Tregagaas' case concerns the relationship between literate theological ideas on sorcery and pagan attitudes to magic. In connecting the case first to paganism and then later to demonization, Stephen A. Mitchell has asked what happened as far afield as remote Norway when Catholic ideology, with its own views on witchcraft and demonic magic, encountered and merged with native Norwegian pagan and half-pagan traditions of sorcery.[22] It is obvious that the existence of local ideas regarding sorcery predated imports from the European Catholic Church.

Works Cited

Primary Sources

Dass, Petter, *The Trumpet of Nordland* (Minneapolis: St Olaf College Press, 1954)

Diplomatarium Norvegicum. Oldbreve til Kundskab om Norges indre og ydre Forhold, Sprog, Slægter, Sæder, Lovgivning og Rettergang i Middelalderen, ed. by Christian C. A. Lange and others, 23 vols (Christiania: Mallings Forladshandel, 1847–2011)

Historia Norwegiae, in *History of Norway and The Passion and Miracles of the Blessed Óláfr*, ed. and trans. by Devra Kunin (London: Viking Society for Northern Research, 2001)

Olaus Magnus, *A Description of the Northern Peoples, 1555*, vol. I, edited by Peter G. Foote (London: Hakluyt Society, 1996)

Reichborn-Kjennerud, I., *Vår gamle trolldomsmedisin V*, in Skrifter utgitt av Det Norske Videnskaps-Akademi i Oslo II. Hist.-Filos. Klasse, No. 1 (Oslo: Dybwad, 1947), pp. 109–11

'To Breve af Biskop Audfind, betræffende en hexeproces i Bergen, Aar 1325' (Meddeelte af Lector P. A. Munch), in *Samlinger til det norske folks sprog og historie*, vol. v, 1st edn (Christiania: Et Samfund, 1837)

Secondary Works

Andrén, Anders, Kristina Jennbert, and Catharina Raudvere, eds, *Old Norse Religion in Long-Term Perspectives: Origins, Changes and Interactions* (Lund: Nordic Academic Press, 2006)

Andersen, Cecilie, *Hr. Petter, Signe-Folk og Satans Træl. En undersøkelse av Petter Dass sin oppfatning av trolldom og hvit magi i andre halvdel av 1600-tallet* (master's thesis, UiT Norges arktiske universitet, 2017) Full text: <https://munin.uit.no/handle/10037/11576> (accessed 22 June 2020)

Arnold, Martin, 'Hvat er tröll nema þat? The Cultural History of the Troll', in *The Shadow-walkers. Jacob Grimm's Mythology of the Monstrous*, ed. by T. Shippey (Arizona: Tempe, 2005), pp. 111–55

---

22 Mitchell, *Witchcraft and Magic*, p. 201.

Bailey, Michael D., *Fearful Spirits, Reasoned Follies. The Boundaries of Superstition in Late Medieval Europe* (Ithaca: Cornell University Press, 2013)

Botheim, Ragnhild, *Trolldomsprosessane i Bergenhus len 1566–1700* (Hovedoppgave i historie, Bergen, 1999)

Bradley, John, 'Kyteler, Alice (ca. 1260/1265 – after 1324)', in *Encyclopedia of Witchcraft. The Western Tradition*, vol. III K-P, ed. by Richard M Golden (Oxford: ABC-CLIO, 2006), pp. 613–15

Decker, Rainer, *Witchcraft and the Papacy. An Account drawing on the formerly secret records of the Roman Inquisition*, trans. by H. C. Erik Midelfort (Charlottesville: University of Virginia Press, 2008)

Figenschow, Stefan, ''The Rise and Extent of Commercial Stockfish Production and Trade in Medieval north-Norwegian Coastal Society' (seminar text, Tromsø 2017)

Haaland, Hilde Elisabeth, *Kirkens fordømmelse og det verdslige samfunnets normer: holdninger til og forståelsen av magisk virksomhet og magikere i norrøn middelalder* (unpublished master's thesis, University of Oslo, 1998)

Hagen, Rune Blix, 'Ragnhild Tregagås', *Norsk biografisk leksikon*, 7 (2003), 301

——, *The Sami — Sorcerers in Norwegian History: Sorcery Persecutions of the Sami* (Karasjok: CálliidLágádus, 2012)

——, 'Witchcraft and Ethnicity: A Critical Perspective on Sami Shamanism in Seventeenth-Century Northern Norway', in *Writing Witch-Hunt Histories: Challenging the Paradigm*, ed. by Marko Nenonen and Raisa Maria Toivo (Leiden: Brill, 2014), pp. 141–66

Heide, Eldar, *Gand, seid og åndevind* (Dr art-avhandling/published doctoral thesis, Universitetet i Bergen, 2006); full text: http://bora.uib.no/handle/1956/4441 (accessed 22 June 2020)

Hutton, Ronald, *The Witch: A History of Fear, from Ancient Times to the Present* (New Haven: Yale University Press, 2017)

Kieckhefer, Richard, 'Magic and its Hazards in the late Medieval West', in *The Oxford Handbook of Witchcraft in Early Modern Europe and Colonial America*, ed. by Brian P. Levack (Oxford: Oxford University Press, 2013), pp. 13–31

Kulturhistorisk leksikon for nordisk middelalder fra vikingetid til reformationstid, vol. XVIII (Copenhagen: Rosenkilde og Bagger, 1974), pp. 655–57 ('Troll' by E. F. Halvorsen)

Kvideland, Reimund, and Henning K. Sehmsdorf (eds), *Scandinavian Folk Belief and Legend* (Oslo: Norwegian University Press, 1991)

Liland, Sigurd, 'Biskop Audfinn og Ragnhild Tregagås', in *Frå Fjon til Fusa* (Nord- og Midhordland sogelag yearbook, Bergen, 1949)

Meylan, Nicolas, 'Magic and Discourses of Magic in the Old Norse Sagas of the Apostles', *Viking and Medieval Scandinavia*, 7 (2011), 107–24

Mitchell, Stephen A., 'Blåkulla and its Antecedents: Transvection and Conventicles in Nordic Witchcraft', *Alvíssmál — Forschungen zur mittelalterlichen Kultur Skandinaviens*, 7 (1997), 81–100

——, 'Heresy and Heterodoxy in Medieval Scandinavia', in *Contesting Orthodoxy in Medieval and Early Modern Europe. Heresy, Magic and Witchcraft*, ed. by Louise Nyholm Kallestrup and Raisa Maria Toivo (Cham: Palgrave Macmillan, 2017), pp. 35–56

——, 'Nordic Witchcraft in Transition: Impotence, Heresy, and Diabolism in 14th-Century Bergen', *Scandia*, 63.1 (1997), 17–33

——, *Witchcraft and Magic in the Nordic Middle Ages* (Philadelphia: University of Pennsylvania Press, 2011)

Nielssen, Alf Ragnar, *Landnåm fra nord. Utvandring fra det nordlige Norge til Island i vikingtid* (Stamsund: Orkana Akademisk, 2012)

Raudvere, Catharina, 'Trolldómr in Early Medieval Scandinavia', in *Witchcraft and Magic in Europe. The Middle Ages*, ed. by Bengt Ankarloo and Stuart Clark (Philadelphia: University of Pennsylvania Press, 2002), pp. 73–171

Rider, Catherine, *Magic and Impotence in the Middle Ages* (Oxford: Oxford University Press, 2006)

——, *Magic and Religion in Medieval England* (London: Reaktion, 2012)

——, 'Women, Men and Love Magic in Late Medieval English Pastoral Manuals', *Magic, Ritual and Witchcraft*, 7.2 (2012), 190–211

Riisøy, Anne Irene, 'Sexuality, Law and Legal Practice and the Reformation in Norway', in *The Northern World: North Europe and the Baltic c. 400–1700 AD, Peoples, Economies and Cultures*, 44 (Leiden: Brill, 2009)

——, *Stat og kirke: rettsutøvelsen i kristenrettsaker mellom sættargjerden og Reformasjone* (published master's thesis, University of Oslo, 2000)

Sandnes, Jørn, 'Fengsel som straff i norsk middelalder', in *Historisk Tidsskrift*, 82.2 (2003), 163–72

Schulz, Katja, *Riesen: Von Wissenshütern und Wildnisbewohnern in Edda und Saga*, Skandinavistische Arbeiten, 20 (Heidelberg: Universitätsverlag, 2004), p. 332.

Stokes, Laura, *Demons of Urban Reform. Early European Witch Trials and Criminal Justice, 1430–1530* (Basingstoke: Palgrave Macmillan, 2011)

Thuv, Therese, *Trolldom før trolldomsprosessenes tid. Saken mot Ragnhild Tregagås og senmiddelalderens syn på magi og trolldom* (unpublished master's thesis, Nord University, 2020)

Tryti, Anna Elisa, 'Andulfinus Audfinn Sigurdsson', in *Norsk biografisk leksikon*; full text <http://nbl.snl.no/Andulfinus_Audfinn_Sigurdsson> (accessed 22 June 2020)

Wilbur, Terence H., 'Troll, an Etymological Note', *Scandinavian Studies*, 30 (1958), 137–39

Zika, Charles, *The Appearance of Witchcraft. Print and Visual Culture in Sixteenth-Century Europe* (London: Routledge, 2007)

Appendix 1: The Latin Text from the Printed Edition *Diplomatarium Norvegicum*, ed. by Lange and others, IX, 113–14

Available online at <http://archive.org/stream/diplomatariumnooohuitgoog/diplomatariumnooohuitgoog_djvu.txt> [accessed 4 November 2019]

No. 93.

8 February 1325. Place: Bergen.

De quadam lapsa in heresim Ragnilda Tregagaas.
In nomine domini amen. Nos Audfinnus dei gratia episco-
pus Bergensis notum facimus universis quod sub anno domini m.o ccc.o
xx.o quinto immediate post octavam epiphanie de septimana in septima-
nam fama publica validusque clamor discretorum nostris auribus defe-
rebant quod Ragnilda dicta Treghagaas, erroris cecitate depressa di-
vini cultus obtestante turbulent(i)a nature, proch dolor peregrina non
solum in innocentium vite existimationisque labefactionem miserabiliter

Vol. IX, 113
sit molita verum eciam ad ipsius creatoris contumeliam in heretice
supersticionis invium detestabilius est prolapsa. Nos igitur predictum
clamorem salva conscientia quadam connivencia captata sub dissimula-
cionis pallio penitus indiscussum pertransire non audentes de fratrum
nostrorum consilio ad inquisicionem descendimus super illo prout postulat
ordo juris, Primo itaque dictam Ragnildam ream citari fecimus ut in festo
beate Agnetis secundo compareret que de statuto comparens super ar-
ticulis de quibus fuerat infamata totam inficiabatur veritatem, hoc vi-
dentes discretos viros videlicet Asbernum de Lundarviik Ketillum de
Haferskor, Hallonem sub Monte Asbernum et Halvardum de Skialbreid
coram quibus fuerat pridem confessata ad diem Martis proximum post
purificationem beate virginis comparituros citavimus, sed ipsam suspi-
cionum presumptionumque podio quasi impositi sceleris obnoxiam secure custodie addiximus qua suspecti set nondum convicti mancipantur
testesque supradicti in personis propriis prefixo termino venientes et
tanquam legittime admissi sacrosanctis evangeliis corporaliter tactis de-
posuere iurati quod anno domini millesimo .ccc.o xxiiij. tercio Nonas
Novembris in hyemali refectorio presbyteri de Fusum se presentes
audivisse quod sepedicta Raghnilda sponte a nullo interrogata fatebatur
articulos qui sequuntur. Scilicet quod prima nocte nuptiarum in thorum Barderi et Bergliote deposuerat quinque panes totidemque pisa una
cum hoc gladium ad eorum caput reposuit cum incantatione detestabili
que subdetur a prefato postmodum die in diem Veneris proximum

Raghnildam citavimus pro veritate de illo negotio lucidius *eruendam,
que determinato die in consistorio nostro comparens modicis commi-
nacionibus super questionibus a balliuo prehabitis si facti seriem diu-
cius subticeret per confessionem articulos detegebat infrascriptos, primo
quod omnes articuli depositi per testes prenominatos veri erant, secundo quod ipsa Raghnilda vivo marito suo se Bardero quatuor vicibus
carnaliter copulaverat, quem tertio et tertio gradu in consanguinitatis
linea contingebat, Jtem quod divine protectioni abrenunciavit et se dyabolo
commendavit, Ad hoc ut inter Barderum Berghliotam dissensionum et
rancorum zizania seminaret, Jtem quod super excitatione dyaboli ad
perficienda predicta verba que subintrant cum incantatione pestilenti
recitavit

Ritt ek i fra mer gondols ondu. æin þer i bak biti annar i
briost þer biti þridi snui uppa þik hæimt oc ofund, oc sidan þesse ord
ero lesen skall spyta uppa þan er till syngzst.

Jtem quod occasione
persuasionum Raghnilde Barderus Bergliota repudiata Halogiam sit pro-
fectus seque fide intermedia constrictam ad eundem ibidem prestolantem
cum primo posset suum iter maturare. Jtem super verbis que orsa fuerat

Vol. IX, 114
quod in Bardero vite necisque teneret potestatem talem interpretationem-
subjunxit quod nisi ipsius voluntati per singula consentiret legittimus
maritus Ragnilde pro incestu et adulterio secum commissis Barderum
vita privaret, Jtem quod secundo die nupciarum sponsum subsannando
in hec verba prorupit, arridet *meus mens quod genitalia Barderi ut
maleficiata non plus valerent ad coitum quam zona ad manum meam re-
voluta. Jtem quod prima nocte nupciarum se absconderet sponso et
sponsa ignorantibus infra thalamum juxta thorum in quo dormiebant,
Jtem interrogata respondit quod hujusmodi incantationes hereticas in
juventute a Solla dicto Sukk didicit quas in hoc casu practicavit.

KAROLINE KJESRUD

The Meaning of Ale: Understanding Political Conflicts in the North in Light of Cultural Practice

Introduction

The political situation in Hálogaland in the early eleventh century is described by Snorri Sturluson in the saga of Óláfr Haraldsson:[1] a man named Sigurðr and his son, Asbjǫrn, gained great respect on their home farm at Þrándarnesi outside Harstad, without yet being the king's men. Sigurðr was the brother of the chieftain Þórir *hundr*. The saga narrative explains that Sigurðr arranged three feasts every year: 'eitt at vetrnóttum, en annat at miðjum vetri, iii. at sumri' (one on winter-night's eve, one on mid-winter's eve, and the third in the summer).[2] Asbjǫrn, Sigurðr's son, continued to arrange these feasts after his father's death, but he soon encountered problems, as the course of seasons grew worse and people's corn harvest failed. Old grain and old provisions had to be used in the preparations for the feasts, and Asbjǫrn had to buy corn wherever he could get it. The problem was, however, that many of the local farmers had insufficient grain for seed the following spring and new bad harvests were expected in the coming years. The situation worsened when the king prohibited all export of corn, malt, and meal from the southern to the northern parts of the country. Asbjǫrn objected to these restrictions. He loaded a ship with objects to sell and set out, together with his men, on a voyage to the south. His purpose was to barter for grain. When the vessel arrived at Qgvaldsnes, Asbjǫrn was met by Þórir *sel* who ran the king's manor. Þórir *sel* inquired who commanded the splendid ship and the purpose of

---

1 Snorri Sturluson, *Heimskringla*, ed. by Finnur Jónsson.
2 Snorri Sturluson, *Óláfs saga hins helga* in *Heimskringla*, ed. by Finnur Jónsson, p. 289, trans. by Laing, chap. 132.

Karoline Kjesrud, Museum of Cultural History, University of Oslo,
karoline.kjesrud@khm.uio.no

Myths and Magic in the Medieval Far North: Realities and Representations of a Region on the Edge of Europe, ed. by Stefan Figenschow, Richard Holt, and Miriam Tveit, AS 10
(Turnhout: Brepols, 2020), pp. 157–178
10.1484/M.AS-EB.5.120524

their voyage. Asbjǫrn explained his request, and Þórir replied with the king's prohibition of selling grain to northern Norway. Asbjǫrn had to continue his journey to one of his relatives, Erlingr *á Sóla*, with the same request. Erlingr welcomed Asbjǫrn warmly, but he was also bound by the king's command. Nevertheless, Erlingr circumvented the king's command and purchased corn and malt for Asbjǫrn in the name of his slaves. Asbjǫrn left Erlingr's place most satisfied and stopped again at Ǫgvaldsnes on his return. Þórir *sel* was upset when he heard about Erlingr's business with Asbjǫrn, and therefore he unloaded the vessel. Even worse, he humiliated Asbjǫrn so that he was brought to tears when he replaced the costly sails on his ship with some older sails of his own. Asbjǫrn went back to Hálogaland deeply shamed and without being able to arrange any feasts that winter.[3] This consequence was hard to swallow.

The main aim of this article is to understand the deeper cultural meanings behind Asbjǫrn's seemingly disproportionate reaction to the regulations of grain import. The saga narrative explains that Asbjǫrn was not able to arrange his seasonal feasts as a major reason for why prohibiting the importation of grains was a problem. Seasonal feasts and other transitional feasts were part of a long, cultural history in Norway, and they all had ale in common as a constituent element. In the following, I will investigate why ale was a crucial component in seasonal and regional feasts for hundreds of years in Nordic culture, and whether this practice had the same implications in the north and in the south.

The application of an interdisciplinary approach to the Old Norse souces will allow an exploration of the range of the cultural impact of ale and ale-rituals in general. The Old Norse word *ǫl* in fact has a wider significance than simply referring to a drink: it also denotes gatherings that involved ale, and the process of brewing (especially that part of the process in which the drink was left for fermentation). These three different meanings of *ǫl* are nonetheless closely related, and it is likely that these elements — the contents of ale, the brewing process, and the ale gatherings — when taken together explain the powerful position that ale has acquired in northern society over hundreds of years. The important status held by ale may have been the reason why the cultivation and trade of grain caused conflict when issues of power were at stake.

This article will shed new light on runic inscriptions from the early Iron Age and Migration Period that have received sparse attention until now, alongside archaeological remains, Eddic poems, saga narratives, and laws from the Viking and Medieval Periods. The investigation across this wide range of sources will enable a deeper understanding of i) the cultural value of ale, and ii) how social rituals may have connected the High North to shared Northern European cultural practices related to ale.

---

3   Snorri Sturluson, *Óláfs saga hins helga*, in *Heimskringla*, ed. by Finnur Jónsson, p. 291.

Ale-Rituals in Norwegian History: Baptism, Funeral, and the Stages In-between

Medieval laws contain various regulations about ale-rituals, which may reflect customs rooted in earlier times. The laws record regulations about *erfi* (funeral / inheritance ale), *barnsǫl* (childbirth ale) (the Norwegian word for childbirth 'barsel' is a shortening of the Old Norse 'barns ǫl' and refers to childbirth ale), and *frelsisǫl* (freedom ale) in the oldest laws. In *Bjarkøyretten*, the oldest urban law from Niðaróss (present-day Trondheim), the law about 'freedom ale' describes how a slave is duty-bound to organize a 'freedom ale' if he acquires his own property (142, also in Frostaþingslög 9–12).[4] The law defined the celebration such that it should consist of nine *mæler* ale[5] and the slave should make the first incision that would kill a ram for the feast during the ritual. The description of the whole event can be identified as a transitional rite in which the slave obtains a new status (the Norwegian word *frelse*, ON *frjáls*, derives from *frēhals <*frīhals- <germ. *frijahalsa*, which means 'freed neck'; this is likely to refer to the opposite of a slave who would have a neck ring,[6] and which could indicate a situation when a slave is emancipated). Additional laws describe the funeral ale and inheritance ale in Chapter 23 in the Gulaþingslög. All of these rituals imply a transitional effect for the participant, meaning that they fall within the definition of *rites de passage* (rites of passage) given by the social anthropologist Arnold van Gennep (1909).[7] These rituals are ceremonies that were organized to ensure the transformation of an individual transformation from one defined status to another. The participant, being an individual or a group of people, needs to separate from his or her former status and get ready for a transformation after a short period of being in limbo. Finally, she / he will incorporate her or his new status and take part in a new collective sphere. Van Gennep argues that since the underlying aim of the ritual is the same, the conducting of the ritual would also be analogous, independent of an underlying theoretical religious approach.[8] The rituals are used with attribution to different religious theories and may thus be considered memories of long-standing practices in a society.[9] In the medieval laws and saga narratives, there are descriptions of more seasonal ceremonies such as 'Christmas ale' and 'mid-winter's ale', as demonstrated by Asbjørn's seasonal festivals. Such ceremonies are, according to van Gennep, also rites of passage, because humans are part of the rhythms of the universe, and

---

4 *Bjarkøyretten: Nidaros eldste bylov*, ed. by Hagland and Sandnes; *Frostatingsloven*, trans. by Sandnes and Hagland; *Gulatingslova*, trans. by Eithun, Rindal, and Ulset.
5 One *mæle* is used for measuring. One *sold* consisted of six *mæler*.
6 Bjorvand and Lindeman, ed., *Våre arveord*, p. 254.
7 van Gennep, *Rites de passage*.
8 van Gennep, *Rites de passage*, p. 22.
9 Connerton, *How Societies Remember*.

the universe and nature is structured around cosmic changes.[10] Arranging seasonal ceremonies / ale-rituals the way Asbjǫrn did in the early eleventh century could have been a sufficient method of demonstrating his position in the local community. The continuous practice of arranging a ritual is not only a synchronic event with positive ramifications for the people in the local community at any given time, it also contributes to a collective commemoration of rituals and practices. This may be one of the reasons explaining why Asbjǫrn *selsbani* finds himself in a difficult position when he is not able to fulfill the seasonal rituals in his local community due to the lack of grain and hence an inability to brew ale.

The medieval laws demonstrate that the word *ǫl* occurs as a denotation for a variety of rituals in medieval society. The Proto-Norse equivalent *alu* appears on a number of runic inscriptions on diverse objects, such as monumental stones, combs, bone fragments, and bracteates, and in a variety of different contexts, especially grave contexts that alter between collective monuments and objects within male or female graves. In Norway, such inscriptions are found with a wide distribution as far north as Alstahaug in Nordland county. The semantic meaning of the word *alu*, ON *ǫl*, may indicate that these inscriptions could refer to a variety of gatherings involving ale, ale-rituals, in the Iron Age, in which the main purpose was to ensure the individual's (or the collective) transition from one status to another — a rite of passage. Thus, the inscriptions themselves, the objects' materiality, and their context are essential for the interpretation.

The alu-inscriptions have been a prevalent topic throughout the last century of runological research.[11] Interpretations of these inscriptions vary, and they include assumptions of the word being a reference to the actual drink ale;[12] the word being a formula with the purpose of keeping evil away due to the word's potential translation to the German *Abwehr*; protection / aversion;[13] or the word being a testimony to a power ceremony / relationship.[14]

Runologist Wolfgang Krause collected a group of magical formulas, *alu*, *lina*, and *laukar*, in a separate chapter in his first collection of inscriptions written in the Older Futhark.[15] Krause interpreted such inscriptions as referring to a cultic practice, and pointed out a symbolical meaning of the word 'protection'. This suggestion has resonated with later scholars in their interpretation of

---

10   van Gennep, *Rites de passage*, p. 23.

11   For an overview of scholarly contributions, I refer to Zimmermann, 'Bier, Runen und Macht', in which she provides a thorough overview of most of the scholarly contributions in the field.

12   See, for example, Høst, *Runer. Våre eldste runeinnskrifter* and 'Trylleordet "alu"', pp. 35–49.

13   See, for example, Krause, *Die Runeninschriften im älteren Futhark*; Imer, 'The Oldest Runic Monuments in the North', pp. 169–212.

14   Zimmermann, 'Bier, Runen und Macht', pp. 45–64.

15   Krause, *Beiträge zur Runenforschung*.

the formulaic-word / single word-inscription,[16] and may have contributed to the drink — and even the word — being associated with magical effects.

Runologist Ute Zimmermann argued in 2014 that the alu-inscriptions on bracteates have functioned in elite contexts to testify to a relationship of power, as gifts from a leader to a devotee, and thus are symbols of status in the Migration Period.[17] The bracteates are pendants in the form of single-sided gold discs, imprinted in relief by a stamp, originally imitating Roman medallions with the emperor's bust or animal ornamentation. Their function can be compared with amulets, presumably with protective functions, and they have been found in Sweden, Denmark, and on large parts of the continent. Could these gifts have been given in particular transitional rituals, for example, from master to servant before or after the warriors were sent into a battle? [18]

The alu-inscriptions may then be read as a reference to the organization or completion of a certain ritual. Some bracteates include the word laþu in the runic inscriptions, which is a proto-Norse word meaning 'invitation'.[19] On the bracteates from Darum I (C 5229, DR BR 9) and Skonager III (DR BR 16) laþu appears together with a name, probably referring either to the inviter or the invitee. The inscription on the Fyn-bracteate (Nat.mus. 8650, DR IK 58) includes both the word laþu and alu, and a name (or a nickname), Howaʀ ('the high one'), who could be the inviter (Fig. 4). In general, the bracteates seem to have been mass-produced, and they may have been tokens of a certain affiliation. In the instances where they also include inscriptions, they may be tokens of a fulfilled transitional ritual and a confirmation of the owner's new status. Zimmermann suggests that the bracteates with alu-inscriptions found in graves could be remnants from drinking rituals in elite contexts. In her opinion, the intoxicating ale would make the journey to the afterlife accessible.[20]

Some bracteates with alu-inscriptions are found in British female graves, as pointed out by the art historian Nancy Wicker. Wicker argues that these bracteates and those with an iconographic representation of a drinking horn should be read as tokens for a ritual other than those of the male bracteates.[21] More precisely, she has suggested them to be understood in relation to the ritual of childbirth.[22] Wicker's observation could serve as an argument for the alu-inscriptions indicating another succession of a transitional rite related to childbirth.

A bronze buckle with a runic inscription (S 66940, N KJ 48) from a Migration Age female grave from Fosse, Jæren in Rogaland, was found together with

16 See, for example, Lundeby and Williams, 'Om Vadstenabrakteatens **tuwa** med et tillegg om Lellingebrakteatens **salu**', pp. 33–40.
17 Zimmermann, 'Bier, Runen und Macht', pp. 51–52, with references.
18 Mees and MacLeod, Runic Amulets and Magic Objects.
19 Bjorvand and Lindeman, ed., Våre arveord, p. 1086
20 Zimmermann, 'Bier, Runen und Macht', pp. 56–57.
21 Wicker, 'Bracteate Inscriptions and Context Analysis', pp. 25–52.
22 Wicker, 'Bracteates and Beverages'.

Fig. 4: 'Fyn bracteate', Fyn in Denmark (Nat.mus. 8650, DR IK 58). The runic inscription reads: HowaR ('the high one') 'laþu' ... 'alu'. Photo: Lennart Larsen, courtesy of Nationalmuseet, Denmark.

human bones, animal bones, pottery, and gaming pieces, but is now lost.[23] The inscription is dated accordingly to AD 375/500–460/470,[24] and is transliterated '*kaa alu*', and interpreted 'Kaa, ale'. Lisbeth Imer suggests the translation '... I protect (?)', and understands the word *alu* as a protective formulaic word. The buckle was probably a personal belonging of the deceased woman in the grave. In light of the British bracteates, the buckle, or the inscription, could derive from an analogous ale-ritual, if not necessarily from a childbirth, maybe from another transitional marking.

There are more objects connected to women that includes alu-inscriptions and thus possibly referring to ale-rituals. A bone comb from Setre, Bømlo in Hordaland, with a runic inscription and neat circle ornamentation (B 8350, N KJ 40) was found in a cave that might have served as dwelling for centuries. The comb was surrounded by fragments of pottery, bones, and various iron

---

23 S6694, Archaeological Museum Stavanger.
24 Imer, 'Runer og runeindskrifter', II, 109.

Fig. 5: Bone fragment from Horvnes, Alstahaug in Nordland
(T 22926/1-74, A372), which includes the inscription *aallu [u]*. Photo: Per
E. Fredriksen, courtesy of NTNU Vitenskapsmuseet.

pieces and is dated to AD 560/70–600.[25] Krause and Jankuhn suggested in
1966 the following reading and interpretation: **hAl mAR mAunA AḷunąAlunąnA**:
'ha[i]l māR mauna a(l)u Nanna alu Nanna', with the translation: 'hail – maid
of maidens – protection – Nanna – protection – Nanna',[26] indicating the word
'*alu*' being a formulaic word meaning protection. Lisbeth Imer (2007; 2011)
transliterates the inscription: **hAl mAR mA unA Alu na Alu nanA**, and refrains
from translating it, but also she recognizes the word *alu* two times.[27]

Another bone comb fragment from Horvnes, Alstahaug in Nordland (T
22926/1-74, A372) includes the inscription *aallu [u]* (Fig. 5).[28] The comb is
dated to the sixth century and was found in an Iron Age female grave consisting
of a number of pearls, buckles, needles, and other combs.[29] This inscription
may be read as a doubling of the word *alu*, and hence translated: 'Ale ale!'.

Yet another bone fragment with a runic inscription (B 4384, N KJ 29) has
been found in a grave context in Ødemotland, Hå in Rogaland, together with
pieces of a bone comb, and pieces of pottery dated to the early Migration Period.
The inscription is dated to AD 460/470–560/570[30] and has been debated ever
since it was found. Ottar Grønvik suggested in 1996 the inscription to illustrate
a ritual of receiving "the holy ale". His reading and interpretation is rather

25 Immer, 'Runer og runeindskrifter', 11.
26 Krause and Jankuhn, *Die Runeninschriften im älteren Futhark*, pp. 90–91.
27 Imer, 'Runer og runeindskrifter', 11, 225.
28 Knirk, James, 'Nyfunn og nyregistreringer 2003', p. 18.
29 Hagland, 'Oppsiktsvekkjande nytt runefunn'; Knirk, 'Nyfunn og nyregistreringer 2003'.
30 Imer, 'Runer og runeindskrifter'.

uncertain: 'Ūha, aure aƀ ykwinu, ai-kund þīnū wū: wēa alu þā-k wiu hnūf, þī-t ī auke kunnu wī!' with the following translation: 'The young [woman], perished from the earth (=is dead), reborn for eternity in your sanctuary (= in heaven). The holy beer I received, I consecrate the horn, so that it (=the beer) may increase therein in the known sanctuary.'[31]

Even though the complete meanings of the N KJ 29 inscription and the N KJ 40 inscription are still debated, the four last inscriptions all include the word *alu*, which may relate the objects to the concept of ale gatherings or ale-rituals. Such transitional rituals may have provided a social and collective protection in the individual's transition from one stage in life to another, for example childbirth rituals, wedding ceremonies, or funerals. A few stone monuments with inscriptions including ale from the same period add more to the understanding of the ale-rituals.

The Tune stone from Østfold (C 2092, N KJ 72) is the longest Proto-Norse runic inscription from Norway, dated to AD 375/400–520/530, and the earliest source indicating jurisdiction and inheritance practices (Fig. 6).[32] The stone (192 cm) has a memorial character and was found in an upright position atop a low burial mound that had been fitted into the churchyard wall surrounding the cemetery at Tune Church. The inscription covers both sides of the stone, and is read and interpreted as follows:

A: *ek WiwaR after Wōdurīdē witandahalaiban worahtō [rūnōR]*
B: *falh Wōdurīdē staina þrijōR dohtriR dālidun arbija āsijōstēR arbijanō*

> (I, WiwaR, in memory of WoduridaR the master of the household, made these runes. I entrusted the stone to WoduridaR. Three daughters arranged the funeral feast, the dearest / most devoted / most divine of the heirs.)[33]

Harald Bjorvand later clarified that the adjective *āsijōstēR* should not be translated as 'the dearest / most devoted / most divine', but simply as the 'closest' relatives.[34]

The word *arbija* is the Proto-Norse word for inheritance ale / funeral ale (*erfi* in Old Norse). The word itself is not related to the word *alu*. Therefore, we cannot really state solely from this inscription that the funeral feast — the *arbija* — involved ale. However, there are other inscriptions from the same time which may indicate that ale was part of burial rituals and grave customs.

The grave slab from Årstad in Sokndal, Rogaland (C 3639, N KJ 58) (121 cm × 78 cm × 13 cm) dates to the period between AD 160–375/400 (Fig. 7), and was found in an upright position outside the western wall of the burial

31 Grønvik, *Frå Vimose til Ødemotland*, pp. 255–67, English translation from www.runenprojekt. uni-kiel.de.

32 Imer, 'Runer og runeindskrifter', II, 418.

33 Spurkland, *Norwegian Runes and Runic Inscriptions*, pp. 38–40.

34 Bjorvand, 'Det besværlige adjektivet på Tunesteinen'.

Fig. 6: The Tune-stone from Tune in Østfold (C 2092, N KJ 72). The stone was erected in a burial field and was later included in the churchyard wall encircling the church of Tune. Now the stone is in the collections at Museum of Cultural History (KHM), Oslo. Photo: Ann Christine Eek, courtesy of KHM, University of Oslo.

Fig. 7: The Årstad grave slab (C 3639, N KJ 58) was found in relation to a grave chamber at the farm Årstad in Sokndal, Rogaland in Norway. Photo: Mårten Teigen, courtesy of KHM, University of Oslo.

chamber in a grave mound.[35] On the side of the stone that faced the grave, a runic inscription is carved. There are two possible readings: 1) 'hīwigaʀ

35 Imer, 'Runer og runeindskrifter', II, 484. Runologist Lisbeth Imer has concluded that the oldest runic monuments in northern society were placed in the grave field from an early age, whereas the placement within the graves was uncommon until the Migration Period, in 'The Oldest Runic Monuments in the North', p. 195.

sar alu (u)ngwināR,[36] and 2) **ˈhiwigaʀ saralu ek wina(ʀ)**ˈ.[37] Scholars have interpreted the inscription differently, from being a magic formula to being a representation of three names 'HiwigaR. Saralu. (?) Engwin',[38] in which two of the names may refer to the deceased, buried people, and the third name to the one who erected the stone.[39] Discussions about this inscription have centred on variations of names,[40] but also on the meaning behind *sar alu*. 'Saralu' does not find any parallels as a name in the proto-Norse. Sophus Bugge interpreted the second line as the *sar* being an adverbial to the word *alu*.[41] Bugge interpreted *alu* as a word for protection, whereas Krause interpreted it as defence, and thus both of them suggested that the inscription is related to some kind of magic in the grave.[42] Another possible way of interpreting the inscription in line with the word division proposed by Bugge and Krause would be to read the sequence with *alu* not as a reference to magic, defence, or protection, but rather as 'ale'. The second line could simply be interpreted as 'Here, ale!', a statement of an ale-ritual that presumably took place when the deceased was buried.[43]

The connection between ale and funerals appears even stronger when we look at the runic monument from Elgesem in Sande, Vestfold, widely dated to the period AD 160–560/570 (C 17791, N KJ 57).[44] This stone was erected with several other stones in the middle of a grave field and holds an inscription consisting of only three runes: *alu*. No information is provided, neither for whom the stone was erected, nor who was responsible for the monument or the runes. The inscription on the Elgesem stone has been crucial for scholars' interpretation of *alu* as a formulaic word. All three aforementioned stones, from Tune, Årstad, and Elgesem, are found in grave contexts in various regions in Norway dating to approximately the same time. Their common grave context speaks about rituals ensuring humans' transformation from one stage in life to another.

This assumption finds support in a Runic monument almost 700 years younger from Skadberg in Rogaland, dated to the twelfth century. The inscription testifies to the same type of ritual as on the Tune-stone, the *erfi*, and it mentions how *ale-men* are involved in the ritual and its preparations (S 3966, N 247).[45] The runic monument is some 3.75 m in height and the inscription is transliterated: **(olh)usmin ræisto stæin þana æf(t)ir skarþa**

---

36 Krause and Jankuhn, *Die Runeninschriften im älteren Futhark*, pp. 130–31.
37 Immer, 'Runer og runeindskrifter', II, 484.
38 Krause and Jankuhn, *Die Runeninschriften im älteren Futhark*, pp. 130–31.
39 Zimmermann, 'Bier, Runen und Macht', p. 46.
40 Spurkland, *Norwegian Runes and Runic Inscriptions*, p. 7; Imer, 'Runer og runeindskrifter', II, 484.
41 Bugge, 'Årstad', p. 232 ff.; Krause and Jankuhn, *Die Runeninschriften im älteren Futhark*, p. 131.
42 Krause and Jankuhn, *Die Runeninschriften im älteren Futhark*, pp. 130–32.
43 This suggestion was discussed briefly by Gerd Høst in *Våre eldste Norske runeinnskrifter*, pp. 87–88.
44 C 17791, Museum of Cultural History; Imer, 'Runer og runeindskrifter', II, 75.
45 N 247, Skadberg in *Norges Innskrifter med de yngre runer*.

(æn) þæir tr(uko) –rfi hans, which has been interpreted as: *The people in the ale-house erected this stone in memory of Skarða, and they drank his funeral ale*. 'The people in the ale-house' is likely to be referring to the people who had gathered for Skarði's funeral. The Old Norse *Ǫlhús* is generally used as a term for a public place, a house used for gatherings of various kinds, often related to specific feasts, such as funeral, childbirth ale, and weddings.[46] The Tune stone from around the fourth century, and the Skadberg stone from the twelfth century, are thus both testimonies to the surroundings and preparations of the funeral ritual.

A protective function is often associated with the alu-inscriptions due to the formulaic appearance of the word. This article shows that another possible interpretation is the word's connotation to ale-rituals, being rites of passage. These rituals were often organized with a protective intention. In such a ceremony, the person celebrated or commemorated would receive protection from people participating in the ritual. These performative acts may have had a certain authority in society. Just by performing them, for example, baptisms, inaugurations, and legal sentences, these performative acts are authoritative. These are all repeated again and again, and through the repetition the performances also display power.[47]

Brewing for Rituals?

Asbjǫrn needed grain to be able to arrange seasonal feasts in his local community and set out to buy grain and malt, not beer, after a bad season. Implicitly we understand that he ought to brew the ale himself, and that brewing equipment existed on northern farms. How people brewed is another question. In the Trøndelag region in mid-Norway, many farmsteads have cultural layers dominated by fire-cracked stones, so-called 'brewing stones', dated to the period AD 600–1600.[48] Such brewing stones are not found at all in northern Norway and Iceland, which could, in Geir Grønnesby's opinion, indicate these areas had unfavourable cultivation conditions, but also other brewing practices. Brewing stones would allow larger amounts of liquid to be brewed.[49]

The kettle is important as a constituent element in the mythological idea of ale and the process of brewing. The Eddic poems tell the story of how Ægir used Hymir's ale kettle when he brewed ale for the gods' banquet.[50] Ægir was only able to brew his magical ale, with barley, in this particular kettle. This

---

46   Hødnebø, 'Ølhus' in *Kulturhistorisk leksikon for nordisk middelalder*, XX, 714.
47   Hall, 'Who Needs Identity?'
48   Grønnesby, 'Hot Rocks! Beer Brewing in Viking and Medieval Age Farms in Trøndelag'
49   Grønnesby, 'Hot Rocks! Beer Brewing in Viking and Medieval Age Farms in Trøndelag', pp. 144–46.
50   The Eddic poems that were first written down in the Middle Ages but presumably transmitted orally for centuries prior to this also contain indications of the constituent elements in ale.

kettle is the main object in *Hymiskviða*. Þórr, the strongest of all the gods, acquired the kettle from the giant Hymir (stanza 39).

Þróttǫflugr kom á þing goða,
oc hafði hver, þannz Hymir átti;
enn véar hverian vel scolo drecca
ǫlðr at Ægis eitt hǫrmeitið.[51]

> (The mighty one came to the council of gods,
> And the kettle he had that Hymir's was;
> So gladly their ale the gods could drink
> In Ægir's hall at the autumn-time.)[52]

Some people practicing traditional ale-brewing of today would prefer bronze cauldrons because they have a generous capability of rapidly heating up liquid.[53] One hundred and twelve imported Roman cauldrons made from copper alloy are recorded from western Norway. One hundred and ten of them were found in graves (with a clear distinction between female and male graves), while two cauldrons were found in bogs.[54] They occur in Norway over a period of over 250 years, but the bog finds are impossible to date.[55] One of these cauldrons, the biggest of them, is the Bjarkøy cauldron (C 18174) with a volume of 200–250 litres (Fig. 8). The cauldron was found in a bog and is dated to the last phase of the Roman Iron Age (AD 300–400). Before becoming parts of the grave goods of prominent people in western Norway, the cauldrons must have been used for cooking of some kind.[56] The Bjarkøy cauldron was heavily worn when it was found, and it may have been linked to the activities at the courtyard site near the location where it was found.[57] Maybe the cauldrons have served as equipment in the production of large quantities of drink for social gatherings on wealthy farms.

The Content of Ale: Possibly Protective?

The most important component in the ale was grain. The Latin word for grain, *ceres*, is the root of the Latin word denoting ale, *cervisia*. Thus, the word ale refers to grain — the essential ingredient in ale. In Germanic languages, the origin of the word ale, *alu* (Proto-Norse),[58] *ǫl* (Old Norse), referred to a drink

---

51   *Edda*, ed. by Neckel and Kuhn, p. 95.
52   *Hymiskviða*, in *The Poetic Edda*, trans. by Bellows, st. 39.
53   Cf. images in Garshol, *Gårdsøl*, pp. 18, 50.
54   Hauken, *The Westland Cauldrons in Norway*.
55   Hauken, *The Westland Cauldrons in Norway*, p. 45.
56   Hauken, *The Westland Cauldrons in Norway*, p. 50.
57   Iversen, 'Courtyard Sites and their Cultic Context', pp. 25–37.
58   At the transition from Proto-Norse to Old Norse, the u-sound dropped out in utterances, whereas 'a' became 'ǫ' by means of u-umlaut.

Fig. 8: The Bjarkøy cauldron (C18174) from Bjarkøy in Harstad, Troms.
Photo: Ove Holst, courtesy of KHM, University of Oslo.

of malted barley.[59] Farmers have cultivated grain for thousands of years in Norway, as far north as Malangen. The crops were used for both food and drink. Regulations about grain cultivation appear in the medieval Norwegian laws, and historical reports about medieval farm life are recorded in the literature.

The earliest historiographer who mentioned the Northern Lights, the midnight sun, and polar ice, Pytheas of Massalia, possibly described northern farm life when he recorded his sailings from France to the North in 325 BC. Pytheas's testimony has been widely discussed for its value as a source for the history of the British Isles and the North, and the geographical areas he describes have been interpreted differently. One of the interpretations is that Pytheas referred to the landscape and people of northern Norway. The text records that Pytheas sailed around the British Isles and to the land he called Thule, which some suggest refer to his sailings along the Norwegian coast, up to Hálogaland. According to Pytheas, the climate in Thule was wet. The people there ate fruits, threshed grain indoors, and they prepared a drink consisting of grain and honey.[60] If Pytheas's description can be trusted, people in the northern Norway used grain in the production of drinks for at least 300 years before Christ. The drink based on grain and honey sounds like a combination of ale and mead. The main ingredient in ale is grain, and honey is the main

59 Bjorvand and Lindeman, eds, *Våre arveord*, p. 1086.
60 Cunliffe, *The Extraordinary Voyage of Pytheas the Greek*.

ingredient in mead. Grain used for beer production was probably introduced on the earliest farms, according to the records of Pytheas.

Truly enough, archaeological excavations at a Bronze Age sheep farm in Sandvika in the High North have revealed some few pollen indicators of *Hordeum* (barley).[61] This shows that cereals could ripen north of the mid-boreal bioclimatic zone where the local climate is good, for example in the fjord districts. The cultivation of cereals has been unsystematic and unstable in the High North due to the shifting climate and variations in the weather; animal husbandry and marine resources must have been more important in the agriculture and economy of these places.[62] The climate crisis in 536 AD must have affected the farmers here; an already limited grazing and cultivation season was even more shortened and the need for winter feed increased.[63] Even so, the long history of ale-rituals in a broader Northern geographical area and the political conflicts in Bjarkøy in the early eleventh century indicate that the social customs of organizing feasts and rituals in the local community required drinks that were made of barley. This may imply that trade and exchange between north and south was important from early on.

In the poem *Lokasenna* (*Loki's quarrel*), barley is personified as *Byggve* (Barleycorn). Loki confronts Byggve in stanza 44:

Hvat er þat iþ litla, er ec þat lǫggra séc,
oc snapvíst snapir?
at eyrom Freys munðu æ vera
oc und qvernom klaca.[64]

(What little creature goes crawling there,
snuffling and snapping about?
At Freyr's ears ever wilt thou be found,
or muttering hard at the mill.)[65]

Barleycorn answers Loki with a characterization of himself (stanza 45). In this stanza, we understand that barley is an essential ingredient in ale:

Byggvir ec heiti, enn mic bráðan qveða
goð ǫll oc gumar
því em ec hér hróðugr, at drecca Hroptz megir
allir ǫl saman.[66]

(Byggvir my name, and nimble am I,
As gods and men do grant;

61 Jensen and Arntzen, 'A Late Bronze Age Sheep Farm North of the Arctic Circle', p. 184
62 Jensen and Arntzen, 'A late Bronze Age Sheep Farm North of the Arctic Circle', pp. 193–98.
63 Iversen, 'Estate Division: Social Cohesion in the Aftermath of AD 536–7'.
64 *Lokasenna*, in *Edda*, ed. by Neckel and Kuhn, p. 105.
65 *Lokasenna*, in *The Poetic Edda*, trans. by Bellows, st. 44.
66 *Lokasenna*, in *Edda*, ed. by Neckel and Kuhn, p. 105.

And here am I proud that the children of Hropt
Together all drink ale.)[67]

Whether Barleycorn's characterization of himself as 'nimble' refers to the fermentation process or to the strong alcohol content of the drink is open to interpretation.

Alcohol is another ingredient in the ale that has caught interest among scholars studying drinking culture in pre-Christian society. The skaldic mead in particular been associated with creativity, and furthermore, creativity as a consequence of intoxication.[68] The consequences of alcohol were well-known, and warnings against intoxication recur in Old Norse literature. The other participants at Æge's drinking banquet explain Loki's wrangling in *Lokasenna* as a consequence of his alcohol consumption (stanza 47):

Qlr ertu, Loki, svá at þú er ørviti,
hví né lezcaðu, Loki?
Þvíat ofdryccia veldr alda hveim
er sína mælgi némanað.[69]

(Drunk art thou, Loki, and mad are thy deeds,
Why, Loki, leavest thou this not?
For drink beyond measure will lead all men
No thought of their tongues to take.)[70]

The ability to ensure alcohol content is related to the fermentation process, and numerous written sources from the Middle Ages describe problems with this process. When problems occurred, the solution was often to approach a supernatural power, a saint or the Virgin Mary, with prayers for their assistance in the process.[71] Together with the contents, the brewing process — fermentation and alcohol content included — was important for ensuring the health-providing quality of the drink, and to make sure the drink was free from bacteria. Many of the herbs used in ale production have the same or similar properties as alcohol — possessing cleansing properties.

Hops (Lat. *Humulus*) were added to ale from quite an early date. This plant performs preservative functions in ale production and ensures the ale's long-lasting qualities. German monasteries and eventually towns developed the use of hops in ale for conservative purposes from the ninth century, a practice that was gradually adopted in northern Europe. Remains of hops (*Humulus lupulus*) are found in Norway and Sweden from the ninth century.[72]

---

67 *Lokasenna*, in *The Poetic Edda*, trans. by Bellows, st. 45.
68 Mundal, 'Heiðrún — den mjødmjølkande geita på Valhalls tak'; Nordvig, 'Skaldemjødens betydning i den oldnordiske kulturkrets'.
69 *Lokasenna*, in *Edda*, ed. by Neckel and Kuhn, p. 105.
70 *Lokasenna*, in *The Poetic Edda*, trans. by Bellows, st. 47.
71 See, for example, *Maríu saga*, ed. by Unger, p. 109.
72 Åsen, *Norske klosterplanter*, p. 239 with references.

The systematic use of hops in ale production took time to implement, but during the Middle Ages it gradually became common. The medieval nun and abbess Hildegard of Bingen described its properties in her *Physica*:

Hops (*hoppho*) is a hot and dry herb, with a bit of moisture. It is not much of use for a human being, since it causes his melancholy to increase, gives him a sad mind, and makes his intestines heavy. Nevertheless, its bitterness inhibits some spoilage in beverages to which it is added, making them last longer.[73]

Archaeological excavations have found female hop plants in layers from AD 900–1000 in Norway, and pollen from male plants have been found in sediments from AD 600–1000 in Trondheim. Finds of the female plant may indicate cultivation of the plant, whereas the male plant may indicate a wild growing plant. Seeds of hops dating from AD 800 have been found in Kaupang in Vestfold.[74] During an excavation of a Viking Age grave from AD 850–950 in 2018, seeds from hops were found in a bailer in the grave.[75] This find indicates the possible use of the hops in drinks, presumably ale, already in the ninth century.

Remnants of hops in cloister gardens may indicate the quantity of ale produced in the monasteries. Here, large quantum and an industrial process were allowed for. As an example, botanist Per Arvid Åsen has shown from the remains of hops that the monastery of Vadstena in Sweden produced 600 litres of ale each day, at a time when 200 people lived in the monastery.[76]

In medical texts from the Middle Ages, descriptions of several herbs that could be suitable for ale-production, especially due to their antibacterial and hence protective properties for the consumer, are provided. For example, yarrow (Lat. *Achillea millefolium*) and plantain (Lat. *Plantago* sp.) are described as having healing and antibacterial properties. Bark from alder (Lat. *Alnus*) and needles from juniper (Lat. *Juniperus*) may also have been included in the oldest recipes.[77] The ale ingredients were associated with protective and health-stimulating properties and the connotations to the word *ale* hint at protection.

The ingredients in ale do possess preservative and cleansing qualities, and the involvement of supernatural and mythological forces in the brewing process afforded the ale with protective qualities. These qualities would be beneficial in transitional rituals, and the meaning of ale as a protective liquid developed throughout the Middle Ages. A Latin diploma dated 8 July 1241 records a correspondence between Pope Gregory IX and the Archbishop of Niðaróss (Trondheim) about Norwegian customs related to baptism.[78]

---

73 *Physica*, trans. by Throop 1998, p. 36.
74 Åsen, *Norske Klosterplanter*, p. 239 with references.
75 Sæther, 'Sikringsundersøkelse av skadet gravminne fra vikingtid'.
76 Åsen, *Norske Klosterplanter*, pp. 238–39 with references.
77 See for example Hildegard von Bingen, *Physica*, trans. by Throop (1998).
78 *DN* I, 26.

In this letter, the Pope sets out his answer to a question proposed by the Norwegian archbishop, who had asked if it was legitimate, in absence of water, to baptize children in ale. The pope replied it was not: Ale was not considered a suitable liquid for baptism in the Roman Church, as it obviously was in selected locations in the north. The correspondence between the pope and the archbishop truly reflects a custom with a certain circulation, since an archbishop from the High North, the periphery of Christendom, discussed the case with the pope. However, this custom was not fully overturned; in certain areas of Norway, ale was still used to baptize children in the eighteenth and nineteenth centuries.[79]

Conclusion

With the aim of tying up all the loose ends in this article it is time to return to the episode with Asbjǫrn *selsbani* in *Óláfs saga Helga* in which the cereal has crucial importance in carrying out seasonal feasts in local communities. Can the protective associations of ale as a beverage also presume the denotation of the word *ǫl* as a gathering?

The narrative of Óláfr Haraldsson in Snorri's *Heimskringla* provides insights into cultural, economic, and social aspects of how seasonal rituals worked in local groups in a society. The saga episode may be read as an example of how important it was to arrange seasonal feasts in local communities. The ale, brewed from grain, was a constituent element in seasonal celebrations. In order to arrange such, the organizers had to be in possession of grain. Keeping up social practices and connecting people across geographical boundaries would implicate trade and exchange of goods between the regions that could produce them.

When Snorri tells of King Óláfr's restrictions on corn exports to northern Norway, he describes so much more than economic regulations: Óláfr interfered in deeply rooted traditions of social and religious customs in northern society. Asbjǫrn was hindered from organizing seasonal festivals in his local community. This deprived him of the opportunity to uphold his important position in the community, and to organize rituals that provided continuity and collective support in the community. Because ale-rituals were repetitive celebrations over a long time span and vast geographical areas, these rituals also embodied cultural and social memories from a longer period of time than the actual scene presented in Snorri's saga about Óláfr Haraldsson.[80] The intensity of Asbjǫrn's humiliation was further exploited when he sought revenge the following year.

After Candlemas (2 February) in AD 1023, Asbjǫrn set out on a new voyage to take revenge, together with ninety men (chap. 124). On 18 April, the vessel

79 Garshol, *Gårdsøl*, p. 79.
80 Connerton, *How Societies Remember*; Hall, 'Who Needs Identity?'.

arrived at Karmey, close to Þórir *sel* at Ǫgvaldsnes. The king was visiting at the same time. When Asbjǫrn went into the hall, he heard Þórir *sel* recounting the story of the events with Asbjǫrn, adding details to the tale that humiliated Asbjǫrn again. Asbjǫrn flew into a rage: he rushed into the hall and struck at Þórir, so that Þórir's head fell upon the table before the king and his body at the king's feet (chap. 124). Skjálgr Erlingsson was at the farm when the incident took place, and he immediately supported his relative Asbjǫrn by taking him to Erlingr Skjálgrsson for assistance (chap. 125). Thereupon, Asbjǫrn's life was saved and he offered himself up into the king's power.

The present investigation aimed at understanding why Óláfr prevented grain exports to the north, and why this was so difficult for the leading men there to accept. The sources discussed in this chapter may reveal how ale was a constituent element in long-standing rituals practised at important stages in people's lives: burial, giving birth, weddings, and other transitional stages. The ale-ritual and the ale itself have possessed protective qualities. By restricting grain exports, Óláfr restricted opportunities to arrange seasonal rituals and rites of passage, because such rituals involved ale.

Works Cited

Manuscripts, Archival Sources, and Other Unpublished Material

Archaeological Finds

Bergen, University Museum of Bergen, B 4384
Bergen, University Museum of Bergen, B 8039
Bergen, University Museum of Bergen, B 8350
Copenhagen, National Museum, C 5229
Copenhagen, National Museum, C 8650
Oslo, Museum of Cultural History, C 2092
Oslo, Museum of Cultural History, C 3639
Oslo, Museum of Cultural History, C 17791
Tromsø, Tromsø Museum, T 22926/1-74
Stavanger, Museum of Archaeology (Arkeologisk Museum), S 66940
Stavanger, Museum of Archaeology (Arkeologisk Museum), S 3966

Primary Sources

Bingen, Hildegard von, *Physica*, trans. by Priscilla Throop (Rochester: Healing Arts, 1998)
Bjarkøyretten: Nidaros eldste bylov, ed. by Jan Ragnar Hagland and Jørn Sandnes (Oslo: Samlaget, 1997)
DN = Diplomatarium Norvegicum. Oldbreve til Kundskab om Norges indre og ydre Forhold, Sprog, Slægter, Sæder, Lovgivning og Rettergang i Middelalderen, ed. by

Christian C. A. Lange, Carl R. Unger, and others, 23 vols (Christiania / Oslo: Mallings Forladshandel, 1847–2011)

Edda. Die Lieder des Codex Regius Nebst Verwandten Denkmälern, ed. by Gustav Neckel and Hans Kuhn (Heidelberg: Winter Universitätsverlag, 1983)

Frostatingsloven, trans. by Jørn Sandnes and Jan Ragnar Hagland (Oslo: Samlaget / Frosta Historielag, 1994)

Gulatingslova = Den eldre Gulatingslova, trans. by Bjørn Eithun, Magnus Rindal, and Tor Ulset, Norrøne tekster, 6 (Oslo: Riksarkivet, 1994)

Maríu saga. Legender om Jomfru Maria og hendes Jertegn, ed. by C. R. Unger (Christiania: Brögger og Christie, 1871)

Norges innskrifter med de ældre Runer, ed. by Sophus Bugge, Norsk Kjeldeskriftsfond (Christiania, A. W. Brøggers Bogtrykkeri, 1891–1903)

The Poetic Edda, trans. by Henry Adams Bellows (Princeton: Princeton University Press, 1936)

Snorri Sturluson, *Heimskringla: Nóregs Konunga Sǫgur*, ed. by Finnur Jónsson (Copenhagen: Gad, 1911)

——, *Heimskringla*, trans. by Samuel Laing (London: Longman, Brown, Green, and Longmans, 1844)

Secondary Works

Bjorvand, Harald, 'Det besværlige adjektivet på Tunesteinen', *Norsk lingvistisk tidsskrift*, 26.1 (2008), 3–12

Bjorvand, Harald, and Otto Lindeman, ed., *Våre arveord: etymologisk ordbok*, Instituttet for sammenlignende kulturforskning, Serie B, Skrifter, 105 (Oslo: Novus, 2000)

Connerton, Paul, *How Societies Remember* (Cambridge: Cambridge University Press, 1989)

Cunliffe, Barry, *The Extraordinary Voyage of Pytheas the Greek: The Man who Discovered Britain*, rev. edn (New York: Walker, 2002)

Enright, Michael J., *Lady with a Mead Cup: Ritual, Prophecy and Lordship in the European Warband from La Téne to the Viking Age* (Dublin: Four Courts, 1996)

Garshol, Lars Marius, *Gårdsøl. Det norske ølet* (Oslo: Cappelen Damm, 2016)

Grønnesby, Geir, 'Hot Rocks! Beer Brewing in Viking and Medieval Age Farms in Trøndelag', in *The Agrarian Life of the North 2000 BC – AD 1000. Studies in Rural Settlement and Farming in Norway*, ed. by Frode Iversen and Håkan Petersson (Kristiansand: Portal, 2016), pp. 133–50

Grønvik, Ottar, *Fra Ågedal til Setre* (Oslo: Universitetsforlaget, 1987)

——, *Frå Vimose til Ødemotland. Nye studier over runeinnskrifter fra førkristen tid i Norden* (Oslo: Universitetsforlaget, 1996)

Hagland, Jan Ragnar, 'Oppsiktsvekkjande nytt runefunn', *Spor*, 2.40 (2005), 16–17

Hall, Stuart, 'Who Needs Identity?', in *Identity: A Reader*, ed. by Paul de Gay, Jessica Evans, and Peter Redman (London: Sage, 2000), pp. 15–30

Hauken, Åsa Dahlin, *The Westland Cauldrons in Norway* (Stavanger: Arkeologisk museum i Stavanger, 2005)

Høst, Gerd, *Runer. Våre eldste runeinnskrifter* (Oslo: Aschehoug, 1976)

Høst Heyerdahl, Gerd, 'Trylleordet "alu"', *Det norske videnskaps-Akademi årbok* (1981), 35–49

Imer, Lisbeth, 'The Oldest Runic Monuments in the North: Dating and Distribution', *Nowele: North-Western European Language Evolution*, 62–63 (October 2011), 169–212

——, 'Runer og runeindskrifter. Kronologi, kontekst og funktion i Skandinaviens jernalder og vikingetid' (unpublished doctoral thesis, University of Copenhagen, 2007)

Iversen, Frode, 'Courtyard Sites and their Cultic Context', in *Religion, Cults and Rituals in the Medieval Rural Environment*, ed. by Cristiane Bis-Worch and Claudia Theune, Ruralia, 11 (Leiden: Sidestone Press Academics, 2017), pp. 25–37

——, 'Estate Division: Social Cohesion in the Aftermath of AD 536–7', in *Agrarian Life of the North 2000 BC –1000 AD: Studies in Rural Settlements and Farming in Norway*, ed. by Frode Iversen and Håkan Petersson (Kristiansand: Portal, 2016), pp. 41–75

Jensen, Christin E., and Arntzen, Johan E., 'A Late Bronze Age Sheep Farm North of the Arctic Circle', in *Agrarian Life of the North 2000 BC–1000 AD: Studies in Rural Settlements and Farming in Norway*, ed. by Frode Iversen and Håkan Petersson (Kristiansand: Portal, 2016), pp. 173–202

Knirk, James, 'Nyfunn og nyregistreringer 2003', in *Nytt om runer. Meldingsblad om runeforskning*, ed. by James E. Knirk (Oslo: Runearkivet, 2004), p. 18

Krause, Wolfgang, *Beiträge zur Runenforschung* (Halle: Niemeyer, 1934)

——, *Runeninschriften im älteren Futhark* (Halle: Niemeyer, 1937)

Krause, Wolfgang, and Herbert Jankuhn, *Die Runeninschriften im älteren Futhark* (Göttingen: Vandenhoeck and Ruprecht, 1966)

Looijenga, Tineke, *Texts and Contexts of the Oldest Runic Inscriptions*, The Northern World, 4 (Leiden: Brill, 2003)

Lundeby, Einar, and Henrik Williams, 'Om Vadstenabrakteatens **tuwa** med et tillegg om Lellingebrakteatens **salu**', *Maal og Minne*, 1–2 (1992), 11–26

McKinnell, John, and others, *Runes, Magic and Religion. A Sourcebook* (Vienna: Fassbaender, 2004)

Mees, Bernard, and Mindy MacLeod, *Runic Amulets and Magic Objects* (Woodbridge: Boydell, 2006)

Mundal, Else, 'Heiðrún — den mjødmjølkande geita på Valhalls tak', in *Eyvindarbók. Festskrift til Eyvind Fjeld Halvorsen 4. mai 1992*, ed. by Finn Hødnebø (Oslo: Institutt for nordistikk og litteraturvitenskap, 1992), pp. 240–47

Nordberg, Andreas, '*Krigarna i Odins sal:* dödsföreställningar och krigarkult i fornnordisk religion' (unpublished doctoral thesis, University of Stockholm, 2004)

Nordvig, Mathias, 'Skaldemjødens betydning i den oldnordiske kulturkrets', in *Drikkekultur i middelalderen*, ed. by Kasper H. Andersen and Sefan Pajung (Aarhus: Aarhus Universitetsforlag, 2014), pp. 27–49

Spurkland, Terje, *I begynnelsen var Futhark* (Oslo: Cappelen, 2001)

——, *Norwegian Runes and Runic Inscriptions* (Woodbridge: Boydell, 2005)

Stamnes, Arne Anderson, 'Effect of temperature change on Iron Age Cereal Production and Settlement Patterns in Mid-Norway', in *Agrarian Life of the North 2000 BC–1000 AD. Studies in Rural Settlements and Farming in Norway*, ed. by Frode Iversen and Håkan Petersson (Kristiansand: Portal, 2016), pp. 27–39

Steinsland, Gro, *Det hellige bryllup og norrøn kongeideologi; en analyse av hierogami-myten i Skírnismál, Ynglingatal, Háleygjatal og Hyndluljóð* (Oslo: Solum, 1991)

——, *Norrøn religion — myter, riter, samfunn* (Oslo: Pax, 2005)

Sæther, Kathryn E., 'Sikringsundersøkelse av skadet gravminne fra vikingtid. Ytre Mosby 28/502. Kristiansand kommune, Vest-Agder', *Rapport Arkeologisk Utgravning* (Kulturhistorisk museum, Universitetet i Oslo, 2018)

van Gennep, Arnold, *Rites de passage. Overgangsriter*, trans. by Erik Ringen (Oslo: Pax, [1909] 1999)

Wicker, Nancy, 'Bracteates and Beverages: alu in Light of the Discovery of a New Bracteate from Scalford', *Reading Runes: Discovery, Decipherment, Documentation. Abstracts for The Eight International Symposium on Runes and Runic Inscriptions*, Nyköping, 2014 <http://www.runforum.nordiska.uu.se/readingrunes/abstracts/wicker/>

——, 'Bracteate Inscriptions and Context Analysis in the Light of Alternatives to Hauck's Iconographic Interpretations', *Futhark — International Journal of Runic Studies*, 5 (2014), 25–43

Zimmermann, Ute 'Bier, Runen und Macht: Ein Formelwort im Kontext', *Futhark — International Journal of Runic Studies*, 5 (2014), 45–64

Åsen, Per Ivar, *Norske klosterplanter* (Kristiansand: Portal, 2014)

Myths and Representations in the Political Consolidation of the North

YASSIN NYANG KAROLIUSSEN

The Origins of Political Organization in the High North: A Study of the Historical and Material Remains of Finnmǫrk, Hálogaland, and the Mythical Ǫmð

Introduction

The toponyms Hálogaland and Finnmǫrk are used in medieval texts that describe the two places very differently: Hálogaland is depicted as a part of the Norwegian kingdom; Finnmǫrk tends to be portrayed as a mystic place situated outside the borders of the realm. The medieval authorities nonetheless seem to have had an interest in the resources existing in this area.

The earliest texts also present the people living in the two places very differently. Finnmǫrk was solely inhabited by the Finns, synonymous with the Sámi population who are presented as heathens, and with a lifestyle and an economy based on hunting and gathering. Marine resources were rich and easily accessible along the coastline of both Finnmǫrk and Hálogaland, and both fishing and the hunting of sea mammals were pursued throughout the Iron Age. Products obtained from these activities contributed both to feeding the inhabitants and producing commodities for exchange. In the interior of Finnmǫrk subsistence was based on hunting game. Hálogaland, by contrast, was largely inhabited by ethnically Norse people. They are described as leading a life similar to the Norse in other parts of the country, living primarily as farmers. The climatic conditions in the Iron Age supported arable agriculture as far north as the Malangen fjord in the northern part of the present-day Troms county, but evidence of Iron Age cereal cultivation has also been found on the island of Kvaløya, situated north of the Malangen fjord.[1] Some Sámi people were also to be found living in Hálogaland.

---

1 Fjærvoll, 'Korndyrkinga i Hålogaland i gammal tid'; Vorren, 'Farm Development at the Arctic Cereal Limit', pp. 161–70.

Yassin Nyang Karoliussen, ykaroliussen@yahoo.no

Myths and Magic in the Medieval Far North: Realities and Representations of a Region on the Edge of Europe, ed. by Stefan Figenschow, Richard Holt, and Miriam Tveit, AS 10
(Turnhout: Brepols, 2020), pp. 181–196

10.1484/M.AS-EB.5.120525

Hálogaland comprised the coastal section of northern Norway, a large area stretching as far as a largely undefined border situated somewhere in the northern part of present-day Troms county. The term Finnmǫrk applied to the coastline north of this point, and to all the lands in the interior. Today, Hálogaland and Finnmǫrk constitute the vast northern region of the state of Norway. The processes by which these northernmost parts of Norway were incorporated into the realm were long-drawn-out; indeed, the final border between Norway and Sweden was established only in 1751 and that between Norway and Russia as late as 1826.

Our meagre written sources do not allow us to construct a clear picture of how this northern region began to be more closely associated with southern regions under a centralized Norwegian authority, a process with its origins in the latter part of the Iron Age and extending well into the Middle Ages. This chapter will therefore examine aspects of that process by looking principally at some of the material remains which provide evidence for early political organization and change in the North.

Ohthere of Hálogaland

The oldest reliable text regarding relations at the end of the Iron Age in present-day northern Norway is the account of Ohthere. This account was written c. 890 AD, when Ohthere from Hálogaland visited the Anglo-Saxon King Alfred of Wessex. Ohthere told the king that he resided far north, farther than any other Norwegian.[2] This account establishes some foundation for where we imagine the seats of the Iron Age chieftains of northern Norway were situated at that time.[3]

Ohthere describes himself as a *Northman*.[4] We cannot be sure what that meant to him, or to the Englishman who wrote down the text. He reports on his interaction with other ethnic groups, including the Sámi, and these peoples are associated with different geographical areas and economic activities. He reports that the Sámi camped and hunted in the great wasteland further north from where he lived, and on the moors east of the coastal areas of the land which were grazed or ploughed. The Sámi economy is further explained when Ohthere relates that he was entitled to collect tribute from them. The products he received were the hides and furs of different kinds of terrestrial or marine animals, feathers from birds, and ivory and bone from marine animals, as well as rope made from their skins. Ohthere himself was active in hunting, especially for whale, walrus, and wild reindeer. In addition to this he

---

2 Bately, 'Ohthere's account', pp. 55–57.
3 Berglund, *Tjøtta-riket*, p. 367; Storli, *Hålogaland før rikssamlingen*, pp. 21–29; Hansen and Olsen, *Samenes historie*, p. 65.
4 Bately, 'Ohthere's Account', p. 55.

had a farm, where he ploughed a small area of land and kept a small number of livestock. He also kept six hundred domesticated reindeer.[5]

Ohthere's report is unique, as it is considered to be a first-hand account of the life of a chieftain living in the northern part of present-day Norway during the late Iron Age. It is often viewed in combination with an economic model introduced by Knut Odner in 1973. This model was developed from Icelandic saga material, as well as from the *Íslendingabók* and *Landnamabók* concerning Icelandic society in the ninth and tenth centuries. In these texts, society appears to be based around the family and the farm. Several farms would be organized into a larger social unit, with one chieftain as the head of this unit. Conflicts with neighbouring farms could then be easily mediated. In the same way, the consolidated farms could more easily resist hostile intruders. The chieftain was entitled to collect a tribute, a share of the surplus produced by the farms he ruled over. This was the basis of his wealth, and through gift exchange he could build alliances with other chieftains and further strengthen his position.[6]

Initially, Odner's model was developed to depict the organization of Iron Age society in the south-western parts of Norway. It seems also to be applicable to Iron Age society in northern Norway, however, and saga descriptions of northern society provides a picture resembling Odner's model. The sagas narrated by Snorri Sturluson provide information about northern Norwegian chieftains organizing blot (sacrifices) and feasts.[7]

Ohthere does not mention the names of any places inhabited by the Sámi, but he refers to the geographical area where he lives as Hálogaland, and as we have seen he describes his own economy as one based on a combination of hunting and farming. In this way, Ohthere's economic utilization differs from that of the Sámi, due to the latter's economy being based exclusively on hunting. Ohthere is distinguishing himself from (at least some of) the Sámi by rank. In the account of Ohthere it is said that Ohthere, amongst others of his peers, received tribute from the Sámi: 'But their wealth consists mostly of the tax (tribute?) that the Finnas pay them'.[8] The collection of tribute and taxes presupposes that the receiver was ranked higher than the giver.[9]

Medieval Texts on Hálogaland and Finnmǫrk

Later texts concerning northern Norwegian society in medieval times describe Sámi occupations as something very different from those of the

5 Bately, 'Ohthere's Account', p. 56.
6 Odner, 'Economic Structures in Western Norway in the Early Iron Age', pp. 105–08.
7 Hansen, *Samisk fangstsamfunn og norsk høvdingeøkonomi*, p. 131.
8 Bately, 'Ohthere's Account', p. 56.
9 Holmsen, 'Finnskatt og nordmannsskatt', pp. 62–63.

Norwegians. Both Adam of Bremen and the anonymous *Historia Norwegie*, probably written respectively in 1075 and *c.* mid-1100,[10] describe historical and ecological conditions in Norway at that time, as seen from the perspective of contemporaneous scholars. In both texts the Sámi way of life is described in distinct chapters.

In the work of Adam of Bremen, the description of the Sámi is set in great contrast to that of the Norwegians. The Norwegians' acceptance of Christianity is particularly emphasized. The Norwegians are described as a peace-loving people. They were farmers, keeping cattle and cultivating the land. The Sámi, on the other hand, are described as heathens and quite unruly. They based their economy on hunting and led a vagrant lifestyle.[11]

Adam of Bremen was a German clergyman who wrote *Gestae Hammaburgensis ecclesiae pontificum*, a work presenting the history of the dioceses belonging to the archdiocese of Hamburg-Bremen. The work consists of four parts, of which the final part presents the conditions of the northern parts of the archdiocese, and it is here that the description of the Sámi and the Norwegians is found. It stands out from the remaining texts by Adam in emphasizing conditions concerning the region's geography, society, and economic adaptation, in addition to its historic conditions.[12] The characteristics put forward by Adam of Bremen are imprinted with his own worldview, with an emphasis on the differences from the life and times that were familiar to him.[13]

The author of *Historia Norwegie* is unknown; he was probably also someone with an ecclesiastical background. The text is clearly inspired by the work of Adam of Bremen, which is obvious due to the similarities between the two texts. *Historia Norwegie* describes the geographical, ecological, and demographic conditions in the Norwegian kingdom at the time it was written. It states that the geographical characteristics of the Norwegian kingdom were divided into three different zones where the inhabitants lived: the *sea land*, the *upper land*, and the *forest land*. The sea land was the coastal area and the upper land was the interior area of present-day southern Norway. Hálogaland was situated within the sea land, and here the Norwegians dwelled with the Sámi, with whom they also traded. The forest land, on the other hand, was exclusively inhabited by the Finns. This was situated to the eastern side of the sea land. *Historia Norwegie* does not stress the Norwegians' way of life to the same extent as Adam of Bremen, but Sámi hunting skills and heathenism are mentioned in the description of the forest land.[14]

The historian Linda Kaljundi has analysed the work of Adam of Bremen, and she has studied how this kind of ecclesiastical historical text dating from

---

10 Koht, *Den eldste Noregs-historia*, p. 5; L. I. Hansen, *Astafjord bygdebok*, p. 55; see also Hansen this volume.
11 Koht, *Den eldste Noregs-historia*, pp. 81–84.
12 Jørgensen, 'The Land of the Norwegians', p. 46; Koht, *Den eldste Noregs-historia*, p. 8.
13 Jørgensen, 'The Land of the Norwegians', p. 5.
14 Koht, *Den eldste Noregs-historia*, pp. 14–16.

the medieval period depicted the development of Christian states in Europe. To legitimize conquering new geographic areas, and to strengthen the Christian community, it was significant to compare developments within Europe with biblical events. One useful tool of rhetoric was to contrast and marginalize heathen people. The portrayal of the challenges lying ahead of the conqueror was achieved by describing the non-Christians, and the geographical areas they dwelt in, as wild and dangerous.[15]

The Archaeology of Hálogaland and Finnmǫrk

The description of the geographical division between Hálogaland and Finnmǫrk put forward in *Historia Norwegie* largely coincides with the archaeological record of Iron Age remains. The Iron Age material along the coastal area south of the northern part of Troms county can be principally connected to the Norse Iron Age population. These remains are often distinct structures in the landscape. The settlements are considered to resemble sedentary farms expressing a cultural affinity to the Germanic settlements farther south. The Iron Age material in the northern part of Troms county and Finnmark county, as well as the interior parts of northern Norway, is mainly connected to the Sámi population. These structures are not as visible in the landscape. They point to a culture and economy founded on hunting. Relying on Odner's economic model, this difference in conspicuousness might be explained by the two groups' different social connections. The Sámi probably occupied a clarified social role in the perception of their collaborators, since they were involved in the Norse population's network of trade as the suppliers of commodities gained from hunting. The Norse population, on the other hand, may have been placed in a more stressful situation, since their cultural identity and social role probably needed to be expressed to different groups of collaborators situated across a greater geographical area.[16]

Earlier, the division of the northern Norwegian landscape was seen as a territorial division, based on the two ethnic groups' different forms of subsistence. The Icelandic text *Rímbegla* (*c.* 1190–1200) states that the northern border of Hálogaland was at the Malangen fjord in the early Middle Ages.[17] As previously mentioned, this has also been regarded as the northern limit for cereal cultivation. Until the 1980s, the general view was that the Sámi Iron Age population had been expelled into the marginal areas of arable land, to the benefit of the Norse farmers. In 1986, the archaeologist Audhild Schanche

---

15 Kaljundi, 'Waiting for the Barbarians', p. 122.
16 Hansen and Olsen, *Samenes historie*, p. 132; see also Barth, 'Introduction', p. 153; Jones, *The Archaeology of Ethnicity*.
17 Hansen, 'Middelaldersamfunnets etniske grenser', p. 63.

analysed the distribution of Iron Age settlement in Hálogaland.[18] Because of the scarce Sámi material in the area, Schanche based her analysis on the presence or absence of remains from Norse Iron Age settlements throughout the landscape. Schanche found the earlier explanation for the settlement pattern insufficient. She stressed the fact that a number of Norse settlements were established on islands where the conditions for cereal farming were not ideal. At the same time, conditions for this activity were rather good in the inner fjords of southern Troms, where Norse Iron Age occupation seems to have been more or less absent.[19] Her study also showed that the Norse settlement tendency to occupy southern and western parts of the landscape also fits the way they inhabited islands.[20] Schanche proposed that the geographical division between the two ethnic groups was based on symbolic expressions of identity and the result of mutual negotiation.[21]

The study of slab-lined pits seemed to support the assumption in Schanche's explanation.[22] These structures are connected to the Sámi group and hunting activities. The pits are frequently found along the coast of Finnmark county, but the greatest concentration of this category is to be found in the northern part of Troms. A few pits are found as far south as Håkøy in Tromsø municipality. The pits appear oval or rectangular openings in the ground, 2–4 m by 1–2 m in size, extending to a depth of 50 cm. The pit interiors are lined with slabs of stone and they often contain the remains of burnt stone and charcoal, as well as traces of animal fat. The pits were used to extract oil from the blubber of marine mammals. Carbon-dating shows that the pits became a normal phenomenon along the coast of Finnmork in around 300 AD, and the use of these pits seems to have peaked around 600–900 AD; they seem to be abandoned after the year 1000. Remains of Sámi Iron Age houses are often found near the slab-lined pits. They appear as the remains of small round house structures, with the hearth placed at the centre. The layout of these house remains seems to resemble the historically known Sámi *rundgamme*. Their unassuming appearance in the landscape differs from house structure remains dating from earlier chronological periods.[23]

The archipelago incorporating Helgøy and Karlsøy, north of Tromsø, is located just on the border between Finnmork and Hálogaland. This is evident from the archaeological record. These islands are covered with cultural remains from both Sámi and Norse Iron Age occupation.[24] Jørn Erik Henriksen views this as an area of mixed ethnicity, in contrast to Arnøy situated to the east,

18 Schanche, *Nordnorsk jernalderarkeologi*.
19 Schanche, *Nordnorsk jernalderarkeologi*, p. 174.
20 Schanche, 'Jernalderens bosetningsmønster', pp. 179–81.
21 Schanche, *Nordnorsk jernalderarkeologi*.
22 Henriksen, 'Hellegropene', p. 101.
23 Myrvoll, 'Excavation of Iron Age sites', p. 83; Hansen and Olsen, *Samenes historie – fram til 1750*, p. 71; Henriksen, 'Hellegropene'.
24 Bratrein, *Karlsøy og Helgøy bygdebok*, pp. 139–54.

where the greatest concentration of slab-lined pits is to be found. Henriksen established the border between Finnmork and Hálogaland at Lyngen.[25] In 1326, a peace and taxation treaty were concluded between the Norwegian kingdom and Novgorod. In this treaty it was stated that the border between the Norwegian and Russian taxation territories should be established at Lyngen. Hansen and Olsen suggest that this medieval border may have had its origins in the Iron Age.[26] At the beginning of the Middle Ages, and the establishment of the Norwegian kingdom, the archaeological material in the Helgøy / Karlsøy region shows a more consistent Sámi character.[27] The border between Finnmork and Hálogaland thus seems to have moved southward in the early Middle Ages.

Iron Age burials marked with mounds are usually interpreted as an expression of Norse ethnicity. The Iron Age burial material in northern Norway, connected to Norse settlement, is nonetheless varied. Analyses that have been carried out on Iron Age grave material in northern Norway show that all Iron Age grave types occur throughout the period. There are, however, some types that occur more frequently than others within limited periods of time. The custom of marking graves with mounds seems to have been practised on a more or less constant basis throughout the Iron Age, although graves without any external grave indicators, so-called flat graves, increased in prevalence during the later part of the Iron Age.[28]

The construction of grave mounds is often interpreted as a family or group's desire to display its power. Large mounds, in particular, are seen as a performance of control. It must have required a lot of labour and a certain number of people to build a mound, so the bigger the mound, the more manpower was necessary. A person, or a family, capable of obtaining a sufficient number of people to spend their time and strength building a mound, either for themselves or for a deceased family member, would have been regarded as being in control of both people and territory.[29]

There are also reasons to believe that grave mounds were erected to demonstrate property and territorial rights. There are several legal documents dating from the Middle Ages, such as Magnus the Law-mender's national law dating from 1274, connecting allodium (an estate held in absolute ownership without service or acknowledgment of any superior), rights to landed property, and kinship to persons buried in heathen grave mounds.[30] In the skaldic poem *Ynglingatal* the kinship and particular king's burial mounds are emphasized.[31]

---

25 Henriksen, 'Hellegropene', pp. 99, 112.
26 Hansen and Olsen, *Samenes historie*, p. 75.
27 Bratrein, *Karlsøy og Helgøy bygdebok*, pp. 201–04.
28 Holand, *Graver og samfunn*, pp. 38–53.
29 Ringstad, 'Graver og ideologi', p. 145; Berglund, *Tjøtta-riket*, p. 33; Storli, *Hålogaland før rikssamlingen*.
30 Skre, *Herredømmet*, pp. 143–44.
31 Skre, *Herredømmet*, p. 202.

Even though the dates of these documents are more recent than the custom of burying people in mounds, it is likely that they are founded on older traditions. This may be the reason why people bothered to build burial mounds, even the smaller ones, instead of not-so-demanding flat graves.

Even though the grave mounds are chiefly most common inside the borders of Hálogaland, there are examples of grave mounds registered within what must be regarded as Finnmǫrk. Sometimes these are considered as dubious or abandoned graves.[32] In other cases, where the mound has been excavated and an actual grave is revealed, it is usually viewed as a Norse individual's burial, even if the grave goods are not unambiguously Norse. The grave location is regarded as far away from the person's domicile or place of birth. The remote burial is explained by death during a journey, colonization, or signs of inter-ethnic marriage.[33]

Studies on northern Norwegian Iron Age burials with mixed ethnic expression have been seen as cases of cultural hybridization.[34] These phenomena, instead of being regarded as anomalies and exotic elements, should be interpreted in their own right. The urge to categorize and label cultural remains spoils the possibility of fully understanding the interaction between people living in the past.[35] This must be applicable to both structures and communities.

The Courtyard Sites

Another archaeological structure strongly associated with Norse Iron Age settlement are the courtyard sites. They appear as assemblies of house foundations placed side by side, with either conjoining or parallel walls. The entrances of the house foundations face a common yard. The overall structure usually forms an unclosed oval or circular shape.[36] There are twenty-six to thirty courtyard sites recorded along the Norwegian coastline; eleven to thirteen of these are located within Hálogaland.[37]

Explanations as to what kind of activity the courtyard sites exhibit have varied over the years. Amongst others, some interpretations are that they were quarterings for the chieftain's troops; that they were the actual residence of the chieftain;[38] or that they were a neutral location for trade between local

32 Schanche, *Graver i ur og berg*, pp. 95–96.

33 Brøgger, *Nord-Norges bosetningshistorie*, p. 51; Gjessing, 'Den fyrste norske busetjinga i finnmark', p. 137; Storli, '*Stallo'-boplassene*, p. 112; Andreassen and Bratrein, 'Finnmark, Bjarkøy and the Norwegian Kingdom', pp. 317–19.

34 Bruun, 'Blandede graver'; Svestad, 'Svøpt i myra'.

35 Bruun, 'Blandede graver', pp. 60–69.

36 Johansen and Søbstad, 'De nordnorske tunanleggene fra jernalderen'.

37 Storli, *Hålogaland før rikssamlingen*; Storli, 'Court Sites of Arctic Norway', p. 128; Iversen, 'Community and Society', p. 2; Brink and others, 'Comments on Inger Storli', pp. 95, 109–10.

38 Berglund, *Tjøtta-riket*, p. 342.

inhabitants and travelling traders.[39] The latest thorough discussion of the sites situated in northern Norway has been carried out by Inger Storli.[40] By using the description of the Icelandic *thing* organization in *Landnámabók* as an analogy, she argues that these sites represent places where delegates from different regions gathered to carry out *thing*.[41] The sites are mostly situated an equal distance from more than one contemporaneous farm. Thus, there is a general comprehension among scholars that the sites represent neutral ground, rather than an expression of power associated with just one family.[42] These courtyard sites appear, then, to be court sites, places where matters were discussed and judgement given. Hereinafter, I will refer to these archaeological phenomena as court sites.

The radiocarbon dates from nine of the northern Norwegian court sites show that eight of them were in use before 600 and only three of the nine showed any sign of continued use after that time. The sites that were in use before 600 had fewer house foundations than the sites which were used after 600. All the sites seem to have gone out of use during the ninth and tenth centuries. Storli interprets this pattern as a sign of a consolidation of power during the later part of the Iron Age in the society of Hálogaland. She views the abandonment of the sites as evidence that this kind of institution went out of use, either because of the introduction of royal supremacy or because the leading families became fewer and each governed a greater territorial area.[43]

Frode Iversen, like Storli, interprets the court sites as locations for holding *thing* meetings. But whereas Storli regards the activities carried out at the court sites as coming to an end as the medieval Norwegian kingdom took form, Iversen sees them from the outset as material remains of the practice of dividing greater territorial areas into administrative units, a practice that continued after the Norwegian kingdom had been established in the Middle Ages.[44]

Iversen points to the fact that *Historia Norwegie* mentions Hálogaland in the same way that it mentions *Gulathing*. The Gulathing was a law province that can be traced back to the eleventh century. Apart from the information provided in *Historia Norwegie*, there is no written record on the development of the law province of Hálogaland.

By combining the law text from Gulathing, the national law of Magnus the Law-mender of 1274, and available population records, Iversen traces the evolvement of the Gulathing law province from the eighth century to

---

39   Urbanczyk, *Medieval Arctic Norway*, pp. 183–85.
40   Storli, 'Court Sites of Arctic Norway'; Storli, *Hålogaland før rikssamlingen*; Storli, 'Tunanleggenes rolle i nordnorsk jernalder'; Storli, 'Barbarians" of the North', pp. 81–103.
41   Storli, *Hålogaland før rikssamlingen*; Storli, 'Court Sites of Arctic Norway'.
42   Storli, 'Court Sites of Arctic Norway', pp. 130–35; Brink and others, 'Comments on Inger Storli'.
43   Storli, 'Court Sites of Arctic Norway', p. 141.
44   Iversen, 'Community and Society'; Iversen, 'Hålogaland blir en rettskrets'.

the thirteenth century in the coastal landscape and parts of the interior landscape of southern Norway.[45] He sees this as a pattern of how increased interaction between smaller communities evolved into larger societies from the later part of the Iron Age.

Iversen proposes that the court sites may be seen in connection with the administrative division of Hálogaland as described in late medieval and early modern texts. He finds a more or less consistent pattern, in that almost all of the court sites that were in use after 600 have additional house plots, compared to the older ones in the vicinity. Iversen interprets this as an indication that the interaction between smaller communities throughout Hálogaland was intensified, expanding into larger administrative units.[46]

The layout of the court sites is also stressed by Iversen. It seems as if the complexes are designed to contribute to the expression of equality between the people using the site. He suggests that equal divisions and distributions of sizes and quantities are an important element in the processes of social negotiation within a society. Their purpose is to prevent conflict and to convey a sense of individual, as well as collective, justice.[47]

The Mythical Ǫmð

Determining exactly where the toponym Ǫmð was situated in the geographical area of Hálogaland has been a subject of debate by scholars. Ǫmð is mentioned in the Saga of St Olaf, written by Snorri Sturlason, probably sometime between 1220 and 1235. The saga is supposed to provide a historical description of the Norwegian King Olav Haraldson's life (995–1030). Snorri clarifies that Ǫmð is situated somewhere in the Hálogaland area, placing it in present-day Trondenes, to the south-west in Troms County.

> 'There was a man named Sigurd Thoreson, a brother of Thorer Hund of Bjarkey Island. Sigurd was married to Sigrid Skjalg's daughter, a sister of Erling. Their son, called Asbjorn, became as he grew up a very able man. Sigurd dwelt at Omð in Thrandarnes'.[48]

Snorri's placing of Ǫmð has been debated. The toponym Thrandarnes, or Trondenes (the contemporary place-name), is situated on Hinnøya. This island forms the south-western coastline of Vågsfjord in the southern part of Troms county. It is accepted that Ǫmð is not a place within the area that is known today as Trondenes. It has been generally concluded that this description is based on Snorri's misunderstanding. Based on its etymology,

45   Iversen, 'Community and Society', pp. 9–11.
46   Iversen, 'Hålogaland blir en rettskrets', pp. 113–15.
47   Iversen, 'Om aritmetikk og rettferdighet', p. 246.
48   Sturalson, 'Saga of Olaf Haraldson (St Olav)'.

Qmð is associated with the island of Andøya,[49] situated north-west of Hinnøya. Andøya forms the north-western coastline of Andfjorden, which inosculates with Vågsfjorden in the east.

In the early twentieth century, the meaning of Qmð as a toponym was interpreted by Oluf and Karl Rygh as 'the island that was jostled and molested by wind and sea'.[50] Later, in 1994, Finn Myrvang interpreted the toponym as deriving from the North Sámi word *omuth* or *omudh*, meaning marsh or mud hole, which also fits the topographical features of Andøya. Myrvang emphasizes that the name of the island could have had a Sámi derivation because the area was inhabited by both Sámi and Norse people during the Iron Age.

In the late nineteenth century, Peter Andreas Munch interpreted the toponym Qmð as the designation of both the landscape and the seascape surrounding Vågsfjorden. This interpretation partly supports Snorri's description, since it includes Hinnøya. In a book published in 2012, Alf Ragnar Nielssen is in agreement with Munch's interpretation. He has studied the Icelandic document *Lándnámabók*, a series of notes on the Scandinavian immigrants settling on Iceland in the period 870–930. It reports that three men, Olaf Bekk, Måne, and Tore Tussepenger, arrived from the realm of Qmð. Nielssen points out that in this text it is said *in* Qmð instead of *on* Qmð. The use of preposition in connection with Qmð indicates that the toponym refers to a greater geographical area, rather than just an island. He suggests that the toponym Qmð refers to Andøya, Bjarkøy, and Trondenes.[51]

In an article published in 2014, the archaeologist Reidar Bertelsen investigated historical, archaeological, and topographical elements relating to the areas around the two fjords, Andfjorden and Vågsfjorden. Bertelsen is of the same opinion as Munch and Nielssen: that the toponym Qmð refers to a greater geographical area than just one island. Bertelsen emphasizes that the sea was the main traffic artery during the Iron Age, and Iron Age grave mounds and the remains of great boathouses were strategically placed along the coasts of both fjords. Concentrations of mounds are found by the three main seaward entrances into the fjords. Boathouses for great ships were placed along the outer parts of the fjords, and in the centre. In addition to this, as mentioned earlier, there are two court sites situated in the area surrounding the fjords: one on Åse, situated on Andøya, and one on Bjarkøy, situated at the intersection point of Andfjorden and Vågsfjorden.

Bertelsen argues that the distribution of these symbols of power throughout the area, and the existence of the court sites, indicate a powerful community. The archaeological record offers no grounds to indicate just one leading farm in the area.[52] Due to the size of Andfjorden, and the importance of the sea

---

49 Hødnebø and Magerøy, 'Redaktørenes fotnoter i Soga om Olav den heilage', p. 322.
50 Rygh and Rygh, *Nordlands amt*, pp. 404–05, 411.
51 Nielssen, *Landnåm fra nord*, p. 78.
52 Bertelsen, 'Qmð og det nordlige Hålogaland', pp. 24–28.

and seaway during the Iron Age, Bertelsen finds it reasonable to believe that this geographical element could have been the point of origin when it comes to naming the whole region.[53]

The view that Qmð is the naming of a greater region is also held by Iversen. He is, in a stronger sense than Bertelsen, combining the court sites with the toponym, and sees it as the name of the northernmost jurisdictional area of Hálogaland. He identifies that Hálogaland was split into three *fylkí*, with Helgeland as the southernmost, Salten and Vestreålen in the middle, and Qmð as the northernmost.

Carbon dates from Storli's court site-study show that the main period of use at the Åse site was 250–600. The site on Bjarkøy was mainly in use between 500 and 900, and thus seems to have succeeded the site at Åse.[54] Iversen points out that the Bjarkøy site contains sixteen house plots while Åse contains only fourteen. As the site on Bjarkøy is situated farther north than the Åse site, Iveresen suggests that this addition was due to the northward expansion in the northernmost jurisdictional area of Hálogaland.[55]

According to Iversen's interpretation, in the main period of the court site on Åse Qmð comprised the area of present-day Vesterålen, Andenes, and Senja.[56] By the time the court site on Bjarkøy was taken in to use, the geographical extensiveness of Qmð had expanded further north, and included Hillesøy and Helgøy, as well.[57] Thus, an increasing part of the population, inhabiting the coastal area of Nothern Norway, was considered as equal citizens of the pre-state organization.

Society and Ethnicity

The early medieval texts portray Hálogaland and Finnmǫrk as two distinct areas with different populations. The lifestyle of the Norwegians is set in contrast to the lifestyle of the Sámi. Ohthere does not contrast his way of life with that of the hunters he met on his northward travels, but he does refer to them as hunters. He reports that he had a farm, and that he did cultivate a little, but that he also went hunting. The ethnic affiliation of Ohthere is thus not entirely clear.

Saga material relates that Iron Age chieftains held feasts to maintain their social network and alliances. Alcoholic beverage made of grain was considered an important element of these feasts.[58] The report stresses that the land

53 Bertelsen, 'Qmð og det nordlige Hálogaland', p. 31.
54 Storli, *Hålogaland før rikssamlingen*, pp. 53, 50.
55 Iversen, 'Community and society', pp. 9–11.
56 Iversen, 'Hålogaland blir en rettskrets', pp. 113–15.
57 Iversen, 'Community and Society', p. 13; Iversen, 'Hålogaland blir en rettskrets', pp. 113–14.
58 Storli, *Hålogaland før rikssamlingen*, pp. 133–34.

Ohthere cultivated was very small, and that in relation to the great number of other products he had access to, this activity does not seem essential from a subsistence perspective. But to enable Ohthere's participation in a greater social network of his peers, access to grain must have been necessary. Is it possible that the cultivation of land carried out by Ohthere is an expression of class, rather than an expression of ethnicity?

As an archaeologist, any thorough investigation of Iversen's retrogressive analyses is beyond the scope of my research. However, it is interesting that the new communities Iversen suggests were added to Qmð are situated north of the Malangen fjord, the proposed border of Norse Iron Age settlement. They are also situated just to the west of the Lyngen fjord, which was suggested as an eastern border between Norse and Sámi occupation. Could the increase in construction and the use of slab-lined pits on the eastern side of the Lyngen fjord be seen as a reaction to Norse society expanding farther north? Both Hillesøy and Karlsøy are situated in an area where cultural expressions often gave an ambiguous impression. Did the administrative regions of Hálogaland comprise only the Norse population within the area? It might be useful to lose the concepts of strict ethnic labels in the study of these local communities with mixed cultural expressions.

Works Cited

Primary Sources

'Ohthere's account', ed. and trans. by Janet Bately, in *Hunters in Transition. An Outline of Early Sámi History*, ed. by Lars Ivar Hansen and Bjørnar Olsen (Leiden: Brill, 2013), pp. 55–57

Snorri Sturlusson, 'Saga of Olaf Haraldsson (St Olav)', in *Heimskringla or The Chronicle of the Kings of Norway*, ed. by Douglas B. Killings and David Widger (The Project Gutenberg EBook of Heimskringla), https://www.gutenberg.org/files/598/98-h/598-h.htm

Secondary Works

Andreassen, Reidun Laura, and Håvard Dahl Bratrein, 'Finnmark, Bjarkøy and the Norwegian Kingdom', in *Hybrid Spaces: Medieval Finnmark and the Archaeology of Multi-Room Houses*, ed. by Bjørnar Olsen, Przemyslaw Urbanczyk, and Colin Amundsen (Oslo: Novus, 2011), pp. 315–27

Barth, Fredrik, 'Introduction', in *Ethnic Groups and Boundaries: The Social Organization of Culture Difference*, ed. by Fredrik Barth (Oslo: Universitetsforlaget, 1969), pp. 9–38

Berglund, Birgitta, *Tjøtta-riket. En arkeologisk undersøkelse av maktforhold og sentrumsdannelser på Helgelandskysten fra Kr. f. til 1700 e. Kr* (unpublished doctoral thesis, University of Trondheim, 1995)

Bertelsen, Reidar, 'Ǫmð og det nordlige Hálogaland — et nytt blikk på P. A. Munchs tanker', in *Endre-boka: postfesumskrift til Endre Mørck*, ed. by Gulbrand Alhaug, Tove Bull, and Aud-Kirsti Pedersen (Oslo: Novus, 2014), pp. 17–36

Bratrein, Håvard Dahl, *Karlsøy og Helgøy bygdebok: folkeliv, næringsliv, samfunnsliv — Fra steinalder til år 1700* (Hansnes: Karlsøy Kommune, 1989)

Brink, Stefan, Oliver Grimm, Frode Iversen, Halldis Hobæk, Marie Ødegaard, Ulf Näsman, Alex Sanmark, Przemyslaw Urbanczyk, Orri Vésteinsson, and Inger Storli, 'Comments on Inger Storli: "Court Sites of Arctic Norway: Remains of Thing Sites and Representations of Political Consolidation Processes in the Northern Germanic World during the First Millenium AD?"', *Norwegian Archaeological Review*, 44.1 (2010), 89–117

Bruun, Inga Marlene, 'Blandede graver — blandede kulturer? En tolkning av gravskikk og etniske forhold i Nord-Norge gjennom jernalder og tidlig middelalder' (unpublished master's thesis, University of Tromsø, 2007)

Brøgger, Anton Wilhelm, *Nord-Norges bosetningshistorie: en oversikt* (Oslo: Universitetsforlaget, 1931)

Fjærvoll, Karl, *Korndyrkinga i Hålogaland i gammal tid: 1500 og 1600-åra* (Svorkmo: Hålogaland historielag, 1961)

Gjessing, Gutorm, 'Den fyrste norske busetjinga i finnmark', *Syn og segn*, 46 (1940), 130–38

Hansen, Lars Ivar, *Astafjord bygdebok: fra eldre jernalder til ca. 1570* (Tennevoll: Lavangen kommune 2000)

——, 'Middelaldersamfunnets etniske grenser', in *Fortidsfortestillinger. Bruk og misbruk av nordnorsk historie. Rapport fra det 27. nordnorske historieseminar. Hamarøy 27.-29.9.2002*, ed. by B. A. Berg and E. Niemi (Tromsø: Universitetet i Tromsø 2004), pp. 59–82

——, *Sámisk fangstsamfunn og norsk høvdingeøkonomi* (Oslo: Novus, 1990)

Hansen, Lars Ivar, and Bjørnar Olsen, *Samenes historie — fram til 1750* (Oslo: Cappelens, 2004)

Henriksen, Jørn Erik, 'Hellegropene: Fornminner fra en funntom periode' (unpublished master's thesis, University of Tromsø, 1995)

Holand, Ingegerd, *Graver og samfunn: samfunnsutvikling og -organisasjon i Nord-Hålogaland i Jernalderen, basert på endringer og variasjon i gravskikk* (unpublished master's thesis, University of Tromsø, 1989)

Holmsen, Andreas, 'Finnskatt og nordmannsskatt', in *Samenes og sameområdenes rettslige stilling historisk belyst – foredrag og diskusjoner på symposium avholdt 7.-9. november 1973*, ed. by B. Bergsland (Oslo: Universitetsforlaget, 1977)

Hødnebø, Finn, and Hallvard Magerøy, 'Redaktørenes fotnoter i Soga om Olav den heilage (første delen)', in *Snorres kongesoger 1*, ed. by F. Hødnebø and H. Magerøy (Oslo: Gyldendal, 1997), pp. 207–344

Iversen, Frode, 'Community and Society: The Thing at the Edge of Europe', *Journal of the North Atlantic*, 8 (2015a), 1–17

——, 'Hålogaland blir en rettskrets', *Heimen*, 52 (2015b), 101–20

———, 'Om aritmetikk og rettferdighet. Tinget i randen av Europa i
Middelalderen', in *Ja, vi elsker frihet*, ed. by Harald Gullbekk (Oslo: Dreyers,
2014), p. 246

Johansen, Olav Sverre, and Tom Søbstad, 'De nordnorske tunanleggene fra
jernalderen', *Viking*, 41 (1978), 9–56

Jones, Sian, *The Archaeology of Ethnicity. Constructing Identities in the Past and
Present* (London: Routledge, 1997)

Jørgensen, Torstein, '"The Land of the Norwegians is the Last in the World":
A Mid-Eleventh-Century Description of the Nordic Countries from the
Pen of Adam of Bremen', in *The Edges of the Medieval World*, ed. by Gerhard
Jaritz and Jaritz Kreem (Tallinn: Central European University Press, 2009),
pp. 46–54

Kaljundi, Linda, 'Waiting for the Barbarians: Reconstructing of *Otherness* in the
Saxon Missionary and Crusading Chronicles, 11th–13th Centuries', in *Medieval
Chronicle V*, ed. by Erik Kooper (Amsterdam: Rodopi, 2008), pp. 113–27

Koht, Halvdan, *Den eldste Noregs-historia, med tilleg: meldingane frå Noreg hos Adam
av Bremen* (Oslo: Det Norske Samlaget, 1921)

Myrvoll, Elin Rose, 'Excavation of Iron Age Sites', in *Hybrid Spaces: Medieval
Finnmark and the Archeology of the Multi-Room Houses*, ed. by Bjørnar Olsen,
Przemyslaw Urbanczyk, and Colin Amundsen (Oslo: Novus, 2011), pp. 83–91

Nielssen, Alf Ragnar, *Landnåm fra nord: utvandringa fra det nordlige Norge til Island
I vikingtid* (Stamsund: Orkana akademisk, 2012)

Odner, Knut, 'Economic Structures in Western Norway in the Early Iron Age',
Norwegian Archaeological Review, 7 (1974), 105–12

Ringstad, Bjørn, 'Graver og ideologi. Implikasjoner fra vestnorsk
folkevandringstid', in *Samfundsorganisation og Regional Variation. Norden
i romersk jernalder og folkevandringstid*, ed. by Charlotte Fabech and Jytte
Ringtvedt (Aarhus: Jysk Arkæologisk Selskab, 1991), pp. 141–50

Rygh, Karl, and Oluf Rygh, *Nordlands amt* (Kristiania: Fabritius, 1905)

Schanche, Audhild, *Graver i ur og berg: Sámisk gravskikk og religion fra forhistorisk til
nyere tid* (Karasjok: Davvi girji, 2000)

———, 'Jernalderens bosetningsmønster i et fleretninsk perspektiv', in *Framskritt
for fortida i nord. I Povl Simonsens fotspor*, ed. by Reidar Bertelsen, Per Kyrre
Reymert, and Astrid Utne (Tromsø: Tromsø Museum, 1989), pp. 171–83

———, *Nordnorsk jernalderarkeologi. Et sosialgeografisk perspektiv* (unpublished
master's thesis, Universitety of Tromsø, 1986)

Skre, Dagfinn, *Herredømmet: bosetning og besittelse på Romerike 200–1350 e. Kr*
(Oslo: Universitetsforlaget, 1998)

Storli, Inger, '"Barbarians" of the North: Reflections on the Establishment of
Courtyard Sites in North Norway', *Norwegian Archaeological Review*, 33.2
(2000), 81–103

———, 'Court Sites of Arctic Norway: Remains of Thing Sites and Representations
of Political Consolidation Processes in the Northern Germanic World during
the first Millenium AD?', *Norwegian Archaeological Review*, 43.2 (2010), 128–44.

———, *Hålogaland før rikssamlingen: politiske prosesser i perioden 200–900 e. Kr* (Oslo: Novus, 2006)

———, '*Stallo'-boplassene: spor etter de første fjellsamer?* (Oslo: Novus, 1994)

———, 'Tunanleggenes rolle i nordnorsk jernalder', *Viking*, 64 (2001), 87–111

Svestad, Asgeir, 'Svøpt i myra — Synspunkter på Skjoldehamnfunnets etniske og kulturelle tilknytning', *Viking, Norsk arkeologisk årbok*, 80 (2017), 129–56.

Urbanczyk, Przemyslaw, *Medieval Arctic Norway* (Warszawa: Semper, 1992).

Vorren, Karl-Dag, 'Farm Development at the Arctic Cereal Limit in Northern Norway: Continuity and Discontinuities', *Vegetation History and Archaeobotany*, 14 (2005), 161–70.

BEN ALLPORT

Norwegian or Northern: The Construction and Mythography of Háleygr Identity, c. 800–1050

Introduction

Since the emergence of Norse historiographical literature, it has been clear that regional identity has played a central role in the development of Norwegian society, with certain regional distinctions first described eight centuries ago demonstrating remarkable longevity. As this volume has made clear, few Norwegian communities have been viewed as distinctly as the residents of northern Norway — Hálogaland, as it was known in Norse texts. In both classical and medieval literature, Hálogaland is a land of contradictions; portrayed as distant, mysterious and unknowable, the region was the first in north-western Scandinavia to be described in any detail, long before even the names of other Norwegian regions had entered the literary record. Thanks to the account of a Northern Norwegian sailor named Ohthere, we are first told of a sense of community uniting the residents of this land in the late ninth century. The members of this community were referred to as the 'Háleygir' (sing. Háleygr) in later sources — one of the most well-attested regional collectives in thirteenth-century saga literature. This can tell us little on its own, however, and in order to attempt to locate this identity in the ninth to mid-eleventh centuries, we must turn to a methodology that combines literature and archaeology in order to build the most secure basis for reconstructing Háleygr identity.

The Reconstruction of Medieval Identities: Theoretical Considerations

Discussions of identity in medieval societies must be approached with a great deal of caution; the nebulous concept of 'identity' is difficult enough

Ben Allport, University of Bergen, Benjamin.Allport@uib.no

Myths and Magic in the Medieval Far North: Realities and Representations of a Region on the Edge of Europe, ed. by Stefan Figenschow, Richard Holt, and Miriam Tveit, AS 10 (Turnhout: Brepols, 2020), pp. 197–214
10.1484/M.AS-EB.5.120526

to define with regard to our modern experiences, let alone the experiences of those who lived a thousand years ago and who left only faint traces in the literary and material records. In the context of this investigation, identity on its most basic level can be understood 'to encompass the self-definition of individuals and social groups and the practices by which they achieved it'.[1] In modern discourse, as Judith Jesch has noted, there is a sense that identity is 'shifting, indeed malleable, constructed and situated rather than essential'.[2] While the extent to which this is applicable to the medieval period has been questioned (notably by Jesch herself), it is uncontroversial to suggest that the variety of concepts or collectives with which an individual can affiliate him / herself results in identity being, to some degree, multilayered. This concept has been explored in a medieval European context by Susan Reynolds, who has drawn attention to the use of the terms '*gentes*', '*nationes*', and '*populi*' to refer to vaguely defined, overlapping collective units of differing levels of political status. She points to the complex interrelationships between groups referred to as Franks, Aquitanians, and Normans to reveal how such communities could be viewed either as subsets of one another or as distinct ethnic units.[3]

Moving to ninth- to eleventh-century Scandinavia, the concept of layers or tiers of collective identity can be corroborated by archaeological central place theory. Central places are sites which functioned as arenas for the renewal of social bonds and the mutual definition of collective identity through political, economic, or religious social rituals. As Dagfinn Skre notes,

> the functions of a central place have a scope beyond the needs of the inhabitants of that place, reaching out to surrounding communities. In order to participate in certain activities or to satisfy some of their public needs […] the inhabitants of a certain area go to the central place.[4]

Central places therefore indicate areas around which communities bound by collective identity may have congregated. Skre points out that central places were organized into a rough hierarchy based on the quantity of social functions they combined: the more functions that can be identified at a single site, the larger the community for which it formed a focal point.[5] In the case of ninth- and tenth-century Norway, a number of sites have been identified as being central places of this higher tier, such as Aure, Åke, Huseby, and, most famously, Borg in Lofoten.[6] These sites are notable for being universally associated with longhouse complexes, an accepted indication of secular power. The archaeological record is imperfect, subject as it is to issues such as selection bias, and it is possible that many central places existed which did

---

1   Allport, 'The Construction and Reconstruction of Regional Collective Identity', p. 82.
2   Jesch, *The Viking Diaspora*, p. 182.
3   Reynolds, 'Government and Community', pp. 87–88.
4   Skre, 'Centrality, Landholding and Trade in Scandinavia', p. 199.
5   Skre, 'Centrality, Landholding and Trade in Scandinavia', p. 199.
6   Hem Eriksen, 'Portals to the Past', p. 50.

not have these associations. On the basis of the evidence we have, however, we may conclude that the arenas in which the largest communities were defined in Norway at this time were most often associated with some level of elite control.

Although it is difficult to ascertain the size of the communities which were served by the highest tier of central places, the broadly spaced distribution of these sites within the boundaries of modern Norway and the limitations posed to long-distance travel by the geography of northwestern Scandinavia make it unlikely that any of these sites could have served a unified community encompassing the entire extent of Norse habitation in this area (in a manner equivalent to, say, the Icelandic *Alþing*, which was founded before 930). The evolution of a communal Norwegian identity continues to be a matter for debate in modern scholarship, but contributions from scholars such as Sverre Bagge have doubted whether a sense of Norway as a political community had even evolved fully by the time the *konungasögur* (Kings' sagas) were being written in the early thirteenth century, arguing that the saga literature conveys a sense of collective pride but not of political uniformity.[7] With regard to central places, the legal assemblies that undoubtedly formed a key communal focal point in Norway from at least the eleventh century remained split into four separate regional jurisdictions (the Gulaþing, Frostaþing, Borgarþing, and Heiðsævisþing) until the late thirteenth century.

Although the extent to which the assembly sites serving these districts maintained their status as central places across these centuries is debateable, the longevity of the regional assemblies at least indicates the difficulty of establishing a 'Norwegian' collective identity on the basis of archaeological sites. The present discussion makes no claims as to whether or not such a collective identity existed in the period under discussion. It instead argues that the highest tier of central places served regional communities, which in turn demands an investigation into what these communities were thought to have been. The importance of central places in the production of social bonds may indicate that regional identity is likely to have played a greater role in the self-definition of residents of north-western Scandinavia than any sense of being collectively 'Norwegian'.

The 'Triangulation' Methodology for the Reconstruction of Regional Identity

The importance attached to central places in the theoretical discussion above hints at their role in the methodology used below to identify regional collectives in the landscape of ninth- and tenth-century Norway. In this chapter — and in the broader research it represents — efforts to reconstruct units of collective

---

7 See, for example, Bagge, 'Nationalism in Norway', pp. 4–7; *Society and Politics*; Opsahl, "'[…] Nonetheless [He] Fulfilled His Obligation Towards the Hirð"', p. 194.

identity in this area have utilized a methodology of 'triangulation' (a term borrowed from sociological studies), whereby statistical analyses of terms of collective identity used in literary sources are combined with archaeological evidence for the distribution of central places and political power centres, thus indicating the broad areas that comprised regional communities.[8] For the reasons stated above, this methodology allows us to reconstruct the most expansive form of collective identity that can be inferred from the highest tier of central places.

This approach holds that both categories of evidence (literary and archaeological) are equally important, and that both are required to reconstruct regional units with any confidence, given that both, on their own, are often problematic. In archaeology, for example, distribution patterns of cultural practices associated with the construction of identity are inadequate as the primary means of constructing identity because in a society comprised of multiple tiers or types of affiliation these varying distribution patterns rarely map neatly onto one another. Furthermore, as analyses of the spread of practices among diasporic communities have indicated, evidence of shared practice does not necessarily imply shared identity; while a diasporic community might share practices with the community from which it had sprung, these were often combined with new practices as a means by which to express both the community's relationship to its origins and its distinctiveness from them.[9] The same or similar dynamics could well account for the distribution patterns of practices throughout Norway. Literary narratives are plagued by their own pitfalls, as their authors were engaged in their own form of identity construction, making us dependent on the perspective of individuals who may be divorced from the 'reality' — temporally and / or geographically.

For the most part, the picture revealed by this methodology results in a relatively clear correlation between rough regional boundaries indicated by power centres and the terms of regional identity which occur in the written record. Along the coast from Viken to Møre, and in the Trondheimsfjord interior, a simple pattern emerges, whereby the distribution of central places (particularly high-status longhouses) indicates that regional communities of broadly similar sizes most frequently coalesced along rivers and fjord systems (as in Rogaland or Sogn, for example). Elites situated on the most fertile land were clustered around key points along these waterways, generally where they met the coast (or, in Trøndelag, the fjord shoreline), allowing them to exercise control over local exchange networks. The close correspondence of central places with sites of secular power in the Norwegian material record holds the key to understanding the extent of the role that local elites must have played in the creation of regional identity, as they must necessarily

---

8 Allport, 'The Construction and Reconstruction of Regional Collective Identity', p. 97.
9 See Abrams, 'Diaspora and Identity in the Viking Age', pp. 17–33; Jesch, *The Viking Diaspora*, p. 69.

have been intimately involved with the practices by which social bonds were constructed and renewed.[10]

As far as southern and western Norway are concerned, the association between power centres and waterways, granting the former control over the regional networks of the latter, has been well documented; most notably, the influential archaeologist Bjørn Myhre tracked the broad phenomenon from the sixth century to the eleventh in a series of seminal articles in the 1980s and 1990s.[11] So far, scholarship that extends the same approach elsewhere has not achieved the same prominence, when it exists at all. When applied to northern Norway, it is clear that geopolitical dynamics continued to play an important role in defining community boundaries; however, the precise nature of these dynamics reflects a clear departure from southern norms, rendered more complex by the unique nature of Norse settlement in the region, strung out along the coastal exterior.

The Reconstruction of Háleygr Identity

It is ironic that the Norse regional identity which was best known in native literature for being mysterious was also the first to be extensively described by external observers. The Latin tradition of *Geographia* incorporated stylized descriptions of the High North and the habits of its inhabitants from the outset of the first millennium AD.[12] Although these accounts often focused on the *Screrefennae* (now understood to be the Sámi), the sixth-century author Jordanes gave a list of Norse tribal names in his *Getica*, a number of which can be identified as the ancestors of certain Viking Age regional names.[13] Among these, and associated in the text with the *Screrefennae*, were the so-called 'Adogit' tribe, whose homeland, alone of all the Germanic tribes listed, was described in detail; this description makes it clear that it is referring to the northernmost Norse population.[14] Although the link is not certain, Mattias Tveitane has suggested that '*Adogit*' is a corruption of '*Alogi*' or '*Halogii*', and can thus be linked to the regional identifier 'Háleygir' and the accompanying regional name 'Hálogaland'.[15]

---

10 Allport, 'The Construction and Reconstruction of Regional Collective Identity', pp. 114–19.
11 Myhre, 'Boathouses as Indicators of Political Organization', pp. 36–60; Myhre, 'Chieftains' Graves and Chiefdom Territories', pp. 169–87; Myhre, 'Boathouses and Naval Organization', pp. 169–83.
12 Valtonen, 'Who Were the *Finnas*?', p. 106.
13 *The Gothic History of Jordanes in English Version*, ed. by Mierow, pp. 56–57; see, for example, Brink, 'People and *land* in Early Scandinavia', p. 92. For the link between the *Screrefenae* and the Sámi, see Valtonen, 'Who Were the *Finnas*?', p. 106.
14 *The Gothic History of Jordanes in English Version*, ed. by Mierow, p. 56.
15 Tveitane, *Fra ord til navn*. For further comment on the origins of this term, see Miriam Tveit's chapter in the present volume.

The Old English text, *Ohthere's Voyage* — which has already received considerable attention in this volume — provides us with the first concrete reference to '*Halgoland*' and the first evidence of a Háleygr expressing his identity. It provides a unique snapshot of the process by which members of two collectives, the Háleygir and the West Saxons of the court of Alfred the Great, constructed and defined their identity in relation to one another. The text should chiefly be interpreted within the literary context in which it appears: incorporated into an Old English translation of Orosius's *Historia Pagani Libri Septem*, it demonstrates its relationship to the tradition of *Geographia*, albeit seemingly as a response or correction to the misconceptions of Ohthere's audience.[16] Ohthere's focus on *Halgoland*, and specifically the lifestyle of a Northern Norwegian chieftain and his relationship with the *Finnas* (Sámi), both reflects his intimate knowledge of the area and, consciously or unconsciously, contributes to the traditional focus of attention upon the High North, a trend that continued to manifest several centuries later in Adam of Bremen's discussion of '*Helgeland*' in the *Gesta Hammaburgensis ecclesiae pontificum*.[17] By the time that authentically native sources start to appear (and before we have the names of many of the collective groups to be found throughout northwestern Scandinavia), we can already see an external perception of the Norse residents of the Arctic region as a unified group. This is both a blessing and a curse, and presages the difficulties posed by the external perspectives of saga narratives when they emerge in the thirteenth century.

For three centuries following *Ohthere's Voyage*, references to the Háleygir are restricted to the cursory attention of skaldic verse. The earliest surviving attestation of the term 'Háleygir' is in the skaldic poem *Hákonarmál*, thought to have been composed by the poet Eyvindr *skáldaspillir* in the second half of the tenth century, at some point after the death of Hákon *góði*, the south-western king in whose memory the verse was composed.[18] The verse refers to the battle of Fitjar (a location in modern Hordaland), fought by Hákon against the Eiríkssons, during which 'hét á Háleygi sems á Holmrygi jarla einbani' (the sole slayer of jarls [Hákon] called upon the Háleygir just as on the Hólmrygir); the group thus appear outside of their native context, participating in a battle fought over 700 km south of their homeland.[19] This sets the precedent for most of the references to members of this community in the more detailed narratives of the thirteenth-century *konungasögur*. It is possible to deduce an even earlier reference to the community, however: the poem *Haraldskvæði*, an early tenth-century composition of Þorbjǫrn *hornklofi* (Horn-cleaver) addressed to Haraldr *hárfagri* (Finehair), contains the kenning

16 See Allport, 'Home Thoughts of Abroad', pp. 263–73.
17 Adam of Bremen, *History of the Archbishops of Hamburg Bremen*.
18 Eyvindr *skáldaspillir* Finnson, *Háleygjatal*, I, 195.
19 Eyvindr *skáldaspillir* Finnson, *Hákonarmál*, I, 177.

'Hǫlga ættar' (the family of Hǫlgi), which refers to a legendary eponymous representative of the community.[20]

It has been noted already in this volume that Hálogaland and its inhabitants were presented as supernatural, unfamiliar, or backward in medieval Norse literature. This presentation has increasingly jarred with the picture painted by archaeological evidence, which suggests that the region must have attained a high degree of economic and political development relative to its neighbours as early as the Viking period. This is indicated most famously by the impressive site at Borg on Vestvågøy, which revealed two immense longhouses, identifying Borg as an elite residence from the fifth century to the tenth. The younger of these longhouses was over eighty metres long and was in use from the seventh century to the mid-tenth, when it was demolished. Combined with the presence of nearby boathouses, a late Iron Age longhouse at nearby Bøstad, and pre-ninth-century assembly sites at Gimsøy and Leknes, Borg points to the existence of a powerful elite situated in the Lofoten islands whose authority lasted for nearly five hundred years.[21] To this we may add increasing evidence for Northern Norwegian integration into exchange networks spanning northern Europe. This is indicated by the remains of a variety of European trade items found at Borg, but is made especially clear through the trade of iron, which Roger Jørgensen suggests was systematically supplied from the Norse regions to the south during this period. As Jørgensen has pointed out, participation in this trade demands a certain level of social organization, as well as maritime technology.[22] Finally, the economic importance of the region is coming into sharper relief, as new evidence pushes the development of organized fisheries (later the cornerstone of the medieval Norwegian economy) further back in time than was previously assumed, hinting at a high level of political organization at a time when it is much harder to find further south.[23]

References to the Háleygr identity in the konungasögur reflect this contradictory impression: the term is used on twelve occasions throughout Heimskringla (the most comprehensive of the konungasögur, composed by Snorri Sturluson in the 1230s), making it one of the most frequently referenced Norwegian regional collectives in this text. It is also one of the most consistently referred to collectives across the konungasögur, regularly appearing in Ágrip af Nóregskonunga sǫgum, Sverris saga, Morkinskinna, and Fagrskinna. Most of these references, however, are in association with individual Háleygir, or — as in Hákonarmál — with military forces, both of which operate beyond their homeland. Hálogaland is portrayed as a far-flung province of

20 Þorbjǫrn hornklofi, Haraldskvæði, I, 108.

21 Munch, Johansen, and Roesdahl, ed., Borg in Lofoten, pp. 12–13.

22 Jørgensen, 'How Did the Natives of North Norway Secure the Supply of Iron?', p. 103. For the trade connections of Borg, see Munch, Johansen, and Roesdahl, ed., Borg in Lofoten, p. 17.

23 Keller, 'Norway in the 10th Century AD', p. 47; Storli, 'Ohthere and His World', p. 90.

the southern kingdom ruled by the successors of Haraldr *hárfagri*. A reigning king does not even venture there before Óláfr Tryggvason (995–1000), who is confronted by supernatural storms and magicians that obstruct his attempts to bring Christianity to the land. Yet it is also clear that the Háleygir were a recognizable, even familiar presence in the landscape of Norwegian regional identities. Given, for example, that Snorri was particularly associated with Jarl Skúli, who was based in Þrándheimr (which broadly corresponds to modern Trøndelag), we may assume that the region's northern neighbours were not wholly unknown to him. At the time the sagas were produced, the Norwegian kings, particularly Hákon Hákonarson (d. 1263), were seeking spiritual justification for extending their political and religious authority ever northwards, a drive that was reflected in contemporary literature.[24] Considering this alongside the consistency with which Hálogaland was depicted as mysterious and supernatural throughout European historiography as a whole, it is likely that the saga portrayal of the Háleygir was dictated more by literary conventions than by reality.

On the other hand, the Háleygr collective identity is unique in appearing to apply to such a broad geographical area without any strong evidence of existing sub-units of identity in either the skaldic verses or the sagas; other identities of a similar geographical scope, such as the 'Þrœndir' (the residents of Þrándheimr) or the 'Upplendingar' (those of the eastern Norwegian interior), were comprised of numerous, well-documented regional collectives of a similar territorial scale to those found in western Norway, where regional boundaries were more clearly delineated by topographical factors. This raises the question of whether such subdivisions of identity existed to any great extent in Hálogaland. Is the sole survival of the overarching demonym 'Háleygir' in literary sources a natural consequence of the sagas' seeming lack of familiarity with Hálogaland and its residents, resulting in a patchy understanding of the distinct communities within it? Or is it possible that this was the dominant communal identity in the region, with the Norse residents of over 600 km of coastline all identifying as Háleygir, to the extent that other, smaller identities lacked as much relevance beyond their highly localized context? In order to answer these questions, it is necessary to turn to archaeological evidence.

In doing so, however, it becomes apparent that the situation was more complex in northern Norway than the neatly delineated regional landscape further south might indicate. The Norse population in Hálogaland was spread thinly along the coast, concentrated on the limited fertile land, and did not extend much beyond the northern limit for grain cultivation. Fjord interiors were inhabited by the Sámi.[25] The dynamic in the south, whereby communities

---

24 Figenschow, 'Comparing the Central Authorities' Expansion into North Norway and Finland', p. 145.

25 Hansen, 'The Dawn of State Formations', p. 31.

arose around entire water networks spreading inland, could not effectively operate further north than the residents of Naumudalr (the *Naumdœlir*). Instead, the archaeological evidence points to a number of elite centres strung out evenly along the Northern Norwegian coastline. This is revealed by the distribution of sites identified as power centres or central places by archaeologists such as Birgitta Berglund and Inger Storli. Those considered active during the ninth to mid-eleventh centuries are spread thinly along the coastline from Torgar in southern Helgeland to Tussøya in central Troms. These locations comprise a mixture of different categories of sites associated with power centres and / or central places. At Borg, Tussøya, Stauran, Arstad, Hunstad, and Skålbunes, there are the remains of longhouses that were occupied at various points throughout the ninth to eleventh century.[26] In Helgeland, Berglund has identified a number of power centres from this period based on various combinations of grave finds, farm mounds, boathouses, and post-eleventh-century evidence: these include Tjøtta, Øysund, Lurøy, Hov, Sandnes, Mo, and Torgar.[27] Finally, at Tjøtta, Steigen, and Bjarkøy, there are the remains of the largest and most long-lived of the oft-discussed *ringformete tunanlegg* (courtyard sites). For the most part, these elite centres consist of one or two closely related sites bearing only a few of the accepted hallmarks of power centres, such as associated boathouses, graves, and other monumental features. In the case of the courtyard sites, the extent to which they should be viewed as elite power centres has been called into question, although their status as central places is undisputed.

The courtyard sites have attracted a great deal of attention in scholarship as a unique category of Norwegian sites used from the fifth century to the tenth, comprising of elliptical arrangements of buildings enclosing a central courtyard. Following the influential work of scholars such as Storli, it is now largely accepted that these sites functioned as assemblies for the surrounding area, with the quantity of buildings at each site giving some indication of the size of the community they served.[28] By the tenth century, only three sites — the largest that have been found — remained in use, located at Tjøtta, Steigen, and Bjarkøy.[29] It has since been argued that these sites formed the basis of distinct communities within Hálogaland. Berglund, for example, argues for the existence of a petty kingdom, dominating sub-Arctic Hálogaland (the district now known as Helgeland), which was centred around modern Tjøtta, where the courtyard site was superseded by a farm mound in the early eleventh century.[30] Frode Iversen has gone so far as to propose that the courtyard sites reflect extraordinarily stable legal districts that had a

---

26 Hem Eriksen, 'Portals to the Past', p. 50.
27 Berglund, 'Continuity and Discontinuity in Viking Power', p. 140.
28 See Storli, *Hålogaland før Rikssamlingen*.
29 Storli, 'Court Sites of Arctic Norway', p. 138.
30 Berglund, 'Changes in the Power Structure around AD 1100 on the North Norwegian Coast', p. 266.

thousand-year pedigree by the sixteenth century, although — in the present author's view — this is based on too generous an interpretation of disparate evidence gathered from across this period.[31] By Iversen's analysis, Hálogaland was split into three legal districts based around these courtyard sites. Ǫmð, which, Iversen argues, stretched north from Vesterålen, was served by the assembly located at Bjarkøy. Steigen was the site of the main assembly for Lofoten and Salten, while sub-Arctic Hálogaland formed a district located around the courtyard site in Tjøtta. Each building at the courtyard sites, according to Iversen, represented a subdivision of the legal district and was intended to house their delegates.[32]

This view is controversial: as Yassin Nyang Karoliussen notes in this volume, the exact location of Ǫmð, for example, is unclear, while the level of legal infrastructure Iversen supposes does not match our current understanding of the nature of political organization in the region at this time. Nevertheless, both Berglund's and Iversen's interpretations might lead us to question the monolithic impression of the Háleygr collective identity conveyed by the literary evidence, as they imply the existence of distinct, separately organized political and / or legal communities. Support for this may even be found in *Heimskringla*, by virtue of the only other collective identity located in Hálogaland to which the saga alludes: Snorri refers twice to the 'Bjarkeyingr' (the residents of Bjarkøy), thus implying that he had a more detailed knowledge of the local political landscapes in the region than the literary conventions outlined above allowed him to admit. Given that this term correlates with the island of Bjarkøy, where a courtyard site was located, we might assume that this corroborates the model of legal communities proposed by Iversen.

Yet there are good reasons to doubt that the term 'Bjarkeyingr' applied to a collective community that extended beyond the small island from which the name derived. No other demonyms listed in the sagas apply to a community which occupied a territory larger than the location it explicitly referred to, whereas, by Iversen's model, the legal community served by the site at Bjarkøy stretched north to the very limits of Norse habitation in modern Troms. In fact, the term — which only appears in *Heimskringla* — is associated with only one individual, Þórir *hundr*, who resided on the island and played a key role in opposing the conversion efforts of Óláfr Haraldsson, eventually leading troops against him at the battle of Stiklarstaðir along with fellow Háleygr, Hárekr of Þjótta (Tjøtta). It is worth noting that the family of the viceroys of Hálogaland at the time Snorri was writing claimed descent from Þórir *hundr*.[33] The term 'Bjarkeyingr' may therefore refer to members of this dynasty, rather than to a broader community, or may have

---

31 Iversen, 'Community and Society', p. 12.
32 Iversen, 'Community and Society', p. 13.
33 Figenschow, 'Comparing the Central Authorities' Expansion into North Norway and Finland', p. 146.

been used as part of an effort on Snorri's part to establish the importance of the family's dynastic heritage in his narrative. Such a ploy would be far from unusual in a narrative catering to the top tier of the medieval Norwegian elite, and corroborates the idea that Hálogaland's isolation from the Norwegian mainstream did not extend beyond its depiction in literature. The apparent coincidence of the link between the term 'Bjarkeyingr' and the courtyard site is unsurprising if one assumes a similar evolution of local power structures to that which is more clearly demonstrated in the archaeological record at Tjøtta; it merely attests to the continuity of power in this area, identifying this island as a significant location in the history of Northern Norwegian political development.

Upon closer inspection, there is little archaeological evidence to support the idea that two or three distinct communities existed within Hálogaland, let alone the intricate legal boundaries proposed by Iversen. As noted previously, the central places that have been identified in Hálogaland were widely spread along the coast; this distinguishes the region from its southern neighbours, where dense clusters of different types of sites at watercourse entrances strongly indicate the existence of communities extending inland. This suggests that, rather than the regional community congregating around a single cluster of land occupied by the elite, it was strung out between different elite centres and central places, whose relative importance might vary. In other words, regional power structures in Hálogaland were not nucleated, as they were further south, but might be better described as linear or nodal.

Having said that, the power centres of Arctic Hálogaland are distributed on either side of the strait separating the Lofoten and Vesterålen archipelagos from the mainland, suggesting a concentration of regional power in this area — albeit one of lesser density than those seen in the south. This reveals the importance of being in a position to access coastal exchange routes (as is particularly clear for the late tenth-century longhouse located at Stauran in Steinsland which overlooks the strait at its narrowest point), but once again the distances between the sites must be taken into account: the younger hall at Borg, for example, is 110 km north of the contemporary longhouse located at Hunstad and 120 km south-west of Stauran (although it is only 80 km north-west of the courtyard site at Steigen). Even allowing for the discovery of other important sites in the future, these distances are too large to imagine that dynasties based at each location could effectively compete for domination of local exchange, a crucial dynamic in regional development south of Hálogaland which resulted in the emergence of nuclei of elite control. Despite its location, Borg was undoubtedly home to a powerful dynasty that was fully integrated into coastal exchange routes, again suggesting that regional power in Hálogaland was not nucleated but was instead spread out between numerous elite centres with roughly equal access to exchange networks. This ability to exert influence over local systems of exchange may have enabled Háleygr chieftains to control the construction of the Háleygr identity: Roger Jørgensen suggests that chieftains in Hálogaland maintained their monopoly over the flow of iron craft items by discouraging local iron extraction, over which they could exert less control than the coastal trade which brought items from regions further south.[34] By acting as conduits for the flow of prestige items as they were disseminated throughout the region from elite-controlled central places, Háleygr chieftains effectively gained the opportunity to dictate their community's perception of what constituted the markers of collective self-definition.

A social structure such as this would explain why the courtyard site assemblies in Hálogaland survived into the tenth century and beyond, long after their southern counterparts were abandoned. More importantly, it could also explain why only the term 'Háleygir' made it into the lexicon of Norwegian regional demonyms, as the dispersed power structure combined with the sparse Norse population would lend itself to strengthening an overarching sense of community. The scattered residents of the coast would be required to travel greater distances to reach the central places (including secular power centres) where the construction and renewal of communal bonds took place. Consequently, we would expect to see a communal identity of broader geographical scope than those found in more densely populated regions, even though it might not have a larger population.

This is not to suggest that sub-units of collective identity did not exist in Hálogaland, but those that did exist are likely to have been highly localized or kin-based — like the Bjarkeyingr — and would not have interfered with the strengthening of broader communal bonds on the occasions when the Hálegyir congregated at central places. Nor should it be assumed that all of these elite centres were of identical power and status. Besides the power and longevity of certain sites being indicated in the archaeological record, the sagas also single out certain chieftains, such as Þórir *hundr* of Bjarkøy and Hárekr of Þjótta, as being particularly powerful. However, as so few Háleygir (let alone their power centres) are named — and in light of the thirteenth-century political considerations already alluded to — there is too little reliable data to confidently establish the most powerful chieftains on the basis of literary material; while sites such as Tjøtta reveal themselves as important in both the literary and archaeological record, undisputedly important sites such as Borg receive no attention in literary sources.

Despite these drawbacks, our understanding of the Háleygr community is only likely to improve as scholarship discovers ever more about the political organization of the area prior to its incorporation into the Norwegian kingdom; we must assume that these findings will nuance or even contradict the impression outlined by the evidence as it currently stands. Yet we must also accept the likelihood that the Norse communities of this north-western corner of Scandinavia were bound by a collective sense of being the Háleygir from at least as early as the late ninth century up to and beyond the time when

---

34 Jørgensen, 'How Did the Natives of North Norway Secure the Supply of Iron?', p. 105.

the sagas were written. Far from being unknown further south, this collective was widely recognized and fully integrated into the lexicon of Norwegian regional communities.

The Háleygir in Norwegian Mythography

Having applied the triangulation methodology to argue for the existence of a strong and distinct Háleygr identity on the basis of both archaeological and literary data, it only remains to supplement this picture by briefly touching upon how this distinctiveness was recognized and perpetuated by the broader Norwegian community, as well as the varying role that the Háleygir played in the Norse peoples' mythologizations of their collective origins.

As suggested, the saga authors' portrayal of Hálogaland as distant and supernatural may be owed in part to contemporary political considerations, such as the drive to extend royal and ecclesiastical authority ever northwards. Yet we must also consider the ramifications of the fact that much of the surviving literature reflects the perspective of a royal dynasty that traced its origins to the southern king, Haraldr *hárfagri*. The tendency to depict the Háleygir as distant and unfamiliar must in part be attributed to the fact that, from the perspective of literature produced under the aegis of a southern monarchy, they were. Located at the northern extremity of the realm, the Háleygir were portrayed as unaccustomed to — and unaccepting of — the concept of royal authority. This is made explicit in *Óláfs saga helga* (part of *Heimskringla*) wherein a major conflict between King Óláfr *helgi* and his recalcitrant subject Erlingr Skjálgsson — the ruler of Hǫrðaland — is initiated by the refusal of Erlingr's Háleygr nephew Ásbjǫrn *selsbani* to pay royal dues. Ásbjǫrn voices his complaints to Erlingr, in response to which 'Erlingr sá til hans ok glotti við tǫnn ok mælti: "Minna vitið þér af konungs ríki, Háleygir, en vér Rygir"' (Erlingr looked at him and grinned and said: 'You know less of the king's power, you Háleygir, than we Rýgir'), providing explicit confirmation of this sentiment.[35] The attitude expressed here through Erlingr may have reflected thirteenth-century perceptions of contemporary political circumstances, wherein the governance of Hálogaland was wholly delegated to a viceroy, a situation not found further south.

Saga accounts suggest that the Bjarkeyingr family had a troubled relationship with the contending royal dynasties of thirteenth-century Norway. In the late twelfth century a member of the family, Víðkunnr Erlingsson, was killed by Bárðr Guthormsson, a prominent member of the *birkibeinar* faction of King Hákon Hákonarson's grandfather, King Sverrir. The family subsequently backed the opposing *baglarr* faction. By the 1230s Bárðr's son Duke Skuli (the patron of Snorri Sturluson) had become Hákon's sole contender in the struggle for

---

35   Snorri Sturluson, *Óláfs saga ins helga*, p. 197.

the Norwegian throne; neither faction is likely to have been appealing to this northern dynasty, strengthening the impression of Hálogaland's distance from royal control.

Another important factor in southern perceptions of the Háleygr community was the latter's relationship with the Sámi who inhabited the northern Norwegian interior. As Miriam Tveit observes in this volume, the indigenous inhabitants of the High North were frequently portrayed as wielders of magic throughout medieval European literature. Besides appearing alongside one another in Jordanes, Ohthere's account provides the earliest written evidence of the relationship between the Háleygir and the Sámi, and although it is likely that at that time the extent of Sámi habitation stretched much further south than Hálogaland, it seems that their association with this region in particular was long-lasting.[36] In *Historia Norwegie*, the anonymous author's brief description of the Háleygir draws attention to their relationship with the Sámi, stating that they 'multum Finnis cohabitant et inter se commercia frequentant' (often live together with the Sámi and have frequent commerce with them).[37] Given that elsewhere the author carefully distinguishes between the parts of Norway inhabited by the Norse and those inhabited by the Sámi, we can assume that, at least to this author and his audience, the Háleygir were defined by their interactions with the Sámi.

While these factors may account for the portrayal of the residents of Hálogaland in the literature of the twelfth and thirteenth centuries, we must also consider the possibility that the Háleygr community played a more significant role in times or places beyond the south-western cultural sphere. So successful was the cultural hegemony imposed by Haraldr *hárfagri*'s successors that only faint elements survive of any alternative cultural zones, yet these elements are sufficient to imply the existence of such a zone based around mid- and northern Norway, beyond the power of the kings in the south-west. During the tenth and early eleventh centuries, this area is primarily associated with the dynasty of the jarls of Hlaðir (Lade), which — according to a tradition attested as early as the twelfth century in the prose texts that preserved the poem — had originated in Hálogaland before relocating to southern Þrándheimr.[38] This dynasty was occasionally able to extend its power over all of the Norwegian seaboard, most notably during the reign of Jarl Hákon Sigurðarson (d. 995) in the last decades of the tenth century, rivalling or even surpassing the power of their southern competitors. Storli has linked the growing authority of the jarls of Hlaðir in the tenth century to

36 For the extent of Sámi habitation from the sixth to eleventh centuries, see Valtonen, 'Who Were the *Finnas*?', p. 106.

37 *Historia Norvegiæ*, ed. by Storm, p. 78. Translation adapted from Phelpstead, ed., *A History of Norway and the Passion and Miracles of the Blessed Óláfr*, p. 3. On this topic, see also Lars Ivar Hansen's contribution to this volume: 'On the View of "the Other" – Abroad and At Home: The Geography and Peoples of the Far North, According to *Historia Norwegiae*'.

38 Eyvindr *skáldaspillir* Finnson, *Háleygjatal*, 1, 194.

the evolution of local power structures seen throughout Hálogaland at this time, such as the transition from courtyard sites to chieftains' farms seen at Tjøtta and Bjarkøy and the abandonment of Borg.[39]

The dynasty was connected to the Háleygr collective identity by the tradition that attaches the name *Háleygjatal* — the enumeration of the Háleygir — to a poem describing Jarl Hákon's ancestry, ostensibly composed by the poet Eyvindr *skáldaspillir* during the jarl's reign. This title is not attested prior to the saga context in which the poem first appears, but widespread intertextual agreement at least implies that it was not an innovation at this time. Scholarly consensus suggests that *Háleygjatal* was modelled stylistically and thematically on the poem known as *Ynglingatal*, which appears to track the genealogy of the Ynglingr dynasty (of which Haraldr *hárfagri* was a member) back to its roots in Uppland, Sweden.[40] Yet, while subsequent authors named *Ynglingatal* after the dynasty it was attached to, *Háleygjatal* was named after the regional community from which the dynasty had originated. It follows the same pattern of tracing a dynasty back to its origins elsewhere (a familiar conceit in dynastic legends of this type), but attributed these origins much closer to home.

Such an attribution grants Hálogaland the same level of cultural authority as Uppland, an area of great political and spiritual significance in the Norse world. The comparison is decreasingly surprising for a region we now know to have played an important economic and political role in the early history of Norway and which had its own spiritual associations. These include the deity associated with Jarl Hákon Sigurðarson and most commonly referred to as Þorgerðr *Hǫlgabrúðr*. The second element of this name, which can be translated as 'the bride of Hǫlgi', has been linked to the Norse interpretation of the meaning of Hálogaland. This indicates, as John McKinnell notes, that it might be best understood as 'the bride of (the rulers of) Hálogaland', again hinting at the role played by the Háleygir in the mythography of the North.[41]

The paucity of literary references that can be traced beyond the hegemony of the Norwegian monarchy ensures that any conclusions about the nature of the cultural role played by the Háleygir during the ninth to eleventh centuries must remain tentative. However, the likelihood that the residents of Hálogaland played such a role is strengthened by the results of the triangulation methodology presented in this research. The combination of archaeological and literary data reveals the strength and unity of a community spread thinly over an immense geographical area, reinforcing the growing consensus about the advanced nature of social and political structures that existed in ninth- to eleventh-century Hálogaland.

---

39 Storli, 'Court Sites of Arctic Norway', p. 138.
40 Fulk, ed., 'Eyvindr *skáldaspillir* Finnson', p. 171.
41 McKinnell, *Meeting the Other in Norse Myth and Legend*, pp. 84–85.

Works Cited

Primary Sources

Adam of Bremen, *History of the Archbishops of Hamburg Bremen*, trans. by Francis J. Tschan (New York: Columbia University Press, 2002)

Eyvindr *skáldaspillir* Finnson, *Hákonarmál*, ed. and trans. by Russell Poole, in *Poetry from the Kings' Sagas 1: From Mythical Times to c. 1035*, 2 vols, ed. by Diana Whaley, Skaldic Poetry of the Scandinavian Middle Ages, 1 (Turnhout: Brepols, 2012), I, 171–94

The Gothic History of Jordanes, in English Version with an Introduction and Commentary by Charles Christopher Mierow (Princeton: Princeton University Press, 1915)

Háleygjatal, ed. and trans. by Russell Poole, in *Poetry from the Kings' Sagas 1: From Mythical Times to c. 1035*, 2 vols, ed. by Diana Whaley, Skaldic Poetry of the Scandinavian Middle Ages, 1 (2012), I, 195–213

Historia Norwegiae, in *Monumenta Historica Norvegiæ: Latinske kildeskrifter til Norges historie i middelalderen*, ed. by Gustav Storm (Kristiania: Brøgger, 1880), pp. 71–124

Snorri Sturluson, *Óláfs saga ins helga*, in *Heimskringla II*, ed. by Bjarni Aðalbjarnarson, Íslenzka fornrit 27 (Reykjavík: Hið Íslenzla fornritfelag, 1945; repr. 2002), pp. 3–415

Þorbjǫrn *hornklofi*, *Haraldskvæði* 14, in *Poetry from the Kings' Sagas 1: From Mythical Times to c. 1035*, 2 vols, ed. by Diana Whaley, Skaldic Poetry of the Scandinavian Middle Ages, 1 (Turnhout: Brepols, 2012), I, 91–117

Secondary Works

Abrams, Lesley, 'Diaspora and Identity in the Viking Age', *Early Medieval Europe*, 20 (2012), 17–33

Allport, Ben, 'The Construction and Reconstruction of Regional Collective Identity in Viking Age Norway', *Quaestio Insularis*, 18 (2007), 78–119

—— , 'Home Thoughts of Abroad: *Ohthere's Voyage* in its Anglo-Saxon Context', *Early Medieval Europe*, 28 (2020), 256–88

Bagge, Sverre, 'Nationalism in Norway in the Middle Ages', *Scandinavian Journal of History*, 20 (1995), 1–18

—— , *Society and Politics in Snorri Sturluson's Heimskringla* (Berkeley: University of California Press, 1991)

Berglund, Birgitta, 'Changes in the Power Structure around AD 1100 on the North Norwegian Coast: The Importance of Waterways and of the Organisation of Trade in Building and in Maintaining Power', in *Rural Settlements and Medieval Europe*, ed. by Guy De Boe and Frans Verhaeghe (Zellik: Instituut voor het Archaeologisch Patrimonium, 1997), pp. 263–70

—— , 'Continuity and Discontinuity in Viking Power on the North Norwegian Coast', in *Papers from the Third Annual Meeting of European Archaeologists at Ravenna 1997: Continuity and Discontinuity from the Late Antique to the Early*

Middle Ages in Europe and across the Mediterranean Basin, 8 vols, ed. by Mark
Pearce and Maurizio Tosi (Oxford: University Press, 1998), pp. 140–44

Brink, Stefan, 'People and *land* in Early Scandinavia', in *Franks, Northmen, and
Slavs: Identities and State Formation in Early Medieval Europe*, ed. by Ildar
Garipzanov, Patrick Geary, and Przemysław Urbańczyk (Turnhout: Brepols,
2008), pp. 87–112

Figenschow, Stefan, 'Comparing the Central Authorities' Expansion into North
Norway and Finland during the Middle Ages', in *Nordens plass i middelalderens
nye Europa*, ed. by Lars Ivar Hansen and others (Stamsund: Orkana, 2011),
pp. 137–51

Fulk, R. D., ed., 'Eyvindr *skáldaspillir* Finnson', in *Poetry from the Kings' Sagas 1:
From Mythical Times to c. 1035*, ed. by Diana Whaley Skaldic Poetry of the
Scandinavian Middle Ages, 1 (Turnhout: Brepols, 2012), I, 171–235

Hansen, Lars Ivar, 'The Dawn of State Formations 800–1550', in *The Barents Region:
A Transnational History of Subarctic Northern Europe*, ed. by Lars Elenius,
Hallvard Tjelmeland, Maria Lähteenmäki, and Alexey Golubev (Oslo: Pax,
2015), pp. 28–84

Hem Eriksen, Marianne, 'Portals to the Past: An Archaeology of Doorways,
Dwellings and Ritual Practice in Late Iron Age Scandinavia' (unpublished
doctoral thesis, University of Oslo, 2015)

Iversen, Frode, 'Community and Society: The *Thing* at the Edge of Europe', *Journal
of the North Atlantic Special Volume*, 8 (2015), 1–17

Jesch, Judith, *The Viking Diaspora* (New York: Routledge, 2015)

Jørgensen, Roger, 'How Did the Natives of North Norway Secure the Supply
of Iron in the Late Iron Age?', in *Exploitation of Outfield Resources: Joint
Research at the University Museums of Norway*, ed. by Svein Indrelid, Kari
Loe Hjelle, and Kathrine Stene (Bergen: University Museum, 2015),
pp. 99–106

Keller, Christian, 'Norway in the 10th Century AD', in *The Neighbours of Poland in
the Tenth Century*, ed. by P. Urbańczyk (Warsaw: Institute of Archaeology and
Ethnicity, Polish Academy of Sciences, 2000), pp. 37–48

McKinnel, John, *Meeting the Other in Norse Myth and Legend* (Woodbridge:
Brewer, 2005)

Munch, Gerd Stamsø, Olav Sverre Johansen, and Else Roesdahl, eds, *Borg in
Lofoten: A Chieftain's Farm in North Norway* (Trondheim: Tapir Academic
Press, 2003)

Myhre, Bjørn, 'Boathouses and Naval Organization', in *Military Aspects of
Scandinavian Society in a European Perspective AD 1–1300: Papers from an
International Research Seminar at the Danish National Museum, Copenhagen,
2–4 May 1996*, ed. by Anne Nørgård Jørgensen and Birthe L. Clausen
(Copenhagen: National Museum, 1997), pp. 169–83

——, 'Boathouses as Indicators of Political Organization', *Norwegian
Archaeological Review*, 18 (1985), 36–60

——, 'Chieftains' Graves and Chiefdom Territories in South Norway in the
Migration Period', *Studien zur Sachsenforschung*, 6 (1987), 169–87

Opsahl, Erik, '"[…] Nonetheless [He] Fulfilled His Obligation Towards the Hirð": Fealty and Politics in Medieval Norway', in *Feudalism: New Landscapes of Debate* (Turnhout: Brepols, 2011), pp. 185–201

Phelpstead, Carl, ed., *A History of Norway and the Passion and Miracles of the Blessed Óláfr*, trans. by Devra Kunin (Exeter: Short Run Press, 2001)

Poole, Russell, ed., 'Háleygjatal', in *Poetry from the Kings' Sagas 1: From Mythical Times to c. 1035*, 2 vols, ed. by Diana Whaley, Skaldic Poetry of the Scandinavian Middle Ages, 1 (Turnhout: Brepols, 2012), I, 195–213

Reynolds, Susan, 'Government and Community', in *The New Cambridge Medieval History Vol. 4, part 1, c. 1024–c. 1198*, ed. by D. Luscombe and J. Riley-Smith (Cambridge: Cambridge University Press, 2004), pp. 86–112

Skre, Dagfinn, 'Centrality, Landholding and Trade in Scandinavia c. AD 700–900', in *Settlement and Lordship in Viking and Early Medieval Scandinavia*, ed. by Bjørn Poulsen and Søren Michael Sindbæk (Turnhout: Brepols, 2011), pp. 197–212

Storli, Inger, 'Court Sites of Arctic Norway: Remains of Thing Sites and Representations of Political Consolidation Processes in the Northern Germanic World during the First Millennium AD?', *Norwegian Archaeological Review*, 43.2 (2010), 128–44

——, *Hålogaland før Rikssamlingen: Politiske prosesser i perioden 200–900 e. Kr* (Oslo: Instituttet for sammenlignende kulturforskning, 2006)

——, 'Ohthere and His World: A Contemporary Perspective', in *Ohthere's Voyages: A Late 9th-Century Account of Voyages along the Coasts and Norway and Denmark and its Cultural Context*, ed. by Janet Bately and Anton Englert, Maritime Culture of the North, 1 (Roskilde: Viking Ship Museum, 2007), pp. 76–99

Tveitane, Mattias, *Fra ord til navn: språklig navnegransking; en artikkelsamling* (Bergen: Universitetsforlag, 1983)

Valtonen, Irmeli, 'Who Were the *Finnas*?', in *Ohthere's Voyages: A Late 9th-century Account of Voyages along the Coasts and Norway and Denmark and its Cultural Context*, ed. by Janet Bately and Anton Englert (Roskilde: Viking Ship Museum, 2007), pp. 106–07

RICHARD HOLT

The Formation of a Norwegian Kingdom: A Northern Counter-Narrative?

There is a traditional account of Norwegian unification, expressed and elaborated in the saga literature of the Middle Ages and repeated by modern historians. In essence, the story was of a nation assembled and ruled through the centuries by a single dynasty of kings, the descendants of Haraldr *hárfagri* (Fine Hair), a local king with an illustrious ancestry. Having earlier vowed not to cut his hair until his destiny was fulfilled, Haraldr won the Battle of Hafrsfjǫrður in maybe 872 and thus brought all of the medieval kingdom of Norway under his rule. And although Haraldr's immediate descendants who succeeded to his kingdom in the decades after his death (in perhaps 932 after an improbably long life) were not all so successful in their rule, nevertheless it was Haraldr's dynasty that was endowed with the legitimacy of kingship and most importantly would provide the hero kings of the late tenth and eleventh centuries — Óláfr Tryggvason, Óláfr Haraldsson, and Haraldr Sigurðarson *harðráði* (Hard Ruler) — who would bring the Norwegians to Christianity and stand as the models of kingly qualities for their successors.

The story grew with the telling to become a national foundation narrative already before the late twelfth century. This chapter will argue that even within this developing grand narrative we find elements of other, alternative narratives which might once have told different stories of national unification, but which long before 1200 had been cast aside by the saga writers, or were retold to fit in with the preferred version of history. It is also possible to shift the geographical focus of the early process of the formation of a single realm. As it stands, the traditional story presents it essentially as occurring in the southern parts of the land; northern Norway is almost entirely marginalized as a peripheral region where little of importance to the state formation process could happen.

It is necessary first to look at the way the accepted national history arose, to consider the basis for the story it tells. When Norwegian historians of the

Richard Holt, UiT The Arctic University of Norway, richard.holt@uit.no

Myths and Magic in the Medieval Far North: Realities and Representations of a Region on the Edge of Europe, ed. by Stefan Figenschow, Richard Holt, and Miriam Tveit, AS 10
(Turnhout: Brepols, 2020), pp. 215–235
© BREPOLS ❧ PUBLISHERS   10.1484/M.AS-EB.5.120527

nineteenth century produced histories of their country in the Middle Ages, it was understandable that they should base their account of the emergence of a Norwegian nation on the histories and Icelandic sagas surviving from the late twelfth and early thirteenth centuries (just as their eighteenth-century predecessor Þormóður Torfason, known as Tormod Torfæus, had done in the first published history of medieval Norway).[1] There were in effect no alternative sources: the earliest surviving written documents produced in Norway date only from the middle of the eleventh century. The Icelanders, by contrast, told tales that went back into a remote past, and which might be considered to have all the authority of age. The reliability of orally transmitted traditions was more easily acceptable in the days before modern research effectively destroyed that illusion; the fragments of archaic, heroic poetry quoted in the sagas — however difficult they might be to understand and interpret — were accepted as confirmation that the saga authors had built their narratives upon reliable traditions of the remote past.[2] Not all historians were convinced, however, that this was a version of history that should be accepted uncritically; there were always those who expressed doubts as to the reliability of the source literature for this narrative.[3] It seemed at the least improbable that any quantity of accurate information could have been conveyed to the writers of the twelfth and thirteenth centuries, separated as they were from the kings they wrote about by a long period in which no written records were made.

It is now accepted that writing about the Norwegian past began with lists of kings compiled in early twelfth-century Iceland by Sæmundr Sigfússon (1056–1133), known also as Sæmundr *fróði* (the Learned), and apparently also by Ari Þorgilsson (1067–1148), similarly referred to as Ari *fróði*. According to the opening words of Ari's *Íslendingabók*, an earlier version he had written had included kings' lives and other genealogies, though further information is lacking.[4] Sæmundr produced a similar historical account of the Norwegian

1   Torfæus, *Historia Rerum Norvegicarum.*
2   Historians of the nineteenth century were generally willing to accept saga evidence after the obviously mythical elements were stripped away: for instance, Keyser, *Norges Historie*; Munch, *Det norske Folks Historie.* Halfdan Koht argued that the sagas are particularly valuable as sources for the times in which they were written, but having been built on an unusually vigorous oral tradition are also repositories of historical facts from distant times: Koht, 'Sagaenes opfatning av vår gamle historie', pp. 379–96. For a similar belief in the capacity of the Icelandic oral tradition to preserve a record of actual events, see Liestøl, *Upphavet til den islandske ættesaga.*
3   In contrast to the Norwegian historiographical tradition of using sagas as sources, Lauritz Weibull's deep scepticism to any historical value the sagas might have for the earlier periods of Norwegian history has become more general of Scandinavian scholarship: Weibull, *Kritiska undersökningar i Nordens historia* and *Historisk-kritisk metod och nordisk medeltidsforskning.* A most useful review of the development of attitudes to saga evidence and its reliability is Helle, 'Hovedlinjer i utviklingen av den historiske sagakritikken', pp. 13–40.
4   Ari Þorgilsson, *Íslendingabók*, p. 3.

kings at around the same time, probably in Latin. Although now lost, Sæmundr's work was the basis for the poem *Nóregs konungatal* (as stanza 40 acknowledges) of about 1190.[5] There the details of the kings' lives are few and scanty, suggesting that Sæmundr's work had similarly been little more than a chronology of a named succession of kings from Haraldr *hárfagri*. The scope and content of neither Ari's nor Sæmundr's work can now be known — just as we cannot know whether they both, independently, gave expression to existing oral traditions or alternatively whether one of them depended on the other as his main source. Further indication that neither compiled much more than an extended list of names may perhaps be found in the three texts written by Norwegians, 'the Norwegian synoptics', which constitute the next body of historical writing we have.

The earliest of these that can be firmly dated is the *Historia de Antiquitate Regum Norwagiensum* by Theodoric, a monk presumably of Niðaróss, which was written not long after 1177 and certainly before 1188.[6] Then there is the anonymous *Historia Norwegie*, which it has been argued might be as early as about 1150, although many would place it rather later.[7] Finally, there is the vernacular *Ágrip af Nóregs konunga sǫgum* of about 1190.[8] None of these has much to say about the Norwegian kings before Óláfr Haraldsson — or indeed about St Óláfr himself. Theodoric tells his readers that it was from the Icelanders that he drew his knowledge, through assiduous inquiry — the Icelanders who had preserved the memory of events and kings in their ancient poetry.[9] Perhaps he implies that he had relied on living informants rather than on texts by Ari or Sæmundr, although he does also name an unidentifiable *catalogus regum Norwagiensium* (a catalogue of Norwegian kings) in assigning a reign of five years to Knútr (Cnut the Great) and his son Sveinn. The reference has been extensively discussed, since at least the time of Gustav Storm in 1873: however, since we know that Sæmundr's work was still extant in Iceland about 1190 when it was used by the author of *Noregs konungatal*, we might assume that Theodoric, too, had been able to make use of it.[10] The sparse details of Theodoric's short history — half of which consists of digressions in the form of classical allusions and long anecdotes — do not fill the reader with confidence that there was any great body of historical knowledge preserved in twelfth-century Iceland. Nor do the other two synoptic works seem to draw on any greater store of knowledge:

---

5 *Nóregs konungatal*, 11, 315.
6 Theodoricus, *Historia*.
7 *Historia Norwegie*, ed. by Ekrem and Mortensen.
8 *Ágrip*, ed. by Driscoll. Theodore M. Andersson, however, regards this date as 'somewhat uncertain' and presents arguments that *Ágrip* may be Icelandic, written in the early thirteenth century: 'Two Ages in *Ágrip*', pp. 93–95.
9 Theodoric, *Historia*, prologue, p. 1.
10 Theodoric, *Historia*, chap. 20, ll. 53–54, p. 33. The identity of this catalogue is discussed extensively by the editors, though without resolution: pp. 92–93 n. 214.

the three texts have much in common, although it remains uncertain how far each of their authors depended on the other two and how far they all made use of common sources. *Ágrip* clearly leans heavily on Theodoric's book, and is perhaps also in part derived from *Historia Norwegie*. The two Latin works, however, appear to have been compiled independently of each other. There is no evidence that one or more unknown works lie behind these three, providing source material common to all; it seems certain that the works of Sæmundr and Ari were the only written sources that were available. The list of six ancestors of Haraldr *hárfagri* in *Historia Norwegie* bears such a close similarity to that given by Ari in the second paragraph of *Íslendingabok* that one cannot doubt that its author had access to this or another text by Ari.[11]

It should also be mentioned that the period around 1180 saw the production of the latest textual version, attributed in its final form generally to Archbishop Eysteinn Erlendsson, of the *Passio et Miracula Beati Olavi*, an account of Óláfr's Christian death with a collection of the miracles attributed to the king and saint.[12] Whilst modern historians might draw a contrast between hagiography and historical writing, we should not assume that its author saw the purpose of his book as being so very different from that of, for example, his contemporary Theodoric. Both wrote down tales from the past so as to point out moral lessons to the reader, and we can no longer say that they necessarily believed implicitly in the truthfulness of their stories: what made the stories worth telling was the example they gave. Actually, the absence of any credible facts about St Óláfr in the *Passio et Miracula Beati Olavi* supports the impression one also receives from Theodoric that, by the 1170s, very little indeed was known in Norway or Iceland about the actions of this king who had long before achieved apotheosis, in his shrine at Niðaróss; his accession was remembered, as was his reputation as a Christianizer, his loss of power in 1028, and his death at Stiklarstaðir (Stiklestad) in 1030 — but nothing more.

In keeping with his mission to write a moralizing history, Theodoric ended his story in 1130, deeming the shameful events and personalities of the following decades as unworthy of record.[13] *Historia Norwegie* and *Ágrip*, like Theodoric, began their story with Haraldr *hárfagri*, but as the latter parts of both texts are now lost it is impossible to be certain of their original length. Presumably much of *Historia Norwegie* is lost as it ends with Óláfr Haraldsson's arrival in Norway in 1015; *Ágrip* ends abruptly in the reign of Ingi *krókhryggr* (Crookback), who succeeded in 1136, and may originally have continued down to the accession of Sverrir Sigurðarson in 1177. Subsequent history writing was

---

11   *Historia Norwegie*, ed. by Ekrem and Mortensen, pp. 78–80; Ari Þorgilsson, *Íslendingabok*, p. 3. A most useful discussion of the sources to all three of these Norwegian texts, and their relationship to each other, may be found in *Ágrip*, ed. by Driscoll, pp. xiii–xviii. Andersson, 'The Two Ages in *Ágrip*', devotes a similarly useful extended footnote to this matter: pp. 94–95 n. 3.

12   *A History of Norway*, ed. Phelpstead.

13   Theodoric, *Historia*, chap. 34, ll. 10–18, p. 53.

concerned with more extensive treatments of recent times and even current events: the earliest known, Eiríkr Oddsson's lost *Hryggjarstykki* written in Iceland perhaps during the 1150s (and known almost entirely from its having been referred to in *Morkinskinna*, and cited extensively by Snorri Sturluson in *Heimskringla*) seems to have concerned itself mainly with the activities of the pretender Sigurðr *slembir* (the Rowdy), who had been active in the period from 1135 until his death in 1139.[14] It was some time before Eiríkr's model caught on, so that further book-length biographies of kings seem not to have been written until the end of the twelfth century. Karl Jónsson, abbot of Þingeyrar, began his biography of King Sverrir Sigurðarson (1177–1202) apparently in the late 1180s, under the direction of the king himself — it was probably finished after Sverrir's death;[15] two monks of Þingeyrar, Oddr Snorrason and Gunnlaugr Leifsson, produced biographies of Óláfr Tryggvason (of which Oddr's survives) at about the same time, and — also in Iceland — someone wrote a biography of the second conversion king Óláfr Haraldsson, known as *The Oldest Saga of St Óláfr*, of which only six fragments have survived.[16]

It was in the 1220s, probably, that the years between 1030 and 1177 first became the subject of extended historical writing, in the collection of kings' sagas now known as *Morkinskinna*.[17] Much of this book dealt with the kings Mágnus Óláfsson and Haraldr Sigurðarson, and with kings Eysteinn and Sigurðr *jórsalafari* (the Crusader), the sons of King Magnús *berfœttr* (Bareleg), in a number of anecdotal episodes. Subsequently, but not long after, the author of the collection known to us as *Fagrskinna* wrote of a longer period, from the time of Hálfdan *svarti* (the Black), the father of Haraldr *hárfagri*, until 1177.[18] These longer books were soon followed, in the 1230s, by Snorri Sturluson's ambitious collection *Heimskringla*.[19] Snorri expanded the timescale of previous writing by composing *Ynglinga saga*, about the supposed antecedents of Haraldr *hárfagri*, and also by writing biographies of the kings — including those of the tenth and eleventh centuries — of much greater length, and containing much more specific detail, than any previous author had done. For his source material, he made use of the earlier kings' sagas, and acknowledged *Hryggjarstykki*. Like the author of *Fagrskinna*, he used *Ágrip*.[20] And like *Morkinskinna* and *Fagrskinna*, his text was laced with stanzas of heroic poetry attributed to named skalds, poets of the past who had composed praise-poems for the kings they served.

---

14 *Morkinskinna*, ed. and trans. by Andersson and Gade, p. 14. Bjarni Guðnason has argued that *Hryggjarstykki* was written as early as 1146–1155: *Fyrsta sagan*.
15 Karl Jónsson, *Sverris saga*, ed. by Indrebø.
16 Oddr Snorrason, *Saga Óláfs Tryggvasonar*; Oddr Snorrason, *The Saga of Olaf Tryggvason*, pp. 2–4; *Morkinskinna*, ed. and trans. by Andersson and Gade, p. 2.
17 *Morkinskinna*, ed. and trans. by Andersson and Gade.
18 *Fagrskinna*, ed. and trans. by Finlay.
19 Snorri Sturluson, *Heimskringla*.
20 *Ágrip*, ed. by Driscoll, p. xii.

It is highly unlikely that Snorri and the other saga authors had any more substantial information about these earlier named kings, other than the sources already mentioned. The earliest written Icelandic sources relied on orally transmitted memories. In *Íslendingabók*, Ari names his sources: important figures he had known in his youth, most of them his own kin, whose memories went back well into the eleventh century and who in turn had preserved family memories from before 1000.[21] We can be sure that this was a strong oral tradition he drew on, particularly when it was concerned with the deeds of immediate ancestors and the high positions they had held in the Church or in the Icelandic structure of government, as well as family descent and title to inherited lands. But it would be naive to regard his record of the period around and before 1000 as trustworthy in all or even most respects, especially when those family links were lacking. Any details of kings before the time of Óláfr Tryggvason that Ari — or Sæmundr — could provide, such as their chronology, their relationships to each other, or their doings, must be regarded as extremely suspect. The text of *Íslendingabók* begins with Ari's statement that the settlement of Iceland began in the reign of Haraldr *hárfagri*, in the same year that St Edmund, King Edmund of East Anglia, was killed by the Danes — that is, 869 (although Ari believed it was 870). His authority was his foster-father Teitr, son of Bishop Ísleifr, and other named people with noted memories, but it is not credible that they could have preserved such a precisely dated memory, especially from a period when dating by the Christian era was presumably not in use in pagan Scandinavia. Ari makes reference to having read an account of St Edmund's life, and most plausibly could not resist the temptation to link northern Europe's greatest saint with his story.[22] His reconstruction of the succession of earlier kings and their chronology — and whatever he and Sæmundr might have written about their deeds — depended on the same corpus of skaldic poetry that Snorri and his contemporaries worked from and cited a century later.

How dependable was skaldic verse as a source for the past? Snorri himself argued in his introduction to *Heimskringla* that the heroic poetry he cited in support of his narrative had been composed for living kings and could hardly have mocked them with stories of brave deeds they had not done. Superficially, that may be an attractive argument, but its ingenuousness tells against it, and, on the contrary, we should assume that this poetry exaggerated and improved on events. This was a genre characterized by its extravagantly allusive style, its kennings, so that its interpretation has never been straightforward or clear. Alistair Campbell expressed the frustration felt by many: 'Norse poets aimed at the artistic decoration of facts known to their hearers rather than at giving information'.[23] Nor is that the only problem with skaldic verse. It is naive to understand these

21 Ari Þorgilsson, *Íslendingabók*, pp. 4, 13.
22 Ari Þorgilsson, *Íslendingabók*, p. 3.
23 *Encomium Emmae Reginae*, ed. by Campbell, p. 66.

poems as finished texts broadly contemporary with the individuals and events to which they refer: their initial composition might often have been later, and furthermore these orally transmitted texts can hardly have remained free from processes of retelling and reconstruction, and indeed wholesale recycling, as skalds used stock expressions and formulations in new contexts.[24] Verses seldom use the names of kings, so that re-use was always possible, as was misattribution by later generations. The early poetry is known only from texts written in the thirteenth century, or later, where stanzas are cited separately; we simply do not know if they are cited in their correct order. And finally, and perhaps most important of all, we must always remember that there was a much greater corpus of verses that the saga authors chose not to cite and which therefore we know nothing of — verses that did not support their narrative, or that perhaps told of other persons and events that the authors did not wish to mention, or verse that they simply did not understand for whatever reason.[25]

The collections of kings' sagas, of which *Heimskringla* was the culmination both in time and by reason of its length and the depth of its narrative, therefore came at the end of a period of perhaps a century of history writing in Iceland, and to a certain extent in Norway as well. It was a period that saw no new sources of information appear about the more distant past, and no new variations on the basic narrative of Norwegian national history. That fact alone might be taken as an argument for the narrative's essential reliability, although it can also be taken to show that the successors of Ari and Sæmundr saw it as their task not to question the basic story these pioneers had told, but instead to elaborate on it. As the century proceeded, the books became longer and longer. In part, this was because they took in the story of the twelfth century as it unfolded, a century well served by written sources such as *Hryggjarstykki*; they also enlarged upon the story of the latter half of the eleventh century, for which there were orally transmitted sources — reliable or not — such as those cited by the author of *Morkinskinna*.[26] But, remarkably, it was also the sagas of the kings of the early eleventh century, and of the tenth century, that expanded in length. Snorri Sturluson could furnish details of the reigns of Haraldr *hárfagri* and his sons that Ari and Sæmundr evidently knew nothing of: he was, for instance, the first to provide a detailed account of Haraldr's programme of conquest — some 350 years previously — that had made him the ruler of all Norway. Snorri's aim had been not to faithfully retell the story

---

24 Claus Krag's important analysis of *Ynglingatal*, described by Snorri as composed by Þjóðólfr ór Hvini, illustrates many of the problems in understanding the content and more importantly the background to verses used by the saga authors. Krag takes up earlier doubts about this poem, supposedly of the ninth century, instead placing its composition firmly into a later Icelandic Christian context: *Ynglingatal og Ynglinge saga*.

25 An excellent discussion of skaldic verses and their uses is: Frank, 'Skaldic Poetry'.

26 The nature of the oral sources available to *Morkinskinna*'s author is discussed by the editors in their introduction, pp. 57–65.

of the past from every available source, but rather to construct an improved narrative for the entertainment and enlightenment of his audience, a narrative that would tell stories worthy of the hero-kings of Norway's past.

Modern historians have dismissed Haraldr's unification of Norway as largely an unhistorical myth. Even so, aspects of the saga accounts — especially Haraldr's reported epic victory at the Battle of Hafrsfjǫrður — are accepted even by the more generally sceptic Claus Krag, and Haraldr's existence as a king of some importance in the south-western part of Norway is not generally disputed.[27] The dismissive treatment of the historical Haraldr by the Icelander Sverrir Jakobsson, who has argued that Haraldr should be seen as a figure of myth and legend without meaningful historical basis — a Norwegian King Arthur, who may or may not have existed but for whom there is no real evidence and who had nothing in common with the hero-king of literature — has clearly not found favour among Norwegian historians.[28] Sverre Bagge expresses what has now become the standard Norwegian view of Haraldr, that whilst he did not create a kingdom covering all of Norway (as later defined), he was a prominent king in the south-west of the land and of contemporary importance.[29] There is actually some support for that in William of Malmesbury's history of the English kings, compiled between 1126 and 1135, where he wrote of a Norwegian King Haraldr, who sent a gift of a ship with a scarlet sail to King Æthelstan of England (924–939).[30] The reference, despite its late date, demands to be taken seriously, as it comes within the section — chapters 132 to 135 of book II — that William wrote after he had completed his main account of Æthelstan's reign because he had subsequently found 'a certain ancient book' (*quodam uolumine uetusto*) he believed was written during Æthelstan's lifetime.[31] Sarah Foot's well-founded and closely argued judgement is that William had indeed succeeded in finding a now-lost source of information about the king's reign dating from the tenth century, having been written perhaps to commemorate Æthelstan's crushing victory over his Scottish and Irish–Scandinavian opponents at *Brunanburh* in 937, or at least soon after his death in 939.[32] That points to a Haraldr active around the 930s — and it should go almost without saying that there is no reason at all to accept preposterous stories of his unfeasibly long life. If there had been any battle at Hafrsfjǫrður some sixty years previously as the culmination of a campaign to conquer all of Norway, it was not fought by this King Haraldr.

---

27 Krag, 'The Early Unification of Norway', pp. 185–89; Helle, 'Norway 800–1200', p. 10.

28 Sverrir Jakobsson, 'Erindringen om en mægtig personlighed', pp. 213–30.

29 Bagge, *From Viking Stronghold to Christian Kingdom*, p. 25. The effect of modern research is undermined, however, when Norwegian schoolchildren are still taught that Haraldr not only created their country but also that he and his sons developed new methods of governing it: Rønning, *Er historiefaget i den norske skolen preget av moderne forskning*, pp. 38–41, 66–67.

30 William of Malmesbury, *Gesta Regum Anglorum* I, pp. xii–xxiii; II, 135.1, p. 217.

31 William of Malmesbury, *Gesta Regum Anglorum*, II, 132, p. 210.

32 Foot, *Æthelstan*, pp. 251–58.

At the same time, we should be sceptical of the saga authors' preserving any real memories of this king. William of Malmesbury, again, when writing of the events of 1066 in England, followed the author of the D manuscript of the *Anglo-Saxon Chronicle* who wrote that it was the king of Norway, *cyng of Norwegon*, Harold *Harfagera*, who fell at the Battle of Stamford Bridge in September of that year.[33] It is a well-remarked feature of the *Anglo-Saxon Chronicle* that it could name the leaders of Scandinavian armies, so that we are confident that English chroniclers, and others, were generally well-informed about their opponents. This D chronicler evidently worked within twenty years of Stamford Bridge; we should expect his report of the name of this Norwegian king, well-known in England because of his ambitions and attempts at conquest both in 1058 and 1066,[34] to have been reliable. It is inconceivable that the chronicler's account was coloured or confused by any memory of another Norwegian king of 150 years earlier, despite the comments of modern editors of the *Chronicle* who have assumed just that.[35] In 1066, we must remember, whatever stories there were preserved in Iceland or Scandinavia of the legendary king had not yet been written down. Gabriel Turville-Petre was puzzled by the fact that this clearly was the name by which Haraldr was known during his lifetime: *harðráði* is not applied to him in any eleventh-century source, or in poetry, but begins to come into regnal lists and the like in the later part of the thirteenth century.[36] Both Judith Jesch and Sverrir, too, argued that the *Anglo-Saxon Chronicle*'s use of the name *hárfagri* should be taken at face value — that this was indeed the name by which King Haraldr Sigurðarson was known to his people.[37] We must admit the possibility that both Haraldr Sigurðarson and a king of the early tenth century might have been known by the same by-name. Yet it is surely more likely that these English references to a Haraldr *hárfagri* in 1066 confirm that the early twelfth-century Icelanders actually had a very imperfect knowledge of the past: that their oral tradition could easily confuse the attributes of a Norwegian king of only fifty years before with those of a semi-mythical king from a distant past. That they assigned the wrong name to the King Haraldr whom they believed had united Norway does not in itself matter; as a sign of the unreliability of the stories they told and then wrote down, however, it certainly does matter.

We simply cannot know whether or not the sagas preserve genuine material telling of the heroic deeds of an early tenth-century Norwegian local king Haraldr, although it seems doubtful. Sverrir Jakobsson argues that the skaldic verses cited in *Fagrskinna* and *Heimskringla*, far from being an

---

33 *Two of the Saxon Chronicles Parallel*, ed. by Plummer, pp. 197, 199.

34 Stenton, *Anglo-Saxon England*, pp. 575, 589–90.

35 For instance, 'The Anglo-Saxon Chronicle', trans. by Tucker, p. 146 n. 3; *Anglo-Saxon Chronicle*, ed. and trans. by Swanton, p. 199 n. 9. Swanton could add, with precise references, that 'Florence, Simeon, Gaimar, and Ordericus all make the same mistake'.

36 Turville-Petre, *Haraldr the Hard-Ruler*, p. 3.

37 Jesch, 'Norse Historical Traditions', p. 144. Sverrir, 'Erindringen om en mægtig personlighed'.

unambiguous poem of praise for Haraldr, are in fact the fragments of quite distinct poems incorrectly attached to his name and which cannot be taken as any sort of evidence or support for the saga of Haraldr.[38] There are no other Scandinavian sources for Haraldr's existence, other than the narratives of the twelfth century.[39] The king of legend may well have had a basis in the living man named by William of Malmesbury, but at the same time we should be careful to distinguish between the historical and the mythical *personæ*. There is no reason to believe that an historical Haraldr unified the land in any meaningful way, nor that he laid foundations for a system of national government — a system that according to Snorri's fanciful account would have made the Norway of 900 as politically advanced and centrally governed as any kingdom in north-west Europe. Nor can Haraldr be accepted as the founder of a royal dynasty, the ancestor of all subsequent Norwegian kings (at least until the impostor King Sverrir Sigurðarson established his line after 1177 — though even then he and his supporters claimed he was of the ancient royal blood). Historians seem willing to accept — without firm evidence it must be said — that Haraldr was succeeded by his sons, Eiríkr *blóðøx* (Bloodaxe) and Hákon *góði* (the Good) (Æthelstan's supposed foster-son), and Eiríkr's son Haraldr *gráfellr* (Greyhide), but that the dynasty ended with them. Despite later stories, there is not a shred of evidence that he was the progenitor of the eleventh-century kings whose existence we can be sure of and through whose activities, dimly perceived, a sovereign and Christian Norwegian monarchy came into existence.[40]

The historian who chooses to write about the early Norwegian monarchy cannot escape the consequences of medieval historical composition. Whilst we may perceive it to be largely a construction of the twelfth century, the absence of earlier written sources means that we will never know to what extent it built upon relatively faithful memories of the past. Nor can we ever know how far it is justified in attempting to construct, in our own time, a counter-narrative to tell another story of early state formation in Norway. The essential difficulty is identifying alternative threads in the historical tradition of that period which might point the way to a different historical narrative, and then evaluating how meaningful they might be. There is one source that stands out, in this respect, which presents alternatives to the Icelandic–Norwegian narrative, and which, moreover, was written down at an earlier date. A century before Theodoric wrote his brief history of the Norwegian kings, Adam of Bremen wrote his history of the archbishops of Hamburg and Bremen.[41] Until the

38 Sverrir, 'Erindringen om en mægtig personlighed', pp. 219–22.
39 Jesch, 'Norse Historical Traditions', pp. 143–45.
40 Krag, 'Norge som odel i Harald Hårfagres ætt', pp. 288–301.
41 Adam of Bremen, *Hamburgische Kirchengeschichte*; Adam of Bremen, *History of the Archbishops of Hamburg-Bremen*.

establishment of the archdiocese of Lund in 1103/4 (followed by Niðaróss in 1152, and Uppsala in 1164), these archbishops had the whole of Scandinavia as their province. A central theme of Adam's book was the conversion of the North under the aegis of Hamburg-Bremen, and in the course of telling that story he also felt impelled to refer to what he loyally regarded as unauthorized missionary activity carried out in defiance of his see's authority. It was also necessary to give some background to his theme, with descriptions of the northern lands, and details — as they seemed relevant — of their kings. It is customary to view Adam's work with suspicion. Whatever he might have heard about the northern parts of Scandinavia, he did not allow the facts to spoil the fanciful and incredible stories he told of these lands in their unenlightened pagan state; in his partiality, moreover, he regarded all who in some way acted against the ecclesiastical authority of his see as transgressors against the faith, or worse. But he is not to be regarded on that ground alone as unreliable: the obvious bias in his writing — his understandable preference for the activities of his own bishops, against those represented as their opponents, such as the English bishops that the different Scandinavian kings often preferred to employ — is transparent and easy to discount. He had no sympathy with what we would interpret as the ambition of the Danish, Norwegian, and Swedish kings to build their own national churches free of German imperial authority, an aim that they would all achieve in the twelfth century when anti-imperial papal policy coincided with Scandinavian national interests.

In at least one respect Adam's work should command our attention. He heard much of what he knew of political events in the century before he wrote — he readily and frequently acknowledged — from the lips of King Sveinn Úlfsson, more generally called Sveinn Ástríðarson or Estridsson, of Denmark, whom he visited in 1068. Sveinn, whose mother Ástríðr was the sister of Knútr *riki*, Cnut the Great, ruled Denmark as king from the time of his cousin Hórðaknútr's or Harthacnut's death in 1042 until his own death in 1074. What he chose to tell Adam of his own family history is not necessarily to be regarded as a reliable version of events, but it is what Sveinn himself believed, or at any rate the version he wished others to believe. Therefore, it has a very special and rare status as a fragment of royal autobiography and stands out from other sources for tenth- and eleventh-century Denmark and Norway, if only for that reason. Moreover, it goes some way to providing an alternative to the Icelandic–Norwegian narrative. We do not know how far, if at all, the twelfth- and thirteenth-century Scandinavian writers used Adam's book; in Denmark, Saxo (in the decades around 1200) took details from it, and it has been argued that Ari read the book when he visited Scandinavia, but otherwise it was only known indirectly in Iceland.[42] But if the Icelanders

---

42 Sawyer and Sawyer, 'Adam and the Eve', pp. 39, 44. Elsa Mundal has argued that Ari knew Adam's book, and indeed used it as the model for *Íslendingabók*: Mundal, '*Íslendingabók*', pp. 111–21.

did have any sort of access to Adam's writings, they chose to ignore those aspects of his story that did not fit in with theirs.

Sveinn told Adam about his own struggle to assert himself against the Norwegian kings Magnús *goði* and Haraldr Sigurðarson in the 1040s and 1050s, a story he made very favourable to himself. When he talked of his own (unfulfilled) claim to the English crown, his insistence that he had been the acknowledged heir of Edward the Confessor confirms this to be a particularly partial account of the situation, a history adjusted to serve current political requirements; it was a year later, in 1069, that Sveinn launched his unsuccessful invasion of England, timed to coincide with rebellions by English opponents of Norman rule.[43] But while his stories of an earlier past are also to be approached with caution, this was a past in which Sveinn himself was not involved and which no longer had political relevance to the world of 1068. Inevitably, as oral history, those stories will be distorted and misrepresented, but the misrepresentations were likely not deliberate, and the distortions only those of time and memory. Modern understanding of social memory, and the value and use of oral testimony in writing history, cautions us against actually believing this to be a coherent account of the past.[44]

The transmission of social memory is always a process of change, of evolution: individuals' misrepresentation even of their own past is insidious and unconscious, a continuous process of reconstruction that matches their changing interests and identity. At the same time, traditional stories and explanations of events 'handed down from generation to generation' have changed and improved with every telling, adapted to fit current expectations and needs. Where traditional poetry is concerned, this might retain its shape much longer than other memories, because its formulations and rhythms encourage retention, which will always be the main argument that there lies a foundation of truth, some rags of genuine memory, behind the developing fantasies of the Icelandic and Norwegian authors of the twelfth and thirteenth centuries. But still, when we read this poetry, like other memories of the past, what we are hearing are the voices of those who told the stories, each time afresh for a new audience. In the case of the details Adam tells us, all that we can be sure of is that these were stories that could be told in the Danish court in the 1060s about individuals who had lived sixty or more years before, and which illustrate how Sveinn and his nearest associates understood their political and religious past, and how they themselves understood the Norwegian monarchy in the time of their fathers and grandfathers.

Sveinn's brief account of Norwegian history had no place for a dynasty of kings descended from any Haraldr *hárfagri*. He told Adam that the first man to seize kingship over Norway was his own great-uncle Hákon, previous

---

43   Stenton, *Anglo-Saxon England*, pp. 602–05.
44   Fentress and Wickham, *Social Memory*. For classic studies of aspects of social memory, see Passerini, *Fascism in Popular Memory*, and Thomson, 'Anzac Memories', pp. 25–31.

to whom there had been only jarls or chieftains, presumably meaning local rulers.[45] Hákon is known from extensive references in Norwegian and Icelandic literature as the jarl of Hlaðir, Hákon Sigurðarson, Hákon *illi* (the Evil). He was king for thirty-five years in the time of King Haraldr Gormsson, called *blátǫnn* (Bluetooth) in Denmark, said Sveinn. Later, Haraldr's son King Sveinn *tjúguskegg* (Forkbeard) of Denmark (Sveinn Ástríðarson's grandfather) found himself at war with another Norwegian king, Óláfr the son of Tryggve. Tryggve had been a pagan; Óláfr was said by many to have become a Christian but by some others to have forsaken the religion. All were agreed, though, that he was a renowned sorcerer and supported magicians, and was known for his divinations based on the ways of birds, so that he was known — in Adam's Latin text — as *Craccaben*, which in Old Norse would presumably be *Krákr beinn* (Crow-leg or Crow-foot).[46] Sveinn's was the earliest story to tell of how Óláfr Tryggvason met his end in a sea battle in the Øresund against both his Norwegian enemies and the Danish king, in defeat leaping from his ship never to be seen again.

One would wish to know more about Hákon, who in the 1060s could be spoken of as Norway's first king. Sveinn seems to have known very little about him, and what he did know may have been of mixed quality, given its nature as orally transmitted memories of a century before. Hákon was driven out by the Norwegians because of his haughtiness, we are told, but was restored by King Haraldr *blátǫnn* of Denmark, who made him improve his treatment of the Norwegian Christians (a reference — if reliable — to a late tenth-century Norwegian church. Haraldr himself is usually regarded as having converted to Christianity in about 965, or in precisely 963 as Michael Gelting has now convincingly argued). A most cruel man, Hákon was descended from giants — an indication that this pagan king had confirmed his kingship in traditional fashion by claiming descent from supernatural ancestors.[47]

Without question, Hákon was a genuine historical figure, from a powerful Norwegian dynasty, who did indeed hold authority in Norway for an extended period before Óláfr Tryggvason began to act as king in Norway in 995. He is a prominent figure in all of the Icelandic–Norwegian literature, accorded his own saga by Snorri Sturluson. As with Adam's depiction of him, he was always presented as a cruel, unrepentant pagan, but on top of that his negative portrayal goes beyond what might be expected even for Hákon 'the Evil', as

---

45 Adam said that Hákon *primus inter Nordmannos regnum arripuit, cum antea ducibus regerentur* (was the first among the Norwegians to seize the kingship, previous to which they had been ruled by dukes): Adam of Bremen, *Hamburgische Kirchengeschichte*, bk II, xxv (22), p. 84.

46 Adam of Bremen, *Hamburgische Kirchengeschichte*, bk II, xl (38), pp. 100–01. This is not an unknown name for a Viking chief, as an Irish–Scandinavian jarl of that name was killed at a battle at Corbridge in northern England in 918: Downham, *Viking Kings*, pp. 148–49.

47 Adam of Bremen, *Hamburgische Kirchengeschichte*, bk II, xxv (22), p. 84; Gelting, 'Poppo's Ordeal', pp. 101–33.

Historia Norwegie called him.[48] Most of what Theodoric wrote about him related to his unrelenting search for Óláfr Tryggvason, whom he knew to be the true king: Óláfr, in contrast with Hákon, is portrayed as a legitimate king by right of descent in the male line from Haraldr *hárfagri*, as well as a hero and a Christian.[49] For *Historia Norwegie*, Hákon, a descendant of Haraldr *hárfagri* only in the female line, was a usurper who controlled all Norway; he refused to be called a king, preferring the title of *jarl* that all his forebears had used.[50] None of the writers accorded him the title of king, thus drawing a sharp line between him — and his sons who ruled Norway between 1000 and 1015 — and the line of supposed descendants of Haraldr *hárfagri* who dominate the sagas and histories.

Whilst it is stressed by all of the Scandinavian authors that it was lust for other men's wives that led eventually to his downfall, the aspect of Hákon's rule that contributed most to his poor reputation by the twelfth century was his generally pro-Danish stance. Both the Scandinavian writers and Adam of Bremen agree that he was, for the most part, an ally of Haraldr *blátǫnn*: in Sveinn Ástríðarson's version of his family history, Hákon was maintained in power by Haraldr, and (as we have seen) forced to tolerate Christianity in Norway. Hákon's kingdom perhaps did not extend to Viken, the region on either side of the Oslofjord, which we know had been under the control of Danish kings in the ninth century and seems again to have been Danish under Haraldr *blátǫnn*. There are indications that the city of Oslo was a foundation of the 970s or 980s, located to serve Danish royal needs for a strategic base which would act as a centre for collecting tribute and trade goods, and perhaps provided with one or more churches.[51] Haraldr's claim on the Jelling stone that he had won for himself all Norway was an exaggeration, but we may infer that he regarded Hákon as his under-king, who provided him with tribute and support. Hákon's sons took refuge in Denmark with Sveinn *tjúguskegg* during the brief interlude of Óláfr Tryggvason's rule, and it was presumably then that Eiríkr Hákonsson married Sveinn's daughter Gyða, a union that would bind the two families together into an even closer alliance for the next thirty years. Eiríkr and Sveinn *tjúguskegg* together would destroy Óláfr Tryggvason's rule at the Battle of Svǫldr, and Eiríkr was apparently content then to rule Norway as his father had done, loyally recognizing Sveinn's suzerainty. As Sir Frank Stenton recognized, it was only with the help of his brother-in-law, 'the most famous warrior in the Scandinavian world', and his Norwegian troops that Sveinn's son, the landless adventurer Cnut the Great, succeeded in winning power in England in 1016 — a contribution for which Eiríkr was rewarded with the mighty earldom of Northumbria, which he held until his death in or

---

48 *Historia Norwegie*, ed. by Ekrem and Mortensen, chap. 16, p. 88.
49 Theodoric, *Historia*, chap. 4, ll. 33–36; chap. 7–10, pp. 8, 10–14.
50 *Historia Norwegie*, ed. by Ekrem and Mortensen, chap. 16, p. 88.
51 Krag, 'The Early Unification of Norway', p. 190; Schia, *Oslo Innerst i Viken*, pp. 122–32.

after 1023.[52] Eiríkr's son, Hákon, was earl of the Worcestershire area of western Mercia between at least 1019 and 1026, and having been installed by Cnut as ruler over Norway after Óláfr Haraldsson's fall in 1028, he drowned at sea in 1030, and the male line of the jarls of Hlaðir came to an end.[53]

What was the basis of Hákon Sigurðarson's power in Norway? According to the Icelandic–Norwegian tradition, he succeeded to a great territorial lordship built up by his forebears. He was jarl of Hlaðir, in wealthy Þrœndalǫg (modern Trøndelag, around Trondheim), but was also by inheritance jarl of Mœrr (Møre) to the south of Þrœndalǫg, and jarl of Hálogaland, the great northern region.[54] It was this latter jarldom that Icelandic-Norwegian literature said had been his family's original patrimony and the foundation of their rise to national dominance. A recent extended study of the rise of the dynasty from its origins until its eventual extinction in the eleventh century, and of its powerbase in early medieval Hálogaland, draws on a wide body of archaeological and other evidence to present a convincing picture of Hákon's family's gradual consolidation of authority.[55] Constituting the whole of Norway north of Þrœndalǫg, the jarldom was rich in the traditional Arctic export products that Ohthere of Hálogaland told King Alfred of in the late ninth century: furs, walrus ivory, eiderdown.[56] By 1000, the region had begun to export large amounts of dried cod, supplying Western Europe's growing demand for stockfish. Hákon's standing during his lifetime is amply demonstrated by the kingly attributes he commanded: the dynastic praise-poem *Háleygjatal* (of which only some sixteen stanzas survive, incorporated mainly into *Heimskringla* and *Fagrskinna*) has been assumed to have been composed in honour of Hákon during the 980s, and traces Hákon's descent from Óðinn.[57]

Intriguingly, Sveinn Ástríðarson also told Adam of Bremen that Hákon was of the stock of Ingvar — *ex genere Inguar* — presumably, that is, of the semi-legendary Ívarr.[58] Historically, Ívarr was the leader of the Great Army that overcame northern and eastern England in the 860s, and who killed King Edmund of East Anglia in 869; in legend, he was Ívarr *inn beinlausi* (the Boneless), the son of the apparently mythical Ragnarr *loðbrók* (Hairy Breeches). Establishing himself during the 870s in Ireland, Ívarr left a host of male descendants who were active as kings of Dublin and the other Irish seaports, and as Viking chieftains over all northern and western Britain and the islands. They remained prominent well after 1000.[59] It is far from

---

52 Stenton, *Anglo-Saxon England*, p. 387.
53 Keynes, 'Cnut's Earls', pp. 57–58, 61–62.
54 For instance, *Ágrip*, ed. by Driscoll, p. 20, or *Historia Norwegie*, ed. by Ekrem and Mortensen, chap. 16, pp. 88–90.
55 Bratrein, *Høvding, Jarl, Konge*.
56 Holmsen, 'Nordnorsk høvding økonomi i vikingtida', pp. 55–60.
57 *Corpus Poeticum Boreale*, I, 251–54.
58 Adam of Bremen, *Hamburgische Kirchengeschichte*, bk II, xxv (22), p. 84.
59 Downham, *Viking Kings*, pp. 1–11, 15–16, 63–67.

impossible that descendants of Ívarr should have chosen to return to pursue active careers in Scandinavia and might moreover have claimed prominent Danish or Norwegian families as kin. There is no reference to Hákon's links with that dynasty in any of the Icelandic or Norwegian literature, either in the sagas or in skaldic poetry; the fact remains, though, that Sveinn Ástríðarson could tell that story about his great-uncle, a generation or two before the Icelanders had even begun to write. But perhaps he, too, was constructing a more exciting family history. Sveinn certainly would have known something of the reputation of the descendants of Ívarr, given both the popularity of fanciful stories of Ragnarr *loðbrók* and his sons, and the many forms of contact that the wider Scandinavian diaspora evidently still maintained in his day; the link may have owed more to creative imagination than to cold fact.

The traditional Norwegian grand narrative, in attributing the important role of nation-building to Haraldr *hárfagri* and his descendants, also lays stress on the regions in the southern part of Norway where these men were held to be active. Snorri Sturluson had Haraldr's original powerbase as Vestfold, on the western side of the Oslofjord; he then extended his activities to the south-western part of the country — having allied himself with the jarl of Hlaðir, Hákon Grjótgarðsson (said to be the grandfather of Hákon Sigurðarson), where he consolidated his kingdom through victory over his various rivals and enemies at the Battle of Hafrsfjǫrður. As the jarl of Hlaðir controlled Þrœndalǫg and northern Norway, the kingdom of Norway was geographically complete. Sverre Bagge expresses the more current opinion that western Norway was Haraldr's power base and the theatre of his activities. The later saga heroes also based themselves in the southern regions of Norway, including Þrœndalǫg, all of them at one time or another serving as the royal power base, according to Bagge.[60] The pattern of activities is based on the sagas, of course; it represents one account of how the Norwegian monarchy developed and is itself an important part of the grand narrative, naming the parts of the realm where important people were active and significant events occurred.

What is striking is the virtual exclusion from the narrative of the North, of Hálogaland, wealthy (as we have seen) in the variety and value of its export products. Why do the sagas and the Norwegian synoptic histories say so little about Hálogaland in connection with the development of the kingdom of Norway? It is not clear, although it might simply reflect the fact that authors based in Iceland or Niðaróss had very little knowledge of the North. Another answer might be the negative attitude to Hákon Sigurðarson and his family. Whilst Adam of Bremen could describe him as king of a realm the core areas of which must have been Hálogaland, Þrœndalǫg, and Mœrr, the version of history that came to prevail reduced his role in the making of Norway.

60 Downham, *Viking Kings*, pp. 25, 33.

Hálogaland stands out as an area that seems to have come under the same authority early, perhaps as early as by 800. Courtyard sites — *tunanlegg* — are a distinctive feature of the Norwegian Iron Age, and are most plausibly interpreted as meeting places for local magnates, for chieftains, gathered together at the *things* where local disputes would be settled.[61] Of twenty-six known sites in Norway, eleven are to be found in northern Norway, spread throughout ancient Hálogaland. Through time, they became fewer and grander until it seems only three of the original eleven functioned, at Tjøtta, Steigen, and Bjarkøy, and these provide few signs of use from the 800s or later. There are always problems in deducing evidence of historical events from material evidence, and particularly when the available dating is not entirely precise, but the conclusion that might be drawn is that this chronological development was indeed a pattern of the concentration of authority over the whole region; given the period in which it was occurring, it would seem to point to the growing dominance of the jarls of Hálogaland, to the point where such meetings of local chieftains became a thing of the past.[62]

At some point, the jarls of Hálogaland extended their authority to Þrœndalǫg, whether by conquest or by marriage, to establish themselves at the traditional cult place of Hlaðir. The picture comes out of the Icelandic–Norwegian historical tradition but seems to be reliable. The move may have been of strategic importance: it is tempting to think, as Johan Schreiner argued as long ago as 1928, and Håvard Dahl Bratrein and Einar Niemi more recently, that, when the wealth of the northern magnates must have depended in large part on the export of luxury goods such as furs and on stockfish, control of the coastline to the south of Hálogaland, giving access to harbours closer to the eventual destinations along the North Sea coasts, would have been highly attractive.[63] It might also be the case that such control would have acquired more urgent importance if local rulers had been taxing or otherwise interfering with northern products on the way south. But whatever the reason, the extension of the jarls' power southwards was a noticeable step in the concentration of authority in Norway — of the slow evolution of Norway into a single entity. The wealth of the jarls and the part it might have played in the emergence of a Norwegian national monarchy was put forward in an extended argument by Andreas Holmsen, who nevertheless continued to stress the importance of a southern Haraldr *hárfagri* and his tenth- and eleventh-century descendants to set beside the northern dynasty's contribution.[64]

According to Holmsen, the jarls of Hlaðir were the losers in Norway's oldest political history, or at least in the stories that were told of those times

---

61 Storli, *Hålogaland før Rikssamlingen*.
62 Storli, *Hålogaland før Rikssamlingen*, pp. 149–58.
63 Schreiner, *Trøndelag og rikssamlingen*; Bratrein and Niemi, 'Inn i rike', I, 150–53.
64 Holmsen, 'Håløygrikdom og vikingrikdom i Norges samling', pp. 61–70.

and events and which were at last taken up by the saga authors.[65] There is an essential truth in the cliché that the winners get to write history. Nevertheless, behind the resultant grand narratives that legitimate and justify the true end, the lineaments at least of what might have been alternative narratives, the versions of history that the losers might have written, are discernable. The grand narrative of the birth of the Norwegian realm is an old one, having begun to take shape perhaps in the late eleventh century, and most clearly in the century that followed. It is also a remarkably persistent narrative; although most aspects of this story have been brought into question, and not least its evidential basis in the writings of the twelfth and thirteenth centuries, its form and even its content still dominate academic historiography. Perhaps for that reason, alternative narratives have been aired only as fragments, and tentatively: despite the equally weak basis of the received history, it seems to have been in practice unchallengeable so that no coherent counter-narrative has ever been written.

Works Cited

Primary Sources

Adam of Bremen, *Hamburgische Kirchengeschichte: Magistri Adam Bremensis Gesta Hammaburgensis ecclesiae pontificum*, ed. by Bernhard Schmeidler, Monumenta Germaniae Historica: Scriptores Rerum Germanicarum (Hannover: Hahn, 1917)

——, *History of the Archbishops of Hamburg-Bremen*, ed. and trans. by Francis J. Tschan (New York: Columbia University Press, 1959); new edn with introduction by Timothy Reuter (New York: Columbia University Press, 2002)

'The Anglo-Saxon Chronicle, 1042–1155', trans. by Susie Tucker, in *English Historical Documents, II, 1042–1189*, ed. by David C. Douglas and George W. Greenaway, 2nd edn (London: Eyre Methuen, 1981)

The Anglo-Saxon Chronicle, ed. and trans. by Michael Swanton (London: Dent, 1996)

Two of the Saxon Chronicles Parallel, ed. by Charles Plummer (Oxford: Clarendon Press, 1892)

Ari Þorgilsson, *Íslendingabók*, trans. and ed. by Siân Grønlie, Viking Society for Northern Research Text Series, 18 (London: Viking Society for Northern Research, 2006)

Ágrip af Nóregs konunga sǫgum, trans. and ed. by Matthew J. Driscoll, Viking Society for Northern Research Text Series, 10 (London: Viking Society for Northern Research, 1995)

---

65   Holmsen, 'Håløygrikdom og vikingrikdom i Norges samling', p. 68.

Encomium Emmae Reginae, ed. by Alistair Campbell, Camden 3rd ser., vol. 72
    (London: Royal Historical Society, 1949)
Fagrskinna, ed. and trans. by Alison Finlay (Leiden: Brill, 2004)
Háleygjatal, in *Corpus Poeticum Boreale*, vol. I, ed. and trans. by Gudbrand
    Vigfusson and F. York Powell (Oxford: Clarendon Press, 1883), pp. 251–54
Historia Norwegie, ed. by Inger Ekrem and Lars Boje Mortensen, trans. by Peter
    Fisher (Copenhagen: Museum Tusculanum Press, 2003)
A History of Norway, and The Passion and Miracles of the Blessed Óláfr, ed. by Carl
    Phelpstead, trans. by Devra Kunin, Viking Society for Northern Research Text
    Series, 13 (London: Viking Society for Northern Research, 2001)
Karl Jónsson, *Sverris saga etter Cod. AM 327 4°*, ed. by Gustav Indrebø (Kristiania:
    Norsk Historisk Kjeldeskrift-Institutt, 1920)
Morkinskinna, ed. and trans. by Theodore M. Andersson and Kari Ellen Gade
    (New York: Cornell University Press, 2000)
Nóregs konungatal, in *Corpus Poeticum Boreale*, vol. II, ed. and trans. by Gudbrand
    Vigfusson and F. York Powell (Oxford: Clarendon Press, 1883), pp. 309–21
Oddr Snorrason, *Saga Óláfs Tryggvasonar af Oddr Snorrason munk*, ed. by Finnur
    Jónsson (Copenhagen: Gad, 1932)
——, *The Saga of Olaf Tryggvason*, ed. and trans. by Theodore M. Andersson (New
    York: Cornell University Press, 2003)
Snorri Sturluson, *Heimskringla: Nóregs Konunga Sǫgur, af Snorri Sturluson*, 4 vols,
    ed. by Finnur Jónsson (Copenhagen: Samfund til Udgivelse af Gamel Nordisk
    Litteratur, 1893–1900)
Theodoricus, *Historia de Antiquitate Regum Norwagiensum*, trans. and ed. by David
    and Ian McDougall, Viking Society for Northern Research Text Series, 11
    (London: Viking Society for Northern Research, 1998)
William of Malmesbury, *Gesta Regum Anglorum*, ed. and trans. by R. A. B. Mynors,
    completed by R. M. Thomson and M. Winterbottom, 2 vols, Oxford Medieval
    Texts (Oxford: Clarendon Press, 1997, 1998)

Secondary Works

Andersson, Theodore M., 'The Two Ages in *Ágrip af Nóregs konunga sǫgum*', in
    Historical Narratives and Christian Identity on a European Periphery, ed. by
    Ildar H. Garipzanov (Turnhout: Brepols, 2011), pp. 93–109
Bagge, Sverre, *From Viking Stronghold to Christian Kingdom: State Formation in
    Norway, c. 900–1350* (Copenhagen: Museum Tusculanum Press, 2010)
Bjarni Guðnason, *Fyrsta saga*, Studia Islandica, 37 (Reykjavik: 1978)
Bratrein, Håvard Dahl, *Høvding, Jarl, Konge: Nord-Norges politiske historie i vikingtid
    — ei annerledes fortelling*, Tromsø Museums Skrifter, 37 (Tromsø: Orkana
    Akademisk, 2018)
Bratrein, Håvard Dahl, and Einar Niemi, 'Inn i riket: politisk og økonomisk
    integrasjon gjennom tusen år', in *Nordnorsk Kulturhistorie*, ed. by Einar-Arne
    Drivenes, Marit Hauan, and Helge Wold (Oslo: Gyldendal, 1994), I, 148–62

Downham, Clare, *Viking Kings of Britain and Ireland: The Dynasty of Ívarr to AD 1014* (Edinburgh: Dunedin Academic Press, 2007)

Fentress, James, and Chris Wickham, *Social Memory* (Oxford: Blackwell, 1992)

Foot, Sarah, *Æthelstan: The First King of England* (New Haven: Yale University Press, 2011)

Frank, Roberta, 'Skaldic Poetry', in *Old Norse Icelandic Literature: A Critical Guide*, ed. by Carol J. Clover and John Lindow, pp. 157–96 (Toronto: University of Toronto Press, 1985), pp. 157–96

Gelting, Michael, 'Poppo's Ordeal: Courtier Bishops and the Success of Christianization at the Turn of the First Millennium', *Viking and Medieval Scandinavia*, 6 (2010), 101–33

Helle, Knut, 'Hovedlinjer i utviklingen av den historiske sagakritikken', in *Leiv Eriksson, Helge Instad og Vinland*, ed. by Jan Ragnar Hagland and Steinar Supphellen, Det Kongelige Norske Videnskabers Selskab, Skrifter 1 (Trondheim: Tapir Akademisk Forlag, 2001), pp. 13–40

——, 'Norway 800–1200', in *Viking Revaluations*, ed. by Anthony Faulkes and Richard Perkins (London: Viking Society for Northern Research, 1993), pp. 1–14

Jesch, Judith, 'Norse Historical Traditions and the *Historia Gruffudd vab Kenan*: Magnús Berfœttr and Haraldr hárfagri', in *Gruffudd ap Cynan: A Collaborative Biography*, ed. by Karen L. Maund (Woodbridge: Boydell, 1996), pp. 117–47

Holmsen, Andreas, 'Nordnorsk høvding økonomi i vikingtida', and 'Håløygrikdom og vikingrikdom i Norges samling', in *Nye Studier i Gammel Historie*, ed. by Andreas Holmsen (Oslo: Universitetsforlaget, 1976), pp. 55–60 and 61–70

Keynes, Simon, 'Cnut's Earls', in *The Reign of Cnut*, ed. by Alexander Rumble (Leicester: Leicester University Press, 1994), pp. 43–88

Keyser, Rudolf, *Norges Historie*, 2 vols (Christiania: Selskabet for folkeoplysningens fremme, 1866, 1870)

Koht, Halfdan, 'Sagaenes opfatning av vår gamle historie', *Historisk Tidsskrift*, 5 (1914), 379–96; repr. in *Rikssamling og Kristendom: Norske Historikere i Utvalg*, ed. by Andreas Holmsen and Jarle Simensen (Oslo: Universitetsforlaget, 1967), pp. 33–44

Krag, Claus, 'The Early Unification of Norway', in *The Cambridge History of Scandinavia*, ed. by Knut Helle (Cambridge: Cambridge University Press, 2003), pp. 184–201

——, 'Norge som odel i Harald Hårfagres ætt', *Historisk Tidsskrift*, 68 (1989), 288–301

——, *Ynglingatal og Ynglingesaga: En studie i historiske kilder* (Oslo: Universitetsforlaget, 1991)

Liestøl, Knut, *Upphavet til den islandske ættesaga*, Instituttet for Sammenlignende Kulturforskning serie A, 10a (Oslo: Aschehoug, 1929)

Munch, Peter Andreas, *Det norske Folks Historie*, 8 vols (Christiania: Chr. Tønsbergs, 1852–1863)

Mundal, Elsa, 'Íslendingabók: The Creation of an Icelandic Christian Identity', in *Historical Narratives and Christian Identity*, ed. by Ildar H. Garipzanov (Turnhout: Brepols, 2011), pp. 111–21

Passerini, Luisa, *Fascism in Popular Memory* (Cambridge: Cambridge University Press, 1987)

Rønning, Steinar, 'Er historiefaget i den norske skolen preget av moderne forskning, eller er historiefaget en dyrkning av nasjonale myter?' (unpublished master's dissertation, University of Tromsø, 2012), <http://hdl.handle.net/10037/4297>

Sawyer, Birgit, and Peter Sawyer, 'Adam and the Eve of Scandinavian History', in *The Perception of the Past in Twelfth-Century Europe*, ed. by Paul Magdalino (London: Hambledon, 1992), pp. 37–51

Schia, Erik, *Oslo Innerst i Viken* (Oslo: Aschehoug, 1991)

Schreiner, Johan, *Trøndelag og rikssamlingen* (Oslo: Det Norske Videnskabs Akademi, 1928)

Stenton, Frank M., *Anglo-Saxon England*, 3rd edn (Oxford: Oxford University Press, 1971)

Storli, Inger, *Hålogaland før Rikssamling: Politiske prosesser i perioden 200–900* (Oslo: Novus, 2006)

Sverrir Jakobsson, 'Erindringen om en mægtig personlighed: Den norsk-islandsk historiske tradisjon om Harald Hårfagre i et kildekritisk perspektiv', *Historisk Tidsskrift*, 81 (2002), 213–30

Thomson, Alistair, 'Anzac Memories: Putting Popular Memory Theory into Practice in Australia', *Oral History*, 18 (1990), 25–31

Torfæus, Tormod, *Historia Rerum Norvegicarum*, 4 vols (Copenhagen, 1711); reissued as *Norges Historie*, ed. by Torgrim Titlestad with translation into Norwegian and English, 3 vols (Bergen: Eide, 2008)

Turville-Petre, G., *Haraldr the Hard-Ruler and his Poets*, The Dorothea Coke Memorial Lecture (London: University College London, 1966)

Weibull, Lauritz, *Historisk-kritisk metod och nordisk medeltidsforskning* (Lund: Gleerup, 1913)

——, *Kritiska undersökningar i Nordens historia omkring år 1000* (Lund: Gleerup, 1911)

STEFAN FIGENSCHOW

Approaches to Mythologized 'Others' in Norwegian Expansion to the North

Introduction

The extension of the medieval Norwegian state and church organizations north- and eastward into northern Fennoscandia has been the subject of increasing scholarly focus over the past decades.[1] The early forays of Christianizing kings Óláfr Tryggvason (r. 995–1000) and Óláfr Haraldsson (r. 1015–1028) into the north laid the foundation for a centuries-long process to integrate Hálogaland and Finnmǫrk in the Norwegian realm. In the early twelfth century, the first royally initiated churches were erected in the north. The reigns of the expansive and ambitious Hákon Hákonarson (r. 1217–1263) and his immediate successors elevated this process to a new level in the thirteenth and early fourteenth centuries. By virtue of the Norwegian realm's involvement in more far-reaching economic systems of international trade and political structures through the late-medieval Scandinavian unions, the integration of the North took on other characteristics. Throughout the Middle Ages, such processes gradually transformed these previously borderless and ethnically complex areas into peripheral regions of national states with centres much further south.

An early in-situ by-product of this development was the gradual downfall and absorption into royal service of the influential northern chieftains at the turn of the first and second millennium. Having apparently carried out a regional centralization process of their own in earlier centuries,[2] a handful

---

1 See, for example, Berg, *Trondenes kannikgjeld*; Bratrein, *Høvding, jarl, konge*; Hansen, 'Fra Nöteborgsfreden til Lappekodicillen'; Hansen, 'The Arctic Dimension of "Norgesveldet"'; Hansen, 'Norwegian, Swedish and Russian "tax lands"'; Hansen, 'Juxta paganos'; Hansen, 'The Successive Integration of Halogaland and Finnmork'; Hansen and Olsen, *Hunters in Transition*; Storli, *Hålogaland før Rikssamlingen*; Urbánczyk, *Medieval Arctic Norway*.
2 See Bratrein, *Høvding, jarl, konge*; Storli, *Hålogaland før Rikssamlingen*.

Stefan Figenschow, UiT The Arctic University of Norway, stefan.figenschow@uit.no

Myths and Magic in the Medieval Far North: Realities and Representations of a Region on the Edge of Europe, ed. by Stefan Figenschow, Richard Holt, and Miriam Tveit, AS 10 (Turnhout: Brepols, 2020), pp. 237–258
10.1484/M.AS-EB.5.120528

of chieftains ruled Hálogaland towards the end of the first millennium. But the chieftains' role as autonomous lay and religious leaders was no longer viable. The gradual arrival of central authority and Christianity put the old political, religious, and social bonds of northern society under threat. The chieftains' centuries-old redistributive economic and social systems had integrated several other ethnic groups — particularly the Sámi — into systems of interaction built on taxation, collecting tribute, plundering, and raids.[3] These inter-ethnic relations were characterized by cooperation and protection, but also by mutual respect and fear. As far as we can tell, this arrangement seems to have been of value to most if not all those partaking, although not necessarily of equal benefit.

Broadly speaking, while — in the case of the Norwegian realm — the Christianized Norse population was increasingly integrated into the developing and expanding kingdom, other ethnic groups were not, at least not as a whole, nor in the same manner. As the differences between the groups increased, it seems reasonable to assume that any feelings of 'otherness' between them grew as well. It has been argued that in processes where a dominant group of people (the in-group, 'self' or 'us', here the Norse and Norwegian central authority) defines one or more different groups and their characteristics (the out-group, 'other', here the further ethnic groups of northern Fennoscandia) as opposite to themselves, the term 'othering' can be applied.[4] Importantly, 'othering' does not merely signify neutral 'difference' but carries with it a disparagement of the 'other'. In the process of 'othering', the out-group is considered fundamentally different or even alien from the in-group. Arguably, this can make 'othering' an important component in the construction of social reality, stabilizing the identity of the in-group at the cost of the 'other', extending social distance between them. As a form of representation, 'otherness' is thus almost exclusively seen in connection with negative attitudes towards the out-group through exorbitant stereotyping, simplistic discrimination, and subjugation. 'Othering' is rendered possible by ignoring individuality and complexity in favour of an essentialist view. The cultural characteristics of the out-group that best suit the biased view of the in-group are designated as explanations for the beliefs and actions of the 'other'.[5] Any representations of 'otherness' in the sources are thus highly subjective, often chosen to attain

---

3 Regarding redistributive systems, see Hansen, *Samisk fangstsamfunn og norsk høvdingeøkonomi*.

4 Jensen, 'Othering, Identity Formation and Agency', pp. 63–64; Jensen, 'Masculinity at the Margins', p. 9; Staszak, 'Other / Otherness', pp. 43. In 1985, G. C. Spivak was the first to use the concept of 'othering' in a systematic way ('The Rani of Sirmur'), but the notion draws upon a number of philosophical and theoretical traditions (see, for instance, de Beauvoir, 'The Second Sex'; Said, 'Orientalism') and has been analysed from several different perspectives (feminist, gender, post-colonial, ethnicity, etc.) during the past few decades.

5 Jensen, 'Othering, Identity Formation and Agency', pp. 64–65; Jensen, 'Masculinity at the Margins', p. 9; Staszak, 'Other / Otherness', pp. 43–46.

specific goals and to further reinforce the power of the in-group over the out-group. It goes without saying that such absolute divisions as 'us' and 'them' cannot be taken at face value in their entirety. This makes it crucial to identify whose subjectivity they represent, and for what reason, when considering the authors' expositions of 'otherness'. Considering these representations in a nuanced way when studying social and political processes such as the approaches of central authority to different ethnic groups as part of state and church expansion makes for an interesting starting point.

As Christianity and a European learned culture took root in the Scandinavian realms, the identities of the people and history of the kingdoms were gradually redefined along the lines of other European kingdoms. Scandinavians, themselves no longer on the outside looking in, at least partly adapted this division to their own relationships with the remaining pagan peoples of Fennoscandia.[6] And nowhere was this more relevant than in the multi-ethnic north. Therefore, part of studying these expansion processes is to examine the approaches chosen by Norwegian authorities in dealing with the 'other', the neighbouring ethnic groups in northern Fennoscandia. However, precisely pinpointing which of the characteristics of the Norse's neighbouring ethnic groups rendered them as distinctly 'other' is difficult. It is reasonable to suppose that a combination of discrepancies in way of life, settlement patterns, social and cultural traditions, language, and religion all played a part, and that the gradual arrival of central authority, Christianity, and increased Europeanization contributed to a stronger distinction between the Norse and the other ethnic groups, perhaps especially — but by no means exclusively — regarding religious issues.

The Norwegian expansion, and consequently their approaches towards other ethnic groups, did not, of course, take place in isolation. Throughout the Middle Ages, Norwegian interests in the North were rivalled by those of the city–state republic of Novgorod. Increasingly from the thirteenth century onwards, inter-Scandinavian relations also became more important as the fates of the three kingdoms became evermore intertwined. Dealing with Fennoscandia's 'others' naturally included the Sámi and the Karelian henchmen and intermediaries of Novgorod. But it also included other less easily identifiable groups such as 'Biarmians', 'Chudes', and 'Kvens'. As kings, churchmen, magnates, and merchants representing the expanding realms gradually extended their influence over the North, the relationships between the different groups took on many different forms. Overall, however, most medieval sources that deal with these 'other' groups quite consistently underline their differences compared to the representatives of the expanding realms, shrouding them in mythical representations and images, contributing heavily to the othering process.

While the reality behind such clear theoretical divisions is obviously never as clear-cut as the sources indicate, considering social and political processes

---

6 Bandlien, 'Norway, Sweden and Novgorod', p. 334.

partly through the lens of such theories can still be productive. This article will use the backdrop of 'otherness' as a starting point for examining two examples of the direct interaction between central authority and inhabitants of the North necessitated by northward expansion. These apparently give evidence of central authority piercing the alienating shrouds brought on by the increased intensity of 'othering'. The two examples stem from the height of the 'Norgesvelde' period.[7] They indicate that the relationship between, on the one hand, the high medieval kings, who spearheaded the Norwegian northward expansion, and on the other, the mythologized Fennoscandian 'others', was more complex and often more pragmatic than the apparent differences between the two might suggest.

As tangible examples of how central authorities dealt with 'other' denizens of the North, it is possible to better understand the actual complexities of attitudes towards different ethnic groups. To this end, we will examine King Hákon Hákonarson's dealings with the Biarmians and his grandson Hákon Magnússon's (r. 1299–1309) dealings with the Sámi.

The Sámi, the Biarmians, and the Norse

When examining the relationship between Norwegian central authorities and other ethnic groups, the specific connection between the Sámi and the Norse stands out. At the advent of the expansion of central authority northward, the relationship between the Norse and the Sámi population was, by all accounts, stable and well-kept for centuries. This was due, among other things, to the critical importance of the Sámi to the aristocracy's redistributive systems. The contemporary source that deals most intimately with the relationship between the Norwegian and the Sámi population is *Historia Norwegie*.[8] Written most probably in the second half of the twelfth century by an unknown clergyman, this Latin history of Norway contains comprehensive descriptions which can

---

7 In medieval documents, the term 'Norgesveldet' (ON 'Noregs veldi', Engl. 'Norwegian dominion' or 'Norwegian lordship') refers to the Norse lands *outside* of mainland Norway in the ocean to the west, the so-called 'skattlands' (tributary lands), which included but were not limited to Orkney, Shetland, the Færoes, Iceland, and Greenland. The eastern border province of Jämtland (in present day Sweden) is also often included due to being run in a very similar way to the Norwegian king's insular realm, as is the northern border province of Finnmǫrk, although it was not considered one of the Norwegian king's 'skattlands'. When used to describe a period of history, 'Norgesveldet' gained popularity around the time of the mid-nineteenth century peak of National Romanticism and commonly refers to the time when the medieval Norwegian monarchy was considered to have been at the height of its political power between *c.* 1227/40 and *c.* 1319/50. See Imsen, 'Introduction', pp. 13, 28–29.

8 For an in-depth analysis of the following, as well as other characteristics of *Historia Norwegie* see Hansen, this volume, pp. 31–69.

only be termed ethnographical, displaying extensive knowledge of the North when compared with similar sources.[9]

The author offers a split description of the relationship between the Sámi and the Norse. On the one hand, he underlines the fundamental characteristics that separate the Sámi from the Norse population, i.e., the 'otherness' of the Sámi. On the other hand, the special qualities of Norwegian–Sámi interaction are emphasized. According to *Historia Norwegie*, the Sámi are undoubtedly ungodly pagan hunters and gatherers who roam the wasteland bordering the kingdom of Norway. They are very different from the devout Norse farmers of Hálogaland, the true inhabitants of the realm.[10] Yet the wilderness that the Sámi inhabit separates the Norwegian kingdom from other pagan peoples further north and east,[11] acting as a buffer zone.[12] Furthermore, the area populated by the Sámi is in another instance seen as the easternmost of three longitudinally divided zones that make up the kingdom of Norway itself.[13] Elsewhere, the *Historia Norwegie* has the Norse and Sámi frequently living together;[14] and while the two latter observations are not the anonymous author's principal way of placing where the Sámi live in relation to the Norse, they do serve to underline his essential ambiguity when dealing with this group of 'others'. The Sámi also pay a large annual tribute to the Norwegian king,[15] identifying them as subjects of the Norwegian crown. *Historia Norwegie*, in addition, provides several other examples of interaction and joint activities between the Sámi and the Norse,[16] providing further evidence of a relatively close relationship, despite the strict dichotomy employed to separate the two. In other words, there is a double connotation when dealing with the Sámi: they are both within and outside the realm of the Norwegian king, and the two peoples enjoy a unique bond despite their differences.[17]

However, it is important not to overdo the degree of comfort between the two peoples, lest one give the impression that the religious ways of the Sámi in the late twelfth century was something the Norwegian authorities took lightly and / or accepted. Even the author of *Historia Norwegie* uses analogies and expressions when describing them that a learned European audience would associate with demons, sin, and dark magic. Other sources contrast the *innate*

---

9 Hansen, 'Om synet på de "andre"', pp. 54–55, 59, 70, 82, Hansen, 'The Arctic Dimension', pp. 209–10, Hansen, this volume, pp. 40–44.

10 *Historia Norwegie*, ed. by Ekrem and Mortensen, pp. 52, 58, 60, 62, 64.

11 *Historia Norwegie*, ed. by Ekrem and Mortensen, pp. 52–54.

12 Hansen, 'Om synet på de "andre"', p. 73, Hansen, this volume, p. 56.

13 *Historia Norwegie*, ed. by Ekrem and Mortensen, p. 52.

14 *Historia Norwegie*, ed. by Ekrem and Mortensen, p. 56.

15 *Historia Norwegie*, ed. by Ekrem and Mortensen, p. 60.

16 *Historia Norwegie*, ed. by Ekrem and Mortensen, pp. 56, 62–64.

17 Hansen, 'Om synet på de "andre"', pp. 70, 73, Hansen, 'The Arctic Dimension of Norgesveldet', pp. 209–13, Hansen, this volume, pp. 53–56. *Historia Norwegie's* complex rendering of Sámi settlement has found many parallels in archaeological investigations and settlement history studies over the last few decades.

Sámi talent for witchcraft with the Norse *need to be taught* such formulas and spells, often from the Sámi.[18] But then again, when accounts of the Sámi being treated unfairly or badly appear in the same corpus of texts, those responsible are consistently labelled as villains and / or punished for their wrongdoing.[19] These contradictory views underline that although special, the relationship between the Sámi and the Norse was a balancing act whose success and apparent stability, at least partly, was probably fuelled by economic interest. This seems true especially on part of the Norse chieftains, and increasingly from the eleventh century, the kings of the Norwegian realm. A relationship between two groups based mainly on shared economic interests is, of course, no guarantee for peaceful coexistence, but the Sámi-Norwegian one has left very little evidence of violent conflict. The increasing cultural and religious differences, it seems, did not stand in the way of trade and economic activity. Most conflicts in medieval northern Fennoscandia regarding economic interests occurred between Norwegians and Novgorod's Karelian representatives in the North and,[20] to a lesser degree, the Biarmians.

We first hear of Biarmians in the earliest written source to come out of the North, *Ohthere's report* to King Alfred (r. 871–899) from the end of the ninth century. This Northern Norwegian chieftain — probably hailing from the area south of the fjord of Malangen — informs us of his relation to a people he refers to as 'Beormas'.[21] The saga corpus provides further information on the Biarmians in *Egils saga Skallagrímsonar* and throughout *Heimskringla* during the reigns of kings such as Haraldr *hárfagri* (r. *c.* 865–*c.* 933), Eiríkr *blóðøx* (r. *c.* 933–935), Haraldr *gráfeldr* (r. *c.* 960–970), Óláfr Haraldsson (r. 1015–1028) and Hákon *Þórisfóstra* (r. 1093–1005) / Magnús *berfœttr* (r. 1093–1103).[22] Common to these accounts are descriptions of the Biarmians as a settled people somewhere on the coast of the White Sea, active in both farming and trade. Precisely classifying the exact ethnic identity and homeland of the Biarmians has been the subject of much scholarly debate, but it is beyond the scope of this article to go into detail regarding this question. Suffice it to say that today's consensus points to the Biarmians being Permian-speaking ancestors of the Komi people or '[…] one of the later-known Balto-Finnic speaking peoples, either the Vots (southern Chudes), the Vepsians (northern Chudes), or the

---

18 Bandlien, 'Trading with Muslims and the Sámi', p. 39.
19 Mundal, 'The Perception of the Saamis', p. 106.
20 Bandlien, 'Trading with Muslims and the Sámi', p. 43; Hansen and Olsen, *Hunters in Transition*, pp. 141–227.
21 *Ohthere's Report*, p. 45.
22 See *Egils saga Skalla-grímssonar*, ed. by Sigurður Nordal and Snorri Sturluson, *Heimskringla*, ed. by Finnur Jónsson. A summary of the most well-known references to the Biarmians in the saga material can be found in Bertelsen, 'Bjarmelandsgåta', pp. 355–58. All in all, the Biarmians or Bjarmaland appear in about thirty medieval sources, most of whom originate from within the Norse world (Koskela, 'Bjarmaland and interaction', pp. 38–39).

Karelians';[23] 'Biarmian' may even have been a functional 'blanket term' that has — over the course of history — enveloped several different ethnic groups crucial to the vast trading networks of northern Fennoscandia as traders and intermediaries.[24] The Biarmians were subject to trading and / or plundering expeditions carried out by individual Norse chieftains such as Ohthere, Þórir *hundr*[25] and — with time — royal representatives, as prospective kings of the realm tightened their grip on the North. The last known such expedition to Bjarmaland mentioned in the sources took place in 1222, recounted to us in *Hákonar saga Hákonarsonar*.[26]

The Biarmians, it seems, are not subject to the same double connotation that applied to the Sámi. The sources' attitude to the Biarmians is remarkably negative,[27] especially contrasted with the intricacies of the Sámi-Norse relationship. Biarmians are consistently seen as true aliens, further removed — in both the geographic and cultural sense — from the authors describing them than the Sámi, consistently underlining their 'otherness'. Unlike the repercussions for mistreating the Sámi, no similar denunciations of those marauding through Biarmian lands can be found. Such activities are widely accepted, if not celebrated.[28] In addition, most, if not all, recorded armed conflicts between the Norse and the Biarmians are instigated by the Norse.[29] This diametrically different attitude to the Biarmians may, as has been pointed out recently by Mervi Koskela Vasaru,[30] be due more to the nature of the sources than the reality of typical contemporaneous Norse-Biarmian relations. The aggressive nature of the incidents portrayed are examples of events that were the bread and butter of most saga writers, consistently concentrating on hero kings, warfare, conflict, and heroism. So even if the episodes themselves reflect reality, the focus of the saga writers may contribute to an exaggerated frequency of violent conflict in relation to other more peaceful circumstances.[31]

It is thus possible that the portrayal of Biarmian–Norse relations owes a lot to the nature and characteristics of the sources themselves, very much

23 Hansen and Olsen, *Hunters in Transition*, p. 149.
24 Hansen and Olsen, *Hunters in Transition*, pp. 149–50, Hansen, 'Interaction between Northern European Sub-Arctic Societies', pp. 45–52.
25 Snorri Sturluson, *Heimskringla*, ed. by Finnur Jónsson, pp. 311–15.
26 Sturla Þórðarson, *Hákonar saga Hákonarsonar*, ed. Sverrir Jakobsson and others, I, 252–53. *Hákonar saga Hákonarsonar* is considered one of the most trustworthy of the kings' sagas, having been written within a few years of Hákon's death in 1263. The fact that the text was composed under the scrutiny of Hákon's son Magnús does however mean that the tendency for propaganda in favour of the royal household is strong. Andersson, *The Sagas of Norwegian Kings*, p. 135.
27 Mundal, 'The Perception of the Saamis', p. 107.
28 Mundal, 'The Perception of the Saamis', p. 107.
29 Koskela Vasaru, 'Bjarmaland and Contacts in the Late-Prehistoric and Early Medieval North', p. 205.
30 Koskela Vasaru, 'Bjarmaland and Interaction in the North of Europe', p. 52.
31 Koskela Vasaru, 'Bjarmaland and Interaction in the North of Europe', pp. 52–53.

in the same way as is normally assumed when considering roughly the same sources' rendering of the relationship between the Sámi and the Norse. The saga authors apparently cared little for the Sámi themselves, only mentioning the Sámi when they played a role in the type of incidents the saga writers usually focus on. This has led to the conclusion that the contact between the Sámi and the Norse — at least the parts that the saga writers knew of — was of a mostly peaceful nature, and therefore not of great interest to their histories. This also fits well with pre-expansion Sámi-Norse interdependence, as described above.

Because our overall knowledge of the medieval Biarmians and the Biarmian–Norse relationship is thoroughly dwarfed by that of the Sámi and the Norse–Sámi relationship, this must remain an enticing hypothesis. Most representations of the Biarmians *are* very negative, and from what we do know it is perhaps equally probable that the Norse–Biarmian relationship *had* been one of enmity, distance, and distrust as portrayed in most sources. And, no matter if the perceived dominance of belligerent encounters between the two peoples hold true or not, we have no reason to assume that the Biarmians were as familiar as the Sámi when considered from a Norwegian viewpoint, seen, for example, in *Historia Norwegie*'s double connotation. In other words, that even the Sámi were clearly 'others' to the medieval authors left no doubt of the 'otherness' of the Biarmians.

Hákon Hákonarson's Biarmian Relief Effort

In the middle of the thirteenth century, with the Norwegian monarchy consolidated after the so-called 'Civil War' period (*c.* 1130–*c.* 1240) and the church firmly ensconced in society and culture, the ambitious kings of the political heyday of the Norwegian medieval realm (*c.* 1240–1319) took centre stage. This period saw its highlight regarding territorial expansion during the reign of Hákon Hákonarson, an ambitious, often successful, and internationally renowned king. His reign navigated the kingdom out of a century of internal strife and into a period of history whose prestige was only rivalled by the glory days of the Viking Age in nineteenth- and early twentieth-century historiography.

The internal consolidation of the realm allowed Hákon to pursue several avenues of international ambition in the latter half of his reign. Attempts to secure and expand Norwegian influence over the northern British Isles brought conflict with the Scottish kingdom, and attempts to further Norwegian interests in Danish Halland and Scania on the western coast of present-day Sweden brought the same with Denmark. The third and in hindsight most feasible of King Hákon's international ambitions was to further his realm's influence in the North. It was during his reign that the long-held boundary of the Malangen fjord — traditionally seen as separating mainly Norse Hálogaland from mainly Sámi Finnmǫrk further north and east — was finally breached. A crucial early step in this process was the erection of a church at Tromsø just north of Malangen *c.* 1250, quite possibly as early as before the end of 1247.[32] The church was later said to be positioned 'close to the heathens' ('*iuxta paganos*'),[33] and a fortification was raised in the vicinity of the church at about the same time.[34]

The foundation of the church at Tromsø appears to stand near the nexus of Hákon's foreign policy in the middle of the thirteenth century. By this time, Hákon had vowed to take part in a crusade twice, at least in part because his illegitimate birth proved troublesome in convincing the papacy to bless him with a proper coronation, which again would serve to refine, legitimize, and secure the status of his lineage. The first vow of 1237 never came to fruition in the classic sense, but the king gained an exemption from his vow in 1241 by promising Pope Gregory IX (r. 1227–1241) to combat and convert the heathen neighbours of his own realm.[35] At some point after the fall of Jerusalem in 1244, Hákon again vowed to go on a crusade, witnessed by a papal letter of 1246.[36] This seems to have triggered Innocent IV's (r. 1243–1254) approval of Hákon's long-awaited coronation.[37] He also granted Hákon and his descendants eternal rights of patronage to any churches built to convert pagans on his realm's frontier[38] and arranged for the Norwegian king to use 1/20 of the realm's ecclesiastical income for three years to finance said crusade.[39] No crusade, nor dispensation, came of this second vow.

Six years later papal correspondence again mentions Hákon having vowed to go on a crusade. The Norwegian king is promised by the pope that the people known as the '*sambite*' would become his subjects should he convert them.[40] The '*sambite*' have been identified as both the Sámi and the Samogitians of the south-eastern Baltic, the former winning ground in present scholarship.[41] Clement V's (r. 1305–1314) decree of 1308 informs us that the church at Tromsø belonged to a special group of fourteen royal chapels subject to *royal* authority and patronage.[42] Hákon had seemingly managed to get what he wanted from the papacy and used his crusade vows to strengthen the Norwegian presence in the North, obtaining royal control of present and future churches on the frontier. The aggressive, centrally initiated Norwegian expansion in the North under Hákon of which the church at Tromsø is a prime example must also be seen in connection with the signing of a peace treaty with Novgorod in

---

32 Trædal, *Kirkesteder og kirkebygninger i Troms og Finnmark*, p. 157.

33 *DN* I, 113.

34 Lind, 'Den gamle borgen Skansen', p. 43.

35 *DN* I, 24.

36 *DN* I, 33.

37 *DN* I, 30–32, 38.

38 *DN* I, 37.

39 *DN* I, 40.

40 *DN* I, 46–48.

41 Hansen and Olsen, *Hunters in Transition*, pp. 157–58; Bandlien, 'Norway, Sweden and Novgorod', p. 343.

42 *DN* I, 113.

1251 after a diplomatic mission from Prince Alexander Nevsky (r. 1236–1263) visited Hákon.[43] The city–state's equally expanding influence in the North increasingly came into conflict with that of the Norwegian realm, and the peace was to be short-lived.

It is as part of the developments around 1250 that we find our first example of particular approaches to the 'other' in medieval expansion in the North. This is recounted to us in *Hákonar saga Hákonarsonar*. In an entry for the first half of the 1240s, we read that King Hákon settled Biarmians fleeing from the ravaging Mongol hordes in the east by giving them the fjord of Malangen after having them Christianized.[44] The account is very brief and contains little detail. No information on the number of settlers or the specifics of their arrival is included, nor any mention of the motivation or possible reward for giving them land to settle on. The lack of detail has not dissuaded discussion.[45] It has been argued that any tangible economic or military significance of the arrival of the Biarmians would be predicated on the settlement of a sizeable group of people, which seems unlikely.[46] No matter how it is considered, it certainly gives pause for thought. Such a non-Norse group who are distinctly classified as 'others' do not seem the most apparent candidates for contributing to securing this borderland for the Norwegian realm.

Almost regardless of the number of Biarmians, it is not too far-fetched to see them as a Christianized group of thankful, and therefore probably loyal, subjects. Their skill in the ways of northern agriculture could have been an integral part of fortifying the Norwegian realm's first steps into consolidating its presence north of the traditional boundaries. Given the contemporary sources and modern historiography's view of the Biarmians as traders, it is not inconceivable that Hákon saw them as potentially important intermediaries in controlling the burgeoning business of exporting arctic resources. Converting and settling the Biarmians would also contribute to keeping them from becoming adherents of Novgorod and the Eastern Orthodox Church. In the very sparsely populated reaches of the North, the number of settlers need not have been very large to make an impact, but regardless of the number the symbolism would be unmistakeable. Hákon's efforts to convert Biarmians and other nearby ethnic groups could serve to underline his role as the defender of Catholic Christianity in the North and to bolster the image of the Norwegian king as a *rex crusesignatus*,[47] even if done in a slightly unusual

---

43 Hansen, 'The Arctic Dimension', p. 215.

44 Sturla Þórðarson, *Hákonar saga Hákonarsonar*, ed. by Sverrir Jakobsson, II, 266.

45 See, for instance, Stang, 'Norges første flyktninger — asiatisk perspektiv'; Bjørgo, 'Norges første flyktninger — norske perspektiv'; Koskela Vasaru, 'Bjarmaland and Interaction in the North of Europe'.

46 See Bjørgo, 'Norges første flyktninger — norske perspektiv', pp. 68–73, for a discussion on the unlikelihood of the number of Biarmians being very significant, for example, in the form of a massive wave of immigration.

47 Svenungsen, *Norge og korstogene*, pp. 205–06.

way. The Norwegian realm's best contribution to the crusades would be as a bulwark defending Christianity from the heathens to the north and east. Being able to boast of the conversion of a few of these eastern 'others' would play right into Hákon's hands, even if they did not make the most obvious candidates for allies.

Throughout, *Hákonar saga Hákonarsonar* attempts to show that Hákon had done more for Christendom than any Norwegian king since Óláfr Haraldsson, and by welcoming the Biarmians to the borderland of Malangen and converting them, Hákon could assert that he too had acted on the pandemonium caused by the marauding Mongols,[48] thus claiming his place among European kings. As shown recently by Theodore M. Andersson, *Hákonar saga Hákonarsonar* idealizes King Hákon to the point that where other saga material accepts '[...] bloodshed as a fact of contemporary history, [...] *Hákonar saga* stands in almost militant opposition to bloodshed'.[49] The actions of King Hákon regarding the Biarmians, recounted in the same source, could be seen in the same light: another example of a powerful monarch following the examples of the greatest kings of the past, but doing it in his own unique way, avoiding bloodshed and making a profit at the same time.

Still, Hákon's amicable approach to the Biarmians was an original interpretation of the contemporary trend of expansion and crusade. Its implementation could have a lot to do with the state of affairs in the North at the time but is still somewhat surprising. Neighbouring expanding central authorities had experienced fatal relapses in their conversion attempts of neighbouring peoples of Fennoscandia. A 1237 letter from Pope Gregory IX (r. 1227–1241) encouraged the bishops of the Swedish realm to save the Catholic faith in Tavastia (Häme), where the apostate population had committed heinous acts against the few remaining Christians, leading to the campaign known as the second Swedish crusade to Finland.[50] Most successful conversion campaigns relied heavily on the presence of central authority over time, but Hákon was apparently satisfied with trusting a group of newly converted Biarmians with obvious eastern affinities with some form of role in his plans.

No matter what the reason behind Hákon's amicable approach to the Biarmians, it differs strongly from most descriptions of the Biarmian–Norse relationship, ignoring their apparent 'otherness'. In many ways, it also differs from what was expected of a king of an expanding realm involved in the crusading rhetoric of the time. This episode is especially interesting in this regard. Perhaps the singularity of Hákon's approach to the fleeing Biarmians is an indication that the actual Biarmian–Norse relationship was more peaceful than most sources — leaning heavily on the eastern people's 'otherness' —

---

48 Bjørgo, 'Norges første flyktninger', pp. 71–72.
49 Andersson, *The Sagas of Norwegian Kings*, p. 135.
50 DS 298; Lind, 'Consequences of the Baltic Crusades', pp. 142–43; Lindkvist, 'Crusades and Crusading Ideology', pp. 123–24.

suggested? It is not impossible that Hákon's approach to the Biarmians was a result of a more general change in the policies of expansion, although that would seem to contradict what we know of similar contemporary processes. Such a change would probably have generated more situations where the Norwegian kings settled members of other ethnic groups in strategic parts of the North as well. Suffice it to say, Hákon's treatment of the Biarmians appears to be a unique occurrence. These examples provide plenty of opportunity to characterize Hákon as pragmatic, but there is no evidence present allowing us to neatly set aside the actions of the king as exclusively driven by practical politics and hardened cynicism. His several crusading vows, northward expansion, and apparent interest in the conversion of the group of Biarmians could also be evidence of a monarch trying to live up to the lofty heights of St Óláfr in his own time, indicating a strong spiritual component present in his decision-making. Worldly and religious motivations do not preclude each other, but the point that the latter may be of importance is still significant.

What we are left with, then, is the impression of the Norwegian king's actions in relation to this group of Biarmian 'others' as quite pragmatic. This is true whether we look at the situation itself or consider it in the broader context of the struggle for influence in northern Fennoscandia between Novgorod and the Norwegian realm or the contemporary trends of the Northern Crusades. Including such a clearly 'other' group as an apparently important element in the northward extension of central authority might seem foolhardy, ambitious, and / or as a stroke of genius. Regardless, it gives indications of a pragmatic attitude to mythologized 'others', a willingness to both take and give chances as part of the push north. It also suggests that the king's decision was probably based on being relatively well informed and having a realistic view of the goings-on in the North, not allowing the contemporaneous pseudo-mythical representations of the Biarmians to cloud his judgement.

Hákon Magnússon and Marteinn, a Real 'King of the North'?

The next example is an investigation of an episode known from the reign of Hákon Hákonarson's grandson, Hákon Magnússon. Early in the fourteenth century, the northward expansion of Norwegian central authority of which Hákon Hákonarson had been such an important proponent two generations earlier was continuing more or less unabatedly.

In 1307, the Norwegian archbishop Jørund (r. 1288–1309) of Niðaróss consecrated a newly raised church at Vardø,[51] and not long after — perhaps around 1330 — Hákon Magnússon had a fortress constructed nearby,

---

51 *Islandske Annaler*, ed. by Storm, p. 74; Bratrein, 'Det eldste Vardøhus', p. 174.

probably in cooperation with the ecclesiastical authorities.[52] Among possible motives for building the fort and church was a mission to Christianize the Sámi population of the area.[53] Vardø would remain the north-easternmost outpost of the Norwegian realm for many centuries to come. Converting the Sámi of the North to Catholicism, and not risking 'losing' them to the influence of Eastern Orthodoxy and Novgorod, could potentially be at least as important to Hákon as converting Biarmians had been to his grandfather. Conversion and at least a semblance of territorial control went hand in hand, and the building of a church was perhaps the most concrete symbol of this. Converting non-Christian Sámi was important, but it is doubtful, given the lack of evidence of armed conflict between the Norse and the Sámi, that any kind of fortification would have been necessary had the installations at Vardø been exclusively orientated towards the Sámi. The solidified presence of central authority in the north-easternmost part of the realm should thus *also* be seen in connection with the increased severity of reciprocal Novgorodian and Norwegian raids along the Arctic coast,[54] as well as the need for a peace agreement between the two in 1326.[55] In other words, we should not underestimate the symbolic nor the strategic value of establishing a relatively strong presence of Norwegian authority this far north and east in the ongoing struggle for supremacy.

In a legal amendment from August 1313, King Hákon Magnússon states, among other decrees, many of which have to do with the North, that any Sámi who accepted baptism would have their court fines reduced by two-thirds for the next twenty years.[56] The king also made it clear that converting the Sámi was the duty of the Norwegian settlers in the area.[57] In an entry for the same year, the Icelandic annals relate that during the summer of 1313 Marteinn the 'Finn [presumably Sámi] king' met with King Hákon,[58] probably in Bergen.[59] Although the latter source does not go into further detail it seems reasonable to consider these two sources in conjunction, the part of the legal amendment regarding the Sámi an apparent product of the meeting between the Norwegian and the Sámi king. It has been assumed that the source's lack of detail in describing the meeting and the resultant agreement between the two kings was well-known at the time, and therefore needed no further explanation.[60] Despite the double connotation regarding the Sámi,

---

52 Hansen, 'Juxta paganos', pp. 313–14; Bratrein, 'Det eldste Vardøhus', p. 181.
53 Urbańczyk, *Medieval Arctic Norway*, p. 227.
54 Hansen, 'The Arctic Dimension', pp. 220–23.
55 *Norges gamle Love* III, 151–53; *DN* VIII, 80; Hansen, 'Juxta paganos', pp. 303–04.
56 *Norges gamle Love* III, 107; *RN* III, 269–70; Hansen and Olsen, *Hunters in Transition*, p. 214;
    Bratrein 'Finnekongen Martin og rikskongen Håkon den femte', p. 2.
57 *Norges gamle Love* III, 107; Urbańczyk, *Medieval Arctic Norway*, p. 227.
58 *Islandske Annaler*, ed. by Storm, p. 393.
59 Bratrein, 'Finnekongen Martin og rikskongen Håkon den femte', p. 3.
60 Bratrein, 'Finnekongen Martin og rikskongen Håkon den femte', pp. 1–2.

a royal meeting with Marteinn — and crucially, the resultant legal action in the aftermath — testifies to an attitude at least not entirely dependant on the understanding of the Sámi as an alien 'other'.

Strengthening and fortifying the Norwegian presence in the furthest north-eastern reaches of the Scandinavian peninsula was not the only ambition of Hákon Magnússon's foreign policy. For a long time, he had been heavily involved in the increasingly complicated inter-Scandinavian affairs, which saw the Norwegian monarchy allied with oppositional forces in both Denmark and Sweden. The latter years of Hákon's reign, especially after 1312, saw increasing Norwegian isolationism regarding inter-Scandinavian politics. This is especially true for the ambition of gaining a territorial foothold in Danish-controlled Halland, and the hope of increasing Norwegian influence on Baltic shipping. This attempted retreat from inter-Scandinavian politics would not spare the Norwegian monarchy from the dynastic chaos of the following years. Still, the increased interest in the denizens of the North seemingly apparent in the amendment of 1313 and the meeting with the Sámi king seems appropriate in a situation where other areas of potential expansion were being cordoned off. Although the rivalry with Novgorod over influence in the North was a serious conflict, it did not entail the same potential consequences for the most populous parts of the Norwegian realm as would an open war with Denmark and / or Sweden. Since the 1260s, it must have become clear to the Norwegian kings that their most realistic and profitable option for attaining lasting success in extending their authority was to be found in the northern parts of Fennoscandia.

Traditionally, and in nearly all but the most recent historiography, medieval efforts to Christianize the population of northern Fennoscandia have been seen as almost exclusively orientated towards the Norse. The mission to convert the Sámi has mostly been seen in conjunction with the mission of Thomas von Westen and others from the turn of the seventeenth and eighteenth centuries. This overly distinctive and simplified but still prevalent dichotomy owes it origin, at least partly, to the equally basic contrast between the Norse population being farmers settled along the coast and the Sámi being semi-nomadic hunter-gatherers of the interior, reinforcing the focus on Sámi 'otherness'. This contrast lacks the fine-tuned methodology of more recent work that takes into account the variations that existed within each ethnic group, especially among the Sámi themselves.[61] The tradition of the Sámi as not being the subject of Christianizing efforts until long after the Middle Ages carries within it the assumption that medieval royalty and other representatives of central authority were not well informed of the situation in the North and / or simply did not care about the 'other' ethnic groups.

This seems not to have been the case for Hákon Hákonarson, and his grandson's meeting with Marteinn seems to suggest something similar. The

---

61   See, for instance, Rasmussen 'The Protracted Sámi Reformation', for an introduction to the protracted nature of the Christianization of the Sámi.

fact that Marteinn is referred to as 'king' might seem a bit surprising. While it is beyond the scope of this article to discuss this in depth, the use of the word '*kongr*' has been taken to mean that Marteinn represented a relatively large Sámi group in a more or less official capacity.[62] It has also been seen as indicating the presence of a more hierarchical Sámi society than most sources confer,[63] even if a few other examples — among them *Ohthere's report* — also suggest the presence of hierarchical structures in Sámi society.[64] The instances where the sources refer to leading men among the Sámi *could*, of course, be a result of the author projecting his own worldview onto the 'other's' society. If this was the case, that would surely mean we would have encountered numerous instances of Sámi kings in the sources. Another possibility is that the contact with the expanding Norse society had resulted in stratification of parts of Sámi society. Widespread stratification nevertheless seems somewhat unlikely, as that too would probably have left us with more instances in the sources where kings of the Sámi are mentioned.

The possibility of a hierarchically structured Sámi society goes against much of what we think we know of Sámi society in the Middle Ages. It is one of the most die-hard conceptions of the society of the Sámi as something 'other'. The practice of describing Sámi society as perpetually egalitarian in many ways resembles the historiographical tradition of seeing Christianization efforts aimed at the Sámi as something that belongs almost exclusively to the eighteenth century and beyond. Here the dichotomy between the Norse and the Sámi is too clear-cut, easily explained, and — at least — partly based on assumptions, where a narrow and stereotypical view of the Sámi is too often employed.[65] For instance, evidence suggests that the ninth, tenth, and eleventh centuries saw at least a partial stratification of Sámi society, mainly 'due to the social options which transactions and contact with the surrounding population provided'.[66] As trading networks widened and mercantile activity increased, it is more than likely that an elite with bonds to the chieftains of the North, based mainly on access to and control over imported goods and luxury items, developed within Sámi society.[67]

Returning to Hákon's decree, regardless of the social station of Marteinn, a reduction of court fines for as long as twenty years seems significant, especially when considering life expectancy in the Middle Ages. In practice, this reduction could last for a person's entire adult life. This circumstance is seldom considered when dealing with this amendment. Of course, a reduction in court fines was only beneficial once an offence was committed,

---

62 Bratrein, 'Finnekongen Martin og rikskongen Håkon den femte', pp. 1–2.
63 Bratrein, 'Finnekongen Martin og rikskongen Håkon den femte', pp. 3–9.
64 *Ohthere's Report*, p. 46 '*Æghwilc gylt be hys gebyrdum*' (Each pays according to his rank [*or* lineage]).
65 Hansen and Olsen, *Hunters in Transition*, p. 7.
66 Hansen and Olsen, *Hunters in Transition*, p. 78.
67 Hansen and Olsen, *Hunters in Transition*, pp. 78–79, 115–16.

so law-abiding citizens would hardly make much economic headway from this type of legal provision. In addition, researchers who have worked in detail on the amendment and its context are unsure of its significance in practice. Some have considered it 'completely insignificant',[68] while others have been satisfied with admitting that we simply do not know what it entailed in practice.[69] It should also be noted that the reduction in fines admitted to the Sámi was applied to other Christian laws three years later. This does not, however, reduce the prospective importance to the Sámi in 1313.[70] A similar decree was issued by King Magnus Eriksson (r. 1319–1364) regarding the Sámi population subject to the Swedish realm in 1340.[71]

No matter the practical outcome of the amendment, we should not disregard the *motivation* behind it. Considering the traditional view of the late Christianization of the Sámi, and the decree's apparent special significance, this would be unwise. The reduction in fines was perhaps considered a good way to 'tempt' remaining non-Christians to convert, but the text also underlines that the plight and poverty of the Sámi is among the reasons for its existence.[72] Further emphasizing royal sympathy — and at the same time admitting that injustice had been taking place — the king demanded that any present high-ranking officials (*lǫgmaðr, sýslumaðr*) should make sure that lower ranking royal or church stewards (*ármaðr*) did not institute false lawsuits against the Sámi, nor extort from them irregular fees or taxes.[73] That representatives of royal authority took liberties when dealing with the Sámi 'other' *could* be seen as further evidence that the king's attitude was not commonplace, and that attitudes towards Sámi 'otherness' facilitated mistreatment. As so often when dealing with sources that have to do with religion, both a seemingly business-like incentive and a more charitable or religious inspiration may be seen as backdrop to the source. I would suggest that these two reasons for the king's announcement should be seen as two sides of the same coin. In fact, the relatively low potential economic yield of Hákon's amendment is a possible indication that the king's religious and social considerations were of prime importance in this situation.

Hákon Hákonarson's treatment of the Biarmians and his grandson's approach to the Sámi three quarters of a century later appear similar in many ways. In meeting with Marteinn, a top-level representative of the Sámi, and then

68 Blom, '*Kongemakt og privilegier i Norge*', p. 354.
69 Hansen and Olsen, *Hunters in Transition*, pp. 295–96 n. 107.
70 Blom, '*Kongemakt og privilegier i Norge*', pp. 355–56. Another important aspect of the 1313 legal amendment is the possibility that if King Hákon did not seek the counsel of the Church in formulating the policies it included, the fact that the king decided to reduce the income of church law fines without the consent of the Church is itself interesting (Blom, '*Kongemakt og privilegier i Norge*', pp. 355–56).
71 DS 3473.
72 RN III, 269.
73 RN III, 269–70.

acting in the form of a royal decree, Hákon Magnússon demonstrated both an interest in, and an understanding of, the situation in and the inhabitants of the North. It is important to note that the options available to Hákon Magnússon, superficially a much less ambitious king than his illustrious grandfather, were very different to those in the middle of the thirteenth century. Nevertheless, neighbouring monarchies and other central powers were fully committed to expanding their territories through military conquest and crusade campaigns, meaning that Hákon Magnússon's more peaceful approach stands out in his era in a way similar to his grandfather. The age-old, mostly stable Sámi–Norwegian relationship does make the younger king's approach somewhat less surprising. Although the sources to their approaches — legal documents vs. an, albeit atypical, king's saga — to the 'other' are dissimilar both in scope and genre, they both contain possible religious, ideological, prestigious, strategic, and charitable elements. It is not beyond the realm of possibility that Hákon Magnússon wanted to style himself a king along the lines of his grandfather. Perhaps more important than attempting to decide which of these factors was the deciding one for the kings' decisions is to establish that their approaches were probably a result of multifaceted motivations. These sought to strengthen the realm and its inhabitants, and the policy — whatever its background — employed by both kings shows that the central authorities' approaches to other ethnic groups are more individual and interesting than an at-a-glance survey of northward expansion of central authority can suggest. They also provide evidence that the Norwegian kings of this era were not guided by prevalent mythical representations nor fear of or suspicion towards the 'otherness' of the North in making their decisions.

Conclusion

A consistent theme of medieval Norwegian central authorities' northern expansion was the promise of economic gain through exploitation of rich natural resources and, often, those producing these resources. Extending and increasing royal and ecclesiastical influence in the North brought increased interaction with several different ethnic groups in the borderless and ethnically diverse northern Fennoscandia. This interaction continued partly along the lines that had bound different peoples together in redistributive economic systems, but the arrival of representatives of both church and state from power bases in the south meant gradual but wide-ranging changes. Soon, pan-European thoughts of conversion, culture, and crusade made an impact in the North, transforming the relationship between the Christian Norse and the 'other'.

The lion's share of Norse sources describing the 'other' of Fennoscandia are rife with representations of 'otherness', although a few sources — in particular *Historia Norwegie* — left the Sámi inhabitants of the North in a curious middle ground, neither adequate as true inhabitants of the Christian Norwegian kingdom nor on par with more alien ethnic groups further east. During the halcyon days of the thirteenth and early fourteenth centuries, Norwegian kings showed relatively remarkable and pragmatic attitudes in their approaches to expansion further north, seemingly acting on insightful knowledge instead of the mythologized stereotypes that existed in contemporaneous literature. This included, especially in the case of Hákon Hákonarson, making use of contemporary European trends when it was considered to be an advantage, but not blindly adopting said strategies or ideologies if they were not. The well-informed knowledge of the mythologized 'others' that the examples demonstrate did not always mean that such 'others' were treated fairly. Rather, it underlines the importance of seeing such approaches to the 'other' and to 'otherness' as part of a wide spectrum of possibilities and attitudes built on information, pragmatism, and a range of considerations not immediately apparent in the stereotypical representations of northern 'others' found in most sources.

While these singular examples cannot be seen as indicative of phenomena that lasted for the entire Middle Ages nor as universal policies expedited by central authorities, considering them can amend the overall impression of the expansion of church and state authority into the North. Thus, these two examples show not only that the nature of the actions of the Norwegian kings of the thirteenth and fourteenth centuries were of an informed and much more pragmatic nature than the views of 'otherness' evident in most contemporaneous narrative sources would suggest, but also demonstrate the futility of dealing with absolute categories such as 'us' and 'them' in general, and especially when writing the medieval history of the inter-ethnic and boundless northern and eastern Fennoscandia.

Works Cited

Primary Sources

DN = *Diplomatarium Norvegicum: Oldbreve til Kundskab om Norges indre og ydre Forhold, Sprog, Slægter, Sæder, Lovgivning og Rettergang i Middelalderen*, ed. by Chr. C. A. Lange, Carl R. Unger, and others, 23 vols (Christiania: Mallings Forladshandel, 1847–2011), <https://www.dokpro.uio.no/dipl_norv/diplom_felt.html, last accessed 011018>

DS = *Diplomatarium Suecanum* <https://sok.riksarkivet.se/sdhk, last accessed 011018>

Egils saga Skalla-grímssonar, ed. by Sigurður Nordal, Íslenzk fornrit, 2. (Reykjavík: Hið íslenzka fornritafélag, 1933)

Hákonar saga Hákonarsonar, Bǫglunga saga, Magnúss saga lagabœtis, ed. by Sverrir Jakobsson, Þorleifur Hauksson, and Tor Ulset, 2 vols, Íslenzk fornrit, 31–32. (Reykjavík: Hið íslenzka fornritafélag, 2013)

Historia Norwegie, ed. by Inger Ekrem and Lars Boje Mortensen, trans. by Peter Fisher (Copenhagen: Museum Tusculanum Press, 2003)

A History of Norway, and The Passion and Miracles of the Blessed Óláfr, ed. by Carl Phelpstead, trans. by Devra Kunin, Viking Society for Northern Research Text Series, 13 (London: Northern Society for Northern Research, 2001; Web publication, 2008, <http://vsnrweb-publications.org.uk/Text%20Series/ Historia&Passio.pdf>

Islandske Annaler indtil 1578, ed. by Gustav Storm (Christiania: Grøndahl and Søns Bogtrykkeri, 1888).

Norges gamle Love indtil 1387, ed. by Rudolf Keyser, Peter Andreas Munch, Gustav Storm and Ebbe Carsten Hornemann Hertzberg, 5 vols (Christiania 1846–1895)

Ohthere's report, ed. and trans. by Janet Bately, 'Text and Translation: The Three Parts of the Known World and the Geography of Europe North of the Danube according to Orosius' Historiae and its Old English Version', in *Ohthere's Voyages: A Late 9th-Century Account of Voyages along the Coasts of Norway and Denmark and its Cultural Context*, ed. by Janet Bately and Anton Englert, Maritime Culture of the North, 1 (Roskilde: Viking Ship Museum, 2007), pp. 40–50

RN = Regesta Norvegica [822–1430]: Kronologisk Fortegnelse over Dokumenter vedkommende Norge, Nordmænd og den norske Kirkeprovins, ed. by Sverre Bagge and others, 10 vols (Christiania: Norsk historisk kjeldskrift-institutt / Riksarkivet, 1898–2015)

Snorri Sturluson, *Heimskringla: Nóregs Konunga Sǫgur*, ed. by Finnur Jónsson (Copenhagen: Gad, 1911)

——, *Heimskringla*, trans. by Alison Finlay and Anthony Faulkes, 3 vols (London: Viking Society for Northern Research, 2011–2015)

Sturla Þórðarson, *Hákonar saga Hákonarsonar*, in *Hákonar saga Hákonarsonar, Bǫglunga saga, Magnúss saga lagabœtis*, ed. by Sverrir Jakobsson, Þorleifur Hauksson, and Tor Ulset, 2 vols, Íslenzk fornrit, 31–32 (Reykjavík: Hið íslenzka fornritafélag, 2013), I, 169–329, and II, 1–267

——, *Soga om Håkon Håkonsson*, ed. by Knut Helle, trans. by Kristian Audne, Norrøne bokverk, 22 (Oslo: Det norske samlaget, 1963)

Secondary Works

Andersson, Theodore M., *The Sagas of Norwegian Kings (1130–1265): An Introduction*, Islandica, 59 (Ithaca: Cornell University Library, 2016)

Bandlien, Bjørn, 'Norway, Sweden and Novgorod. Scandinavian Perceptions of the Russians, Late Twelfth — Early Fourteenth Centuries', in *Imagined Communities on the Baltic Rim, from the Eleventh to the Fifteenth Centuries*, ed. by Wojtek Jezierski and Lars Hermanson, Crossing Boundaries: Turku Medieval and Early Modern Studies, 4 (Amsterdam: Amsterdam University Press, 2016), pp. 331–52

——, 'Trading with Muslims and the Sámi in Medieval Norway', in *Fear and Loathing in the North: Jews and Muslims in Medieval Scandinavia and the Baltic Region*, ed. by Jonathan Adams and Cordelia Heß (Berlin: de Gruyter, 2015), pp. 31–48 de Beauvoir, Simone, *The Second Sex* (London: Vintage Classics, 1997; first published in French in 1949)

Berg, Sigrun Høgetveit, 'Trondenes kannikgjeld — makt og rikdom gjennom seinmellomalder og reformasjon' (unpublished doctoral thesis, University of Tromsø, 2014)

Bertelsen, Reidar, 'Bjarmelandsgåta', *Haaløygminne*, 77.1 (1996), 355–62

Bjørgo, Narve, 'Norges første flyktninger – norsk perspektiv på Troms 1242', *Historisk tidsskrift*, 61 (1982), 68–73

Blom, Grethe Authén, *Kongemakt og privilegier i Norge inntil 1387*, Scandinavian University Books (Oslo: Universitetsforlaget, 1967)

Bratrein, Håvard Dahl, 'Bjarkøy og Finnmork', *Ottar*, 208.5 (1995), 14–27

——, 'Det eldste Vardøhus', *Håløygminne*, 83.3 (2002), 173–82

——, 'Finnekongen Martin og rikskongen Håkon den femte', *Håløygminne*, 82.1 (2001), 1–10

——, *Høvding, jarl, konge. Nord-Norges politiske historie i vikingtid. Ei annerledes fortelling*, Tromsø Museums skrifter, 37 (Stamsund: Orkana Akademisk, 2018)

——, 'Passio Olavi, et kildested om Finnmarks-fisket på 1100-tallet', *Håløygminne*, 79.1 (1998), 117–21

Hansen, Lars Ivar, 'The Arctic Dimension of "Norgesveldet"', in *The Norwegian Domination and the Norse World c. 1100–c. 1400*, ed. by Steinar Imsen (Trondheim: Tapir Academic Press, 2010), pp. 199–228

——, 'Fra Nöteborgsfreden til Lappekodicillen, *c.* 1300–1751: Folkegrupper og statsdannelse på Nordkalotten med utgangspunkt i Finnmark', in *Grenser og grannelag i Nordens historie*, ed. by Steinar Imsen (Oslo: Cappelen akademisk forlag, 2005), pp. 362–86

——, 'Fredstraktaten mellom Norge og Novgorod av 1326', *Middelalderforum*, 3.1–2 (2003), 4–28

——, 'Interaction between Northern European Sub-Arctic Societies during the Middle Ages: Indigenous Peoples, Peasants and State Builders', in *Two Studies on the Middle Ages*, ed. by Magnus Rindal, KULTs skriftserie, 66 (Oslo: Research Council of Norway, 1996), pp. 31–96

——, 'Juxta paganos: The Delineation of the Religious Frontier in the North', in *'Ecclesia Nidrosiensis' and 'Noregs veldi': The Role of the Church in the Making of Norwegian Domination in the Norse world*, ed. by Steinar Imsen, 'Norgesveldet' occasional papers, no. 3 (Trondheim: Akademika Publishing, 2012), pp. 301–31

——, 'Norwegian, Swedish and Russian "tax lands" in the North', in *Taxes, Tributes and Tributary Lands in the Making of Scandinavian Kingdoms in the Middle Ages*, ed. by Steinar Imsen, 'Norgesveldet' occasional papers, no. 2 (Trondheim: Tapir Academic Press, 2011), pp. 295–330

——, 'Om synet på de "andre" — ute og hjemme. Geografi og folkeslag på Nordkalotten ifølge *Historia Norwegiae*', in *Olavslegenden og den latinske historieskriving i 1100-tallets Norge*, ed. by Inger Ekrem, Lars Boje Mortensen, and Karen Skovgaard-Petersen (Copenhagen: Museum Tusculanums Forlag, 2000), pp. 54–88

——, *Samisk fangstsamfunn og norsk høvdingeøkonomi* (Oslo: Novus, 1990)

————, 'The Successive Integration of Hålogaland and Finnmǫrk into the
    Realm of the King of Norway', in *Rex Insularum: The King of Norway and his
    "Skattlands" as a Political System c. 1260–c. 1450*, ed. by Steinar Imsen (Bergen:
    Fagbokforlaget, 2014), pp. 347–70

Hansen, Lars Ivar, and Bjørnar Olsen, *Hunters in Transition: An Outline of Early
    Sámi History*, The Northern World, 63 (Leiden: Brill, 2014)

Henriksen, Jørn Erik, 'Kulturmøte og identitet på Finnmarkskysten i tidlig
    historisk tid. Tolkninger basert på arkeologiske analyser av mangeromstufter'
    (unpublished doctoral thesis, UiT The Arctic University of Norway, 2016)

Imsen, Steinar, 'Introduction', in *Rex Insularum: The King of Norway and his
    "Skattlands" as a Political System c. 1260–c. 1450*, ed. by Steinar Imsen (Bergen:
    Fagbokforlaget, 2014), pp. 13–32

Jensen, Sune Qvotrup, 'Masculinity at the Margins — Othering, Marginality
    and Resistance among Young Marginalized Ethnic Minority Men', *NORMA:
    International Journal for Masculinity Studies*, 5.1 (2010), 6–26

————, 'Othering, Identity Formation and Agency', *Qualitative Studies*, 2.2 (2011),
    63–78

Johnsen, Oscar Albert, *Finmarkens politiske historie: Aktmæssig fremstillet*,
    Videnskapsselskapets Skrifter, 2, Historisk-filosofisk klasse, 1922, vol. 3.
    (Kristiania: Dybwad, 1923)

Koskela Vasaru, Mervi, 'Bjarmaland and Contacts in the Late Prehistoric and
    Early Medieval North', in *Fibula, Fabula, Fact: The Viking Age in Finland*,
    ed. by Joonas Ahola and Frog with Clive Tolley, Studia Fennica Historica, 18
    (Helsinki: Finnish Literature Society, 2014), pp. 195–218

————, 'Bjarmaland and Interaction in the North of Europe', *Journal of Northern
    Studies*, 6.2 (2012), 37–58

Lind, John H., 'Consequences of the Baltic Crusades in Target Areas: The Case
    of Karelia', in *Crusade and Conversion on the Baltic Frontier 1150–1500*, ed. by
    Alan V. Murray (Aldershot: Ashgate, 2001), pp. 133–51

Lind, Keth, 'Den gamle borgen Skansen', in *Tromsøboka den andre*, II (Tromsø:
    Tromsøboka AS, 2000), pp. 36–47

Lindkvist, Thomas, 'Crusades and Crusading Ideology in the Political History of
    Sweden, 1140–1500', *Crusade and Conversion on the Baltic frontier 1150–1500*, ed.
    Alan V. Murray (Aldershot: Ashgate, 2001), pp. 119–33

Mundal, Else, 'The Perception of the Saamis and their Religion in Old Norse
    Sources', in *Shamanism and Northern Ecology*, ed. by Juha Pentikäinen,
    Religion and Society, 36 (Berlin: de Gruyter, 1996), pp. 97–116

Olsen, Bjørnar, Przemysław Urbańczyk, and Colin P. Amundsen, ed., *Hybrid
    Spaces: Medieval Finnmark and the Archaeology of Multi-Room Houses*,
    Instituttet for sammenlignende kulturforskning Serie B, Skrifter, 139 (Oslo:
    Novus, 2011)

Rasmussen, Siv, 'The Protracted Sámi Reformation — Or the Protracted
    Christianizing Process', in *The Protracted Reformation in Northern Norway,
    Introductory Studies*, ed. by Lars Ivar Hansen, Rognald Heiseldal Bergesen, and
    Ingebjørg Hage (Stamsund: Orkana Akademisk, 2014), pp. 165–83

Said, Edward W., *Orientalism* (London: Penguin, 1995; first published in 1978)

Spivak, Gayatri Chakravorty, 'The Rani of Sirmur: An Essay in Reading the Archives', *History and Theory*, 24–3 (1985), 247–72

Stang, Håkon, 'Norges første flyktninger — asiatisk perspektiv på Troms 1242', *Historisk tidsskrift*, 60 (1981), 337–61

Staszak, Jean-François, 'Other / Otherness', in *International Encyclopedia of Human Geography*, ed. by Rob Kitchin and Nigel Thrift (Amsterdam: Elsevier, 2009), pp. 43–47

Storli, Inger, *Hålogaland før Rikssamlingen: Politiske prosesser i perioden 200–900 e. Kr* (Oslo: Novus forlag, 2006)

Svenungsen, Pål Berg, 'Norge og korstogene. En studie av forbindelsene mellom det norske riket og den europeiske korstogsbevegelsen, *c.* 1050–1380' (unpublished doctoral thesis, University of Bergen, 2016)

Trædal, Vidar, 'Kirkesteder og kirkebygninger i Troms og Finnmark før 1800' (unpublished doctoral thesis, University of Tromsø, 2008)

Urbánczyk, Przemysław, *Medieval Arctic Norway* (Warsaw: Semper, 1992)

Index of People and Places

Page numbers in italics refer to maps and images.

Adam of Bremen: 13, 24, 26–27, 29–30, 32, 40–41, 43, 53, 184, 202, 224–30
Ægir: 73, 168
Æthelstan, King of England: 222, 224
Agnarr: 103–105, 112–14
Åke: 198
Aldra: 100
Alexander Yaroslavich Nevsky (Александр Ярославич Невский), Prince of Novgorod, Grand Prince of Kiev and Vladimir: 55, 246
Alfred the Great, King of Wessex: 182, 202, 229, 242
Alice Kyteler, Dame: 150
Alstahaug: 160, 163
Alsten: 100
Alþing: 199
Áma: 76
Án: 87
Andfjorden, Andfjord: 191
Andøya: 25, 108 n. 37, 191
Andulfinus Audfinn Sigurdsson, bishop of Bergen: 144
Ångermanland: 53
Arctic: 26, 53, 81, 88, 91
    Circle: 25, 74
    coast: 249
    Hálogaland: 207
    High: 79–80, 86
    Norway: 86
    Ocean: 80–84
    region: 145
    sub-: 205–06
Ari fróði Þorgilsson: 216–18, 220–21, 225

Arinnefja: 79, 82, 85, 90
Arngrímr: 76
Arnøy: 186
Årstad: 164, 166, 167
Ásbjǫrn selsbani (Sigurðarson): 157–58, 160, 168, 174–75, 190, 209
Åse, court site: 192
Ásmundr the Berserk-Killer: 82
Augustine, bishop of Hippo, St: 12
Aure: 198
Austrvik: 86
Avignon: 146, 148, 150

Baltic: 145, 245
    countries: 80
    region: 22
    Sea, the: 43
Bárðr Guthormsson: 209
Bárðr Snæfellsáss: 80–81
Barents Sea, the: 14
Beloozero: 62
Bergen: 102, 143–46, 148, 154, 249
Bestla: 75
Biarmia, see Bjarmaland
Bjarkey Island, see Bjarkøy
Bjarkøy (Bjarkey Island): 171, 190–92, 205–06, 208, 211, 231
Bjarmaland: 48, 84, 99, 242 n. 22, 243
Blesanergr: 83–84
Bodø: 100, 111 n. 53
Bolga: 100
Bólm: 77
Bǫlþorn: 75
Bømlo: 162

Borg, Lofoten: 198, 203, 205, 207–08, 211
Bøstad: 203
Brana: 84, 88–89
Búri: 75
Byggve (Barleycorn): 171

Claudius Ptolemy: 23, 27
Clement V, Pope: 245

Dass, Petter: 147
Denmark: 42, 52, 97, 161, 162, 224–25, 227–28, 244, 250
Devil, the alias Satan: 125, 145, 147, 149, 151
Dofri: 81
Dofrum, Dovrefjell: 73
Drífa: 73
Dumbr: 80–82, 85
Dumbshaf: 79–80, 82–84, 86, 91
   see also Arctic Ocean
Dvina: 58
   River: 62, 64

Edmund (St Edmund), King of East Anglia: 220, 229
   see also St Edmund
Egill: 82
Eiríkr blóðøx (Haraldsson), King of Norway: 224, 242
Eiríkr Hákonsson, Earl of Northumbria and Jarl of Hlaðir: 228
Eiríkr Oddsson: 219
Eiríkssons, the: 202
Elgesem: 87
Élivágar: 75, 77
Erlingr á Sóla (Skjálgsson): 158, 175, 209
Europe: 11–13, 19, 146–48, 185
   central parts of: 32
   Christian: 13
   continental: 20
   northern (incl. 'northerly areas'): 12, 21, 31, 74, 147, 172, 203

north-western: 224
southern: 23, 26
western: 11, 16, 22
Eysteinn Erlendsson, Archbishop of Niðaróss: 218
Eysteinn Magnússon, King of Norway: 219
Eyvindr skáldaspillir (Finnson): 75, 96, 98, 109, 110, 202, 211

Far North: 11–13, 15–16, 19–21, 24–30, 32, 39, 44, 71–73, 76–80, 82, 84–91, 96, 98–99, 143, 145–46
Feima: 87
Fennoscandia: 22
   northern (incl. 'the north of'): 11, 13, 18–19, 27 n. 50, 57–60, 120, 126, 237–39, 242–43, 247–48, 250, 253–54
Finland: 50, 57–62, 73, 247
Finnmark: 51, 59–60, 73 n. 7, 98, 127, 129, 130, 185–86
   see also Finnmǫrk
Finnmǫrk (Finnmark): 14, 31, 50, 73, 77, 81, 86, 89, 143, 145, 181–83, 185–88, 192, 237, 240 n. 7, 244
Fitjar, battle of: 202
fjords: 50, 98, 125, 191
   of southern Troms: 186
   see also Andfjorden; Hafrsfjǫrðr; Lyngen; Malangen; Ófótansfjörðr; Oslofjorden; Trondheimsfjorden; Vågsfjord
Forað, Forat: 86–87
Fornjótr: 73–75, 81
Freyja: 111–12, 114
Freyr: 109 n. 43, 110–12
Frigg: 103–05, 111–12, 114
Froan, archipelago: 100–01
Frosti: 73, 81–82
Fusa: 143–44

Gandvík, see White Sea, the
Gästrikland: 83
Geaimmejávri, Lake: 130

Geirrøðr: 103–106, 112–14
God: 21, 27, 32, 51, 53
Gói: 73
Górr: 73
Götaland: 53
Greenland: 26, 31, 80, 83, 240 n. 7
Gregory IX, Pope: 173, 245, 247
Gregory of Tours: 29
Grímr, son of Hergrímr: 76–77
Grímr, son of Kettil: 87, 89
Grund: 85
Guðmundr of Glæsisvellir, King of
    far-northern giants: 84–85
Gulf of Bothnia: 24, 43, 57–58, 73
Gull-Þórir, Gold-Þórir: 84
Gunnlaugr Leifsson, monk of
    Þingeyrar: 219

Hafrsfjǫrðr (Hafrsfjord), battle of:
    215, 222, 230
Hákon Eiríksson, Earl of
    Worcestershire area of western
    Mercia and Jarl of Hlaðir: 229
Hákon góði (Haraldsson), King of
    Norway: 202, 224
Hákon Grjótgarðsson, Jarl of Hlaðir:
    230
Hákon Hákonarson, King of Norway:
    55, 204, 209, 237, 240, 242, 244–48,
    250, 252, 254
Hákon illi (Sigurðarson), Jarl of
    Hlaðir: 75, 82, 105–06, 109, 113,
    210–11, 226–30
Hákon Magnússon, King of Norway:
    240, 248–250, 253
Hákon Þórisfóstra, King of Norway:
    242
Håkøy: 186
Hálfdan svarti: 219
Halgoland. See Hálogaland
Halland: 244, 250
Hallbjörn Half-Troll: 86–87
Hálogaland: 14, 17–18, 25, 31, 47–56,
    58 n. 57, 64, 75–77, 81–82, 86–87,
    95–103, 107–11, 113–14, 143, 145,

157–58, 170, 181–93, 197, 201–11,
    229–31, 237–38, 241, 244
Halsingland, see Hälsingland
Hälsingland: 50, 57–58
Halten, fishing bank: 101
Hamburg: 31
Hamburg-Bremen, archbishopric: 24,
    26, 41, 43, 184, 224–25
Häme, Tavastia: 247
Haraldr blátǫnn (Gormsson), King of
    Denmark: 227–28
Haraldr gráfellr (Eiríksson), King of
    Norway: 224
Haraldr harðráði (Sigurðarson), King
    of Norway: 18, 215, 223
Haraldr hárfagri, King of Norway: 18,
    202, 204, 209–11, 215, 217–21, 223,
    226, 228, 230–31, 242
Hárekr of Þjótta (Tjøtta): 206, 208
Haukr: 89–90
Heiðr: 90
Helgeland: 99, 192, 202, 205
Helgi: 85
Helgøy: 186–87, 192
Helluland: 82–84, 88, 91
Helsingjabotn, see Gulf of Bothnia
Hergrímr Halftroll: 76–77
Herodotus: 21
High North: 158, 171, 174, 181, 201–02,
    210
Hilda, daughter of Þráinn svartaþurs:
    96
Hildigunnr: 88
Hillesøy: 192–93
Hinnøya: 16, 190–91
Hlaðir, Lade: 17, 75, 82, 105, 109, 113,
    210, 227, 229–31
Hlér: 73
Hofgarða-Refr Gestsson: 99
Honorius Augustodunensis: 41
Hórðaknútr (Harthacnut) Knutsson:
    225
Hordaland: 162, 202
Hov: 205
Hrafnista: 86–87, 89

Hrímnir: 87, 89
Hrólfr: 73
Hugla: 100
Hunstad: 205, 207
Huseby: 198
Hymir: 169

Iceland: 14–15, 17, 24, 26, 31, 39, 42 n.
    12, 43 n. 18, 71, 82, 97, 106, 113, 123,
    168, 191, 216–21, 223, 225, 230, 240
    n. 7
Ilmen, Lake: 128
Ingi *krókhryggr* (Haraldsson), King of
    Norway: 218
Innocent IV, Pope: 245
Ireland: 150, 229
Ísleifur, bishop of Iceland: 26
Ívarr *inn beinlausi*: 229–30

Jæren: 108 n. 37, 161
Jämtland (Jamtland): 50, 53, 240 n. 7
Jamtland, *see* Jämtland
Jan Mayen: 80
Járnhauss: 89
Jelling: 228
John XXII, Avignon Pope: 148, 150
Jökull: 73, 88
Jordanes: 22–26, 28, 201, 210
Jørund, Archbishop of Norway: 248
Jósteinn: 83
Jǫtunheim(ar): 75–77, 79–80, 82, 85

Karasjok: *130*
Karelia: 50, 57, 59
Karelian Isthmus: 59
Kári: 73
Karl Jónsson, abbot of Þingeyrar: 219
Karlsøy: 186–87, 193
Kautokeino: *127*
Ketill *hœngr* Hallbjarnarson: 82,
    86–87
Kilkenny: 150
Kirjalabotn: 83

Knútr *riki* (Sveinnsson) (Cnut the
    Great), King of England, Denmark,
    and Norway: 217, 225, 228–29
Kola Peninsula: 39, 55, 59, 64
Kunna: 100
Kvaløya: 181
Kvenland: 43, 50, 57, 61 n. 68, 73, 81

Ladoga: 52
    Lake: 59, 62
Læstadius, Lars Levi: 124
Láhpojohka, Lake: *127*
Landegode: 100
Lapland: 147
Leknes: 203
Lofoten Isles: 24, 95, 97, 101, 106–08,
    113, 145, 198, 203, 206–07
Logi: 73
Loki: 171–72
Lovund: 100
Lund, archdiocese: 225
Lurøy: 205
Lyngen, Lyngen fjord: 59, 128, 187, 193
Lyngstuva: 55

Magnús *berfœttr* (Óláfsson), King of
    Norway: 219, 242
Magnus Eriksson, King of Norway
    and Sweden: 252
Magnús *goði* (Óláfsson), King of
    Norway: 219, 226
Malangen, fjord: 50, 170, 181, 185, 193,
    242, 244–47
Mannheimar: 76
Mardǫll, *see* Freyja
Marteinn, 'Finn' (Sámi) king: 248–52
Meløy: 100
Mjöll: 73, 81
Mo: 205
Mœrr (Møre): 110 n. 47, 200, 229–30
Moskenes maelstrom: 24
Múspellsheimr: 75

Naumudalr, Namdal(en): 50, 96–97, 99, 111 n. 53, 113, 205
Niðaróss, archdiocese: 225
Niðaróss, Trondheim: 65, 105–06, 113, 159, 173, 217–18, 230, 248
Nikel: 25
Njǫrðr: 111–12
Nóatún: 111
Nordland: 17, 54, 99–101, 105, 107, 109, 111 n. 53, 113, 122, 147 n. 10, 160, 163, 163, 170
Nórr: 73
Norrbotten: 58
North Calotte: 39, 39, 60
see also Fennoscandia, northern
North Sea: 28–29, 39, 231
North, the: 12–13, 15–16, 18, 20–21, 23–32, 53, 56, 60, 64, 71, 73, 78, 81, 83, 87, 98, 144–45, 157, 170, 174–75, 179, 182, 185, 211, 225, 230, 237, 239–51, 253–54
see also Far North; High North
northern world: 14, 19–20, 26
Norway: 11, 13, 15–18, 25, 29, 31, 43, 47–48, 50, 52–54, 56, 72, 73, 77, 90–91, 95, 108 n. 37, 110 n. 46, 111, 121, 122, 123, 127, 128, 129, 130, 131, 143, 146–51, 158, 160, 164, 166, 167, 169–70, 172–74, 182–83, 184, 198–200, 209–11, 216, 218, 221–31, 240
  Arctic: 86, 145
  central: 75
  coastal: 110
  king of: 59, 223, 227
  kingdom of: 18, 54, 64, 215, 230, 241
  medieval: 16, 149, 216
  mid: 126, 168, 210
  north-east of: 127
  northern (incl. 'northernmost parts, northern regions'): 11, 14, 24, 54, 65, 75, 81–82, 95–97, 99, 108, 112, 129, 158, 168–70, 174, 182, 185, 187, 189, 192, 197, 201, 204, 210, 215, 229–31

  present-day (incl. 'modern'): 129, 183, 199
  southern: 18, 97, 108 n. 36, 110 n. 46, 126, 184, 190, 201, 230
  south-western parts: 183, 222
  western (incl. 'western part of, west coast of'): 108, 114, 143, 145, 148–49, 169, 201, 204, 230
Norwegian kingdom: 12, 16–18, 56, 181, 184, 187–89, 208, 215, 241, 253
  see also Norway, kingdom of
Norwegian realm: 232, 237–38, 242, 246–50
Norwegian ríki, see Norwegian realm
Novgorod: 59–60, 63, 128, 187, 239, 242, 245–46, 248–250

Oddr Snorrason, monk of Þingeyrar: 41, 77, 219
Oddr, son of Grímr, son of Kettil: 87–88, 99
Óðinn: 75, 77, 79, 83, 96, 103–106, 112–14, 229
Ófótansfjörðr: 82
Ófóti: 82
ǫgn Álfasprengi: 76–77
ǫgvaldsnes, Avaldsnes: 157–58, 175
Ohthere of Hálogaland: 30, 57, 62, 182–83, 192–93, 197, 202, 210, 229, 243
Óláfr helgi (Haraldsson) (St Óláfr), King of Norway, St: 18, 51–52, 98, 110 n. 46, 157, 174–75, 206, 209, 215, 217–19, 229, 237, 242, 247–48
Óláfr Tryggvason, King of Norway: 18, 110 n. 46, 204, 215, 219–20, 227–28, 237
Olaus Magnus: 31, 43, 64, 147
ǫmð: 17, 181, 190–93, 206
Onega: 58
  Lake: 62
Øresund: 227
Orkney: 74, 240 n. 7
Orosius: 30, 202
Os: 145

Oslo: 165, *166*, *170*, 228
Oslofjorden, Oslofjord: 105, 106 n. 34,
    228, 230
Østfold: 164, *165*
Øysund: 205

Paulus Diaconus, Paul the Deacon: 23
Pomponius Mela: 49
Procopius: 24–26, 28
Pytheas of Massalia: 170–71
Pliny the elder: 21, 29–30

Ragnarr *loðbrók*: 229–30
Ragnhildr *tregagás*, Ragnhild
    Tregagaas: 15, 143–50
Raknarr: 83
Rauðfeldr: 81
Rauðgrani: 83
Reinesfjellet: 99
Riphean Mountains: 19, 29
Risaland: 79–80, 85, 88
Rogaland: 108 n. 37, 161, 163–64, *166*,
    167, 200
Røst: 96, 101–02, 108
    see also Útrǫst, Utrøst
Russia: 25, 39 n. 2, 63, 79, 128, 182

Sæmingr: 75
Sæmundr *fróði* Sigfússon: 41, 216–18,
    220–21
Salten: 107 n. 35, 192, 206
Sande: 167
Sandflesa: 101
Sandnes: 205
Satan *alias* Devil, the: 125, 145, 147,
    149, 151
Saxo Grammaticus: 63, 225
Scandinavia: 11, 15, 22, 23 n. 23, 24–25,
    112, 198, 223, 230
    northern: 30, 74, 147, 225
    northwestern: 197, 199, 202, 208
    pagan: 220
Scandza: 23–26, 28
    see also Scandinavia
Senja: 192

Sigurd Thoreson, *see* Sigurðr
    Þórirsson
Sigurðr *jórsalafari* (Magnússon), King
    of Norway: 219
Sigurðr *slembidjákn/slembir*
    (Magnússon): 15, 219
Sigurðr Þórirsson: 157
Skadberg: 167–68
Skaði: 75
Skålbunes: 205
Skelkingr, king of the trolls: 82, 85
Skjálgr Erlingsson: 175
Skúli Bárðarson, Norwegian jarl and
    later duke: 204, 209
Snær: 73–74, 81
Snorri Sturluson: 61, 73–74, 78–79,
    87, 97, 111 n. 53, 157, 174, 183, 190–91,
    203–04, 206–07, 209, 219–221, 224,
    227, 230
Sogn: 108, 200
Sokndal: 164, *166*
Solinus: 42
Sørle Sukk: 15, 145
St Edmund: 220
    see also Edmund, King of East
    Anglia
St Óláfr: 51, 217–18, 248
    see also Óláfr *helgi* (Haraldsson)
St Petersburg: 128
Stállo: 124–26, 128, 134
Stauran: 205, 207
Steigen: 205–07, 231
Stiklarstaðir, Stiklestad: 206, 218
Svaði: 73, 83–84
Svalbarði, Svalbard: 80
Svarfaðardal: 96–97
Sveinn Ástríðarson (Estridsson), King
    of Denmark: 225, 227–30
Sveinn Knutsson, King of Norway:
    217
Sveinn *tjúguskegg* (Haraldsson), King
    of Denmark: 227–28
Sveinn Úlfsson. *See* Sveinn
    Ástríðarson

Sverrir Sigurðarson, King of Norway:
209, 218–19, 222–24
Svitjod: 52
Svoldr, battle of: 228
Svolvær: 99
Sweden: 53, 59, 83, 110 n. 46, 121, 123,
126–27, 131, 161, 172–73, 182, 211, 240
n.7, 244, 250
northern: 127
southern: 23 n. 23
Swedish realm: 247, 252

Tacitus: 24 n. 26, 49
Tavastia, see Häme
Theodoric, (probably) monk of
Niðaróss: 40, 217–18, 224, 228
Þjótta (Tjøtta): 205–08, 211, 231
Þorbjǫrn hornklofi (Horn-cleaver):
202
Thorer Hund, see Þórir hundr
(Þórirsson)
Þorgerðr Hörgatröll: 82, 86, 211
alias Þorgerðr Hölgabrúðr, Þorgerðr
Hǫlgabrúðr, and Þorgerðr
Hörgabrúðr
Þórir hundr (Þórirsson): 157, 206, 208
Þórir sel: 157–58, 175
Þorleifr jarlsskáld Rauðfeldarson: 96,
105–06
Þormóður Torfason alias Tormod
Torfæus: 216
Þórr: 77, 79, 83–84, 169
Þorri: 73
Þorsteinn svarfaðr: 96
Þráinn svartaþurs: 96
Thrandarnes, see Þrándarnesi,
Trondenes
Þrándarnesi, Trondenes: 157, 190–91
Þrándheimr (roughly, Trøndelag):
204, 210
see also Þrœndalǫg
Þrœndalǫg, Trøndelag: 17, 95–96,
100–01, 107, 108 n. 37, 109, 110 n. 47,
111, 113–14, 168, 200, 204, 229–31
see also Þrándheimr

Thule: 24, 24 n. 25, 26, 170,
Tjøtta, see Þjótta
Tomma: 100
Torga: 100
Torgar: 205
Troms: 17, 54, 60, 123, 128–29, 181–82,
185–86, 190, 205–06
Tromsø: 143 n. *, 186, 244–45
University of: 11
Trøndelag, see Þrœndalǫg
Trondenes, see Þrándarnesi
Trondheimsfjorden,
Trondheimsfjord: 200
Tryggve Olafsson: 227
Tussøya: 205

Uppland: 211
Utfroan: 101
Útgarðr: 78, 104, 107
Útrøst, Utrøst: 14, 96–97, 100 n. 18,
101–03, 105–14
see also Utfroan, Útgarðr; Utvega
Utrøst, see Útrøst
Utvega: 101

Værøy: 102
Vågakallen: 99
Vågan: 99
Vågsfjord: 190
Valr: 83–84
Vardø: 248–49
Vatnsnes: 86
Vega: 101
Vegestav: 48
Vesterålen: 108 n. 37, 145, 192, 206–07
Vestfold: 167, 173, 230
Vestvågøy: 203
Víðkunnr Erlingsson: 209
Vígharðr: 90
Vignir: 88
Viken: 200, 228
Vilhjálmr, king of Valland: 89
Vínland: 82

Wessex: 182
West, the: 57, 120
White Sea, the: 14, 39 n. 2, 59–60,
    62–64, 73, 76, 84, 87, 89–91, 242
William of Malmesbury: 222–24

Ymir: 75–75, 80
Ymisland: 76–80

Zavoločje: 62–63

General Index

Page numbers in italics refer to maps and images.

Adogit: 25, 201

Æsir: 75, 111–12, 114

Ágrip af Nóregs konunga sǫgum: 41, 203, 217–19

alcohol: 172

  see also ale; beer; fermentation; mead

ale: 15, 157–58, 160–64, 167, 168 n. 50, 169–75

  and baptism: 174

  barnsǫl (childbirth ale): 159, 168

  brewing: 158, 160, 168–69, 172

  Christmas: 159

  drinking: 16, 160, 172–73

  erfi (funeral/inheritance ale): 159, 164, 168

  frelsisǫl (freedom ale): 159

  gatherings: 158, 164

  house: 168

  kettle: 168

  mid-winter's: 159

  -rituals: 16, 158–60, 162, 164, 168, 171, 174–75

  wedding: 168

Alþing: 199

alveland: 98

amazons: 24, 43

amendment, legal: 249–252

ancestors: 60–63, 71 n. 1, 74, 77, 127–28, 201, 218, 220, 227, 242

ancient: 18–21, 27, 49, 57, 62, 72, 74, 76–77, 114, 120–21, 131, 136, 150, 217, 222, 224, 231

Anglo-Saxon Chronicle: 223

animals: 26, 28–29, 42, 48–50, 98, 119, 126, 182

Áns saga bogsveigis: 87

archbishops: 41, 43, 173–74, 218, 225, 248

ármaðr: 252

Årstad grave slab (incl. 'Årstad stone'): 164, *166*, 166–67

assembly sites, *see* courtyard sites

authorities: 11, 23, 181

  central: 13, 210–11, 238–40, 247–50, 253–54

  ecclesiastical (incl. 'church'): 148, 209, 225, 249, 254

  imperial: 225

  Norwegian: 182, 239, 241, 249

  political: 204

  regional: 17, 229, 231

  religious: 204

  royal: 209, 245, 250, 252

  secular: 146, 148

  state: 254

  temporal: 146

authority, *see* authorities

authors: 12, 16, 20, 24, 27–28, 124, 200, 211, 218, 221, 226, 228, 230, 239, 243–44

  saga: 209, 216, 220–21, 223, 232, 244

  see also writers

Baglarr: 209

Baltic: 250

  groups: 60

  -Finnish: 62–63

baptism: 125, 159, 168, 173–74, 249

barbarians: 27, 30, 43,
Bárðar saga Snæfellsáss: 80
barley: 15, 168, 170–71
bealljegoahti: 121
beaver: 42, 49, 124
beer: 164, 168, 171
    see also alcohol; ale; mead
beings: 12, 14–15, 71–72, 91, 98–99,
    101–02, 110, 112
Beormas, *see* Biarmians
berserk: 76–77, 124
Biarmian: 62–63, 243–44, 247–48
Biarmians: 56, 62–64, 239–40,
    242–44, 246–49, 252
Birkarler: 58, 63
bishops: 24, 26, 144–46, 148, 150, 220
Bjarkeyingr: 206–09
Bjarkøyretten: 159
Bjarms, *see* Biarmians
blubber oil: 186
boathouses: 191, 203, 205
boats: 31, 51, 57, 86, 98–99, 107, 110
bonds: 96, 208
    economic: 251
    social: 198–99, 201, 238
bones: 75
    animal: 122, 129–30, 162, 182
    fragments: 160, 162–63
    human: 162
border: 21, 48–50, 53, 57 n. 55, 121, 145,
    181–82, 185–88, 193, 237, 240 n. 7,
    241, 253
    -land: 32, 73 n. 7, 246–47
Bósa saga ok Herrauðs: 85
bracteates: 160–62
    Fyn: 161, *162*
brothers: 73, 83, 95, 103–04, 106, 110,
    113–14
buffer zone: 27, 56, 64, 241

Carta Marina: 31
cauldrons: 107, 169
    Bjarkøy: 169, *170*
    see also kettle
cave: 29, 84, 103–04, 162

central places: 17, 198–200, 205,
    207–08
centres: 12, 20, 237
    administrative: 12
    elite: 205, 207–08
    power: 200–01, 205, 207–08
    religious: 91
cereal: 171, 174, 181, 185–86
    see also barley; cultivation; corn;
    grain
chaos: 21, 112, 114, 250
charcoal: 106, 122, 186
chieftains: 17–18, 125, 157, 183, 188, 192,
    208, 211, 227, 229–31
    Háleygr: 98, 207–08, 238
    northern: 182–83, 202, 237–38,
    242–43, 251
children: 73, 80, 103, 129, 144, 172, 174,
    222 n. 29
Christian: 13, 16, 20–22, 27, 29–30,
    32, 39, 44, 51, 53–54, 64, 103, 150,
    185, 218, 220, 221 n. 24, 224, 227–28,
    252–53
    non-: 43–44, 249
    pre-: 16, 21, 172
Christianity: 20, 24, 29, 32, 54, 56,
    112, 182, 204, 215, 227–28, 238–39,
    246–47
Christianization: 11, 135, 250 n. 61,
    251–52
Christianizing: 18, 29, 237, 250
Chud: 63–64, 128 135, 239, 242
Chudes, *see* Chud
church: 12, 18, 99, 102, 144, 164, 228,
    237, 244–45
    as institution ('the Church'): 29, 54,
    148, 151, 174, 220, 244
    Eastern Orthodox: 246, 249
    -men: 239
    national: 225
    Norwegian: 41, 227
    organization: 54, 237,
    -yard: 164, *165*
climate crisis of 536: 171

coast: 19 n. 1, 50, 55, 59–60, 77, 80, 83,
    86, 98, 100–01, 108 n. 37, 109–11, 113,
    191, 200, 204, 208, 244, 250
    Arctic: 86, 249
    Hálogaland: 86, 207
    -line: 83, 181–82, 188, 190–91, 204–05
    North Sea: 231
    Norwegian: 95, 98, 105, 112, 125, 170
    of Finnmark: 186
    White Sea: 59, 62, 64, 242
cod: 98, 229
    see also stockfish
combs: 160, 162–63
communities: 26, 56, 64, 125, 132–33,
    188, 190–91, 193, 197–200, 204–07
    boundaries: 201
    Christian: 185
    cultural: 64
    diasporic: 200
    Háleygir: 197, 202–03, 207–08,
        210–11
    legal: 206
    local: 132, 160, 168, 171, 174, 193
    Norse: 208
    Norwegian: 198, 209
    political: 199
    regional: 199–200, 207, 209, 211
    Western: 134
composition: 13, 202, 221
    ethnic: 12, 63
    historical: 224
conditions: 24, 46, 72, 132, 136, 184
    breeding: 22–23
    climatic: 123, 181
    cultivation: 168, 186
    ecological: 184
    economic: 184
    environmental: 64, 123
    geographical: 61, 184
    natural: 13, 19, 119
    physical: 28, 30
    social: 11, 184
consolidation: 17, 45–46, 189, 229, 244
    political: 12, 16, 179
contexts: 132, 160, 221

cultural: 127, 129, 135
    economic: 122
    elite: 161
    European: 107
    grave: 160, 167
    historical: 136
    indigenous: 120–21
    legal: 135
    Sámi: 128, 132–33
    social: 120
    West Sámi: 128
corn: 109, 157–58, 174
court sites, *see* courtyard sites
court: 23, 147 n. 10, 149,
    case: 135, 143–44
    ecclesiastical: 144
    fines: 251
    papal: 148
    records: 147
    royal: 202, 226
courtyard sites (*tunanlegg*): 17,
    189–92, 203, 205–06, 208
creatures: 26–28, 30, 81–82, 85–87, 120
crops: 97–98, 170
crusades: 245, 247, 253
    Northern: 248
Čud, *see* Chud
cultivation: 158, 168, 170–71, 173, 181,
    185, 193
    northern limit of: 204
cults: 82, 231
cultural: 13, 45, 55–56, 119, 133–34,
    158–59, 174, 210–11, 243
    authority: 211
    characteristics: 238
    complex: 39, 44
    differences: 242
    differentiation: 60–61
    divisions: 53
    elements: 45–46
    expressions: 45–46, 193
    heritage: 121, 136
    history: 158
    hybridization: 188
    identity: 185

imagination: 71–72, 91
landscape: 119
layers: 168
meaning: 158
memories: 174
practices: 157–58, 200
remains: 186, 188
sphere: 113, 210
tradition: 101 n. 20, 239
traits: 45, 98, 112
see also culture
culture: 15–16, 18, 44–45, 111–12, 131,
    133, 185, 244
drinking: 172
European: 12, 239, 253
fisherman-farmer: 95, 97
Nordic: 158
oral: 16
Sámi: 15, 135
static: 120–21
Western: 27
customs: 159, 164, 171, 173–74

Danish: 42, 57, 225–28, 230, 244, 250
daughter: 73–76, 81, 85, 87, 89, 96, 111,
    164, 190, 228
De Animalibus: 43
De philosophia et ratione mundi: 42
death: 31, 81, 89, 111–12, 114, 145, 148,
    157, 188, 202, 215, 218–19, 222, 225,
    228, 243 n. 26
decree:
    clerical: 146
    papal: 245
    royal: 249, 251–53
demonic: 21, 146, 148–49, 151
demonology: 149
descendants: 18, 22, 215, 228–31, 245
Descriptio Cambriae: 42
diabolism: 144, 149
dragons: 21, 83–84
drink: 28, 103–05, 158, 160–61, 169–70,
    172
drinking: 125
    see also ale drinking

dynasty: 207
    Bjarkeyingr: 206
    northern: 210–11, 229–31
    Norwegian (incl. 'of Norwegian
        kings'): 18, 215, 227
    of Hlaðir: 17, 210–11
    royal: 209, 224, 226
    Ynglingr: 110, 211

economy, redistributive: 125, 238, 240,
    253
Edda, Poetic: 14, 168–69, 170–71
    see also poems; poetry
Edda, Prose: 73–74, 78–79, 87, 111
    see also poems; poetry
Eggum stone: 97, 108, 112, 114
*Egils saga einhenda ok Ásmundar
    berserkjabana*: 79, 82, 90
Egils saga Skallagrímssonar: 50, 57
Elgesem stone: 167
elites: 98, 124, 148, 161, 199–200, 203,
    207, 251
    centres: 205, 207–08
    Norwegian: 207
elves: 98, 101, 103, 110–12
English: 11, 41, 61, 63, 89, 147 n. 10, 202,
    222–23, 225–26
erotic: 88, 104–05
    knowledge: 104–05
    pleasure: 145
ethnicity: 44–45, 186–87, 192–93, 238
    n. 4
ethnographic(al): 40, 120, 128–31, 241
    conditions: 64
    descriptions: 44, 54, 130
    evidence: 129
    interpretations: 128
    understanding: 120
evil: 12, 26, 53, 81, 87, 103, 146–47, 149,
    150, 160, 227
expansion: 12–13, 16–18, 59, 63, 192,
    237, 239–40, 244–48, 250, 253–54
export: 97–98, 157, 174–75, 229–32, 246
Arctic products: 182, 193, 229, 246

Fagrskinna: 203, 219, 223, 229
family: 74, 85–87, 96, 102, 110, 183,
    187, 189, 203, 206–07, 209, 220, 225,
    228–30
farmers: 50, 52, 87, 95, 97, 102–03,
    112–13, 157, 170–71, 181, 184–85, 241,
    250
    see also fishermen-farmers
farms: 55, 97–98, 103–05, 107, 158, *166*,
    168–69, 170–71, 175, 183, 185, 189,
    191–92, 205, 211
father: 73, 75, 81, 85–87, 89, 96, 103–04,
    106, 157, 219, 226, 228
    fore-: 109
    foster-: 81, 106, 220
    founding: 22
    grand-: 75, 209, 226–27, 230, 249, 253
    Great: 114
feasts: 16, 85, 157, 159, 164, 168, 171, 174,
    183, 192
    mid-winter's eve: 158–59
    summer: 157
    winter-night's eve: 157
Ferðavisur: 99
fermentation: 158, 172
fertility: 111, 144
Finnar, see Sámi
Finnas, see Sámi
Finnish: 43, 57–62
Finns, *see* Sámi
fire: 41, 73, 75, 84, 147 n. 10, 168
fireplaces: 122, 129
firney: 97, 108–09, 111–13
fish: 17, 31, 51, 97–98, 102–04, 108–11
    see also cod; stockfish
fisheries: 97, 101, 203
fishermen: 51, 95, 97–107, 108 n. 37,
    109–13
fishermen-farmers: 95, 97, 103, 112–13
fishing: 14, 48 n. 27, 51, 95, 97–98,
    101–03, 107, 108 n. 37, 110–11, 114, 181
Flateyjarbók: 73–74, 90, 96, 105
flesh: 28, 48, 125
fog: 30, 105–06

folklore: 14–15, 95, 99, 113–14, 120, 128,
    132–34, 136
food: 103, 105, 170
forest: 47, 50, 73 n. 7, 78, 107, 125, 184
fornaldarsögur: 14, 71–72, 78, 82, 85, 91
frontier: 245
frost: 23, 30, 73, 81–82, 87, 91
    -giants: 75–76, 78, 80
Fundinn Noregr: 73–75, 91
furs: 57–58, 98, 128, 182, 229–31

gand: 52, 146–47
Gandul (*gondols*): 146
    spirits of: 15, 143–44, 146
gatherings: 16, 150, 158, 160, 164,
    168–69
genealogies: 43, 216
German: 19 n. 1, 24, 42, 57, 60, 160, 172,
    184, 225
Germanic: 24, 49, 60, 63 n. 73, 64, 124,
    169, 185, 201
Gesta Danorum: 27
Gesta Hammaburgensis ecclesiae
    pontificum: 24, 40, 202
Getica: 22, 23 n. 18, 24 n. 25, 201
giants: 14, 71–91, 99, 109 n. 43, 120, 124,
    135, 169, 227
    frost-: 75–76, 78, 80
    see also Hrímþursar; trolls
Ginnungagap: 74
gods: 14, 74–75, 77, 79, 83–85, 98–99,
    103, 105, 110–14, 168–69, 171
    demi-: 21
    -lings: 52
    Æsir: 75, 111–12, 114
    Vanir: 103, 107, 111–14
    see also Ægir; Búri; Freyja; Freyr;
        Frigg; Njǫrðr; Óðinn; Þórr (in
        names index)
gondols, see Gandul
grain: 15, 28, 97–98, 145, 157–58, 160,
    168–71, 174–75, 192–93, 204
graves: 16, 129, 160–64, *166*, 166–67,
    173, 187–88, 205
    female: 160–62, 169

goods: 169, 188
male: 169
material: 187
mounds: 166, 187–88, 191
Grímnismál: 14–15, 95–96, 103, 105–06, 112–14
Gríms saga loðinkinna: 89
Gulaþing, Gulathing: 159, 189, 199
Gulaþingslög (the Gulaþing law): 159
Gull-Þóris saga: 84
Gylfaginning: 74

habitat: 42, 46, 54, 57
habitation: 78, 91, 125, 199, 206, 210
hafgufa: 31
hafrkitta: 31
hafstrambr: 31
Hákonar saga Hákonarsonar: 62, 243, 246–47
Hákonarmál: 202–03
Háleygir (sing. *Háleygr*): 17, 25, 110, 114, 197, 201–04, 208–11
Háleygjatal: 75, 97, 109, 211, 229
Hálfdans saga Brönufóstra: 84, 88
Hálfdans saga Eysteinssonar: 83
Halten lore: 101, 103, 113
Hämäläiset, Tavastians: 59, 61–62
Haraldskvæði: 202–03
Hauks þáttr hábrokar: 89
heathen: 24, 27, 29, 32, 48, 51, 53–54, 56, 64, 83, 181, 184–85, 187, 245, 247
Heimskringla: 16, 41 n. 7, 61–62, 74, 98, 174, 203, 206, 209, 219–21, 223, 229, 242
Helga þáttr Þórissonar: 85
heresy: 146, 148–50
heroes: 16, 22, 31, 79, 81–82, 84–86, 88, 91, 230
kings: 18, 215, 222, 228, 243
Hervarar saga ok Heiðreks: 76–78, 80, 85, 91
hieros gamos: 104
Historia de Antiquitate Regum Norwagiensium: 40, 217

Historia de Gentibus Septentrionalibus: 43, 64
Historia Naturalis: 21, 30
Historia Norwegie: 13–15, 31–32, 39–44, 47–56, 61–64, 110, 184–85, 189, 210, 217–18, 228, 240–41, 244, 253
Historia Pagani Libri Septem: 202
historicity: 124, 134
historiography: 129, 204, 232, 244, 246, 250
holmes: 98–99
Hólmrygir: 202
holy: 96, 104, 146, 163–64
hops: 172–73
Horned Finns, *see* Sámi
Hrafnistasögur: 30, 86, 88
Hrímþursar, frost giants: 75
Hryggjarstykki: 219, 221
hunters: 14, 28, 52, 58, 60, 192, 241, 250
hunting: 28, 49, 58, 74, 97, 107, 120, 123–24, 126, 134, 181–86, 192
husband: 81, 103, 145
Hversu Noregr byggðist: 73–74, 81, 90–91
Hymiskviða: 169
Hyndluljóð: 82 n. 42, 87
Hyperboreans: 21

Icelanders: 31, 71, 110, 216–17, 222–23, 225, 230
Icelandic: 16, 30, 41, 50, 71, 73, 77, 84, 91, 183, 185, 189, 191, 199, 216–17, 220–21, 226–27, 230, 249
-Norwegian: 44, 224–25, 227, 231
identity: 11, 13, 15, 39–40, 45, 82, 121, 136, 186, 197–98, 216, 238–39
collective: 17, 198–200, 204, 206–09, 211
construction: 200
cultural: 185
ethnic: 44–46, 58, 60, 242
fisherman: 105
Háleygr: 197, 201–09
in medieval societies: 197
Norse: 17

Norwegian: 17, 199
regional: 17, 197, 199, 201
religious: 46
social: 15
symbolic expressions of: 186
tiers of: 17, 198
trollish: 100
imagination: 71–72, 74, 88, 91, 107, 230
Imago mundi: 42
impotence: 144–45, 147, 149
indigenous: 132–34, 136
groups: 121, 133
peoples: 120, 133
inheritance: 150, 159, 164, 229
inscriptions, runic: 108, 111, 158,
160–64, 166–67
-*alu*: 160–62, 168
integration: 76, 125, 133, 135, 203, 237
interaction: 12, 39, 50, 53, 56, 60–61, 79,
145, 182, 188, 190, 210, 238, 240–41,
253
inter-ethcnic: 18, 188, 238, 254
intermediaries: 63, 128, 239, 243, 246
iron: 98, 124–25, 134, 162, 203, 208
see also *ruovdegakte*
Iron Age: 61–62, 95, 98, 107, 160, 163,
181–83, 185–87, 191–93
early: 97–98, 158
late (incl. 'latter part of the'): 16–17,
111, 182–83, 187, 189–90
Roman: 169
Íslendingabók: 183, 216, 218, 220, 225
n. 42
Íslendingasögur: 71, 80
Itinerarium Cambriae: 42

jarldom: 17, 229
jarls: 75, 96, 202, 210, 227–29, 231
of Hálogaland: 229–31
of Hlaðir: 17, 75, 82, 105–06, 109–10,
210–11, 227, 229–31
Jarlsníð: 105–06
Jelling stone: 228
Jökuls þáttr Búasonar: 88
Jǫtunn: 72–73, 79, 99

joyous island: 95, 101–03, 111, 113
jurisdiction: 54, 148, 164, 192, 199

Karelian: 59–60, 63–64, 128, 135, 239,
242
kettle: 168–69
Kirjarlers: 53
knowledge: 13, 20–21, 28–30, 41, 55, 64,
76–77, 96, 102, 104–06, 114, 121, 131,
133, 135, 148, 202, 206, 217, 223, 230,
241, 244, 254
academic: 132–33
erotic: 104–05
first-hand: 12, 32
holy ruler-: 104
ruler-: 104–05, 114
traditional: 132–33
Komi: 62–63, 242
konungasögur: 17, 71, 199, 202–03,
219–21, 243
Kvæn, *see* Kven
Kven: 53, 56–59, 62–63, 239
kvenna: 30, 76, 81

lagdømme, see law province
lagting (provincial court assembly):
54
lakes: 50, 57, 110
Landnamabók: 97, 183, 189, 191
landscapes: 14–15, 17, 28, 32, 73, 75,
84, 119–21, 123, 126, 128–29, 136, 170,
185–86, 190, 199
coastal: 43, 190
cultural: 119
mountain: 122
mythical: 21
naming: 46
political: 206
regional: 204
sacred: 135
Sámi: 120, 128, 131, 134–35, 186
studies: 15
Laps/Lapps, *see* Sámi
Lausavisar: 98
law: 146, 158–60, 252

canon: 146, 148
divine: 104
medieval: 159–60, 170
national: 187, 189
province: 47–48, 50, 189
sentence: 146, 168
urban: 159
legal districts: 205–06
legends: 16–17, 121, 132, 135–36
Sámi: 15, 121, 128, 134–35
leidang: 54
lifestyle: 14, 18, 24, 46, 181, 184, 192, 202
literature: 11, 15, 19, 30, 51, 79, 134, 170,
199, 201, 207, 209–10, 213, 216, 222
Old Norse (incl. 'Icelandic-
Norwegian, medieval Norse'):
71, 96, 114, 172, 203–04, 227,
229–30, 254
saga: 44, 120, 197, 199, 215
lǫgmaðr: 252
Lokasenna: 171–72
longhouse: 198, 200, 203, 205, 207
Lule Sámi area: 123

magic (incl. 'magical'): 11–16, 21, 24,
26, 32, 37, 52–53, 73, 77, 85, 105,
143–51, 160–61, 167–68
black: 144
dark: 241
formula: 160, 167
love: 149–50
poison and image: 148
rites: 146, 148–49
rituals: 15, 143, 145–46, 148,
Sámi: 13–15, 17, 135, 143, 145, 210,
241–42
shamanistic: 14
skilled in (*fjǫlkunnig*): 81
spells: 29, 144, 147, 242
magnates: 98
see also chieftains
male: 31, 84, 99–100, 160–61, 169, 173,
228–29
malt: 15–16, 157–58, 168
manifestation: 79, 91

mappae mundi: 20, 27
marriage: 59, 96, 149, 188, 231
mead: 170–72
see also alcohol; ale; beer
memories: 61, 159, 164, 168, 174, 202,
217, 220, 223–24, 226–27
collective: 132, 136
Sámi folk: 15, 124
social: 226
Middle Ages: 12, 19, 120, 123–24,
127–28, 130–31, 148–50, 168 n. 50,
172–73, 182, 187, 189, 215–16, 237,
239, 250–51, 254
Early: 12–13, 17, 22, 27, 32, 40, 54, 58,
60–61, 63–64, 185, 187
High: 12, 19, 32, 40, 60, 63–64
Late: 58, 63, 144, 146, 150
midnight sun: 25, 28, 170
Migration Age/Period: 158, 161, 163,
166 n. 35
monks: 146, 219
monsters: 12, 27–30, 43, 83–84, 86
sea: 13, 19, 21, 31, 53
monuments: 119–21, 127, 132, 134, 160,
164, 166 n. 35, 167
Morkinskinna: 203, 219, 221
mother: 59, 75, 81, 89, 225
foster-: 87–88, 90
Great: 114
step-: 89
motif: 95–97, 101, 103–04, 113
folkloric (incl. 'folktale'): 78, 91,
105, 113
Leit-: 42
literary: 79
'take your time': 102, 105, 113
mounds: 111 n. 35, 187
burial/grave: 164, 166, 187–88, 191
farm: 205
myths: 12–13, 15–16, 21, 29, 37, 110, 114,
128 n. 48, 136, 179, 222
foundation (incl. 'founding'):
17–18, 72–75
northern: 12, 74

origin: 22–24, 31, 71–72, 75, 78, 81,
    88, 91, 104
Sámi: 119–21, 124, 128, 131–36

narratives: 18, 41, 72, 74, 132, 174, 207,
    216, 220–22, 224–25
    academic: 133
    counter-: 215, 224
    foundation: 215
    grand: 215, 230–32
    saga: 157–59, 202
negotiations: 45, 136, 186, 190
neighbours: 56, 97, 102
networks: 17, 145, 201, 231
    exchange: 200, 203, 207
    trade: 17, 243, 251
nomadic: 14
    semi-: 49, 52, 250
non-human: 71–72, 91, 119–20
Norðrsetudrápa: 74
Nóregs konungatal: 217
Norgesveldet: 240 n. 7
Northern lights: 170
Norwegian synoptics, the: 217
    see also Ágrip, Historia Norwegie;
        Historia de Antiquitate Regum
        Norwagiensium
Norwegian: 12, 15–18, 31, 44–45,
    47–50, 52, 54, 58, 60, 101, 146–47,
    197, 200, 208–09, 244–45, 250
    authorities: 238–41, 248–49, 253
    authors: 16, 226
    charters/documents: 143–44, 150
    church/ecclesiastical province:
        41, 227
    coast (incl. 'coastline, seaboard'):
        95, 98, 112, 125, 170, 188, 205, 210
    community: 197, 209
    economy: 203
    elite: 207
    expansion: 239–40, 244–45
    family: 31, 96, 230
    historians: 62, 215, 222
    history: 12, 159, 226, 231
    identity: 17, 199

interior: 204, 210
kings: 18, 50, 190, 204, 216–17,
    222–27, 240–41, 244–50, 253–54
laws: 146, 170
monarchy: 16, 209, 211, 224, 226,
    230–31, 240 n. 7, 244, 250
nation: 216
national history: 221–22
non-Norwegian: 13, 18
northern Norwegian (incl. 'north
    Norwegian'): 15, 25, 60, 103, 106,
    109 n. 41, 147, 182–83, 188–89, 197,
    202–03, 207, 242
population: 240
presence: 245, 250
provinces: 25
regional identities: 203–04
regions: 197
-Russian: 55
-Sámi: 241
state: 18, 44, 50, 237
unification (incl. 'unification of
    Norway'): 215, 222

offerings: 52, 98–99, 104
Ohthere's account/report: 62, 182–83,
    202, 210, 242, 251
ǫl: 158–60, 169–71, 174
    -hús: 168
Óláfs saga helga: 61, 174, 209
Óláfs saga Tryggvasonar: 77, 91
Oldest Saga of St Óláfr, the: 219
Origo Gentis Langobardorum: 23
origo: 21–24
Orkneyinga saga: 72–73
Orosius: 27
Örvar-Odds saga: 80, 88, 99
other, the: 28, 111, 239–40, 236, 238,
    248, 250, 252–54
othering: 238–40
otherness: 18, 20–21, 27–29, 31–32,
    238–41, 243–44, 247–48, 250,
    252–54

pagan: 13, 16, 24, 51, 83, 151, 220, 225, 227
gods: 74, 77, 79, 83–85
half-: 151
peoples: 239–41
society: 22, 30
paganism: 12, 53, 99, 151
pagans: 18, 27, 245
Passio et Miracula Beati Olavi: 51–53, 210 n. 37, 218
peace agreement, *see* treaty
Permian: 242
Physica: 173
pilgrimage: 146
Pite Sámi area: 127–28
pitfall traps: 120, 124, 126–28, 134–35
see also reindeer; system, trapping; trapping systems
pits, slab-lined: 186–87, 193
poems (incl. 'verse'): 219, 221, 224
Eddic: 79, 87, 95–96, 99, 158, 168–69
skaldic: 41 n. 7, 187, 202–04, 220–21, 223
see also *Edda, Poetic*; *Edda, Prose*
poetry: 217, 223
heroic: 216, 219–20
skaldic: 97, 108, 216–17, 219–23, 226, 230
see also *Edda, Poetic*; *Edda, Prose*
poets: 75, 96, 110, 202, 211, 219–20
see also skalds
population: 22–23, 26, 39, 54, 58, 60, 63, 71, 75, 91, 189, 192, 247, 250–51
coastal: 114, 192
farming: 14, 49
Finnish-speaking: 58–59, 62
Háleygir: 25
local: 18
multi-ethnic: 13
Norse: 30, 125, 185, 192–93, 201, 204, 208, 238, 240–41, 250
Norwegian: 145
Sámi: 31, 143–45, 181, 185, 192–93, 240–41, 249, 252
Vepsian: 63

pottery: 162–63
power: 15–16, 54, 96, 114, 147, 158, 160–61, 175, 207–10, 218, 228–31, 239–40
-base: 75, 229–30, 256
central: 16, 253
centres: 200–01, 205, 207–08
consolidation of: 189
display of (incl. 'expression of, symbols of'): 168, 187–89
secular: 198
social: 54
state: 44, 50
structure: 207–08, 211
supernatural: 172
priest: 83, 101–03, 105, 113, 147
Procopius: 24–26, 28
Proto-Norse: 160–61, 164, 167, 169

radiocarbon dating/dates: 122, 126, 189
regional assemblies: 199
reindeer: 28, 49, 124
domesticated: 183
herding/pastoralism: 123
hunting: 120, 123, 126–28
pitfall traps: 124, 126–28, 134–35
wild: 124,127, 127, 182
representations: 19–21, 27, 40, 161, 167, 179, 226, 238–39, 244, 253–54
mis-: 226
mythical: 239, 248, 253
over-: 114
riddarasögur: 71
rights: 55, 58–59, 128, 228
historic Sámi: 15
of indigenous groups: 121
of patronage: 245
property: 187
territorial: 187
usufruct: 131
Rimbegla: 50, 185
risi, see giants
rituals: 13, 15–16, 37, 58, 114, 129, 131, 135, 159–61, 167–68, 174–75
ale-: 16, 158–64, 167–68, 171, 174–75

burial: 164
magic: 143, 145–46, 148
political: 15
protective: 168–69, 173–75
rites of passage: 159, 168, 175
Sámi: 15, 131
seasonal: 160
sites: 15, 131, 135
transitional: 159, 161, 164, 173
see also offering sites
rock: 14, 29, 75–76, 91, 99, 126, 129
rocky: 97, 129
Romana et Getica, see Getica
rundgamme: 186
ruovdegakte: 124
Rýgir: 209

saga: 14–15, 17, 30–31, 71–91, 125, 150,
   157–59, 174, 183, 190–92, 202–11, 216,
   219, 223–24, 226–30
accounts: 209, 222
authors (incl. 'writers'): 72, 84, 91,
   209, 215–16, 220–23, 232
   see also authors; writers
Icelandic sagas, *see Íslendingasögur*
kings' sagas, *see konungasögur*
knights' sagas, *see riddarasögur*
legendary sagas, *see fornaldarsögur*
literature: 44, 120, 197, 199, 215
narratives: 157–59, 202
tradition: 90
sailors: 31
sambite: 245
Sámi: 14–18, 27, 31, 39, 44, 47–65, 71 n.
   1, 75–76, 96, 98, 101, 119–36, 143–47,
   181–87, 191–93, 201–02, 204, 210,
   238–45, 249–53
as *Finnar*: 15, 71, 73, 86 n. 56
as *Finnas*: 183, 202
as *Finns*: 47–48, 51, 61–62, 181, 184
as Horned Finns: 53, 56, 60–61
as Laps/Lapps: 51, 147
as pagans or heathens: 51–52, 54,
   184, 241, 249
as *Screrefennae*: 201

as *Skridfinns*: 27, 29–30
as wielders of magic: 210
beliefs: 124
Coastal: 54
contexts: 128, 132–33
culture: 15, 135
elite: 251
folk memory: 15
kings: 248–51
magic of: 13–15, 17, 135, 143, 145, 210,
   241–42
myths: 119–21, 124, 128, 131–36
North (language): 191
-Norwegian: 242, 253
offering sites: 120, 129–31, 134–35
place names: 128
Proto-: 60–61
ritual sites (incl. 'places'): 15,
   129–30, 135
rituals: 15, 131
settlement: 47, 49–50, 52–54, 56, 59,
   65, 241 n. 17
society: 123–25, 251–52
Stállo house grounds as: 122–26,
   134–35
taxation of: 55, 59, 123–26, 128, 134,
   183, 238, 241, 249–50, 252
traditions: 125, 130–31, 134–35
Samogitians: 245
Samsons saga fagra: 79–80, 85
Scandinavian: 11–13, 16, 21 n. 7, 24, 27,
   97, 147, 149, 191, 216 n. 3, 223–25, 228,
   230, 237
inter-: 239, 250
Irish-: 222, 227n. 46
peninsula: 24, 28, 250
realms: 239
Scandinavians: 12, 21 n. 7, 76, 239
Scottish: 222, 244
Screrefennae, see Sámi
sex: 88–90, 144–45, 149–50, 238 n. 4
shaman: 14–15, 51
shamanistic, *see* shaman
siida: 125
sister: 73, 96, 190, 225

Skadberg stone: 167–68
skalds: 219–21
    see also poems; poets; poetry
Skarvene fra Utrøst (The Cormorants
    from Utrøst): 102
skeaŋka: 125
Skiðblaðnir: 111
Skírnismál: 87
Skridfinns, see Sámi
snow: 14, 23–24, 28–30, 49, 73–75, 91,
    98, 125
society: 11, 16, 28, 102, 119, 143, 159–60,
    168, 174, 183, 189–90, 192–93, 200,
    244
    agricultural: 15
    northern: 13, 158, 166 n. 35, 174, 183,
        238
    northern Norwegian: 15, 183
    Norwegian: 197
    pagan: 22, 30
    pre-christian: 172
    Sámi: 123–25, 251–52
son: 73, 75–77, 81, 83–85, 87–88, 105,
    157, 190, 209, 217, 220, 224, 227–29,
    243 n. 26
    foster-: 89, 103, 224
sorcerers (troll, trollfolk): 12, 24,
    105–06, 113, 144, 146–50
sorcery (trolldom): 15, 76, 106, 146–51
spells: 15, 29, 89, 101, 113, 144, 147, 242
spirits: 15, 22, 25, 52, 82, 98, 100,
    143–44, 146–47
Stállo house grounds: 120–29, 134–35
state: 49, 54, 135, 185, 225, 239, 253–54
    building (incl. 'formation'): 11, 16,
        215, 224
    city-state: 128, 239, 246
    national: 12, 237
    Norwegian (incl. 'state of
        Norway'): 18, 44, 50, 182, 237
stereotypes: 12, 15, 18, 121, 131, 135, 150,
    254
stockfish: 97, 107, 229, 231
    see also cod; fish
stone: 82, 97, 121, 126, 129–31, 186

brewing: 168–69
circles: 129–31
-hurling: 99
monuments: 160, 164
rune-: 97, 108
    see also Årstad grave slab; Eggum
        stone; Elgesem stone; Jelling
        stone; Skadberg stone; Tune
        stone
Sturlaugs saga starfsama: 81, 86
subsistence: 107, 181, 185, 193
supernatural: 12, 14, 17, 19–21,
    71–72, 74, 79–88, 91, 99, 102, 172–73,
    203–04, 209, 227
    islands: 95–96, 101–102, 106–13
        see also joyous island
superstition: 95–97, 110–12
    Devilish: 52
Sverris saga: 203, 219
Swedish: 58, 124–25, 225
    crusade: 247
    -Russian: 57, 59
sysler: 54
sýslumaðr: 252
system: 14, 28, 44, 46, 54, 62, 64 n. 77,
    78, 133, 200, 224
    economic: 58–59, 207, 237–38, 240,
        253
    redistributive: 125, 238, 253
    trade: 58–60, 238
    trapping: 126–28
        see also pitfall traps

tales: 12–14, 16, 22, 24, 71, 84, 90–91,
    95, 100, 101 n. 20, 102, 105, 175, 216,
    218
    see also Utrøst tales
Tavastians, see Hämäläiset
tax, taxes, see taxation
taxation: 47, 55, 60, 85, 187, 231, 238
    of the Sámi: 55, 59, 123–26, 128, 134,
        183, 238, 252
    see also tribute
theologians: 146–47
Þokuvísur: 15, 105–07

Þorleifs þáttr jarlaskálds: 95–97, 105, 113

Þorsteins saga bæjarmagns: 85

Þroendir: 204

Þurs (troll): 72, 99

Topographica Hiberniae: 42

topography: 57, 78, 126

trade: 14–17, 51, 57–60, 107, 123, 125–26,
    128, 145, 158, 171, 184–85, 203, 208,
    228, 237, 242

traditional (incl. 'traditionally'): 12,
    14, 44–46, 75, 107, 124, 128, 134, 169,
    202, 215, 226–27, 229–31, 244, 246,
    250, 252
    account: 111, 215

traditions: 12, 19 n. 1, 40, 44–46, 76,
    90, 95–102, 111–14, 120–21, 124,
    130–36, 174, 188, 201–02, 210–11,
    216–17, 224, 231, 238 n. 4, 239, 250–51
    Far North: 96
    folk: 98
    indigenous oral: 134, 136
    oral (incl. 'orally transmitted'): 100,
        120, 127, 131–36, 216–17, 220, 223
    pagan: 151
    saga: 90
    Sámi: 125, 130–31, 134–35
    skaldic: 16

trapping systems: 126–28
    see also pitfall traps

treaty: 57 n. 55, 59, 157, 245

triangulation methodology: 199–201,
    209, 211

tribes: 22–24, 28, 53, 201

tribute: 18, 47, 50, 52, 55, 75, 125, 182–83,
    228, 238, 241
    see also taxation

Trojan: 22, 74

trolldom, see sorcery

trolls: 14, 31, 71–72, 78–82, 84–91, 96,
    99–100, 103–05, 112–13, 124
    see also giants

trollkvenna heiti: 99

Tuftefolket på Sandflæsa (The Elves on
    Sandflæsa): 103

Tune stone: 164, 165, 167–68

turf: 107, 121, 123, 127, 129

ultima thule: 21

uncle: 103–05
    great-: 226, 230

ungodly: 21, 32, 52, 241

utmark: 107–08

Utrøst complex: 95, 101–03, 110, 113

Utrøst tales: 95–97, 101–02, 104, 107,
    109–14

Valdimars saga: 80

Vepsians: 62–64, 242

Viking Age/Period: 11, 96, 110 n.
    46; 47, 125, 127, 134–35, 173, 201, 203,
    244

vikings: 30, 83–84, 124, 158, 227 n. 46,
    229

villains: 124, 133–34, 242

Völsunga saga: 87

Votes: 62–63

walrus: 182, 229

warriors: 74–75, 124, 134, 161, 228

wasteland: 48–49, 52–53, 56, 62, 64, 91,
    182, 241

waterways: 96, 200–01

weather: 71, 73–74, 106, 123, 171

wedding: 144, 148, 164, 168, 175

whales: 31, 89, 98, 182

wilderness: 18, 48, 62, 85–88, 91, 241

wind: 81, 106, 191
    north: 21, 30, 73, 147

winter: 16, 24–26, 42 n. 15, 74–75,
    80–81, 84, 87, 91, 123, 125, 157–59
    darkness: 25, 28
    dwellings (incl. 'habitation'): 123,
        125
    feed: 171
    fisheries: 97–98, 107, 113
    solstice: 26

witch: 107
    -burning: 150
    -craft: 15, 29, 143–44, 146–47, 149–51
    -hunts: 149–50

trials: 15, 146–47, 149–50
women: 30, 43, 78 n. 28, 81, 86–88,
    98–99, 149–50, 162
writers: 12, 20–22, 24–25, 27, 31–32, 47,
    61, 72, 216, 225, 228
    see also authors; saga authors

Ynglinga saga: 41, 74–75, 110 n. 46, 219
Ynglingatal: 41, 187, 211, 221 n. 24
Ynglingr dynasty: 110, 211

zones: 20, 47, 171, 184, 241
    buffer: 27, 56, 64, 241
    coastal: 47
    cultural: 210
    forest: 47
    middle: 47
    temperate: 20

Acta Scandinavica:

Cambridge Studies in the Early Scandinavian World

All volumes in this series are evaluated by an Editorial Board, strictly on academic grounds, based on reports prepared by referees who have been commissioned by virtue of their specialism in the appropriate field. The Board ensures that the screening is done independently and without conflicts of interest. The definitive texts supplied by authors are also subject to review by the Board before being approved for publication. Further, the volumes are copyedited to conform to the publisher's stylebook and to the best international academic standards in the field.